Religious Liberty and the American Founding

Religious Liberty and the American Founding

Natural Rights and the Original Meanings of the First Amendment Religion Clauses

VINCENT PHILLIP MUÑOZ

THE UNIVERSITY OF CHICAGO PRESS   CHICAGO AND LONDON

The University of Chicago Press, Chicago 60637
The University of Chicago Press, Ltd., London
© 2022 by The University of Chicago
Published 2022
Printed in the United States of America

30 29 28 27 26 25 24 23 22 21   1 2 3 4 5

ISBN-13: 978-0-226-82142-9   (cloth)
ISBN-13: 978-0-226-82144-3   (paper)
ISBN-13: 978-0-226-82143-6   (e-book)
DOI: https://doi.org/10.7208/chicago/9780226821436.001.0001

Library of Congress Cataloging-in-Publication Data

Names: Muñoz, Vincent Phillip, author.
Title: Religious liberty and the American founding : natural rights and the original meanings
    of the First Amendment Religion Clauses / Vincent Phillip Muñoz.
Description: Chicago : University of Chicago Press, 2022. |
    Includes bibliographical references and index.
Identifiers: LCCN 2022006343 | ISBN 9780226821429 (cloth) |
    ISBN 9780226821443 (paperback) | ISBN 9780226821436 (ebook)
Subjects: LCSH: United States. Constitution. 1st Amendment. | Freedom of religion—
    United States. | Constitutional law—United States—History—18th century. |
    Church and state—United States. | Founding Fathers of the United States—Attitudes.
Classification: LCC KF4783 .M859 2022 | DDC 342.7308/52—dc23/eng/20220415
LC record available at https://lccn.loc.gov/2022006343

FOR JENNIFER CABANISS MUÑOZ

A popular Government, without popular information, or the means of acquiring it, is but a Prologue to a Farce or a Tragedy; or, perhaps both. Knowledge will forever govern ignorance: And a people who mean to be their own Governors, must arm themselves with the power which knowledge gives. — James Madison

Letter to W. T. Barry

August 4, 1822

Contents

Preface

This book aims to recover certain ideas about political liberty. It presents to the best of my abilities the American Founders' understanding of the inalienable natural right of religious liberty and how that understanding might inform a construction of the First Amendment Religion Clauses of the United States Constitution.

I wrote this book in an attempt to better appreciate the American Founders' understanding of natural rights and natural rights constitutionalism. My primary purpose is not to advocate for the implementation of those ideas here and now. I do not thoroughly attempt to answer the question of whether it would be desirable to mold our constitutional practice so that it better approximates the Founders' constitutionalism. To address that question well would require considerations and arguments that lie beyond the scope of this study.

To address the question at all, however, does require the knowledge that this book attempts to present. Before determining whether we should attempt to return to the American Founders' constitutionalism or, for that matter, whether we have significantly improved upon and surpassed their political thinking, we have to understand the Founders. This book attempts to present that understanding regarding the natural right of religious liberty.

I am sympathetic to some aspects of the Founders' constitutionalism but, at the same time, I do not favor some of the results its implementation would produce. Constitutional politics is a complex sport. The path to victory may or may not involve adopting the Founders' strategies. My task is not to advocate for the Founders' constitutionalism, but to present it accurately and, I hope, with clarity and insight. This book will be successful if the reader better understands the American Founders and thereby can assess independently to what degree it would be prudent to attempt to restore their philosophical and constitutional principles in contemporary political life.

Natural Rights and the First Amendment Religion Clauses

It is now no more that toleration is spoken of, as if it was by the indulgence of one class of people, that another enjoyed the exercise of their inherent natural rights. For happily the Government of the United States, which gives to bigotry no sanction, to persecution no assistance requires only that they who live under its protection should demean themselves as good citizens, in giving it on all occasions their effectual support. — George Washington

Letter to the Hebrew Congregation at Newport, Rhode Island (1790)[1]

Upon being elected America's first president, George Washington received numerous congratulatory letters from religious associations around the country. Washington's responses, which he knew would be circulated, offered the new nation a civics lesson on the principle of religious liberty. To the Quakers, whose pacifist beliefs frequently put them at odds with military leadership during the Revolutionary War, Washington declared,

> The liberty enjoyed by the People of these States, of worshipping Almighty God agreeable to their Consciences, is not only among the choicest of their Blessings, but also of their Rights.[2]

1. George Washington to the Hebrew Congregation in Newport, Rhode Island, August 18, 1790, in *Papers of George Washington: Presidential Series*, 6:285.

2. George Washington to the Society of Quakers, October 1789, in *The Papers of George Washington: Presidential Series, September 1789–January 1790*, ed. Dorothy Twohig (Charlottesville: University Press of Virginia, 1993), 4:266. This opening paragraph borrows from

The following year, in 1790, he wrote the beautiful passage that serves as the epigraph of this chapter. Washington's identification of conscientious worship of God as a natural right reflects the Founding Fathers' common understanding. We no longer understand, however, what the Founders meant when they declared religious liberty to be an "inherent," "natural," or "inalienable" right. One purpose of this book is to remedy our intellectual amnesia and thereby make possible a reconsideration of the Founders' natural rights constitutionalism.

It is ironic that we so little understand the Founders' political philosophy of church and state, since originalism has arguably influenced no other area of constitutional law more.[3] When faced with its first significant Free Exercise Clause case in *Reynolds v. United States* (1879), and then its first significant Establishment Clause case in *Everson v. Board of Education* (1947), the Supreme Court turned to the Founders for guidance.[4] It has continued to do so ever since. Of the nine current justices on the Court, at least six have cited the Founders in a church-state opinion.[5] And

---

Vincent Phillip Muñoz and Kevin Vance, "How the Founders Agreed about Religious Freedom but Disagreed about the Separation of Church and State," in *The Wiley Blackwell Companion to Religion and Politics in the U.S.*, ed. Barbara McGraw (Oxford, UK: John Wiley & Sons, 2016), 85–97.

3. Andrew P. Koppelman, in *Defending American Religious Neutrality* (Cambridge, MA: Harvard University Press, 2013), 78, writes: "In the interpretation of the religion clauses, perhaps more than in any other field of constitutional law, both the Court and commentators feel impelled to make originalist arguments."

4. *Reynolds. v. United States,* 98 U.S. 145 (1879); *Everson v. Board of Education,* 330 U.S. 1 (1947). Cases prior to *Everson* that involved the Establishment Clause include *Bradfield v. Roberts,* 175 U.S. 291 (1899); *Quick Bear v. Leupp,* 210 U.S. 50 (1908); *Arver v. United States,* 245 U.S. 366 (1918).

5. See, e.g., *Hosanna-Tabor Evangelical Lutheran Church and School v. Equal Employment Opportunity Commission,* 565 U.S. 171, 184 (2012) (Roberts, C. J.) ("The Establishment Clause prevents the Government from appointing ministers, and the Free Exercise Clause prevents it from interfering with the freedom of religious groups to select their own. This understanding of the Religion Clauses was reflected in two events involving James Madison, 'the leading architect of the religion clauses of the First Amendment.'"); *Rosenberger v. Rector & Visitors of the University of Virginia,* 515 U.S. 819, 854–56 (1995) (Thomas, J., concurring) (citing and discussing Madison); *Zelman v. Simmons-Harris,* 536 U.S. 639, 717 (2002) (Breyer, J., dissenting) ("The [Religion] Clauses reflect the Framers' vision of an American Nation free of the religious strife that had long plagued the nations of Europe."); *Town of Greece v. Galloway,* 572 U.S. 565, 600–603 (2014) (Alito, J., concurring) (discussing the Founders' actions concerning legislative prayer); *Trinity Lutheran v. Comer,* 582 U.S. ___, slip op. at 12–13 (2017) (Sotomayor, J., dissenting) (citing and discussing Madison); *Town of Galloway v. Greece,* 572 U.S. 565, 619–20 n.1) (2014) (Kagan, J., dissenting) (citing Madison, Jefferson, and Washington).

As of July 2021, Justices Neil Gorsuch, Brett Kavanaugh, and Amy Barrett, the three most recently appointed justices, have not yet cited a Founding Father or the Founders in a

not only the Court's conservatives do so.[6] Even Justice William Brennan, perhaps the Court's leading twentieth-century critic of originalism, said of the Establishment Clause, "I believe that the line we must draw between the permissible and the impermissible is one which accords with history and faithfully reflects the understanding of the Founding Fathers."[7]

The consensus that the Founders' understanding should serve as a guide has produced neither agreement nor coherence in church-state jurisprudence. Indeed, it has produced the opposite; it seems that almost any and every church-state judicial position can invoke the Founders' support. Regarding the Establishment Clause, justices have argued both that the Founders erected a "wall of separation" between church and state, and that they never intended to erect a "wall."[8] Some justices say the First Amendment demands government neutrality toward religion,[9] or neutrality

---

Supreme Court church-state opinion. Judge Kavanaugh did cite the Founders in an Establishment Clause case while he was on the Court of Appeals for the DC Circuit. See *Newdow v. Roberts*, 603 F. 3d 1002, 1018 (2010) (Kavanaugh, J., concurring) (discussing the practices of George Washington and the First Congress), and Justice Gorsuch signed Justice Alito's originalist concurring opinion in *Fulton v. City of Philadelphia*, 593 U.S. ___ (2021).

6. See, e.g., *American Legion v. American Humanist Association*, 588 U.S. ___, slip op. at 3, 4, 17 (2019) (Ginsburg, J., dissenting) (citing Madison, Jefferson, and Washington). Donald L. Drakeman, in "Which Original Meaning of the Establishment Clause Is The Right One?" in *The Cambridge Companion to the First Amendment and Religious Liberty*, ed. Michael D. Breidenbach and Owen Anderson (New York: Cambridge University Press, 2020), 378, writes:

Perhaps the most remarkable aspect of the Supreme Court's church-state jurisprudence is that justices generally considered very liberal (e.g., Black, Rutledge, Brennan, and Sotomayor) as well as those categorized as quite conservative (e.g., Rehnquist, Scalia, and Thomas) have all embraced a historical approach to the establishment clause. Church-state constitutional battles seem almost invariably to be about the founding era.

7. *Abington School District v. Schempp*, 374 U.S. 203, 294 (1963).

8. *Everson v. Board of Education*, 330 U.S. 1, 16 (1947) (Black, J.) ("In the words of Jefferson, the clause against establishment of religion by law was intended to erect 'a wall of separation between church and State'"); *Wallace v. Jaffree*, 472 U.S. 38, 92 (1985) (Rehnquist, J., dissenting) ("It is impossible to build sound constitutional doctrine upon a mistaken understanding of constitutional history, but unfortunately the Establishment Clause has been expressly freighted with Jefferson's misleading metaphor for nearly 40 years"). For a critique of separationist jurisprudence on historical and other grounds, see Philip Hamburger, "Separation and Interpretation," *Journal of Law and Politics* 18 (2002): 7–64.

9. See, e.g., *Trump v. Hawaii*, 585 U.S. ___, slip op. at 1 (2018) (Sotomayor, J., dissenting) ("The United States of America is a Nation built upon the promise of religious liberty. Our Founders honored that core promise by embedding the principle of religious neutrality in the First Amendment."); *Masterpiece Cakeshop v. Colorado Civil Rights Commission*, 584 U.S. ___, slip op. at 3 (2018) ("When the Colorado Civil Rights Commission considered this case, it did not do so with the religious neutrality that the Constitution requires.")

between religion and irreligion,[10] or neutrality that does not exclude or endorse religion,[11] or neutrality plus separation;[12] others, only that government not prefer one religion over others;[13] still others that the Founders were not concerned with neutrality at all, but rather with state coercion of religion.[14] Some eschew the attempt to develop a grand unifying theory at all;[15] others recognize an "overarching set of principles," and also that each category of cases "has its own principles based on history, tradition, and precedent."[16] Justice Clarence Thomas has suggested that all these positions are probably incorrect because the Establishment Clause was originally about federalism.[17]

10. *Board of Education of Kiryas Joel Village School District v. Grumet*, 512 U.S. 687, 703 (1994) (Souter, J.) ("The anomalously case-specific nature of the legislature's exercise of state authority in creating this district for a religious community leaves the Court without any direct way to review such state action for the purpose of safeguarding a principle at the heart of the Establishment Clause, that government should not prefer one religion to another, or religion to irreligion.").

11. *Rosenberger v. Rector & Visitors of the University of Virginia*, 515 U.S. 819, 839 (1995) (Kennedy, J.) ("We have held that the [Establishment Clause] guarantee of neutrality is respected, not offended, when the government, following neutral criteria and evenhanded policies, extends benefits to recipients whose ideologies and viewpoints, including religious ones, are broad and diverse."); *Rosenberger v. Rector & Visitors of the University of Virginia*, 515 U.S. 819, 846 (1995) (O'Connor, J., concurring) ("This insistence on government neutrality toward religion explains why we have held that schools may not discriminate against religious groups by denying them equal access to facilities that the schools make available to all").

12. *Rosenberger v. Rector & Visitors of the University of Virginia*, 515 U.S. 819, 877 (1995) (Souter, J., dissenting) (arguing that neutrality "does not alone satisfy the requirements of the Establishment Clause, as the Court recognizes when it says that evenhandedness is only a 'significant factor' in certain Establishment Clause analysis, not a dispositive one").

13. *Wallace v. Jaffree*, 472 U.S. 38, 99 (1985) (Rehnquist, J., dissenting) ("The evil to be aimed at, so far as those who spoke were concerned, appears to have been the establishment of a national church, and perhaps the preference of one religious sect over another; but it was definitely not concerned about whether the Government might aid all religions evenhandedly").

14. *Lee v. Weisman*, 505 U.S. 577, 640 (1992) (Scalia, J., dissenting) ("The coercion that was a hallmark of historical establishments of religion was coercion of religious orthodoxy and of financial support by force of law and threat of penalty.").

15. *Rosenberger v. Rector & Visitors of the University of Virginia*, 515 U.S. 819, 852 (1995) (O'Connor, J., concurring) ("When bedrock principles collide, they test the limits of categorical obstinacy and expose the flaws and dangers of a Grand Unified Theory that may turn out to be neither grand nor unified. The Court today does only what courts must do in many Establishment Clause cases—focus on specific features of a particular government action to ensure that it does not violate the Constitution").

16. *American Legion v. American Humanist Association*, 588 U.S. ___, slip op. at 3–4 (2019) (Kavanaugh, J. concurring).

17. *Elk Grove Unified School District v. Newdow*, 542 U.S. 1, 45 (2004) (Thomas, J., concurring) ("I would take this opportunity to begin the process of rethinking the Establishment

The range of constructions for the Free Exercise Clause is not as extensive but is equally divergent and divisive. In *Fulton v. City of Philadelphia* (2021), Justice Samuel Alito wrote a lengthy concurring opinion, signed by Justices Thomas and Gorsuch, contending that the Free Exercise Clause provides religious exemptions from burdensome laws, a construction also advanced by Justice Sandra Day O'Connor and defended by Michael McConnell, arguably the nation's most distinguished church-state originalist.[18] Other justices and leading scholars, including Justice Antonin Scalia and Philip Hamburger, have argued that following the Founders does not require support for a First Amendment right to exemptions.[19] In short, church-state originalism has failed to deliver conclusive accounts for either the Establishment Clause or the Free Exercise Clause. And that is not the worst of it. It has produced contradictory results for each clause and has also manufactured tensions between the clauses.[20] As a result, First Amendment church-state matters remain—as Justice Thomas described Establishment Clause jurisprudence more than two decades ago—"in hopeless disarray."[21]

Clause. I would acknowledge that the Establishment Clause is a federalism provision, which, for this reason, resists incorporation.").

18. *Fulton v. City of Philadelphia*, 593 U.S. ___ (2021) (Alito, J., concurring). See, also, Justice O'Connor's dissenting opinion in *City of Boerne v. Flores*, 527 U.S. 501 (1997), which relies heavily on Michael W. McConnell, "The Origins and Historical Understanding of Free Exercise of Religion," *Harvard Law Review* 103 (1990): 1409–1517.

19. See Justice Scalia's concurring opinion in *City of Boerne v. Flores*, 527 U.S. 501 (1997), which cites Philip Hamburger, "A Constitutional Right to Religious Exemption: An Historical Perspective," *George Washington Law Review* 60 (1992): 915–48.

20. See Justice Rehnquist's dissenting opinion in *Thomas v. Review Board of the Indiana Employment Security Division*, 450 U.S. 707, 720–21 (1981). See also Kent Greenawalt, *When Free Exercise and Nonestablishment Conflict* (Cambridge, MA: Harvard University Press, 2017).

21. *Rosenberger v. Rector and Visitors of the University of Virginia*, 515 U.S. 819, 861 (1995). More recently and only slightly more moderately, Justice Samuel Alito wrote, "Pinning down the meaning of a 'law respecting an establishment of religion' has proved to be a vexing problem." *American Legion v. American Humanist Association*, 588 U.S. ___, slip op. at 12 (2019). In the same case, Justice Gorsuch (slip op. at 7) wrote, "As the plurality documents, our 'doctrine [is] in such chaos' that lower courts have been 'free to reach almost any result in almost any case,'" quoting Michael W. McConnell, "Religious Participation in Public Policy Programs: Religious Freedom at the Crossroads," *University of Chicago Law Review* 59 (1992): 119.

Regarding the United States Supreme Court's church-state jurisprudence as a whole, Nelson Tebbe, in *Religious Freedom in an Egalitarian Age* (Cambridge, MA: Harvard University Press, 2017), 7, writes:

Current law is complex and often contradictory. And no one has identified a single tenet or rubric that is capable of organizing all of First Amendment law. Instead, the

This disarray does not owe to a dearth of originalist scholarship. A veritable cottage industry exists on the subject of religious liberty and the American Founding. Nonetheless, and as presumptuous as I fear this will sound, this book contends that we have neither grasped the Founders' natural rights understanding of religious liberty nor accurately appreciated how it would inform First Amendment church-state jurisprudence. *Religious Liberty and the American Founding* attempts to provide this understanding by accomplishing three things:

- documenting and explaining the Founders' understanding of religious liberty as an inalienable natural right.
- uncovering what we can *and cannot* determine about the original meaning of the First Amendment's Religion Clauses.
- in light of the foregoing, constructing a natural rights jurisprudence for the First Amendment's Religion Clauses and explaining how the approach could adjudicate First Amendment church-state issues.

I should make clear that my aim is not to provide a systematic argument for the adoption of a natural rights jurisprudence of religious liberty. While I am sympathetic to some aspects of the Founders' political and constitutional thinking, my purpose is not advocacy and my goals are more modest. I hope instead to present a historically and philosophically sound account of the Founders' church-state constitutional thought that will equip the reader (a) to better evaluate how the Founders have been used and misused, especially by judges, (b) to consider with greater depth and understanding whether we ought to attempt to implement the Founders' church-state natural rights constitutionalism, and (c) should we choose

---

doctrine is driven by multiple commitments. Perhaps for that reason, the law seems immune to systematization or meaningful simplification.

More colorfully, Paul Horwitz, in *The Agnostic Age: Law, Religion, and the Constitution* (New York: Oxford University Press, 2011), xii, writes:

The Establishment Clause and the Free Exercise Clause . . . have occasioned endless debate and confusion. It is so common and so obligatory nowadays to begin any serious work on law and religion in the United States by describing this confusion that the computers of American law and religion scholars might as well come with a macro key to save them the time and trouble of hunting down the usual sources. Instead, a keystroke would vomit forth words and phrases like "incoherent," "chaotic, controversial and unpredictable," "in shambles," "schizoid," "confused," and "a complete hash." And that is just what law and religion scholars are likely to say when they are feeling generous. On bad days, they may say something *really* unpleasant.

to follow their lead, to facilitate a more accurate application of the Founders' natural rights political thought to contemporary constitutional issues.

As noted, Supreme Court justices repeatedly invoke the Founders in church-state cases. Whatever one thinks about looking to the past to guide the present, if history is to be consulted, one should consult the most accurate and comprehensive historical accounts available. Toward that end, I hope this book will contribute to the ongoing scholarly effort to better understand the Founders' constitutionalism of religious liberty. I also hope that it will be useful to citizens whose civic responsibilities include keeping a watchful eye over those whose duties include fidelity to our Constitution and the liberties it is meant to protect. One of this book's findings, we shall see, is that the Founders have been misused in a number of important church-state opinions.

This book also aims to contribute to the broader scholarly discussion of whether we ought to attempt to return to the Founders' understanding for our constitutional practice. It does so from a perspective somewhat different than most originalists. At the core of the originalist method is the proposition that a legal text's original meaning ought to govern us.[22] That might be true in a narrow and immediate sense, especially as it applies to the role of judges in a constitutional republic. But that a text's original meaning is thus and such is not a compelling reason to follow it in a more comprehensive sense. Unjust and ill-considered laws have original meanings too, and one should not be eager to give them effect even if obligated to do so. Ultimately, the most persuasive reason to adopt the Constitution's original meaning is that its meaning helps to make the Constitution a *good* constitution. I do not think it sufficient, therefore, only to know the Constitution's original meaning. We necessarily must make judgments about its merits.[23] To make considered judgments, we need to understand

22. Originalists offer different accounts of why the Constitution's original meaning is binding, but most accept what Larry Solum calls "the fixation thesis" (the linguistic meaning of the constitutional text was fixed at the time each provision was framed and ratified) and "the public meaning thesis" (constitutional meaning is fixed by the understanding of the words and phrases and the grammar and syntax that characterize the linguistic practices of the public and not by the intentions of the framers). See Robert W. Bennett and Lawrence B. Solum, *Constitutional Originalism: A Debate* (Ithaca, NY: Cornell University Press, 2011), 4. For a defense of the relevance of intentions within originalism, see Donald L. Drakeman, *The Hollow Core of Constitutional Theory: Why We Need the Framers* (New York: Cambridge University Press, 2020).

23. Kathleen Brady, in *The Distinctiveness of Religion in American Law: Rethinking Religion Clause Jurisprudence* (New York: Cambridge University Press, 2015), 9, helpfully writes regarding originalism:

the mind of the lawgiver and how desirable it would be to follow it. I attempt, therefore, to present the Founders' understanding of religious liberty; to explore the political, philosophical, and theological reasons that guided it; and to explain how the Founders' approach would resolve leading church-state issues.

Just as my authorial orientation differs from those originalists who accept the Constitution's original meaning only because it is the original meaning, I am not inclined to agree with conservatives who are disposed to follow tradition because it offers a path that is tried and true. I do not believe that the old is the same as the good. At the same time, and unlike many (though certainly not all) progressives, I do not start from the premise that the Founders' thought is outdated or impoverished because it is old or is the thought of elite white men, some of whom owned slaves. We may, in fact, find any number of reasons to disagree with or disregard the Founders. Those conclusions, however, must follow from arguments, not from a presumed intellectual or moral superiority, faith in progress, or bias against the past. I attempt to take the Founders' political and constitutional thought seriously and understand it on its own terms with as few preconceived notions as possible. Only by doing so, I believe, can we then place ourselves in a position to judge its suitability for our own times.

The Argument

In this book I attempt to demonstrate the following:

- Founding-era (1776–91) state declarations of rights and constitutions, as well as the Founders' philosophical and theological political writings, reveal that the

---

Such an approach would not, by itself, be sufficient to convince scholars whose method of constitutional interpretation is not closely tied to history but, rather, draws more on normative analysis. These scholars demand an account of religion's distinctiveness that is persuasive today and principles for decision making that are compelling in their own right.

Making a similar point, Jack M. Balkin, in "The New Originalism and the Uses of History," *Fordham Law Review* 82 (2013): 653, contends:

... Although lawyers use adoption history to appeal to powerful features of American cultural memory, originalist arguments are usually not dispositive unless supported by other kinds of reasons. Precisely because these arguments appeal to ethos and tradition, they will normally not be persuasive unless the audience can plausibly accept the values of the adopters as their own, or can recharacterize them so that they can plausibly accept them as their own.

Founders' most authoritative understanding of religious liberty is that it is an inalienable natural right.

- The First Amendment's framers left the original meanings of the First Amendment's Religion Clauses underdetermined. We can know something about the texts' original meanings, but there is no clear, unambiguous original public meaning of what constitutes an "establishment" of religion or the "free exercise" thereof. To construe the text, accordingly, we must go beyond the text.

- An originalist construction of the Religion Clauses consistent with the First Amendment's text and the Founders' most authoritative understanding would be based on the Founders' conception of religious liberty as an inalienable natural right.

  - For the Free Exercise Clause, an inalienable natural rights construction would prohibit Congress and the states (assuming incorporation) from making laws that exercise jurisdiction over religious exercises as such. Thus constructed, the Free Exercise Clause would prohibit state actions that punish, prohibit, mandate, or regulate religious beliefs or exercises as such.

  - For the Establishment Clause, an inalienable natural rights construction would prohibit Congress and the states (assuming incorporation) from exercising the functions of a church and from delegating government's coercive authority to churches, especially in matters of taxation and financial contributions.

Corresponding contributions I hope this book makes include:

- Elucidating the Founders' inalienable natural rights political philosophy and explaining why an approach to religious liberty jurisprudence based on it captures the Founders' most authoritative understanding.
- Explaining what we can know and what we likely *cannot know* about the original meaning of the First Amendment's Religion Clauses, thereby clarifying why we have to go beyond the First Amendment's text to elaborate its meanings.
- Presenting a natural rights construction of the Religion Clauses based on the Founders' political philosophy of inalienable natural rights.

Jurists have long recognized that the First Amendment Religion Clauses lack clear meanings, but they have never clearly explained why, or forthrightly acknowledged the implications for church-state originalism. The cause of the clauses' underdetermined meanings lies in part in the unique circumstances that led to the creation of the Bill of Rights. Many, if not most, of the individuals who drafted the First Amendment did not think it was necessary. It was the Constitution's critics, the Anti-Federalists, who called for amendments, including a declaration of rights that recognized religious liberty. Anti-Federalists were not numerous enough to prevent the Constitution's ratification, but they did elicit a promise of amendments from the Constitution's supporters, the Federalists, during the ratification debates. These amendments were then drafted in the First Congress, a body dominated by Federalists. The drafting records reflect the Federalists' lack of enthusiasm for amendments. As I will show in detail, the aim of many in the First Congress was to get amendments drafted, not to draft precise amendments. This background is not the whole story. Still, it helps explain why the First Congress could draft text without a clear and precise original meaning.

The Supreme Court has not acknowledged what the texts' underdetermined character means for church-state jurisprudence. Take, for example, *Reynolds v. United States* (1879), the Court's first major Free Exercise Clause case. Writing for the Court, Chief Justice Morrison Waite noted that "the word 'religion' is not defined in the Constitution," and that therefore "we must go elsewhere, . . . to ascertain its meaning. . . ."[24] "Elsewhere" turned out to be Thomas Jefferson's 1802 letter to the Danbury Baptist Association, which, the chief justice said,

> may be accepted almost as an authoritative declaration of the scope and effect of the amendment thus secured. Congress was deprived of all legislative power over mere opinion, but was left free to reach actions which were in violation of social duties or subversive of good order.[25]

Good reasons may exist to turn to Jefferson—I myself will do so in chapter 3, though for different reasons than Chief Justice Waite did—but Waite's quick move from unclear constitutional text to Jefferson's Danbury letter both overlooked and precipitated a number of complications and difficulties. First and foremost, what he said about the relationship between the First Amendment's Religion Clauses and Jefferson's Danbury letter is not really true; no evidence exists to suggest that the scope and

24. *Reynolds v. United States*, 98 U.S. 145, 162 (1879).
25. *Reynolds v. United States*, 98 U.S. 145, 164 (1879). Daniel L. Dreisbach, in *Thomas Jefferson and the Wall of Separation between Church and State* (New York: New York University Press, 2002), 181n71, notes that Chief Justice Waite misquoted Jefferson. Jefferson's actual language is that "Congress was deprived of all legitimate power," not "legislative" power. Dreisbach reports that the transcription error originated with a mistake by the editor of the edition of Jefferson's works cited by Waite.

effect of the Free Exercise Clause was intended to distinguish beliefs from actions and to deny government authority over the former. Moreover, Waite perpetrated a sort of jurisprudential sleight of hand. He claimed to be merely interpreting the text—supposedly uncovering its original meaning through his knowledge of the Founding—when in reality he used Jefferson to create meaning.[26]

In the language of contemporary constitutional theory, Waite "constructed" the Free Exercise Clause. I don't fault Waite for making a construction. My argument, in fact, is that the First Amendment Religion Clauses' underdetermined character means that they must be constructed. I fault Waite, rather, for his lack of candor, for his inadequate justification for turning to Jefferson, and for adopting Jefferson's idiosyncratic belief-action doctrine. Unfortunately, the Court has frequently followed Waite's example in its church-state jurisprudence.[27] The Founders and Founding-era actions are too often cited with little justification, and citations to authority tend to take the place of reasoned argumentation.[28]

26. For a fascinating history of the *Reynolds* decision and the backstory of Chief Justice Waite's turn to the Founders, see Donald L. Drakeman, *Church, State, and Original Intent* (New York: Cambridge University Press, 2010), 21–73.

27. About *Everson v. Board of Education* (1947), Michael W. McConnell, "Establishment at the Founding," in *No Establishment of Religion: America's Original Contribution to Religious Liberty*, ed. T. Jeremy Gunn and John Witte Jr. (New York: Oxford University Press, 2012), 46, writes:

> One would never know from the justices' careless description of history that no small number of the "freedom-loving colonials" considered official sanction for religion natural and essential, that the movement toward disestablishment was hotly contested by many patriotic and republican leaders, and that there were serious arguments—not mere "feelings of abhorrence"—on both sides of the issue. The justices never analyzed any of the books, essays, sermons, speeches, or judicial opinions setting forth the philosophical and political arguments in favor of an establishment of religion, and relied on only one, perhaps unrepresentative, example among the hundreds of arguments made against the establishment.

Donald L. Drakeman titles his chapter on *Everson* in his book *Church, State, and Original Intent*, "*Everson*: A Case of Premeditated Law Office History."

28. It is not hard to understand at least one reason why this happens. To oversimplify, the basic dilemma (or opportunity, depending on one's point of view) is as follows. Courts have authority to enforce the Constitution but only to enforce the Constitution, which means that judges are supposed to find the Constitution's meaning within the Constitution. If a text is unclear, a judge has to go beyond the text to find meaning; but going beyond the text, especially when no precedents exist, might be, or appear to be, illegitimate. If a jurist (or scholar) goes beyond the text to the Founding Fathers, however, it's as if he or she is not really going beyond the text itself, because the Founding Fathers authored the text. Grounding an extratextual opinion in the Founders' thought or practice thus gives the opinion the appearance of legitimacy,

There is a more coherent way to integrate respect for the Constitution's original design and the need to develop meaning. Using the distinction between "interpretation" and "construction" recently introduced by leading constitutional theorists, I explain how we can, by utilizing the Founders' political philosophy of religious liberty, elaborate constitutional doctrines for the Religion Clauses that cohere with the Constitution's text and are (mostly) consistent with what we can determine about the text's original meaning.[29] Unlike Waite, I acknowledge that I am offering a construction of the text, not simply applying its original meaning. Such candor about the necessity of construction will, I hope, spur more robust conversations about whether we are interpreting the Founders correctly and about what evidence is most relevant to develop the First Amendment Religion Clauses consistently with their original design.

This project of originalist construction expands the range of Founding-era evidence considered and develops a more precise articulation of the Founders' philosophical principles. Church-state originalism is dominated by interpretations of Jefferson and Madison, in no small part because of the prominent roles they played in foundational Supreme Court cases, notably Chief Justice Waite's *Reynolds* opinion and the opinions of Justices Hugo Black and Wiley Rutledge in *Everson v. Board of Education* (1947). I, too, recognize the importance of Jefferson and Madison, but I also attempt to place Virginia and its statesmen in their proper historical context by offering a more wide-ranging and thorough investigation of the Founding-era state church-state provisions than typically has been done.

Founding-era state constitutions and declarations of rights are a treasure trove of underappreciated documentary evidence about how the Founding generation generally thought about religious liberty and the proper separation of church and state. To highlight just one example, the 1778 South Carolina Constitution is the one and only Founding-era state constitution that expressly established a religion. It offers particularly helpful insight into what a Founding-era religious establishment was; but for reasons that

---

or at least of increased legitimacy. Citing the Founders' authority, moreover, may relieve the judge of the need to articulate independent reasons for his or her legal doctrine. The Founders thus exercise a sort of gravitational pull, especially in church-state matters, since the Supreme Court has a long history of invoking their authority.

29. I say "mostly consistent" with what we can know about the text's original meaning because the incorporation of the Establishment Clause remains an insuperable difficulty, as I will discuss in chapters 5 and 7.

are not readily apparent, South Carolina's actual establishment has never figured prominently in church-state jurisprudence or scholarship.

Other states, too, shed light on the Founders' understanding of religious liberty. The period between 1776 and 1791 (marking the adoption of the Bill of Rights) was one of tremendous constitutional activity at the state level. Twelve states adopted constitutions, and eight prefaced their constitutions with declarations of rights that served to articulate fundamental political principles. These founding constitutions ought to carry great weight in our understanding of the Founding generation's political and constitutional thinking.[30] They embody the reason and will of the American people acting in their most sovereign political capacity. They offer evidence from every region of the new nation. Church-state matters, furthermore, were primarily state issues at the time. In these state charters, we can find the Founding generation's considered and collective political and constitutional thought about religious liberty and the separation of church and state.[31] Given that the Supreme Court turned to one of the Founding-era states (Virginia) in its first significant Free Exercise and Establishment Clause opinions, it is surprising that the Court and scholars have not more thoroughly investigated all the Founding-era states so as to understand the Founding generation's views as a whole.[32]

30. Donald S. Lutz, "The State Constitutional Pedigree of the U.S. Bill of Rights," *Publius* 22 (1992): 28, concludes:

> The immediate background for the U.S. Bill of Rights was formed by the state bills of rights written between 1776 and 1787. Madison effectively extracted the least common denominator from these state bills of rights, excepting those rights that might reduce the power of the federal government. Almost every one of the twenty-six rights in the U.S. Bill of Rights could be found in two or three state documents, and most of them in five or more.

31. Although I consult the Founding-era state charters for somewhat different reasons, it should be noted that consulting the charters does go toward resolving the "summing" problem. A difficultly that has relentlessly dogged originalism is that it is quite difficult to locate the Founders' shared original intentions or the original public understanding for any given provision. This is why originalism in practice has tended to privilege a few leading individuals or states, a description that certainly fits much church-state originalism. Indeed, the movement by originalist scholars to a focus on the text's original public meaning is in part a response to the summing problem. Taken as a whole, the Founding-era state charters may offer a way to determine the original public meaning of at least some of the Constitution's provisions.

32. I do not mean to suggest that church-state scholars have completely overlooked the Founding-era states and how they might inform First Amendment church-state jurisprudence. For work on the subject, see *Disestablishment and Religious Dissent: Church-State Relations in the New American States 1776–1833*, ed. Carl H. Esbeck and Jonathan J. Den Hartog

These state documents and their church-state provisions provide the pivotal evidence of this study. In every region of the country, Founding-era states recognized religious liberty to be an inalienable natural right. To identify the inalienable natural rights understanding as the Founders' most authoritative view is to contend that other competing accounts—including "neutrality," "accommodation," "separation," "nonendorsement," "minimizing political division," and "tradition"—do not capture the deepest understanding of the Founders' thought. Though some of these accounts may state some individual Founder's view or partially reflect the Founders' more general position, a jurisprudence constructed to further one or more of these alternative notions inevitably departs from the essence of the Founders' inalienable natural rights understanding.

To conclude that the Founders shared a common view of the principle of religious liberty does not imply that they agreed about every church-state matter. My review of the Founding-era states illustrates both how the Founders agreed about the principle of religious liberty and how they disagreed about the proper separation of church and state. Their agreement about fundamental principles did not preclude disagreements about secondary matters. This finding will help us better understand the drafting debates over the First Amendment in the First Congress. It also explains why I prioritize religious free exercise over church-state separation when I offer my constitutional constructions.

Developing constitutional constructions on the basis of the inalienable natural rights character of religious liberty requires a new approach to the First Amendment Religion Clauses.[33] My findings clash with those reached by leading church-state originalists, both on and off the bench. For the Free Exercise Clause, I challenge the conventional wisdom, most

---

(Columbia: University of Missouri Press, 2019); Ellis M. West, *The Free Exercise of Religion in America: Its Original Constitutional Meaning* (Cham, Switzerland: Palgrave Macmillan, 2019); Mark D. McGarvie, "Disestablishing Religion and Protecting Religious Liberty in State Laws and Constitutions (1776–1833)," in *No Establishment of Religion*, 70–99; John K. Wilson, "Religion under the State Constitutions, 1776–1800," *Journal of Church and State* 32 (1990): 753–73; G. Alan Tarr, "Religion under State Constitutions," *Annals of the American Academy of Political and Social Science* 496 (1988): 65–75.

33. Of course, no one begins at the beginning. My work builds upon Philip Hamburger's scholarship on natural rights and religious liberty, including "A Constitutional Right to Religious Exemption: An Historical Perspective"; "Natural Rights, Natural Law, and American Constitutions," *Yale Law Journal* 102 (1993): 907–60; *Separation of Church and State* (Cambridge, MA: Harvard University Press, 2002); "More Is Less," *Virginia Law Review* 90 (2004): 835–92.

powerfully articulated by Michael McConnell and recently championed by Justices Alito, Thomas, and Gorsuch, that the Founders' constitutionalism requires a presumptive right of exemptions from religiously burdensome laws. I will argue that a more thorough understanding of the Founders' principle of inalienable natural rights leads to the conclusion that exemptions from burdensome laws, while constitutionally permissible, are not a natural or constitutional right. Regarding the Establishment Clause, I challenge the "strict separationist" construction first articulated by the Court in *Everson v. Board of Education* (1947) and championed most recently by Justices Ginsburg, Sotomayor, and Kagan. To the extent that the Founders believed religious establishments to be noxious (and not all the Founders did), it was because they believed that establishments fostered a politics that tended toward the violation of the principle of religious liberty. Founders who advocated against religious establishments did not advance nonestablishment as its own independent principle, as "separationists" tend to do, but rather opposed establishments to better secure the fundamental principle of the natural right of religious liberty.[34] I also present an alternative to "accommodationist" constructions. Typically championed by conservatives, including several on the current Supreme Court, "accommodationist" constructions tend to rely on the Founders' post-1789 church-state practices alone, and thus fail to identify those practices that are inconsistent with the Founders' own principles.[35] My constructions correspond to no existing approach, and they do not fall into what are usually considered either the "conservative" or "liberal" positions on church-state matters.

While the Founders remain a significant force in the Supreme Court's jurisprudence, contemporary church-state scholars advance approaches based on seemingly everything but natural rights: liberal egalitarianism,[36]

34. Among the merits of reconsidering the Founders' approach is that it offers an opportunity to harmonize the First Amendment's Religious Clauses, avoiding the Court's sometimes contradictory constructions.

35. See, e.g., Justice Scalia's dissenting opinion in *Lee v. Weisman*, 505 U.S. 577 (1992), and sections 2 and 2-A of Justice Kennedy's opinion for the Court in *Town of Greece v. Galloway*, 572 U.S. 565 (2014), which was joined by Chief Justice Roberts and Justices Scalia, Thomas, and Alito.

36. Among the many varieties of church-state liberal egalitarianism, see Martha C. Nussbaum, *Liberty of Conscience: In Defense of America's Tradition of Religious Equality* (New York: Basic Books, 2008) (emphasizing equality as nondomination/nonsubordination); Christopher L. Eisgruber and Lawrence G. Sager, *Religious Freedom and the Constitution* (Cambridge, MA: Harvard University Press, 2007); Cécile Laborde, *Liberalism's Religion* (Cambridge, MA: Harvard University Press, 2017).

neutrality,[37] social coherence theory,[38] religion's distinctiveness,[39] religion's lack of distinctiveness,[40] constitutional agnosticism,[41] tradition,[42] multiple traditions,[43] the scholar's own creative thinking,[44] or the rejection of theoretical foundations.[45] The natural rights understanding should at least be considered as a serious alternative.[46] And, of course, other countries have their own constitutional traditions; articulating and explaining the natural rights understanding will contribute to comparative constitutional analyses and allow scholars of comparative law to include the American Founding among their case studies.[47]

37. See, e.g., Koppelman, *Defending American Religious Neutrality*; Douglas Laycock, "Formal, Substantive, and Disaggregated Neutrality toward Religion," *DePaul Law Review* 39 (1990): 993–1018; McConnell, "Religious Freedom at a Crossroads." For helpful overviews of "neutrality" in the church-state context, see Emily R. Gill, *Free Exercise of Religion in the Liberal Polity* (Cham, Switzerland: Palgrave Macmillan, 2019), 25–68.

38. See, e.g., Tebbe, *Religious Freedom in an Egalitarian Age*.

39. See, e.g., Brady, *Distinctiveness of Religion in American Law*; Christopher C. Lund, "Religion is Special Enough," *Virginia Law Review* 103 (2017): 481–524.

40. See, e.g., Micah Schwartzman, "What if Religion Is Not Special?" *University of Chicago Law Review* 79 (2012): 1351–1427; Laborde, *Liberalism's Religion*, 3.

41. See, e.g., Horwitz, *Agnostic Age*.

42. See, e.g., Marc O. DeGirolami, "First Amendment Traditionalism," *Washington University Law Review* 97 (2020): 1653–86; Marc O. DeGirolami, "The Traditions of American Constitutional Law," *Notre Dame Law Review* 95 (2020): 1123–81.

43. See, e.g., John Witte, Jr. and Joel A. Nichols, *Religion and the American Constitutional Experiment: Essential Rights and Liberties*, 4th ed. (New York: Oxford University Press, 2016).

44. See, e.g., Noah Feldman, *Divided by God: America's Church-State Problem—and What We Should Do about It* (New York: Farrar, Straus and Giroux, 2005).

45. See, e.g., Stanley Fish, "Mission Impossible: Settling the Just Bounds between Church and State," *Columbia Law Review* 97 (1997): 2255–2333; Marc O. DeGirolami, *The Tragedy of Religious Freedom* (Cambridge, MA: Harvard University Press, 2013); Larry Alexander, "Liberalism, Religion, and the Unity of Epistemology," *San Diego Law Review* 30 (1993): 763–97; Steven D. Smith, *Foreordained Failure: The Quest for a Constitutional Principle of Religious Freedom* (New York: Oxford University Press, 1995); Steven D. Smith, *Getting over Equality: A Critical Diagnosis of Religious Freedom in America* (New York: New York University Press, 2001).

46. For a still-relevant discussion of the unfavorable disposition toward natural rights in American constitutional jurisprudence, see Hadley Arkes, *Beyond the Constitution* (Princeton, NJ: Princeton University Press, 1990), 11–16. Michael McConnell has presented the leading natural rights account of the Free Exercise Clause. As noted, and as will be developed throughout this study, I offer an alternative interpretation of the Founders' natural rights understanding. For helpful overviews of recent church-state scholarship, see Brady, *Distinctiveness of Religion*, chapters 1 and 2; Horwitz, *Agnostic Age*, chapters 1 and 2; DeGirolami, *Tragedy of Religious Freedom*, part 1.

47. Examples of comparative constitutional accounts focusing on religious liberty include Gary Jeffrey Jacobsohn, *The Wheel of Law: India's Secularism in Comparative Constitutional Context* (Princeton, NJ: Princeton University Press, 2003); Christian Joppke, "Beyond the Wall

Plan of the Work

This study proceeds in three parts. Part 1 explains the Founders' political philosophy of religious freedom. Through an examination of pre-1787 state declarations of rights and state constitutions, it identifies the Founders' core understanding of religious freedom: that the right to worship according to conscience is an inalienable natural right. Chapter 1 presents the evidence for this finding, as well as the evidence that the Founders understood the right to be possessed by all individuals, not just Christians.

Chapter 2 explains the Founders' constitutional understanding of inalienable rights by reviewing their social compact theory of government. The chapter develops two points that are especially important: the all-but-forgotten distinction between alienable and inalienable natural rights, and that natural rights have natural limits. In the Founders' understanding, the natural right to religious liberty was not limited by reasonable legislation consistent with the political common good, even if it limited some religiously motivated acts.

Chapter 3 presents the philosophical and theological arguments that led the Founders to conceive of religious liberty as an inalienable natural right. Here we see that Jefferson and Madison are of fundamental importance, for they articulated the underlying philosophical reasoning that corresponds with the Founding-era states' recognition of the natural rights understanding of religious liberty. We also see that their rightly famous documents were not the only arguments made in favor of natural rights. Dissenting Protestants also championed the idea that religious liberty is an inalienable natural right, a conclusion they reached from scripture and Christian theology. Through a review of Jefferson's Enlightenment philosophy, Madison's natural theology, and the Baptist preacher Isaac Backus's Christian theology, I show how the Founders achieved their own version of an "overlapping consensus" and employed both reason and revelation to support the idea that all individuals possess an inalienable right of religious liberty.

---

of Separation: Religion and the American State in Comparative Perspective," *International Journal of Constitutional Law* 14 (2016): 984–1008; *Law, Religion, Constitution: Freedom of Religion, Equal Treatment, and the Law*, ed. Durham, Ferrari, Cianitto, Thayer (London: Routledge, 2013); Witte and Nichols, *Religion and the American Constitutional Experiment*, 249–75. See also Ran Hirschl and Ayelet Shachar, "Competing Orders? The Challenge of Religion to Modern Constitutionalism," *University of Chicago Law Review* 85 (2018): 425–55.

Chapter 4 concludes part 1 by explaining that while the Founders agreed about the core meaning of religious liberty as an inalienable right, they disagreed about its scope. The more liberal church-state Founders held a more expansive view of religious freedom that, in their understanding, broadly limited the scope of legitimate state action.[48] The more republican church-state Founders held a narrower view of religious liberty that provided more constitutional space for the adoption of majoritarian church-state policies. Both "expansive liberals" and "narrow republicans," as I shall call them, understood their own positions to be compatible with the natural right of religious freedom; they disagreed about the extent to which that right limited democratic governance, and whether it was politically prudent for government to support religion directly.

Understanding how the Founders agreed about the principle of religious liberty but disagreed about the separation of church and state will help us grasp what is determinable about the original meanings of the First Amendment's Religious Clauses, which is the subject of part 2. Chapters 5 and 6 discuss the demands for and drafting of the Establishment and Free Exercise Clauses. I pay close attention to the amendments' drafting records in the First Congress, since they most clearly reveal what we can and cannot determine about the texts' original public meanings. The essential finding of part 2 is that both the Establishment Clause and Free Exercise Clause must be constructed.

Part 3 then offers an originalist construction of the Religion Clauses based on the inalienable natural rights understanding explained in part 1. Chapter 7 articulates a method for originalist constructions, which I call "text and design," and then applies that method to the Free Exercise and Establishment Clauses. Chapter 8 explores how these constructions would adjudicate a number of significant church-state issues by applying the proposed constructions to a number of actual First Amendment cases.

The conclusion presents what I consider to be some of the better arguments for and against the natural right constructions.

*   *   *

Let me offer one additional thought about this study. While it is focused on the issue of religious liberty, I hope the book will be helpful to those

---

48. I use "liberal" here in the sense of eighteenth-century classical liberalism, not in the sense of twentieth- and twenty-first-century progressivism.

NATURAL RIGHTS AND THE RELIGION CLAUSES

interested in the political and constitutional thought of the American Founders more generally. In it, one will find a corrective to the misunderstanding of the Founding advanced by a number of "postliberal" critics. My friend and Notre Dame colleague Patrick Deneen, to take the most noteworthy example, contends that "liberalism has failed because liberalism has succeeded," that the liberal political project, of which the American Founding is the exemplar, was bound to fail on account of its impoverished philosophical foundations.[49] Professor Deneen asserts that liberalism is "most fundamentally constituted by a pair of deeper anthropological assumptions that give liberal institutions a particular orientation and cast: (1) anthropological individualism and the voluntaristic conception of choice, and (2) human separation from and opposition to nature."[50] At least as applied to the political thought of the American Founding, this statement is mistaken. The Founders' natural rights constitutionalism, as this book shows, embraces neither of these "anthropological assumptions." The Founders distinguished liberty from license, and they firmly judged that the law of nature — objective morality — required political authorities to recognize and protect natural rights. The American Founding brought forth neither a "procedural republic" nor a democracy committed to "neutrality toward competing conceptions of the good," but a constitutional republic dedicated to political liberty grounded in the "laws of nature and nature's God."[51]

The Founders protected religious liberty because they held it to be an inalienable natural right. If the Founders were correct, we ought to consider following them not primarily because they are *our* founders or the authors of *our* Constitution, but because they help us better understand and realize the demands of justice. If what George Washington wrote in 1790 to the Hebrew Congregation in Newport is true, and the liberty to worship God according to conscience is one of our inherent natural rights as human beings, we ought to understand the nature and meaning of that right, so as to better protect it. To the extent this book improves

49. Patrick Deneen, *Why Liberalism Failed* (New Haven, CT: Yale University Press, 2018), 179.

50. Deneen, *Why Liberalism Failed*, 31. See also Adrian Vermeule, "Integration from Within," *American Affairs* 2 (2018), 202–13.

51. See Harry V. Jaffa, "Thomas Aquinas Meets Thomas Jefferson," *Interpretation: A Journal of Political Philosophy* 33 (2006): 177–84; Harry V. Jaffa, "The American Founding as the Best Regime: The Bonding of Civil and Religious Liberty," in *The Rediscovery of America: Essays by Harry V. Jaffa on the New Birth of Politics*, ed. Edward J. Erler and Ken Masugi (Lanham, MD: Rowman & Littlefield, 2019), 121–44.

our knowledge of America's founding principles, contributes to a better understanding and jurisprudence of the First Amendment's Religion Clauses, and facilitates a more thorough understanding and realization of the blessings of liberty, I hope it will be useful to the legal community, and of interest and benefit to citizens generally.

PART I

Philosophy: The Founders' Political Philosophy of Religious Liberty

CHAPTER ONE

The Founders' First Agreement

Religious Liberty Is a Natural Right
Possessed by All Individuals

W hen President Washington wrote to the Hebrew Congregation of
Newport, Rhode Island, that "it is now no more that toleration is
spoken of," he may have had in mind the drafting of Virginia's 1776 Declaration of Rights. One of the American Founding's first official acts, the
declaration committed Virginia to the protection of the natural right of
religious freedom, a guarantee that soon would be recognized in nearly
every state of the union. This chapter documents two points: (1) the
Founders' common understanding of religious freedom was that it is a
natural right, and (2) they understood that right to be possessed by all
individuals.[1] I start with these elementary points in part because today the
pursuit of "neutrality"—rather than the protection of the natural right
of liberty—plays a central role in church-state scholarship and jurisprudence, and in part because the universal character of the Founders' political philosophy—that they held natural rights to be possessed by all individuals, not just white men—is underappreciated today.[2]

---

1. This chapter draws on material that first appeared in Vincent Phillip Muñoz, "If Religious Liberty Does Not Mean Exemptions, What Might It Mean? The Founders' Constitutionalism of the Inalienable Rights of Religious Liberty," *Notre Dame Law Review* 91 (2016):
1387–1417; Vincent Phillip Muñoz, "Church and State in the Founding-Era State Constitutions," *American Political Thought* 4 (2015): 1–38.
2. On the role of "neutrality" in the Supreme Court's recent jurisprudence, see, for example, *American Legion v. American Humanist Association*, 588 U.S. ___, slip op. at 2 (2019),

The proximate cause of the drafting of Virginia's Declaration of Rights was the Second Continental Congress's May 1776 call for each colony to prepare a constitution appropriate for an independent state. In Virginia, that task fell primarily to George Mason.[3] Mason drafted two distinct documents, a declaration of rights and a constitution. Due to our experience with the federal Bill of Rights, we think of declarations of rights as the part of a constitution that protects individual rights by specifying legal restrictions on governmental power. This is not the function they originally served. The early Founding-era state declarations of rights were not legal documents in the sense of constitutional law. Rather, they were written as a sort of preamble that served to educate citizens and officeholders about the fundamental rights of individuals and the principles of free government.[4]

(Kagan, J., concurring) (praising the majority opinion's "respect for the Nation's pluralism, and the values of neutrality and inclusion that the First Amendment demands"); Justice Kennedy's seven-member Court opinion in *Masterpiece Cakeshop v. Colorado Civil Rights Commission*, 584 U.S. ___, slip op. at 3, (2018) ("When the Colorado Civil Rights Commission considered this case, it did not do so with the religious neutrality that the Constitution requires"); *Trump v. Hawaii*, 585 U.S. ___, slip op. at 1 (2018) (Sotomayor, J., dissenting) ("The United States of America is a Nation built upon the promise of religious liberty. Our Founders honored that core promise by embedding the principle of religious neutrality in the First Amendment").

For the role of "neutrality" in church-state scholarship, see, e.g., Andrew P. Koppelman, *Defending American Religious Neutrality* (Cambridge, MA: Harvard University Press, 2013); Douglas Laycock, "Formal, Substantive, and Disaggregated Neutrality toward Religion," *DePaul Law Review* 39 (1990): 993–1018; Emily R. Gill, *Free Exercise of Religion in the Liberal Polity* (Cham, Switzerland: Palgrave Macmillan, 2019), 25–68.

3. Mason would later represent the state at the 1787 Constitutional Convention in Philadelphia and become a leading Anti-Federalist, in part because the Constitution lacked a bill of rights. For discussions of the drafting of the 1776 Virginia Declaration of Rights and Mason's role in it, see Daniel Dreisbach, "George Mason's Pursuit of Religious Liberty in Revolutionary Virginia," in *The Founders on God and Government*, ed. Dreisbach, Hall, and Morrison (Lanham, MD: Rowman and Littlefield, 2004), 207–49; Bernard Schwartz, *The Great Rights of Mankind: A History of the American Bill of Rights* (New York: Oxford University Press, 1977), 67–72.

4. For further discussion of Founding-era state declarations of rights and their purposes, see Donald S. Lutz, *Popular Consent and Popular Control: Whig Political Theory in the Early State Constitutions* (Baton Rouge: Louisiana State University Press, 1980), 61–71; Robert C. Palmer, "Liberties as Constitutional Provisions 1776–1791," in *Liberty and Community: Constitution and Rights in the Early American Republic*, with introduction by Frederick Schauer (New York: Oceana Publications, Inc., 1987), 55–148; G. Alan Tarr, *Understanding State Constitutions* (Princeton, NJ: Princeton University Press, 1998), 76–81; John J. Dinan, *Keeping the People's Liberties: Legislators, Citizens, and Judges as Guardians of Rights* (Lawrence: University Press of Kansas, 1998), 2; Marc W. Krumen, *Between Authority and Liberty: State Constitution Making in Revolutionary America* (Chapel Hill: University of North Carolina Press, 1999), 37–49.

Mason opened his initial draft with a resounding statement of natural rights:

That all Men are born equally free and independant [*sic*], and have certain inherent natural Rights, of which they can not by any Compact, deprive or divest their Posterity; among which are the Enjoyment of Life and Liberty, with the Means of acquiring and possessing Property, and pursueing [*sic*] and obtaining Happiness and Safety.

Mason also specifically addressed religious freedom:

that all Men shou'd enjoy the fullest Toleration in the Exercise of Religion, according to the Dictates of Conscience.[5]

The Virginia convention adopted most of Mason's draft declaration with only minor revisions. But a young James Madison took issue with Mason's use of "Toleration," proposing in its place "the full and free exercise" of religion.[6]

5. The full text of Mason's initial proposal regarding religious toleration was as follows:

That as Religion, or the Duty which we owe to our divine and omnipotent Creator, and the Manner of discharging it, can be governed only by Reason and Conviction, not by Force or Violence; and therefore that all Men shou'd enjoy the fullest Toleration in the Exercise of Religion, according to the Dictates of Conscience, unpunished and unrestrained by the Magistrate, unless, under Colour of Religion, any Man disturb the Peace, the Happiness, or Safety of Society, or of Individuals. And that it is the mutual Duty of all, to practice Christian Forbearance, Love and Charity towards Each other.

Selections from Mason's initial draft and the final adopted text of the 1776 Virginia Declaration of Rights can be found in Dreisbach, "George Mason's Pursuit of Religious Liberty in Revolutionary Virginia," 234–36.

6. The full text of Madison's initial proposed revision was as follows:

That Religion or the duty we owe to our Creator, and the manner of discharging it, being under the direction of reason and conviction only, not of violence or compulsion, all men are equally entitled to the full and free exercise of it according to the dictates of conscience; and therefore that no man or class of men ought, on account of religion to be invested with peculiar emoluments or privileges; nor subjected to any penalties or disabilities unless under the color of religion, any man disturb the peace, the happiness, or safety of Society. And that it is the mutual duty of all to practice Christian forbearance, love, and charity, towards each other.

The text can be found in Irving Brant, *James Madison: The Virginia Revolutionist* (New York: Bobbs-Merrill, 1941), 245. According to Thomas E. Buckley, S.J., *Church and State in Revolutionary Virginia, 1776–1784* (Charlottesville: University Press of Virginia, 1977), 18–19,

"Toleration" might suggest that the state possesses legitimate authority over religious duties, such that their exercise is a civil privilege that could be granted or revoked by the state at will. "Full and free exercise," by contrast, better accorded with the meaning and grounding of inherent natural rights.[7] As Thomas Paine would write a few years later,

> Toleration is not the *opposite* of intoleration, but is the *counterfeit* of it. Both are despotisms. The one assumes to itself the right of withholding liberty of conscience, and the other of granting it. The one is the Pope, armed with fire and faggot, and the other is the Pope selling or granting indulgences. The former is church and state, and the latter is church and traffic.[8]

The Virginia convention appears to have agreed, adopting the following language in Article 16:

> all men are equally entitled to the free exercise of religion, according to the dictates of conscience. . . .[9]

Describing the Virginia Declaration in 1778, Mason wrote, "We have laid our new government upon a broad foundation, and have endeavored to provide the most effectual securities for the essential rights of human nature, both in civil and religious liberty. . . ."[10]

Madison's initial proposed text was submitted for consideration by Patrick Henry, and his second proposed revision was submitted by Edmund Pendleton. See also Carl H. Esbeck, "Virginia," in *Disestablishment and Religious Dissent: Church-State Relations in the New American States, 1776–1783*, ed. Carl H. Esbeck and Jonathan J. Den Hartog (Columbia: University of Missouri Press, 2019), 140–43.

7. Brant, *James Madison*, 247–48.

8. Paine's emphasis. Thomas Paine, *The Rights of Man*, pt. 1 [1791] in *The Founders' Constitution*, ed. Kurland and Lerner (Indianapolis. IN: Liberty Fund, n.d.; originally published in Chicago: University of Chicago Press, 1987), 5:95. For a brief and helpful overview of the concept and practice of toleration in post-Reformation Europe, see Jack N. Rakove, *Beyond Belief, beyond Conscience: The Radical Significance of the Free Exercise of Religion* (New York: Oxford University Press, 2020), 13–40.

9. For discussions of the significance and meaning of Madison's proposed changes to Mason's text, see Dreisbach, "George Mason's Pursuit of Religious Liberty in Revolutionary Virginia," 211–15; Vincent Phillip Muñoz, *God and the Founders: Madison, Washington, and Jefferson* (New York: Cambridge University Press, 2009), 32–34.

10. Letter from George Mason to Colonel George Mercer, October 2, 1778, in *Principles and Acts of the Revolution in America,* ed. Hezekiah Niles (New York: A. S. Barnes, 1876), 303. Mason's letter continued as follows: "The people become every day more and more attached to it; and I trust that neither the power of Great Britain, nor the power of hell will be able to

Virginia's express recognition of inherent rights and its affirmation that *all* men are entitled to the "free exercise of religion" mark the official beginning of the new nation's commitment to religious freedom.[11] Madison biographer Irving Brant called Virginia's 1776 Declaration of Rights an "epochal" act of statesmanship. Its proclamation of religious freedom, he wrote, "asserted, for the first time in any body of fundamental law, a natural right which had not previously been recognized as such by political bodies in the Christian world."[12]

Did the Founders Share a Common Understanding of Religious Liberty?

Other states soon followed Virginia's lead. Before turning to them, however, let me note a significant methodological difficulty endemic to Founding-era studies in general and to originalist legal inquiry in particular. Given that the American Founding was a collective action undertaken by numerous individuals and several distinct political bodies, one might ask whether we can identify a unitary set of "founding political principles." Does any single voice or document adequately represent and capture the seemingly diverse views of the Founders as a whole? Who counts as a "Founder"? And what counts as an authoritative "Founding document"?[13] Such questions are particularly germane to historical scholarship on religious freedom. My own previous work on the church-state political thought of James Madison, George Washington, and Thomas

---

prevail against it." It should be noted that, in what became Article 1, the Virginia Convention changed Mason's "inherent natural rights" to "inherent rights." Earlier in his letter to Mercer, Mason had written that his original draft "received few alterations, some of them I think not for the better." For a discussion of the changes made to Article 2, see Helen Hill Miller, *George Mason: Gentleman Revolutionary* (Chapel Hill: University of North Carolina Press, 1975), 149.

11. I do not mean to imply, of course, that religious freedom or the idea of a natural right to religious freedom was absent or unknown prior to the Founding. Regarding the latter, see, for example, the discussion of Elisha Williams in chapter 3.

12. Brant, *James Madison*, 190, 249.

13. Though focused more specifically on interpreting the Constitution's text than on the "Founders' understanding" generally, Larry Solum's account of the "summing problem" is at least partially applicable to this issue. See Robert W. Bennett and Lawrence B. Solum, *Constitutional Originalism: A Debate* (Ithaca, NY: Cornell University Press, 2011), 87–88. See also Paul Brest, "The Misconceived Quest for the Original Understanding," *Boston University Law Review* 60 (1980): 204–38.

Jefferson emphasizes their differences and disagreements.[14] Scholarship
focusing on the "forgotten Founders" adds more voices to an already ca-
cophonous conversation.[15] Noting all these diverse voices, some scholars
go so far as to deny that any shared position or any single "Founders'
understanding" of religious liberty exists.[16]

The Founders did, in fact, share a conception of religious liberty notwithstanding some important disagreements, as will be discussed in chapter 4. We can speak confidently of the Founders' common understanding
because they themselves produced several authoritative documents articulating a consistent political philosophy. Between 1776 and 1786, twelve
states drafted state constitutions.[17] (I include Vermont, which did not become a state until 1791, but which drafted a constitution in 1777 and then
revised it in 1786.) Eight of these twelve states also drafted declarations of
rights. These early state charters, penned in every part of the new nation,
are the collective voice of the citizens of the several Founding-era states
acting in their sovereign capacities as self-constituting and self-governing
political societies. As one scholar has noted, they "represent the most
authoritative expression of the consensus of the founding generation."[18]
Justice Samuel Alito has recently written that they "provide the best evidence of the scope of the right embodied in the First Amendment."[19] In

14. Muñoz, *God and the Founders*.

15. *The Forgotten Founders on Religion and Public Life*, ed. Dreisbach, Hall, Morrison
(Notre Dame, IN: University of Notre Dame Press, 2009).

16. David Sehat, *The Myth of American Religious Freedom* (New York: Oxford University
Press, 2011), 13–29.

17. Rhode Island and Connecticut simply revised their existing colonial charters by removing all references to the British Crown. The colonies of South Carolina and New Hampshire adopted short provisional constitutions in early 1776, but rewrote their constitutions in
1778 and 1784, respectively.

18. Thomas G. West, *The Political Theory of the American Founding: Natural Rights, Public
Policy, and the Moral Conditions of Freedom* (New York: Cambridge University Press, 2017),
175. Cf. Edward J. Erler, *Property and the Pursuit of Happiness: Locke, the Declaration of
Independence, Madison, and the Challenge of the Administrative State* (Lanham, MD: Rowman and Littlefield, 2019), 221, contending that "the States can hardly be said to represent the
standard for religious freedom as it was understood by the founders."

19. *Fulton v. City of Philadelphia*, 593 U.S. ___, slip op. at 33 (2021) (Alito, J., concurring). In
City of Boerne v. Flores, 521 U.S. 507, 553 (1997) (O'Connor, J., dissenting), Justice O'Connor
similarly stated that the Founding-era state provisions offer "perhaps the best evidence of
the original understanding of the Constitution's protection of religious liberty. After all it is
reasonable to think that the States that ratified the First Amendment assumed that the meaning of the federal free exercise provision corresponded to that of their existing state clauses."

About the pre-1787 state constitutions, church-state scholar Michael W. McConnell, in
"The Origins and Historical Understanding of Free Exercise of Religion," *Harvard Law Review* 103 (1990), 1456, has written:

these founding constitutions, the Founders set forth a coherent and consistent understanding of religious liberty. Agreement was not complete, as we will see; but it was sufficiently common to warrant talk of the Founders' shared principle.

The Founders' Recognition of Religious Liberty as a Natural Right

The early Founding-era state charters reveal that the Founders held religious liberty to be a natural right possessed by all individuals.[20] As table 1 shows, all eight state declarations of rights drafted between 1776 and 1786 included statements of religious freedom. Five states (Delaware, Pennsylvania, North Carolina, Vermont, New Hampshire) explicitly identified religious worship according to conscience as a natural and inalienable right. Three states (Virginia, Maryland, Massachusetts) did not. But Massachusetts and Maryland included natural rights language elsewhere in their declarations of rights, and adopted text protecting religious liberty that was consistent with, if not suggestive of, the natural rights understanding.[21]

These state constitutions provide the most direct evidence of the original understanding [of the Free Exercise Clause], for it is reasonable to infer that those who drafted and adopted the first amendment assumed the term "free exercise of religion" meant what it had meant in their states. The wording of the state provisions thus casts light on the meaning of the first amendment.

20. On the American Founders' belief in and commitment to protecting natural rights more generally, see West, *Political Theory of the American Founding*, 19–42; Michael P. Zuckert, *The Natural Rights Republic: Studies in the Foundation of the American Political Tradition* (Notre Dame, IN: University of Notre Dame Press, 1996); Michael P. Zuckert, "Natural Rights in the American Revolution: The American Amalgam," in *Launching Liberalism: On Lockean Political Philosophy* (Lawrence: University Press of Kansas, 2002), 274–93; Randy Barnett, "A Law Professor's Guide to Natural Law and Natural Rights," *Harvard Journal of Law and Public Policy* 20 (1997), 655. Of course, not all scholars agree that natural rights were central to the American Founding. See, e.g., J. G. A. Pocock, *The Machiavellian Moment: Florentine Political Thought and the Atlantic Republican Tradition* (Princeton, NJ: Princeton University Press, 1975); John Phillip Reid, *Constitutional History of the American Revolution: The Authority of Rights* (Madison: University of Wisconsin Press, 1986).

21. Article 1 of the 1780 Massachusetts Declaration of Rights begins by declaring, "All men are born free and equal, and have certain natural, essential and unalienable rights. . . ." Article 2 then declares, "It is the right as well as the duty of all men in society . . . to worship the Supreme Being." The religion article of Maryland's 1776 Declaration of Rights does not identify religious liberty as a natural right, but refers to natural rights elsewhere in the same article. *The Federal and State Constitutions, Colonial Charters, and Other Organic Laws of the United States*, 2nd edition, ed. Ben Perley Poore (Washington: Government Printing Office, 1878), 1:957, 819.

And we have already discussed the 1776 Virginia Declaration of Rights and how its religious freedom provision embodied the natural rights understanding—a view the state would embrace definitively when, in 1786, it adopted Jefferson's Statute for Religious Freedom and its proclamation that religious liberty is "of the natural rights of mankind."[22]

22. "A Bill for Establishing Religious Freedom in Virginia," in Vincent Phillip Muñoz, *Religious Liberty and the American Supreme Court: The Essential Cases and Documents*, updated edition (Lanham, MD: Rowman and Littlefield, 2015), 605. I limit my discussion to the state charters adopted prior to 1787 on the premise that doing so will help us grasp how religious liberty was understood prior to and at the time of the First Amendment's adoption. Regarding the problems of interpreting the original meaning of a constitutional provision on the basis of a law passed after its adoption, see Ellis M. West, *The Free Exercise of Religion in America: Its Original Constitutional Meaning* (Cham, Switzerland: Palgrave Macmillan, 2019), 25–29.

Examining the constitutions of state governments that entered the union after the First Amendment was adopted, however, would confirm the natural rights understanding. Of the ten states that entered the Union between 1792 and 1820, nine included protections for the right to religious freedom. Of these nine states, seven recognized the right to worship God as a "natural and indefeasible" or "natural and unalienable" right. Mississippi's 1817 and Alabama's 1819 constitutions did not expressly declare religious freedom to be an inalienable natural right, but they embraced the natural rights social compact understanding of government, and their constitutional protections are consistent with the natural rights understanding. Louisiana's 1812 constitution did not contain a bill of rights or a provision related to religious freedom. After Missouri's entry into the Union in 1820, no state entered the Union until Arkansas in 1836. The relevant religious freedom text from these states is below. Volume and page numbers in parentheses refer to Poore's *Federal and State Constitutions*.

Kentucky (1792) Article 12. "That all men have a natural and indefeasible right to worship Almighty God according to the dictates of their own consciences. . . ." (1:654)

Tennessee (1796) Article 11, Section 3. "That all men have a natural and indefeasible right to worship Almighty God according to the dictates of their own consciences; . . ." (2:1673)

Ohio (1802) Article 8, Section 3. "That all men have a natural and indefeasible right to worship Almighty God according to the dictates of their conscience; . . ." (1:1461)

Louisiana (1812) [No religious freedom provision or bill of rights]

Indiana (1816) Article 1, Section 3. "That all men have a natural and indefeasible right to worship Almighty God, according to the dictates of their own consciences: . . ." (2:500)

Mississippi (1817) Article 1, Section 3. "The exercise and enjoyment of religious profession and worship, without discrimination, shall forever be free to all persons in this State; . . ." (1:1055)

Illinois (1818) Article 8, Section 3. "That all men have a natural and indefeasible right to worship Almighty God according to the dictates of their own consciences; . . ." (1:446)

Alabama (1819) Article 1, Section 3. "No person within this state shall, upon, any pretence, be deprived of the inestimable privilege of worshipping God in the manner most agreeable to his own conscience; . . ." Section 4. "No human authority ought, in any case whatever, to control or interfere with the rights of conscience." (1:33)

Maine (1820) Article 1, Section 3. "All men have a natural and unalienable right to worship Almighty God according to the dictates of their own consciences, . . ." (1:1788–89)

Missouri (1820) Article 8, Section 4. "That all men have a natural and indefeasible right to worship Almighty God according to the dictates of their own consciences; . . ." (2:1114)

When the Founders spoke of "natural" rights, they meant to distinguish them from "acquired" rights, or what we today often call "civil" rights.[23] Natural rights, in the Founders' understanding, exist prior to government. They are "natural" in the sense that neither the state nor any other human authority creates them. They are "inherent" in the sense that they inhere in the individual on account of human nature. Washington's prose in his letter to the Hebrew Congregation in Newport—"It is now no more that toleration is spoken of, as if it was by the indulgence of one class of people, that another enjoyed the exercise of their inherent natural rights"— reflects the Founders' shared natural rights understanding that religious liberty belongs to the individual independently of, and prior to, any state recognition or state action.[24] "Toleration" is no longer spoken of because religious freedom is not granted by the state; rather, just governments recognize and secure individuals' natural right of religious liberty.

The eight Founding-era states that adopted declarations of rights provide the clearest and most authoritative evidence that the Founders widely recognized religious liberty as a *natural* right. As documented in table 1, five of these states explicitly identified religious liberty as a natural right; the other three discussed natural rights elsewhere in their declarations, and adopted religious liberty provisions consistent with that framework. These declarations were designed to educate the American people about their rights and the corresponding responsibilities of government; precisely speaking, most were not judicially enforceable legal documents akin to the Federal Bill of Rights.[25] Like the Declaration of Independence,

23. Philip Hamburger, "Natural Rights, Natural Law, and American Constitutions," *Yale Law Journal* 102 (1993), 908.

24. For a complementary discussion of natural rights in the context of freedom of speech, see Jud Campbell, "Natural Rights and the First Amendment," *Yale Law Journal* 127 (2017): 249–321.

25. Dinan, *Keeping the People's Liberties*, 2. In this light, consider the following comment from John Marshall during the Virginia convention that ratified the Constitution:

Does our [Virginia] Constitution direct trials to be by jury? It is required in our bill of rights, which is not a part of the Constitution. Does any security arise from hence? . . . The [Virginia] bill of rights is merely recommendatory. Were it otherwise, the consequence would be that many laws which are found convenient would be unconstitutional.

Jonathan Elliot, *The Debates in the Several State Conventions on the Adoption of the Federal Constitution, as Recommended by the General Convention at Philadelphia, in 1787*, 2nd edition (Washington: Taylor and Maury, 1836), 3:56. Article 8 of the 1776 Virginia Declaration of Rights stated, "That in all capital or criminal prosecutions a man hath a right . . . to a speedy trial by an impartial jury of twelve men of his vicinage." *Federal and State Constitutions*, 2:1909. As Lutz, in *Popular Consent and Popular Control*, 62, 65–67, further explains,

TABLE I. **Recognition of the right to religious liberty in pre-1787 Founding-era state declarations of rights and state constitutions***

Founding-era state declarations of rights

VA 1776	Sec. 16. That religion, or the duty which we owe to our Creator, and the manner of discharging it, can be directed only by reason and conviction, not by force or violence; and therefore all men are equally entitled to the free exercise of religion, according to the dictates of conscience; and that it is the mutual duty of all to practice Christian forbearance, love, and charity towards each other.
DE 1776	SECT 2. That all men have a natural and unalienable right to worship Almighty God according to the dictates of their own consciences and understandings; and that no man ought or of right can be compelled to attend any religious worship or maintain any ministry contrary to or against his own free will and consent, and that no authority can or ought to. be vested in, or assumed by any power whatever that shall in any case interfere with, or in any manner controul the right of conscience in the free exercise of religious worship.
PA 1776	II. That all men have a natural and unalienable right to worship Almighty God according to the dictates of their own consciences and understanding: And that no man ought or of right can be compelled to attend any religious worship, or erect or support any place of worship, or maintain any ministry, contrary to, or against, his own free will and consent: Nor can any man, who acknowledges the being of a God, be justly deprived or abridged of any civil right as a citizen, on account of his religious sentiments or peculiar mode of religious worship: And that no authority can or ought to be vested in, or assumed by any power whatever, that shall in any case interfere with, or in any manner controul, the right of conscience in the free exercise of religious worship.
MD 1776	XXXIII. That, as it is the duty of every man to worship God in such manner as he thinks most acceptable to him; all persons, professing the Christian religion, are equally entitled to protection in their religious liberty; wherefore no person ought by any law to be molested in his person or estate on account of his religious persuasion or profession, or for his religious practice; unless, under colour of religion, any man shall disturb the good order, peace or safety of the State, or shall infringe the laws of morality, or injure others, in their natural, civil, or religious rights; nor ought any person to be compelled to frequent or maintain, or contribute, unless on contract, to maintain any particular place of worship, or any particular ministry....
NC 1776	XIX. That all men have a natural and unalienable right to worship Almighty God according to the dictates of their own consciences.
MA 1780	II. It is the right as well as the duty of all men in society, publicly and at stated seasons, to worship the Supreme Being, the great Creator and Preserver of the universe. And no subject shall be hurt, molested, or restrained, in his person, liberty, or estate, for worshipping God in the manner and season most agreeable to the dictates of his own conscience, or for his religious profession or sentiments, provided he doth not disturb the public peace or obstruct others in their religious worship.
NH 1784	V. Every individual has a natural and unalienable right to worship GOD according to the dictates of his own conscience, and reason; and no subject shall be hurt, molested, or restrained in his person, liberty or estate for worshipping GOD, in the manner and season most agreeable to the dictates of his own conscience, or for his religious profession, sentiments or persuasion; provided he doth not disturb the public peace, or disturb others, in their religious worship.
VT 1786	III. All men have a natural and unalienable right to worship Almighty God, according to the dictates of their own consciences and understandings, as in their opinion shall be regulated by the word of GOD; and that no man ought, or of right can be compelled to attend any religious worship, or erect or support any place of worship, or maintain any minister, contrary to the dictates of his conscience; nor can any man be justly deprived or abridged of any civil right as a citizen, on account of his religious sentiments, or peculiar mode of religious worship; and that no authority can, or ought to be vested in, or assumed by any power whatsoever, that shall in any case interfere with, or in any manner control the rights of conscience, in the free exercise of religious worship: Nevertheless, every sect or denomination of Christians ought to observe the Sabbath or the Lord's day, and keep up some sort of religious worship, which to them shall seem most agreeable to the revealed will of God.

TABLE I. (*continued*)

Founding-era state constitutions

NJ 1776	XVIII. That no person shall ever, within this Colony, be deprived of the inestimable privilege of worshipping Almighty God in a manner agreeable to the dictates of his own conscience; nor, under any pretence whatever, be compelled to attend any place of worship, contrary to his own faith and judgement; nor shall any person, within this Colony, ever be obliged to pay tithes, taxes, or any other rates, for the purpose of building or repairing any other church or churches, place or places of worship, or for the maintenance of any minister or ministry, contrary to what he believes to be right, or has deliberately or voluntarily engaged himself to perform. XIX. That there shall be no establishment of any one religious sect in this Province, in preference to another; and that no Protestant inhabitant of this Colony shall be denied the enjoyment of any civil right, merely on account of his religious principles....
NC 1776	XXXIV. That there shall be no establishment of any one religious church or denomination in this State, in preference to any other; neither shall any person, on any presence whatsoever, be compelled to attend any place of worship contrary to his own faith or judgment, nor be obliged to pay, for the purchase of any glebe, or the building of any house of worship, or for the maintenance of any minister or ministry, contrary to what he believes right, or has voluntarily and personally engaged to perform; but all persons shall be at liberty to exercise their own mode of worship: — *Provided*, That nothing herein contained shall be construed to exempt preachers of treasonable or seditious discourses, from legal trial and punishment.
GA 1777	LVI. All persons whatever shall have the free exercise of their religion; provided it be not repugnant to the peace and safety of the State; and shall not, unless by consent, support any teacher or teachers except those of their own profession.
NY 1777	XXXVIII. And whereas we are required, by the benevolent principles of rational liberty, not only to expel civil tyranny, but also to guard against that spiritual oppression and intolerance wherewith the bigotry and ambition of weak and wicked priests and princes have scourged mankind, this convention doth further, in the name and by the authority of the good people of this State, ordain, determine, and declare, that the free exercise and enjoyment of religious profession and worship, without discrimination or preference, shall forever hereafter be allowed, within this State, to all mankind: *Provided*, That the liberty of conscience, hereby granted, shall not be so construed as to excuse acts of licentiousness, or justify practices inconsistent with the peace or safety of this State.
SC 1778	XXXVIII. That all persons and religious societies who acknowledge that there is one God, and a future state of rewards and punishments, and that God is publicly to be worshipped, shall be freely tolerated.

*Texts in this table can be found in *Federal and State Constitutions*, with the exception of the provision of the 1776 Delaware Declaration of Rights, which for unclear reasons does not appear in Poore's edition: 2:1909 (VA), 2:1541 (PA), 1:819 (MD), 2:1410 (NC), 1:957 (MA), 2:1281 (NH), 2:1868 (VT), 2:1313 (NJ), 2:1413–14 (NC), 1:383 (GA), 2:1338 (NY), 2:1626 (SC). Text of the 1776 Delaware Declaration of Rights can be found in *Founders' Constitution*, 5:5–6. This table is adapted from one in Muñoz, "Church and State in the Founding-Era State Constitutions," 11.

the nonlegal character of the state declarations is evinced by the use of "ought" as opposed to "shall." In Founding documents at the time, "ought" was used to describe desirable political norms whereas "shall" was used to specify binding legal rules associated with the formal instruments of government.

Rakove, *Beyond Belief, beyond Conscience*, 76, notes that in Pennsylvania and Massachusetts the declarations were incorporated into the text of their respective constitutions and thus acquired legal force. For discussions of the Founding-era state declarations of rights, including the relationship between the declarations of rights and constitutions, see Vincent Phillip

they state the foundational principles of the American government, which is why they expressly employ the phrase "natural rights."

Of the four Founding-era states that adopted new constitutions but did not draft declarations of rights, three (New Jersey, Georgia, New York) adopted legal protections for religious liberty consistent with the natural rights understanding but, as one might have expected, without specific natural rights language. The Founding-era state declarations of rights functioned as statements of principles; constitutions established positive law. Natural rights language was appropriate for the former but less so for the latter. As table 1 shows and as we will discuss below, only South Carolina adopted the older language of "toleration."

The Founders' Recognition That Religious Liberty Is Possessed by All Individuals

The Founders held that the natural right of religious liberty belongs to individuals on account of their human nature, and, accordingly, is possessed by all individuals. In chapter 3, I will discuss the leading Founders' philosophical and theological arguments for the natural right to religious liberty and how those arguments substantiate its universal character. At present, it suffices to note that, as table 1 reveals, the texts of the state declarations of rights reflect the Founders' affirmation of that character. Six states use the phrase "all men" (Virginia, Delaware, Pennsylvania, North Carolina, Vermont, Massachusetts); "men" in this sense is properly understood as the generic noun demarcating all human persons. New Hampshire refers to "every individual." Maryland somewhat confusingly seems to restrict the protection of religious liberty only to those "who profess the Christian religion"; but in the immediate sequel, the text drops this restriction, declaring that, "*no person* ought by any law to be molested in his person or estate on account of his religious persuasion or profession, or for his religious practice"—which suggests a more universal protection.[26] The use of "all

---

Muñoz, "Church and State in the Founding-Era State Constitutions," *American Political Thought* 4 (2015): 1–38; Tarr, *Understanding State Constitutions*, 76–81; Krumen, *Between Authority and Liberty*, 37–49.

26. Emphasis added. According to Michael D. Breidenbach, "Church and State in Maryland: Religious Liberty, Religious Tests, and Church Disestablishment," in *Disestablishment and Religious Dissent*, 314, the committee that drafted Maryland's text did not keep a record of its proceedings, so "their voiced intentions are lost to history."

men," "every individual," or "no person" in all eight documents is telling, for those documents employ more restrictive language when referring to other, nonnatural rights and privileges such as eligibility for political office.[27] With the possible exception of Maryland, the eight state declarations of rights recognize that all individuals possess the right of religious liberty, an understanding that reflects the Founders' underlying natural rights philosophy.

Three of the four states that drafted constitutions but not declarations of rights also affirm the universal character of religious liberty. As table 1 shows, the religious freedom protections in the New Jersey, Georgia, and New York state constitutions encompass all individuals. Article 18 of New Jersey's 1776 Constitution declares, "That no person shall ever . . . be deprived of the inestimable privilege of worshipping Almighty God in a manner agreeable to the dictates of his own conscience." Article 56 of the 1777 Georgia Constitution states, "All persons whatever shall have the free exercise of their religion." Article 38 of New York's 1777 Constitution, similarly, extends "to all mankind" "the free exercise and enjoyment of religious profession and worship, without discrimination or preference."

Of the twelve states that adopted new constitutions between 1776 and 1786, only South Carolina failed to recognize the right of religious liberty. Article 38 of the 1778 South Carolina Constitution provides only that "all persons and religious societies who acknowledge that there is one God, and a future state of rewards and punishments, and that God is publicly to be worshipped, shall be freely tolerated." Not coincidentally, South Carolina was the only Founding-era state to erect an official religious establishment. The next sentence of Article 38 declares, "The Christian Protestant religion shall be deemed, and is hereby constituted and declared to be, the established religion of this State."[28] The state, however, soon reversed course. The establishment text was deleted in the state's 1790 constitution and replaced with the following:

> The free exercise and enjoyment of religious profession and worship, without discrimination or preference, shall forever hereafter be allowed within this State to all mankind.[29]

27. Muñoz, "Church and State in the Founding-Era State Constitutions," 27–30.

28. Chapter 7 considers South Carolina's establishment of Christianity and how it sheds light on the Founders' understanding of what constituted an establishment of religion.

29. Constitution of South Carolina, 1790, Article 8, Section 1, *Federal and State Constitutions* 2:1632–33.

By 1790, all twelve states that had adopted a declaration of rights and/or a new constitution recognized that all individuals possess the right to religious freedom (again, noting the complexities of Maryland's 1776 Declaration of Rights).

As noted, two states, Rhode Island and Connecticut, did not draft declarations of rights or adopt new constitutions during the Founding era. After the Revolutionary War, Rhode Island continued to be governed under its 1663 Royal Charter, which provided robust religious freedom for all individuals:

> No person within the said colony, at any time hereafter, shall be any wise molested, punished, disqualified, or called into question for any difference of opinion in matters of religion ... every person may at all times freely and fully enjoy his own judgment and Conscience in matters of religious concernments.[30]

In 1784, Connecticut enacted "An Act Securing the Rights of Conscience in Matters of Religion, to Christians of every Denomination in this State," which held that

> no Persons in this State, professing the Christian Religion, who soberly and conscientiously dissent from the Worship and Ministry by Law established in the Society wherein they dwell, and attend public Worship by themselves, shall incur any Penalty for not attending the Worship and Ministry established, on the Lord's Day, or on Account of their Meeting together by themselves on said Day, for public Worship in a Way agreeable to their Consciences.[31]

Connecticut is the one Founding-era state after 1790 that clearly limited freedom of worship to Christians.[32] The universal character of religious freedom is the overwhelmingly dominant expression of the Founders' understanding.

30. *Federal and State Constitutions* 2:1596–97. For a brief discussion of the 1663 Rhode Island Charter and its protections for religious liberty, see Patrick T. Conley and Robert G. Flanders Jr., *The Rhode Island State Constitution: A Reference Guide* (Westport, CT: Prager, 2007), 6–7.

31. "An Act Securing the Rights of Conscience in Matters of Religion, to Christians of every Denomination in this State," in *Acts and Laws of the State of Connecticut, in America* (New London: Timothy Green, 1784), 21–22.

32. For a helpful discussion of church-state relations in Connecticut before, during, and after the Founding era, see Robert J. Imholt, "Connecticut: A Land of Steady Habits," in *Disestablishment and Religious Dissent*, 327–50.

To say that religious liberty was extended to all individuals (except in Connecticut and possibly Maryland) is not to say that every Founding-era state adopted a principle of religious nondiscrimination in matters of civil rights. Today we tend to presume that natural equality (including our equal enjoyment of our natural rights) dictates nondiscrimination in civil rights.[33] The state of Virginia adopted this position with regard to religious freedom, as we shall discuss in chapter 4.[34] But most Founding-era states distinguished civil protections for natural rights from civil protections for nonnatural or acquired rights.[35] The acknowledgment of the equal natural rights of all individuals was not necessarily understood to require the equal extension of, or equal protection for, nonnatural or acquired civil rights within society.[36]

The failure to appreciate the Founders' distinction between natural and acquired rights has led some to conclude—mistakenly—that the Founders limited religious freedom only to Christians or even just to Protestants.[37] To take a notable example, in the Ten Commandments case, *Van Orden v.*

33. See, for example, Akhil Reed Amar, "What the Same-Sex Marriage Opinion Should Have Said (and Almost Did)," *Slate.com*, July 10, 2015 (accessed July 27, 2015), http://www.slate.com/blogs/outward/2015/07/10/supreme_court_gay_marriage_what_kennedy_s_opinion_should_have_said.html. See also Justice Clarence Thomas's concurring opinion in *Rosenberger v. Rector and Visitors of the University of Virginia*, 515 U.S. 819, 854–55 (1995); Justice Antonin Scalia's dissenting opinion in *Locke v. Davey*, 540 U.S. 712, 726–27 (2004).

34. Jefferson's Virginia Statute stated that "our civil rights have no dependance [*sic*] on our religious opinions." "A Bill for Establishing Religious Freedom in Virginia," in Muñoz, *Religious Liberty and the American Supreme Court*, 604–5. Madison's original draft of what became the First Amendment's Religion Clauses included the provision, "The civil rights of none shall be abridged on account of religious belief or worship." *Annals of the Congress of the United States, 1789–1834* (Washington: Gales and Seaton, 1789), 1:451.

35. Muñoz, "Church and State in the Founding-Era State Constitutions," 11–12, 27–32.

36. Hamburger, "Natural Rights, Natural Law, and American Constitutions," 908, 918–22. A textual example of how the Founders both recognized the universal character of natural rights and also limited civil rights and privileges can be found in Sections 2 and 3 of the 1776 Delaware Declaration of Rights, in *Founders' Constitution* 5:5–6:

> Sect. 2. That all men have a natural and unalienable right to worship Almighty God according to the dictates of their own consciences and understandings. . . .
>
> Sect. 3. That all persons professing the Christian religion ought forever to enjoy equal rights and privileges in this state. . . .

37. For a helpful discussion of the distinction between natural and civil rights in the political thought followed by the Founders, see Gary L. McDowell, "The Limits of Natural Law: Thomas Rutherforth and the American Legal Tradition," *American Journal of Jurisprudence* 37 (1992), 65. For a different account, mistaken in my view, that sees a tension between the Founders' statements of equal natural rights and their practice of religion-based limitations on civil rights, see Sehat, *The Myth of American Religious Freedom*, 17–18.

Perry (2005), Justice John Paul Stevens criticized an originalist approach to the First Amendment's Religion Clauses because, in his words, "many of the Framers understood the word 'religion' in the Establishment Clause to encompass only the various sects of Christianity." Justice Stevens's dissenting opinion continues:

> The evidence is compelling. Prior to the Philadelphia Convention, the States had begun to protect "religious freedom" in their various constitutions. Many of those provisions, however, restricted "equal protection" and "free exercise" to Christians, and invocations of the divine were commonly understood to refer to Christ.[38]

Justice Stevens is not wrong that some state constitutions limited equal protection of acquired civil rights to Christians. But he is wrong to suggest that "many" of the Founding-era states limited "free exercise" rights to Christians.[39] As I have just noted, prior to 1790, twelve of the fourteen Founding-era states declared that *all individuals* possess the right to the free exercise of religion, and only Connecticut unambiguously limited religious liberty to Christians. One suspects that Justice Stevens's misreading owes in part to a lack of careful attention to the texts, and in part to the assumption that because some state declarations granted "equal rights and privileges" only to Christians, they similarly limited free exercise rights. To repeat, the Founders distinguished natural rights from acquired civil rights. When they recognized the natural right to religious freedom in state declarations of rights, and protected it constitutionally, they did so for all individuals. Only South Carolina (until 1790) and Connecticut clearly limited the rights of religious free exercise to Christians.

I have focused on the early Founding-era state declarations of rights and constitutions because they are the most authoritative evidence for the American Founders' shared political principles. Religious freedom's status as a natural right was also recognized in other contexts. Political sermons, important political pamphlets and documents, state legislation, and debates between Anti-Federalists and Federalists over the Constitution's

---

38. *Van Orden v. Perry*, 545 U.S. 677, 726–27 (2005).

39. The one Founding-era state constitution that Justice Stevens could have cited to support his interpretation of the Founders as parochial Christians is South Carolina's 1778 Constitution. See Constitution of South Carolina, 1778, Article 38, *Federal and State Constitutions* 2:1626.

ratification all identified religious freedom as a natural right.[40] To take a relatively unknown but revealing example, Rhode Island's official ratification of the Constitution included a declaration of natural rights principles. The document, which is dated May 29, 1790, begins:

> We, the delegates of the people of the state of Rhode Island and Providence Plantations, duly elected and met in Convention, having maturely considered the Constitution for the United States of America, ... and having also seriously and deliberately considered the present situation of this state, do declare and make known, —
> I. That there are certain natural rights of which men, when they form a social compact, cannot deprive or divest their posterity, ...

Article 4 then declares:

> IV. That religion, or the duty which we owe to our Creator, and the manner of discharging it, can be directed only by reason and conviction, and not by force and violence; and therefore all men have a natural, equal, and unalienable right to the exercise of religion according to the dictates of conscience; and that no particular religious sect or society ought to be favored or established, by law, in preference to others.[41]

New York's document officially ratifying the Constitution, dated July 28, 1788, similarly declares the exercise of religion to be a "natural and unalienable right":

> That the people have an equal, natural, and unalienable right freely and peaceably to exercise their religion, according to the dictates of conscience; and that no religious sect or society ought to be favored or established by law in preference to others.[42]

---

40. For an illuminating discussion of the Founders' understanding of natural rights and natural law as communicated through religious sermons in eighteenth-century Congregational New England, see Hamburger, "Natural Rights, Natural Law, and American Constitutions." For extensive documentation of the Founders' natural rights consensus, including but not limited to the natural right of religious liberty, see Terry Brennan, "Natural Rights and the Constitution: The Original 'Original Intent,'" *Harvard Journal of Law and Public Policy* 15 (1992): 965–1029.

41. *Elliot's Debates* 1:334. Article 4 follows Virginia's proposed constitutional amendment. See the discussion in chapter 5.

42. *Elliot's Debates* 1:328.

As I will discuss in chapter 3, the Founders embraced the idea of a natural right to religious freedom because they understood it to be discoverable through philosophical reasoning and supported by Christian theology. Before turning to those arguments, however, I will explain what the Founders meant when they identified religious liberty as an "unalienable" natural right. That is the subject of chapter 2.

CHAPTER TWO

The Founders' Second Agreement

Social Compact Theory, Freedom of Worship, and Religious Liberty as an Inalienable Right

In chapter 1, I attempted to show that the Founders held religious liberty to be a natural right possessed by all individuals. I noted that five states (Delaware, Pennsylvania, North Carolina, New Hampshire, and Vermont) explicitly identified the right to worship God according to one's conscience as an "unalienable" natural right, and that three other state declarations of rights adopted language consistent with that understanding. Grasping what the Founders meant by "unalienable" takes us to the core of the Founders' natural rights constitutionalism of religious freedom.

To understand the concept of the inalienability of religious freedom, we must review the basic features of the Founders' social compact theory of government. Its fundamental starting point is the "self-evident truth" that all individuals are created equal. This chapter begins, accordingly, with a discussion of the Founders' understanding of political equality and how it forms the basis of their conceptions of political consent and inalienable natural rights. The chapter then explains what the Founders meant when they labeled religious freedom an "unalienable" natural right, and how they understood the natural right of religious freedom to have natural limits. By refamiliarizing ourselves with the Founders' social compact political philosophy, we will see, first, that they understood the freedom of worship to be the core of the inalienable right to religious freedom; and, second, that the Founders understood freedom of worship to be both categorical and bounded.

The Founders' adoption of social compact theory can be seen across the Founding-era state declarations of rights and constitutions, but perhaps nowhere more clearly than in the 1784 New Hampshire Bill of Rights. For brevity's sake, I will closely examine the first five articles of that document rather than the Founding-era state charters more generally.[1]

The Founders' Social Compact Theory:
Natural Equality and Natural Rights

The first two articles of the 1784 New Hampshire Bill of Rights read as follows:

1. Parts of this chapter first appeared in Vincent Phillip Muñoz, "If Religious Liberty Does Not Mean Exemptions, What Might It Mean? The Founders' Constitutionalism of the Inalienable Rights of Religious Liberty," *Notre Dame Law Review* 91 (2016): 1387–1417. Of the Founding-era state declarations of rights, Marc W. Kruman, in *Between Authority and Liberty: State Constitution Making in Revolutionary America* (Chapel Hill: University of North Carolina Press, 1997), 40, writes (criticizing Gordon Wood):

> The declarations, though sometimes treated as hodgepodges of principles and rights, represented strikingly coherent statements of principle. They differed from one another in particulars but not in their general design and goal. All of the declarations avowed that the people created government by compact, that only the people could regulate their government, and that rulers possessed no part of sovereign authority. They then delineated rights that could not be infringed upon by magistrates but could be altered or abrogated by legislatures, and described others that could not be violated by any branch of government, including the legislature.
>
> Drawing upon John Locke, other political writers, and English constitutional tradition, the declarations began with sketches of either the origins of society or the origins of government.

For other discussions of social compact theory and the creation of Founding-era state constitutions, see Gordon S. Wood, *The Creation of the American Republic, 1776–1787* (New York: W. W. Norton, 1969), 282–91; Ronald M. Peters, Jr., *The Massachusetts Constitution of 1780: A Social Compact* (Amherst: University of Massachusetts Press, 1978). For accounts that interpret the political theory of the Founding-era states to be more varied than the account presented here, see Daniel J. Elazar, "The Principles and Traditions Underlying State Constitutions," *Publius* 12 (1982): 11–25; Donald S. Lutz, *Popular Consent and Popular Control: Whig Political Theory in the Early State Constitutions* (Baton Rouge: Louisiana State University Press, 1980).

For accounts of social compact theory in the Founding more generally, see Andrew C. McLaughlin, "Social Compact and Constitutional Construction," *American Historical Review* 5 (1990): 467–90; Edward S. Corwin, "The Basic Doctrine of American Constitutional Law," *Michigan Law Review* 12 (1914): 247–76; Thad W. Tate, "The Social Contract in America, 1774–1787," *William and Mary Quarterly* 22 (1965): 375–91; Harry V. Jaffa, *A New Birth of Freedom: Abraham Lincoln and the Coming of the Civil War* (Lanham, MD: Rowman and Littlefield, 2000), 44–50; Jud Campbell, "Republicanism and Natural Rights at the Founding," *Constitutional Commentary* 32 (2017): 85–112.

ARTICLE I. All men are born equally free and independent; therefore, all government of right originates from the people, is founded in consent, and instituted for the general good.

II. All men have certain natural, essential, and inherent rights; among which are—the enjoying and defending life and liberty—acquiring, possessing and protecting property—and in a word, of seeking and obtaining happiness.[2]

Article I begins with the fundamental principle of American constitutionalism: that all men are by nature free and equal.[3] Thomas Jefferson captured the Founders' common understanding at the end of his life while writing about the meaning of the Declaration of Independence:

May it be to the world what I believe it will be, (to some parts sooner, to others later, but finally to all), the signal of arousing men to burst the chains under which monkish ignorance and superstition had persuaded them to bind themselves, and to assume the blessings and security of self-government. . . . The general spread of the light of science has already laid open to every view the palpable truth that the mass of mankind has not been born with saddles on their backs, nor a favored few booted and spurred, ready to ride them legitimately, by the grace of God.[4]

Horses are not born with saddles on their backs, but most of us nonetheless think it legitimate that men break horses, saddle them, and ride them for their own purposes. A good owner should treat his steed humanely, of course, but men may legitimately use horses in ways that primarily benefit

2. *The Federal and State Constitutions, Colonial Charters, and Other Organic Laws of the United States*, 2nd edition, ed. Ben Perley Poore (Washington: Government Printing Office, 1878), 2:1280.

3. I use "men" here as the Founders did—i.e., to refer to all human beings. For a discussion of the centrality of human equality in the American political tradition, see Harry V. Jaffa, *Crisis of the Strauss Divided: Essays on Leo Strauss and Straussianism, East and West* (Lanham, MD: Rowman and Littlefield, 2012), 234–39.

It goes without saying that the meaning of equality and whether the Founders were actually devoted to it have generated no shortage of political and academic controversy. See, e.g., Thurgood Marshall, "Reflections on the Bicentennial of the U.S. Constitution," *Harvard Law Review* 101 (1987): 1–5. For a discussion of and response to scholars who deny that the Founders were truly devoted to the equality of all men, see Thomas G. West, *Vindicating the Founders: Race, Sex, Class, and Justice in the Origins of America* (Lanham, MD: Rowman and Littlefield, 1997), 1–36.

4. Thomas Jefferson, Letter to Roger Weightman, June 24, 1826, in *The Portable Thomas Jefferson*, ed. Merrill D. Peterson (New York: Penguin Books, 1977), 585.

the owner. Men also may govern horses without their consent because of the species inequality between mankind and animals; horses are incapable, at the level of root capacity, of rational consent.[5] Jefferson's point is that no similar inequality exists among men. No man may legitimately rule another man as a man may rule an animal because all men, by nature, have an equal title to exercise dominion over their own life and liberty.[6] "All men are created equal" means that no man is, by nature, the rightful ruler of any other man.[7]

James Wilson, a signer of the Declaration of Independence and one of President Washington's appointees to the inaugural Supreme Court, articulated the same understanding of equality in his *Lectures on Law*. It is worth quoting Wilson at length:

> When we say, that all men are equal; we mean not to apply this equality to their virtues, their talents, their dispositions, or their acquirements. In all these respects, there is, and it is fit for the great purposes of society that there should be, great inequality among men. . . .
>
> But however great the variety and inequality of men may be with regard to virtue, talents, taste, and acquirements; there is still one aspect, in which all men in society, previous to civil government, are equal. With regard to all, there is an equality in rights and in obligations; there is that "jus aequum," that equal law,

5. Of course, not everyone agrees with the idea of species inequality. See, e.g., Peter Singer, "Speciesism and Moral Status," *Metaphilosophy* 40 (2009): 567–81.

6. Harry V. Jaffa, in "Thomas Aquinas Meets Thomas Jefferson," *Interpretation* 33 (2006): 179, explains the Declaration's teaching about equality as follows:

> There is only one respect however in which "all men" (meaning all human beings) are held to be equal. That is in what John Locke calls "dominion." By nature, no man is the ruler of another. There is no natural difference between one human being and another, such as there is between the queen bee and the workers or drones. Nor is there any such difference between one human being and another, as there is between any man, and any dog or horse or chimpanzee, by reason of which the one is the ruler and the other is the ruled. Jonathan Swift to the contrary notwithstanding, men ride horses by self-evident natural right. The "enslavement" of the horse by his rider is not against nature, and is therefore not unjust. But the enslavement of one human being by another violates that same order of nature which justifies the rider of the horse.

7. Michael P. Zuckert, *Launching Liberalism: On Lockean Political Philosophy* (Lawrence: University of Kansas Press, 2002), 212–13. The proposition that "all men are created equal" or that "all men are born equally free and independent" does not undercut parents' rightful rule over and responsibility for their children. For a discussion of the compatibility of the liberal principle of natural equality and the rightful rule of parents over children, see Thomas G. West, "Locke's Neglected Teaching on Morality and the Family," *Society* 50 (2013): 472–76. Natural equality means that among adults, no person by nature or divine grant rightfully exercises political authority over another person.

in which the Romans placed true freedom. The natural rights and duties of man belong equally to all. Each forms a part of that great system, whose greatest interest and happiness are intended by all the laws of God and nature. These laws prohibit the wisest and the most powerful from inflicting misery on the meanest and most ignorant; and from depriving them of their rights or just acquisitions. By these laws, rights, natural or acquired, are confirmed, in the same manner, to all. . . . As in civil society, previous to civil government, all men are equal; so, in the same state, all men are free. In such a state, no one can claim, in preference to another, superiour right: in the same state, no one can claim over another superiour authority.[8]

Men are equal in their natural dominion over their own lives. This fundamental equality in freedom lies at the foundation of the Founders' conception of natural rights.

The Founders' idea of natural rights involves an authority to do freely those things an individual is able to do, and the reciprocal immunity from being coerced on account of those activities.[9] It expresses the individual's legitimate inherent authority to do or not to do something; e.g., to exercise religion or not. The concept presupposes the individual's competence to judge for himself whether to exercise the right. It also presumes, as Harvey Mansfield Jr. notes, "that the thing to which one has a right is possible to do. One cannot have a right to an impossible condition, such as immortality. . . ."[10]

8. James Wilson, *Lectures on Law* (chapter 7, "Of Man as a Member of Society"), in *Collected Works of James Wilson*, ed. Kermit L. Hall and Mark David Hall (Indianapolis, IN: Liberty Fund, 2007), 1:636–38.

9. Mark Blitz, in *Conserving Liberty* (Stanford, CA: Hoover Institution Press, 2011), 15, helpfully defines the concept of rights as follows:

> A right is an authority to reflect, prefer, choose, use, proceed, and act that we justly possess. As an authority, it is not a mere privilege or opportunity. As an authority to reflect, prefer, choose, use, proceed, and act, a right is freedom of self-direction, not a particular outcome or a bare state of being unobstructed. As justly possessed or deserved, a right is not something stolen or usurped. An inalienable right is an authority one cannot give up, unlike a fleeting possession. The individual natural rights with which we are endowed, therefore, are individual authorities to reflect, prefer, choose, use, proceed, and act that always belong to us.

See also S. Adam Seagrave, *The Foundations of Natural Morality: On the Compatibility of Natural Rights and the Natural Law* (Chicago: University of Chicago Press, 2014), 73, which offers the following definition of natural rights: "a basis for moral claims residing within or deriving from the individual."

10. Harvey C. Mansfield Jr., "Responsibility versus Self-Expression," in *Old Rights and New*, ed. Robert A. Licht (Washington: AEI Press, 1993), 97.

The American natural rights tradition nearly always recognizes life, liberty, and property, the three natural rights listed in Article 2 of the New Hampshire Bill of Rights. The natural rights to life and liberty reflect the fact that every man possesses dominion over his own life—which, again, is to say that no other man possesses such authority by nature. The natural right to property follows from a man's rightful freedom to labor and to enjoy the fruits of his labor.[11]

Life, liberty, property, and other natural rights are *natural* in the twofold sense that men possess them on account of their human nature, and that they exist in the state of nature; i.e., independently of political society. Such rights, accordingly, are not granted by the state or by any human authority.[12] In the Founders' political thought, legitimate political authority is constituted in order to recognize and protect natural rights.[13]

The Founders' Social Compact Theory: Consent and the Ends of Government

Article 3 of the 1784 New Hampshire Bill of Rights states:

> III. When men enter into a state of society, they surrender up some of their natural rights to that society, in order to insure the protection of others; and, without such an equivalent, the surrender is void.[14]

11. For helpful discussions of the Founders' understanding of the natural right to property, see James W. Ely, *The Guardian of Every Other Right: A Constitutional History of Property Rights*, 3rd edition (New York: Oxford University Press, 2008), 26–58; Eric R. Claeys, "Takings, Regulations, and Natural Property Rights," *Cornell Law Review* 88 (2003), 1566–74; Chester James Antieau, "Natural Rights and the Founding Fathers: The Virginians," *Washington and Lee Law Review* 17 (1960): 65–68.

12. Cf. Michael P. Zuckert, *The Natural Rights Republic: Studies in the Foundation of the American Political Tradition* (Notre Dame, IN: University of Notre Dame Press, 1996), 73–78.

13. Consider Article 1 of the 1776 Pennsylvania Declaration of Rights, which begins:

> WHEREAS all government ought to be instituted and supported for the security and protection of the community as such, and to enable the individuals who compose it to enjoy their natural rights, and the other blessings which the Author of existence has bestowed upon man. . . .

Federal and States Constitutions, 2:540. See also James Wilson's chapter, "Of the Natural Rights of Individuals," in his *Lectures on Law* in *Collected Works of James Wilson*, 2:1053–83 (esp. 1061–62); James Madison, "Property," in *The Founders' Constitution*, ed. Philip B. Kurland and Ralph Lerner (Indianapolis, IN: Liberty Fund, n.d.; originally published Chicago: University of Chicago Press, 1987), 1:598–99.

14. *Federal and State Constitutions*, 2:1280.

Political authority is necessary because individuals often fail to respect the limits of their own natural liberties by violating the natural rights of others.[15] To better secure their natural rights, men enter into society and "surrender" their natural authority to protect their own rights, receiving civil protections in exchange.

Let me clarify how individuals "enter into a state of society" and, then, address in what sense rights are "surrendered." The formation of a political society includes two analytically distinct steps.[16] James Madison provides one of the Founders' clearest statements on the subject:

> The idea of a compact among those who are parties to a Government is a fundamental principle of free Government. The original compact is the one implied or presumed, but nowhere reduced to writing, by which a people agree to form one society. The next is a compact, here [in the United States] for the first time reduced to writing, by which the people in their social state agree to a Government over them.[17]

Individuals take the first step when they agree to leave the state of nature and to form a political society. Madison, following Locke, calls this the "original compact."[18] The original compact exists among all the individuals who are parties to it, rather than between the government and the people. Individuals take the second step when, in Madison's words, "the people in their social state agree to a Government over them." The second step involves the adoption of a form of government and constitutional rules. After forming a society, members of the "original compact" specify how the political power of the community will be arranged, divided, exercised, etc.

According to Locke and Madison, unanimity establishes (and then simple majority rule governs) the initial civil society; constitutions, however, can legitimately empower one person, a few, many, or some combination

---

15. Consider Madison's argument in *Federalist* 10 of the naturalness and inevitability of factious behavior.

16. A different version of this and the next paragraph first appeared in Vincent Phillip Muñoz, "Two Concepts of Religious Liberty: The Natural Rights and Moral Autonomy Approaches to the Free Exercise of Religion," *American Political Science Review* 110 (2016): 372.

17. James Madison, letter to Nicholas. P. Trist, February 15, 1830, in *Founders' Constitution*, 1:240.

18. Gary Rosen, *American Compact: James Madison and the Problem of Founding* (Lawrence: University of Kansas Press, 1999), 3, 6, 10, 88.

No vo

thereof.[19] Regarding the first step, Madison writes, "each individual, being previously independent of the others, the compact which is to make
them one Society, must result from the free consent of *every* individual."[20]
Unanimous consent to the original compact is required because all individuals are naturally free. This is the precise meaning of "founded in
consent" in Article 1 of the 1784 New Hampshire Bill of Rights.[21] Being
naturally free, individuals have no obligation to join any particular political community; only consent legitimates the exercise of political authority
by some over others. For those individuals born into a political community
(presumably, most individuals), natural human freedom means that they
have a natural right to emigrate and renounce their membership in the
community of their birth.[22]

Consent is necessary to establish legitimate government, but the consent of the governed alone is not sufficient to legitimate political rule.
Legitimate governments actually secure the "general good," understood
first and foremost as the liberty of the naturally free and independent individuals who form the social compact.[23] As stated in Article 3 of the 1784

19. John Locke, "The Second Treatise of Government," chapter 8, sections 95–99, and
chapter 10, section 132, in *Two Treatises of Government*, student edition, ed. Peter Laslett
(Cambridge: Cambridge University Press, 1988), 331–33, 354.

20. Emphasis in the original. Madison, "Sovereignty" (1835), in *The Writings of James
Madison*, ed. Gaillard Hunt (New York: G. P. Putnam's Sons, 1900), 9:570.

21. For a penetrating discussion of the Founders' understanding of the relationship be-
tween the idea of human equality and the principle of government by consent, see Harry V.
Jaffa, "Equality, Liberty, Wisdom, Morality, and Consent in the Idea of Political Freedom,"
Interpretation 15 (1987): 3–28.

22. The Founders' views of tacit consent and the natural right to emigrate are set forth
most clearly by James Wilson, who writes in "Of Man as a Member of Society," in the series
Lectures on Law, in *Collected Works of James Wilson*, 1:642:

It may be observed, that every man being born free, a native citizen, when he arrives
at the age of discretion, may examine whether it be convenient for him to join in the
society, for which he was destined by his birth. If, on examination, he finds, that it will
be more advantageous to him to remove into another country, he has a right to go,
making to that which he leaves a proper return for what it has done in his favour, and
preserving for it, as far as it shall be consistent with the engagements, which his new
situation and connexions may require, the sentiments of respect and attachment.

23. In his essay "Property," *Founders' Constitution*, 1:598, James Madison writes,

This term ["property"] in its particular application means "that dominion which one
man claims and exercises over the external things of the world, in exclusion of every
other individual." In its larger and juster meaning, it embraces every thing to which a
man may attach a value and have a right; and which leaves to every one else the like
advantage. In the former sense, a man's land, or merchandize [*sic*], or money is called
his property. In the latter sense, a man has a property in his opinions and the free

New Hampshire Bill of Rights, if the government fails to protect those rights, "the surrender is void."

Though the New Hampshire Bill of Rights speaks of a "surrender" of rights, that term was not universally accepted among the Founders in their writings on social compact theory. James Wilson, one of the most thoughtful and notable opponents of this language, wrote at length to reject explicitly the idea that individuals "surrender," "sacrifice," or "give up" their natural rights in order to protect them.[24] Wilson disliked the notion of a "surrender," which he attributed to Burke, because it suggested that "under civil society, man is not only made *for*, but made *by* the government: he is nothing but what the society frames: he can claim nothing but what the society provides. His natural state and natural rights are withdrawn altogether from notice...."[25] Wilson feared that "surrender" might suggest that natural rights no longer exist within or inform the political community, which is obviously incorrect if the principal object of government is to secure natural rights.

The difference between the lawyerly Wilson and the 1784 New Hampshire Bill of Rights is likely more semantic than real.[26] Theophilus Parsons, an influential jurist who would become Chief Justice of the Supreme Judicial Court of Massachusetts, helpfully addresses this very point in *The Essex Result*, which offers one of the most thoughtful Founding-era accounts of the Founders' social compact theory of natural rights. Parsons, the document's probable author, writes:

> All men are born equally free. The rights they possess at their births are equal, and of the same kind. Some of those rights are alienable, and may be parted with for an equivalent. Others are unalienable and inherent, and of that importance,

---

communication of them. He has a property of peculiar value in his religious opinions, and in the profession and practice dictated by them. He has a property very dear to him in the safety and liberty of his person. He has an equal property in the free use of his faculties and free choice of the objects on which to employ them. In a word, as a man is said to have a right to his property, he may be equally said to have a property in his rights. . . . Government is instituted to protect property of every sort; as well that which lies in the various rights of individuals, as that which the term particularly expresses. This being the end of government, that alone is a just government, which impartially secures to every man, whatever is his own.

24. Wilson, *Collected Works of James Wilson*, 2:1053–61.

25. Wilson's emphasis. *Collected Works of James Wilson*, 2:1058. Tom West pointed out to me that it is not altogether clear that Wilson interprets Burke accurately on this point.

26. Jud Campbell, "Natural Rights and the First Amendment," *Yale Law Journal* 127 (2017): 274.

that no equivalent can be received in exchange. Sometimes we shall mention the surrendering of a power to controul [*sic*] our natural rights, which perhaps is speaking with more precision, than when we use the expression of parting with natural rights—but the same thing is intended.

For two reasons, "surrendering . . . a power to controul" more precisely describes the process of entering the social compact than "parting with" natural rights. First, individuals can always reacquire their natural rights upon invoking the inalienable right to revolution. Even alienable natural rights are not *irrevocably* alienated; they can always be reclaimed. *The Essex Result* states:

> The equivalent every man receives, as a consideration for the rights he has sur-rendered, . . . consists principally in the security of his person and property. . . . For if the equivalent is taken back, those natural rights which were parted with to purchase it, return to the original proprietor, as nothing is more true, than ALLEGIANCE AND PROTECTION ARE RECIPROCAL.[27]

Second, and more relevantly, individuals do not surrender their natural rights in the sense that they relinquish each right's underlying principle of justice. The state is given power to secure natural rights, not eviscerate them.

We can clarify this second point by introducing a distinction implicit in the Founders' social compact theory. There are two aspects of natural rights, which we might call the "what" and the "how." The "what" refers to the normative content of the right; the "how" refers to the power to secure the right. The right's substantive content—the "what"—can be stated as a rule of justice; e.g., "An individual rightfully possesses the fruits of his own labor." The power to secure a natural right—the "how"—pertains to those aspects of legislative, executive, and judicial authority that are nec-essary for individuals to be able to enjoy their rights. When Parsons writes in *The Essex Result* that it is more precise to "mention the surrendering of a power to controul our natural rights" than to "use the expression of parting with natural rights," he means that we alienate only the "how" of natural rights, not the "what." James Wilson's comments cited above

27. Emphasis in the original. *The Essex Result*, April 29, 1778, in *Founders' Constitution*, 114–15. For a discussion of this point, see Thomas G. West, *The Political Theory of the Ameri-can Founding: Natural Rights, Public Policy, and the Moral Conditions of Freedom* (New York: Cambridge University Press, 2017), 136–38.

reflect the same concern. Wilson disliked the term "surrender" because it could be interpreted to mean that individuals also alienated the moral content of their natural rights, thereby losing the solid ground of justice from under their feet, and were reduced to "claim[ing] nothing but what the society provides."

"Surrender," however, is not a wholly inappropriate term. Individuals do surrender something of their alienable natural rights upon entering the social compact. Most clearly, they surrender their natural executive powers to judge violations of their rights and, correspondingly, to use force to protect and restore their rights—that is, they surrender the means or the "how" of protecting their natural rights.

An example might be helpful. The natural right to acquire property includes the liberty to employ one's body to take unappropriated goods from nature's common stock, subject only to the limitations of the law of nature—in other words, one can legitimately catch as many fish as one can consume in a non–privately owned lake, as long as a sufficient amount is left for others. In the state of nature, every individual has the power to judge and enforce the law of nature. In our example, our fisherman—let's call him Dominic—possesses the authority to judge how many fish he can catch without exhausting the lake's supply and harming his neighbors. The potential complication, of course, is that other fishermen have the same authority to judge and enforce the law of nature. Let's say two other fishermen—Madeleine and Sophie—are standing on the lakeshore, and they believe Dominic has hauled in so many fish that the lake's supply will now be exhausted. In their judgment, he has violated the law of nature. According to the law of nature, Madeleine and Sophie possess authority to punish Dominic for taking too many fish. Dominic, however, disagrees with their judgment. He believes he has taken a fair number of fish and has respected nature's law, and thus that Madeleine and Sophie's aggression toward him is itself a violation of the law of nature. The lack of a clear rule to specify the law of nature, and of an authority that promulgates, enforces, and judges violations of that law, inevitably leads to conflict.

The "what" in our example is the natural right to acquire fish by one's own labor; the "how" is limiting one's catch so as to leave sufficient fish for others. To protect the natural right of acquisition (the "what"), individuals alienate their power over the rules of fishing (the "how"). They create a political authority and give it power to pass laws that regulate fishing—say, by specifying that one cannot fish in certain ways, at certain times, in certain places, or take more than a certain amount—so as to facilitate their natural right to acquire property via fishing.[28]

To summarize: individuals *do not* surrender their alienable natural rights in the sense that (a) they can never reacquire them or (b) they relinquish the claim of justice underlying them. Upon entering the social compact, individuals grant authority to the government to secure their natural rights. They do this by alienating their executive power of the state of nature, a power that necessarily includes discerning the contours and boundaries of natural rights.

Through this mutual surrender of natural executive power and recognition of one another's rights, naturally free and independent individuals become members of one society, and fellow citizens. Even in society, individuals still retain some residual executive authority to protect their natural rights. An individual, for example, can defend herself—that is to say, she can invoke her natural executive power—when her life is threatened and no recourse to civil authority is possible. And, of course, the right of revolution is never surrendered. But in the main, individuals "surrender" their natural executive power in exchange for civil protections that better secure their rights. This mutual recognition of one another's rights, and mutual consent to form one civil and political association, allow naturally free and independent individuals to become fellow citizens in a single society governed by the rule of law. The primary aim of the political society, therefore, is to protect natural rights, as stated perhaps most clearly by James Wilson:

> Government, in my humble opinion, should be formed to secure and to enlarge the exercise of the natural rights of its members; and every government, which has not this in view, as its principal object, is not a government of the legitimate kind.[29]

Any well-constituted government, according to Wilson, will enhance Dominic's, Madeleine's, and Sophie's enjoyment of their natural right to fish.

---

28. "Regulate" in this sense might be defined as "adjusting conditions so as to facilitate." See George Sutherland, "The Constitutional Aspect of Government Ownership," address at the Missouri Bar Association meeting, September 29, 1915, in *Proceedings of the Thirty-Third Annual Meeting of the Missouri Bar Association* (Springfield, MO: Inland Printing and Binding, n.d.), 102. See also Claeys, "Takings, Regulations, and Natural Property Rights," 1553–54.

29. Wilson, *Collected Works of James Wilson*, 2:1061. The passage is from Wilson's chapter, "Of the Natural Rights of Individuals," in his *Lectures on Law*. For a discussion of the extent to which a regime dedicated to the protection of rights can go "beyond" rights to protect "rights infrastructure," see Zuckert, *Launching Liberalism*, 226–28.

The Founders' Social Compact Theory: Inalienable Rights

However, individuals do not transfer authority over *every* right when they enter the social compact. Article 4 of the 1784 New Hampshire declaration states:

> IV. Among the natural rights, some are in their very nature unalienable, because no equivalent can be given or received for them. Of this kind are the RIGHTS OF CONSCIENCE.[30]

The concept of inalienability has a precise meaning in the Founders' social compact constitutionalism. Inalienable rights are, as the name suggests, those rights that cannot be alienated — that is, those over which individuals cannot, and hence do not, grant the state authority. Such rights cannot be alienated, either because of the nature of the right itself or because such a transfer would always run contrary to self-interest.[31]

In his Virginia Statute for Religious Liberty, Jefferson identifies religious opinions as inalienable on the grounds that the nature of belief formation prevents us from delegating authority over beliefs to any other individual or group of individuals. As we will discuss in more detail in chapter 3, Jefferson argues that because opinions follow evidence alone, we cannot consent to follow the dictates of others.[32] In *Notes on the State of Virginia*, he arrives at the same conclusion by reference to religious obligations:

> But our rulers can have authority over such natural rights only as we have submitted to them. The rights of conscience we never submitted, we could not submit. We are answerable for them to our God.[33]

In his "Memorial and Remonstrance," James Madison also emphasizes our duties to the Creator in his account the inalienable character of

---

30. Emphasis in the original. *Federal and State Constitutions*, 2:1280–81.

31. Jean Yarbrough, "Jefferson and Property Rights," in *Liberty, Property, and the Foundations of the American Constitution*, ed. Ellen Frankel Paul and Howard Dickman (Albany: State University of New York Press, 1989), 66. For a brief discussion of the concept of "inalienable rights," see Zuckert, *Launching Liberalism*, 218–20.

32. For an elaboration of Jefferson's argument on this point, see Vincent Phillip Muñoz, *God and the Founders: Madison, Washington, and Jefferson* (New York: Cambridge University Press, 2009), 85–87.

33. Thomas Jefferson, *Notes on the State of Virginia*, query 17, in *The Portable Thomas Jefferson*, ed. Merrill D. Peterson (New York: Penguin Books, 1975), 210.

religious free exercise.[34] Each individual must fulfill his own obligations to God, Madison argues, because the duty itself is "to render to the Creator such homage and such only as he believes to be acceptable to him." The personal character of religious obligation—that the worshipper himself must be sincere in his worship and personally believe such worship is required by the Creator—makes religious free exercise an inalienable right. As Madison states,

> If a member of Civil Society, who enters into any subordinate Association, must always do it with a reservation of his duty to the General Authority; much more must every man who becomes a member of any particular Civil Society, do it with a saving of his allegiance to the Universal Sovereign.[35]

In accord with the social compact theory articulated by leading Framers like Jefferson and Madison and accepted by the Founders generally (as is apparent in the early Founding-era state declarations of rights), the Founders protected the inalienable right of religious free exercise primarily by limiting governmental jurisdiction over it.[36] In the Founders' social compact constitutionalism, government acquires only the authority granted to it by the people.[37] When they said the rights of conscience are "unalienable," they meant that authority over the rights of conscience is

34. For further discussion of this point, see the discussion of Madison's political thought in chapter 3.

35. James Madison, "Memorial and Remonstrance against Religious Assessments," 1785, in Vincent Phillip Muñoz, *Religious Liberty and the American Supreme Court: The Essential Cases and Documents*, updated edition (Lanham, MD: Rowman and Littlefield, 2015), 606–7. Madison makes the same point in his 1835 essay "Sovereignty," in *Writings of James Madison*, 9:570–71, where he writes:

Whatever be the hypothesis of the origin of the *lex majoris partis*, it is evident that it operates as a plenary substitute of the will of the majority of society for the will of the whole society; and that sovereignty of the society as vested in & exercisable by the majority, may do anything that could *rightfully* done by the unanimous concurrence of the members; the reserved rights of individuals (of conscience for example) in becoming parties to the original compact being beyond the legitimate reach of sovereignty, wherever vested or however viewed.

36. For an elaboration of this point, see Muñoz, "Two Concepts of Religious Liberty," 369–74.

37. For a thoughtful and revealing discussion that addresses how contemporary liberal egalitarians address jurisdictional boundaries between religion and the state, see Cécile Laborde, *Liberalism's Religion* (Cambridge, MA: Harvard University Press, 2017), 160–71. Laborde's notion of the social contract starts with the state, not with individuals in a prepolitical state of nature. No conception of inalienable natural rights exists in her approach, and she

not, and cannot be, granted to the government. Delaware (1776), Pennsylvania (1776), and Vermont (1777 and 1786) articulated this point with precision in their declarations of rights, which all stated:

> No authority can or ought to be vested in, or assumed by any power whatever that shall in any case interfere with, or in any manner controul the right of conscience in the free exercise of religious worship.[38]

The natural right of religious free exercise remains "unalienated"; individuals retain what they possessed prior to and outside of civil society. Individuals do not grant government authority over the "how" aspect of religious free exercise. Government possesses no legitimate authority to determine what constitutes the obligations we owe to God, how we fulfill them, or whether we fulfill them at all. The political authority created by the consent of the people lacks sovereignty over the rights of conscience in the free exercise of religion.

Article 5 of the 1784 New Hampshire Bill of Rights specifies the meaning of this lack of sovereignty:

> V. Every individual has a natural and unalienable right to worship GOD according to the dictates of his own conscience, and reason; and no subject shall be hurt, molested, or restrained in his person, liberty or estate for worshipping GOD, in the manner and season most agreeable to the dictates of his own conscience, or for his religious profession, sentiments or persuasion; provided he doth not disturb the public peace, or disturb others, in their religious worship.[39]

We tend to speak broadly about "the natural right of religious liberty," as I myself have done thus far. The Founders were more precise. What is inalienable is the right to worship God according to conscience. From the government's absence of sovereignty over that particular right, the Founders derived an immunity for all persons ("no subject") from punishment ("shall be hurt, molested, or restrained in his person, liberty or estate") on account of religious exercises, beliefs, or profession ("for worshipping GOD,

---

concludes, accordingly, that "states, not churches, have . . . the authority to define their own spheres of competence, as well as those of other institutions" (p. 165).

38. *Founders' Constitution*, 5:5 (DE); *Federal and State Constitutions*, 2:1541 (PA), 2:1859, 1868 (VT). See also Vincent Phillip Muñoz, "Church and State in the Founding-Era State Constitutions," *American Political Thought* 4 (2015): 14–15.

39. Emphasis in the original. *Federal and State Constitutions*, 2:1281.

in the manner and season most agreeable to the dictates of his own conscience, or for his religious profession, sentiments or persuasion"), with certain limitations ("provided he doth not disturb the public peace . . ."), which we shall discuss in the third part of this chapter.

The absence of governmental authority to hurt, molest, or restrain individuals on account of their religious worship, beliefs, or affiliation is the very core of the Founders' understanding of religious freedom. Every state that drafted a new constitution between 1776 and 1786, except Virginia and South Carolina, recognized and protected freedom of religious worship and belief.[40] Virginia, in its 1776 Declaration of Rights, had only recognized that "all men are equally entitled to the free exercise of religion, according to the dictates of conscience." The commonwealth did soon pass specific legal rules to protect religious free exercise, when it adopted Jefferson's statute in 1786. That legislation is reflected in table 2.

As table 2 shows, some states included additional text explicitly recognizing citizens' freedom *from* compelled worship. Prohibitions against compelled worship follow the same logic as freedom of worship: jurisdiction over religious worship as such is not granted to the state; accordingly, worship as such remains beyond the state's sovereignty; therefore, the state may neither prohibit nor mandate forms or religious worship. As Madison says in his "Memorial and Remonstrance," "The Religion then of every man must be left to the conviction and conscience of every man." Madison does not leave individuals' freedom from coerced worship in doubt:

> We cannot deny an equal freedom to those whose minds have not yet yielded to the evidence which has convinced us. If this freedom [of religious exercise] be abused, it is an offense against God, not against man: To God, therefore, not to man, must an account of it be rendered.[41]

Without jurisdiction over religious exercise as such, the state lacks authority to prohibit or compel either believers or nonbelievers. In this way, the Founders' concept of religious freedom was designed to protect all individuals, including nonbelievers and atheists.[42]

40. Muñoz, "Church and State in the Founding-Era State Constitutions," 12–17.

41. James Madison, "Memorial and Remonstrance Against Religious Assessments," in *Religious Liberty and the American Supreme Court*, 606–7.

42. It might be argued that the state of Massachusetts deviated from the founding consensus on this point. Article 3 of its 1780 Declaration of Rights invests the state legislature

	Freedom of worship and belief	Freedom from compelled worship
VA 1786 (VSRF)	VSRF: . . . no man . . . shall be enforced, restrained, molested, or burthened in his body or goods, nor shall otherwise suffer, on account of his religious opinions or beliefs; but that all men shall be free to profess, and by argument to maintain, their opinions in matters of religion	VSRF: . . . no man shall be compelled to frequent or support any religious worship, place, or ministry whatsoever . . . .
NJ 1776	XVIII. That no person shall ever . . . be deprived of the inestimable privilege of worshipping Almighty God in a manner agreeable to the dictates of his own conscience; . . .	XVIII. . . . nor [shall any person], under any presence whatever, be compelled to attend any place of worship, contrary to his own faith and judgment; . . .
DE 1776	*SECT 2. . . . and that no authority can or ought to be vested in, or assumed by any power whatever that shall in any case interfere with, or in any manner controul the right of conscience in the free exercise of religious worship.*	*SECT 2. . . . and that no man ought or of right can be compelled to attend any religious worship or maintain any ministry contrary to or against his own free will and consent, ...*
PA 1776	*II. . . . and that no authority can or ought to be vested in, or assumed by any power whatever, that shall in any case interfere with, or in any manner controul, the right of conscience in the free exercise of religious worship.*	*II. . . . no man ought or of right can be compelled to attend any religious worship, or erect or support any place of worship, or maintain any ministry, contrary to, or against, his own free will and consent: . . .*
MD 1776	*XXXIII. . . . wherefore no person ought by any law to be molested in his person or estate on account of his religious persuasion or profession, or for his religious practice; . . .*	*XXXIII. . . . nor ought any person to be compelled to frequent or maintain, or contribute, unless on contract, to maintain any particular place of worship, or any particular ministry. . . .*
NC 1776	XXXIV. . . all persons shall be at liberty to exercise their own mode of worship. . . .	XXXIV. . . . neither shall any person, on any pretence whatsoever, be compelled to attend any place of worship contrary to his own faith or judgment, . . .
GA 1777	ART. LVI. All persons whatever shall have the free exercise of their religion; . . .	
NY 1777	XXXVIII. . . . the free exercise and enjoyment of religious profession and worship, without discrimination or preference, shall forever hereafter be allowed, within this State, to all mankind. . . .	
VT 1777/ 1786	*III. . . . no authority can, or ought to be vested in, or assumed by any power whatsoever, that shall, in any case, interfere with, or in any manner controul, the rights of conscience, in the free exercise of religious worship. . . .*	*III. . . . no man ought, or of right can be compelled to attend any religious worship, or erect or support any place of worship, or maintain any minister, contrary to the dictates of his conscience; . . .*
SC 1778		

continues

TABLE 2. (*continued*)

	Freedom of worship and belief	Freedom from compelled worship
MA 1780	*II. And no subject shall be hurt, molested, or restrained, in his person, liberty, or estate, for worshipping God in the manner and season most agreeable to the dictates of his own conscience, or for his religious profession or sentiments, . . .*	*III. And the people of this commonwealth have also a right to, and do, invest their legislature with authority to enjoin upon all the subject an attendance upon the instructions of the public teachers aforesaid [Protestant teachers of piety, religion, and morality], at stated times and seasons, if there be any on whose instructions they can conscientiously and conveniently attend.*
NH 1784	*V. . . . no subject shall be hurt, molested, or restrained in his person, liberty or estate for worshipping GOD, in the manner and season most agreeable to the dictates of his own conscience, or for his religious profession, sentiments or persuasion; . . .*	

*Texts in this table can be found in *Federal and State Constitutions*, with the exception of the texts from the 1786 Virginia Statute for Religious Freedom and the 1776 Delaware Declaration of Rights, the latter of which, for unclear reasons, does not appear in Poore's *Federal and State Constitutions*: 2:1313 (NJ), 2:1541 (PA), 1:819 (MD), 2:1413–14 (NC), 1:383 (GA), 2:1338 (NY), 2:1859, 1868 (VT), 1:957 (MA), 2:1281 (NH). Text of the Virginia Statute can be found in *Religious Liberty and the American Supreme Court*, 605. Text of the 1776 Delaware Declaration of Rights can be found in *Founders' Constitution*, 5:5. This table is adapted from a table in Muñoz, "Church and State in the Founding-Era State Constitutions," 18–19.
Italicization indicates that the text appears in a declaration of rights. All other text appears in state constitutions with the exception of Virginia, the text of which is taken from Jefferson's 1786 Statute for Religious Freedom.

The Founders' jurisdictional protection for religious freedom might seem narrow, at least to contemporary eyes. Their inalienable natural rights understanding removes a relatively small (though fundamentally important) area of human liberty from governmental jurisdiction: the state lacks legitimate authority to punish or compel religious exercises and professions as such. From a more robust historical perspective, however, the Founders' teaching is revolutionary. Removing the salvation of souls from the legitimate purposes of government by denying governmental author-

---

with power "to enjoin upon all the subject an attendance upon the instructions of the public teachers aforesaid [Protestant teachers of piety, religion, and morality], at stated times and seasons. . . ." But then, as if the drafters knew they were about to go a step too far, the article immediately limits this power: "if there be any on whose instructions they can conscientiously and conveniently attend." Article 3 of the 1780 Massachusetts Declaration of Rights comes close to authorizing compelling religious worship, but it does not actually do so. For a discussion of the contemporaneous debates surrounding these provisions, see Peters, *Massachusetts Constitution of 1780*, 32–34. See also pp. 50–56 for Peters's not altogether persuasive interpretation of these debates. The relevant text can be found in *Federal and State Constitutions*, 1:957.

ity over the exercise of religion as such marks a revolution in political philosophy and political authority. Indeed, limiting governmental authority over religion is at the core of the Founders' liberalism. As I shall discuss both in chapter 4 and in part 3 of this study, translating this core liberal principle into constitutional rules is not without complication or difficulty. But it remains revolutionary.

The Boundaries of the Natural Right of Religious Free Exercise

To say that the Founders recognized elements of the natural right of religious free exercise as inalienable is not to say that they held *every* religiously motivated action to be immune to legal prohibition or regulation. We tend to think of rights, or at least natural rights, as categorical protections or absolute immunities not susceptible to state limitation or prohibition. Regarding the nonalienated aspects of the natural right of religious free exercise, those descriptions are true in one sense (as discussed above), but not in another. In the Founders' understanding, all natural rights have natural limits. To speak more precisely, the Founders understood the natural right of religious liberty to be categorical but not unbounded.[43] Understanding the legitimate boundaries of the natural right of religious free exercise helps to explain more precisely what specific types of state action it was understood to prohibit.

I have frequently used the cumbersome modifier "as such," as in, for example, "religious worship as such." The phrase "as such" is intended to capture the distinction between (1) outlawing a practice *on account of its religious character* and (2) enacting a general prohibition that incidentally outlaws a religious practice. A municipal ordinance that specifically prohibits the Catholic Mass is an example of the former; an ordinance that requires traffic control for all gatherings that draw two hundred vehicles or more might be an example of the latter.

An often-used example may be helpful: the Aztec religious practice of human sacrifice. Would its prohibition be consistent with the Framers' unalienable natural rights understanding? The answer, clearly, is yes. The

43. Cf. Ellis M. West, *The Free Exercise of Religion in America: Its Original Constitutional Meaning* (Cham, Switzerland: Palgrave Macmillan, 2019), 186–87, who finds the Founders on this point "confusing and contradictory." West asks: "How can a right be absolute if it can be denied under certain circumstances?" I attempt to provide the Founders' answer to West's question in this section.

Founders did not understand the right of religious liberty to include the freedom to do anything provided that it is religiously motivated. They understood the natural boundaries of natural rights to be established by the law of nature.

In his *Lectures on Law*, James Wilson offers perhaps the most developed account of how nature establishes both the grounds for and limits of our rightful liberty:

> Nature has implanted in man the desire of his own happiness; she has inspired him with many tender affections towards others, especially in the near relations of life; she has endowed him with intellectual and with active powers; she has furnished him with a natural impulse to exercise his powers for his own happiness, and the happiness of those, for whom he entertains such tender affections. If all this be true, the undeniable consequence is, that he has a right to exert those powers for the accomplishment of those purposes, in such a manner, and upon such objects, as his inclination and judgment shall direct; provided he does no injury to others; and provided some publick interests do not demand his labours. This right is natural liberty. Every man has a sense of this right. Every man has a sense of the impropriety of restraining or interrupting it. Those who judge wisely, will use this liberty virtuously and honourably: those, who are less wise, will employ it in meaner pursuits: others, again, may, perhaps, indulge it in what may be justly censured as vicious and dishonourable. Yet, with regard even to these last, while they are not injurious to others; and while no human institution has placed them under the control of magistrates or laws, the sense of liberty is so strong, and its loss is so deeply resented, that, upon the whole, more unhappiness would result from depriving them of their liberty on account of their imprudence, than could be reasonably apprehended from the imprudent use of their liberty....
>
> The laws of nature are the measure and the rule; they ascertain the limits and the extent of natural liberty.[44]

"In a state of natural liberty [the state of nature]," Wilson writes later in his *Lectures on Law*, "everyone is allowed to act according to his own inclination, provided he transgress not those limits, which are assigned to him by the law of nature...."[45] The law of nature, he further explains, con-

44. Wilson, *Collected Works of James Wilson*, 1:638–39.
45. Wilson, *Collected Works of James Wilson*, 2:1056. For further discussion of the Founders' understanding of the natural law boundaries on natural rights, with particular reference

tains two basic maxims, both of which are made known to us through our reason and common sense: that no man should injure another man, and that lawful engagements voluntarily made should be faithfully fulfilled.[46]

In the Founders' understanding, to have a right to do X does not imply that one can do anything to secure, enact, or practice X. The right to do X means the right to secure, enact, or practice X in a manner consistent with the law of nature. The Founders often expressed the natural law boundaries on the exercise of natural rights in terms of respecting the equal rights of others. As Jefferson stated in a private letter, "No man has a natural right to commit aggression on the equal rights of another."[47] The young Alexander Hamilton made the same point in his 1775 "Farmer Refuted" essay. Hamilton rejects the Hobbesian notion that the possession of natural rights implies that men are perfectly free from all moral restraints in the state of nature and that moral obligation only arises from the agreement to enter into civil society. He writes,

---

to James Wilson, see Hadley Arkes, *Beyond the Constitution* (Princeton, NJ: Princeton University Press, 1990), 62–65.

46. Wilson, *Collected Works of James Wilson*, 1:498, 2: 1062. Wilson defines "injury" as follows: "An injury is a loss arising to an individual, from the violation or infringement of his right." In Wilson, *Collected Works of James Wilson*, 2:1087. For a discussion of the moral foundations of James Wilson's account of natural law and natural rights, see Justin Buckley Dyer, "James Wilson, Necessary Truths, and the Foundations of Law," *Duquesne Law Review* 56 (2018): 49–71; Justin Buckley Dyer, "Reason, Revelation, and the Law of Nature in James Wilson's *Lectures on Law*," *American Political Thought* 9 (2020): 264–84. Cf. Philip Hamburger, "Natural Rights, Natural Law, and American Constitutions," *Yale Law Journal* 102 (1993): 924, which emphasizes "enlightened self-interest" in his account of the Founders' understanding of the law of nature:

> Being equally free [by nature], individuals did not have a right to infringe the equal rights of others, and, correctly understood, even self-preservation typically required individuals to cooperate—to avoid doing unto others what they would not have others do unto them. In this way, the assumptions about humans and, particularly, human liberty in the state of nature—that individuals in the state of nature were equally free and that such individuals should seek to preserve their liberty—were considered to be foundations upon which humans could reason about cooperative behavior for the preservation of that liberty. These assumptions could, in fact, be used to justify rules that bore a striking resemblance to some of the social duties of traditional morality.... Thus, America derived social obligations from enlightened self-interest ... and therefore could talk about natural law both as a law of human nature and as the foundation of moral rules.

47. Thomas Jefferson, letter to Francis Walker Gilmer, June 7, 1816, in *The Works of Thomas Jefferson*, ed. Paul L. Ford (New York: Knickerbocker Press, 1905), 534.

Good and wise men, in all ages, have embraced a very dissimilar theory. They have supposed, that the deity, from the relations, we stand in, to himself and to each other, has constituted an eternal and immutable law, which is, indispensably, obligatory upon all mankind, prior to any human institution whatever. This is what is called the law of nature. . . .

Hamilton identifies God as the author of and authority behind the law of nature, but he does not conclude that only those people who have access to divine revelation or God's prophets are subject to the law. God endowed man with rational faculties, he says, through which man can discern both his interests and his duties. The law of nature, therefore, is

binding over all the globe, in all countries, and at all times. No human laws are of any validity, if contrary to this; and such of them as are valid, derive all their authority, mediately, or immediately, from this original.

"Hence, in a state of nature," Hamilton emphasizes, "no man had any *moral* power to deprive another of his life, limbs, property or liberty. . . ."[48]

Even though it makes some sense to envision the law of nature as limiting natural rights, the Founders did not understand it to do so.[49] Rather, the law of nature sets boundaries on the exercise of a natural right.[50] The scope of any natural right, in other words, does not extend to actions that injure another. The saying, "you have no right to do wrong," captures this meaning insofar as "wrong" is defined in terms of violations of the natural moral law consisting, primarily, of the natural rights of others.[51] As the saying goes, my right to swing my arm ends at the tip of your nose.

The Founders understood the law of nature and natural rights to be consistent with one another. The latter was part of the former. To say that all men are naturally free and equal in their natural rights was, for the Founders, to say that no man has a moral right to exercise his liberty in a

48. Alexander Hamilton, "The Farmer Refuted," February 23, 1775, in *Selected Writings and Speeches of Alexander Hamilton*, ed. Morton J. Frisch (Washington: AEI Studies, 1985), 20.

49. For a helpful discussion of this point, see Hamburger, "Natural Rights, Natural Law, and American Constitutions," 944–49.

50. For a discussion of the natural law limitations on the natural right of freedom of speech, see Campbell, "Natural Rights and the First Amendment," 268–80.

51. Hadley Arkes, "A Natural Law Manifesto or an Appeal from the Old Jurisprudence to the New," *Notre Dame Law Review* 87 (2012): 1246.

manner that infringes another's equal freedom.[52] One Founding-era Vermont minister stated the matter thus:

> All have, most certainly, an equal right to freedom and liberty by the great law of nature. No man or number of men, *has* or *can* have a right to infringe the natural rights, liberties, or privileges of others. . . . [53]

Jefferson, to give just one further example, wrote:

> Of Liberty then I would say that, in the whole plenitude of its extent, it is unobstructed action according to our will: but rightful liberty is unobstructed action according to our will, within the limits drawn around us by the equal rights of others. I do not add 'within the limits of the law'; because law is often but the tyrant's will, and always so when it violates the right of an individual.[54]

To return to our Aztec example: a law that prohibits murder, when applied to a religiously motivated killing such as ritual human sacrifice, does not violate the natural right of religious free exercise as the Founders understood it, because the exercise of natural rights does not license the violation of others' natural rights, including the right to life. No religious free exercise right exists to sacrifice another human person, regardless of a religious motivation—even a sincere motivation—for such an action.

Several Founding-era state declarations of rights reflect the natural law boundaries of the natural right of religious free exercise. After declaring

---

52. For a discussion of this point, including multiple citations to Founding-era writers, see Hamburger, "Natural Rights, Natural Law, and American Constitutions," 922–30.

53. Quoted in Hamburger, "Natural Rights, Natural Law, and American Constitutions," 927. The quotation is from Peter Powers's 1778 election sermon "Jesus Christ Is the True King and Head of Government." Elisha Williams had said much the same thing nearly forty years earlier:

> This natural freedom is not a liberty for every one to do what he pleases without any regard to any law; for a rational creature cannot but be made under a law from its Maker: But it consists in freedom from any superiour power on earth, and not being under the will or legislative authority of man, and having only the law of nature (or in other words, of its Maker) for his rule.

Elisha Williams, "The Essential Rights and Liberties of Protestants," (1744) in *Political Sermons of the American Founding Era, 1730–1805*, ed. Ellis Sandoz (Indianapolis, IN: Liberty Fund, 1990), 56.

54. Thomas Jefferson to Isaac H. Tiffany, April 4, 1819, in *Thomas Jefferson: Political Writings*, ed. Appleby and Ball (New York: Cambridge University Press, 1999), 224.

that no individuals should be "hurt, molested or restrained" on account of religious worship, profession, sentiments, or persuasion, Article 5 of the 1784 New Hampshire Bill of Rights adds the boundary proviso, "provided he doth not disturb the public peace, or disturb others, in their religious worship." As table 3 shows, six other Founding-era states had similar provisions in their declarations of rights (Maryland, Massachusetts) or constitutions (New Jersey, North Carolina, Georgia, New York).

The meaning of these boundary provisos has been a matter of significant dispute. Michael McConnell has interpreted them to provide a balancing standard for religious liberty exemptions, a position that Justice Samuel Alito adopted in *Fulton v. City of Philadelphia* (2021).[55] According to McConnell's interpretation, Article 5 of the New Hampshire Bill of Rights should be construed to afford religious citizens exemptions from generally applicable laws in all cases except when an exemption would "disturb the public peace, or disturb others, in their religious worship"—a standard that he suggests would in many cases favor exemptions.[56]

If McConnell and Alito's reading is correct, and if the Founders understood the right of religious liberty to require exemptions from generally applicable laws, we would expect balancing-standard provisos to accompany free exercise text in every relevant Founding-era declaration of rights or constitution.[57] That provisos are absent from the Delaware, Pennsylvania, and Vermont Declarations of Rights, not to mention Jefferson's Virginia Statute, casts some doubt on the plausibility of their reading.

A more fundamental reason explains the provisos' presence and absence: they were written to communicate the natural law limits on the natural right of religious free exercise. As discussed above, the Founders did not understand religious liberty (or any other natural right) to be without boundaries. The exercise of natural rights was always understood not to license actions that interfered with others' prerogatives to exercise their natural rights. Strictly speaking, boundary provisos were not needed, because natural rights are by their nature bounded. The Founders' understanding of natural rights did not include the liberty to disturb the public peace or act licentiously, regardless of whether boundary provisos were textually specified. The provisos' superfluity helps to explain why some states included them while others did not. And it must be remembered

55. *Fulton v. City of Philadelphia*, 593 U.S. ___, slip op. at 33–39 (2021) (Alito, J., concurring).

56. Michael W. McConnell, "The Origins and Historical Understanding of Free Exercise of Religion," *Harvard Law Review* 103 (1990): 1461–66.

57. Muñoz, "Church and State in the Founding-Era State Constitutions," 13–17.

TABLE 3. **Boundary provisions on religious free exercise**[*]

	Protection for religious free exercise	Boundary provision
VA 1786 (VSRF)	VSRF: ... no man shall be compelled to frequent or support any religious worship, place, or ministry whatsoever, nor shall be enforced, restrained, molested, or burthened in his body or goods, nor shall otherwise suffer, on account of his religious opinions or belief; but that all men shall be free to profess, and by argument to maintain, their opinions in matters of religion, and that the same shall in no wise diminish, enlarge, of affect their civil capacities.	
NJ 1776	XVIII. That no person shall ever ... be deprived of the inestimable privilege of worshipping Almighty God in a manner agreeable to the dictates of his own conscience; ...	XIX. ... all persons, professing a belief in the faith of any Protestant sect, who shall demean themselves peaceably under the government ... shall fully and freely enjoy every privilege and immunity, enjoyed by others their fellow subjects.[†]
DE 1776	*SECT 2. ... and that no authority can or ought to be vested in, or assumed by any power whatever that shall in any case interfere with, or in any manner controul the right of conscience in the free exercise of religious worship.*	
PA 1776	*II. ... and that no authority can or ought to be vested in, or assumed by any power whatever, that shall in any case interfere with, or in any manner controul, the right of conscience in the free exercise of religious worship.*	
MD 1776	*XXXIII. ... wherefore no person ought by any law to be molested in his person or estate on account of his religious persuasion or profession, or for his religious practice; ...*	*XXXIII. ... unless, under colour of religion, any man shall disturb the good order, peace or safety of the State, or shall infringe the laws of morality, or injure others, in their natural, civil, or religious rights; ...*
NC 1776	XXXIV. ... all persons shall be at liberty to exercise their own mode of worship: ...	XXXIV. *Provided,* That nothing herein contained shall be construed to exempt preachers of treasonable or seditious discourses, from legal trial and punishment.
GA 1777	ART. LVI. All persons whatever shall have the free exercise of their religion; ...	ART. LVI. ... provided it be not repugnant to the peace and safety of the State; ...
NY 1777	XXXVIII. The free exercise and enjoyment of religious profession and worship, without discrimination or preference, shall forever hereafter be allowed, within this State, to all mankind; ...	XXXVIII. Provided, That the liberty of conscience, hereby granted, shall not be so construed as to excuse acts of licentiousness, or justify practices inconsistent with the peace or safety of this State.

continues

TABLE 3. (*continued*)

	Protection for religious free exercise	Boundary provision
VT 1786	*III. . . . no authority can, or ought to be vested in, or assumed by any power whatsoever, that shall in any case, interfere with, or in any manner control, the rights of conscience, in the free exercise of religious worship: . . .*	
MA 1780	*II. And no subject shall be hurt, molested, or restrained, in his person, liberty, or estate, for worshipping God in the manner and season most agreeable to the dictates of his own conscience, or for his religious profession or sentiments, . . .*	*II. . . . provided he doth not disturb the public peace or obstruct others in their religious worship.*
NH 1784	*V. . . . no subject shall be hurt, molested, or restrained in his person, liberty or estate for worshipping GOD, in the manner and season most agreeable to the dictates of his own conscience, or for his religious profession, sentiments or persuasion; . . .*	*V. . . . provided he doth not disturb the public peace, or disturb others, in their religious worship.*

*Texts in this table can be found in Poore's *Federal and State Constitutions,* with the exception of the texts from the 1786 Virginia Statute for Religious Freedom and the 1776 Delaware Declaration of Rights, the latter of which, for unclear reasons, does not appear in Poore's edition: NJ (2:1313), PA (2:1541), MD (1:819), NC (2:1414), GA (1:383), NY (2:1338), VT (2:1868), MA (1:957), NH (2:1281). Text of the Virginia Statute can be found in *Religious Liberty and the American Supreme Court,* 605. Text of the 1776 Delaware Declaration of Rights can be found in *Founders' Constitution,* 5:5. This table is adapted from one appearing in Muñoz, "Church and State in the Founding-Era State Constitutions," 14–15.
†Whether the limiting provision in article 19 was meant to apply to the provisions of article 18 is unclear.
Italicization indicates that the text appears in a declaration of rights. All other text appears in state constitutions with the exception of Virginia, the text of which is taken from Jefferson's 1786 Statute for Religious Liberty.

that early Founding-era declarations of rights were not constitutional law akin to the federal Constitution's Bill of Rights. One of their primary purposes was to educate newly independent Americans about their natural rights, including the limits of those rights. To interpret the boundary provisions as precise rules of constitutional law is to fail to read them in light of their proper historical context.

Misreadings of these boundary provisions have contributed to a consequential misinterpretation of the Founders' understanding of the right of religious free exercise. As I shall discuss in chapter 6 and further develop in chapters 7 and 8, the inalienable character of religious worship neither involves nor entails a right of exemption from general laws. The Founders sought to protect religious freedom, first and foremost, by recognizing fixed and categorical limits on what governing authorities can legitimately do, as opposed to exempting religious individuals from burdensome but otherwise legitimate generally applicable laws.

*   *   *

The argument I have made in chapters 1 and 2 can be summarized as follows:

- The Founders acknowledged and recognized that all persons possess a natural right of religious free exercise. This is demonstrated by the early Founding-era state declarations of rights and constitutions.
- The Founders understood the natural right of religious worship according to conscience to be "unalienable"; therefore, they held that the state lacked sovereign authority over religious exercises as such.
- The absence of sovereignty over religious exercises as such led the Founders to declare two specific, reciprocal, core religious liberty immunities from state power:
  - No individual could be punished (in the Founders' language, "hurt, molested, or restrained") on account of religious opinions, profession, or observances as such.
  - No individual could be compelled to embrace, profess, or observe religious beliefs or practices.
- The Founders understood natural rights to have natural limits. An individual's exercise of his natural rights does not extend to interference with other individuals' natural rights.

Religious worship according to conscience, properly understood as a natural "unalienable" right, is the foundational political principle animating the Founders' thinking on matters of church and state. Whatever other disagreements the Founders had about church-state matters (the topic of chapter 4), they agreed on the existence of the "unalienable" natural right of worship according to conscience, and that individuals do not alienate authority over religious worship to the state upon becoming members of the social compact. I will address the extent to which natural rights principles influenced the drafting of the First Amendment's Religion Clauses in part 2 of this book, and how the Founders' natural rights principles might be constructed into constitutional rules in part 3. We will be able to approach those questions more thoughtfully, however, if we first address the Founders' underlying philosophies and theologies of the inalienable natural right of religious freedom. That is the subject of chapter 3.

The Foundations of the Founders' Agreements

The Founders' Philosophies and Theologies of the Natural Right of Religious Liberty

All the great writers of antiquity were part of the aristocracy of masters, or at least they saw that aristocracy established without dispute before their eyes; their minds, after expanding in several directions, were therefore found limited in that one, and it was necessary that Jesus Christ come to the earth to make it understood that all members of the human species are naturally alike and equal. — Tocqueville, *Democracy in America*[1]

I have documented in chapters 1 and 2 how the Founding-era state dec- larations of rights and constitutions recognize that every individual pos- sesses the natural right of religious liberty. But why did the Founding gen- eration hold the right to worship according to conscience to be inalienable? On what foundations did this commitment rest? Is the idea of a natural right of religious freedom just an article of their religious faith? Does the Founders' political creed have a philosophical foundation?

This chapter addresses those questions by explaining how leading Found- ers appealed to both reason and revelation—sources of knowledge they held to be compatible and mutually reinforcing—to ground their political thinking about religious freedom. While the Founders' natural rights rea- soning may have fallen out of fashion, understanding it is essential to un- derstanding their political philosophy and constitutional design.[2] And to

1. Alexis de Tocqueville, *Democracy in America*, vol. 2, part 1, chapter 3, trans. Harvey C. Mansfield and Delba Winthrop (Chicago: University of Chicago Press, 2000), 413.
2. For an exploration of the early-twentieth-century critique of natural rights political philosophy, a critique that remains dominant today, see James W. Ceaser, "Progressivism and

the extent that the Founders offer philosophical arguments based on natural reason, they remain capable, at least in principle, of persuading even skeptical minds today.[3] The Founders' theological arguments, furthermore, can still resonate with those who share or are open to their articles of faith.

This chapter begins with Thomas Jefferson, one of the more religiously skeptical Founding Fathers, and the epistemological argument he offers in the Virginia Statute for Religious Liberty.[4] It then turns to James Madison's natural theology of religious freedom. It concludes by surveying the Christian political writings of Isaac Backus, one of the era's most influential preachers. Backus's Christian account of the natural right to religious freedom complements the accounts of his more philosophical contemporaries. Together, Jefferson, Madison, and Backus present the leading Founding-era philosophical and theological arguments for the natural right to religious freedom.

Jefferson's Philosophy of the Natural Right to Religious Liberty

Jefferson's Virginia Statute for Religious Liberty has long been recognized as one of the Founding generation's most authoritative defenses of religious freedom. Harvard historian Bernard Bailyn declared it "the most important document in American history bar none."[5] For our purposes, the importance of the statute lies in its audacious claim

---

the Doctrine of Natural Rights," in *Natural Rights Individualism and Progressivism in American Political Philosophy*, ed. Paul, Miller, and Paul (New York: Cambridge University Press, 2012), 177–95.

3. In this context, the following observation by Paul Horwitz in *The Agnostic Age: Law, Religion, and the Constitution* (New York: Oxford University Press, 2011), xii, is apt:

> Questions of religious freedom ultimately cannot be satisfactorily answered without at least some attempt to grapple with the broader question of religious truth. In this simple fact lies much of what we have seen in the realm of law and religion scholarship: dissatisfaction, approaching a state of utter misery.

4. For a study of Jefferson's religious beliefs, see Gregg L. Frazer, *The Religious Beliefs of America's Founders: Reason, Revelation, and Revolution* (Lawrence: University Press of Kansas, 2012), 125–63.

5. Quoted in Daniel L. Driesbach, "Religion and Legal Reform in Revolutionary Virginia," in *Religion and Political Culture in Jefferson's Virginia* (Lanham, MD: Rowman and Littlefield, 2000), 211n39. Histories of Virginia's battle to establish religious freedom that focus on Jefferson include Thomas E. Buckley, S.J., *Establishing Religious Freedom: Jefferson's Statute in Virginia* (Charlottesville: University of Virginia Press, 2013); John A. Ragosta, *Religious Freedom: Jefferson's Legacy, America's Creed* (Charlottesville: University Press of Virginia, 2013).

that the rights hereby asserted are of the natural rights of mankind, and that if
any act shall be hereafter passed to repeal the present or to narrow its operation, such act will be an infringement of natural right.[6]

Though enacted as regular legislation, the statute invokes "natural right"
for its authority, and concludes that future legislatures would be unjust to
rescind its protections.

The statute offers theological and prudential arguments, but I will focus
on its epistemology, since that is how the statute authoritatively defends
the natural right of religious freedom.[7] I will also examine Jefferson's original draft, as opposed to the final, slightly modified text that the Virginia
legislature adopted, because the original more clearly reveals Jefferson's
underlying philosophical argument.

Jefferson's bold opening focuses on the nature of the mind's operations:

> Well aware that the opinions and belief of men depend not on their own will,
> but follow involuntarily the evidence proposed to their minds; that Almighty God
> hath created the mind free, and manifested his supreme will that free it shall
> remain by making it altogether insusceptible of restraint. . . .

Two related aspects of the mind's operations drive Jefferson's argument:
that it involuntarily adheres to the evidence it finds persuasive, and that it
cannot be restrained. Both observations echo the teachings of John Locke,
whom we know Jefferson carefully studied.[8] In *A Letter Concerning Tolera-*

---

6. "A Bill for Establishing Religious Freedom in Virginia," in *Religious Liberty and the
American Supreme Court: The Essential Cases and Documents*, revised edition, ed. Vincent
Phillip Muñoz (Lanham, MD: Rowman and Littlefield, 2015), 604–5. All subsequent refer-
ences to the Virginia Statute in this chapter will be omitted.

7. For an analysis of the statute's philosophical, theological, and prudential arguments, see
Vincent Phillip Muñoz, *God and the Founders: Madison, Washington, and Jefferson* (New York:
Cambridge University Press, 2009), 82–97. The next four paragraphs are derived, in part, from
pages 85–92 in that volume.

8. See "Notes on Locke and Shaftesbury," in *The Papers of Thomas Jefferson*, ed. Julian P.
Boyd (Princeton, NJ: Princeton University Press, 1953), 1:544–51. S. Gerald Sandler sets forth
a side-by-side comparison of Locke's *Letter Concerning Toleration*, Jefferson's notes on the
Letter, and Jefferson's "Bill for Establishing Religious Freedom" that documents Jefferson's
indebtedness to Locke. S. Gerald Sandler, "Lockean Ideas in Thomas Jefferson's Bill for Establishing Religious Freedom," *Journal of the History of Ideas*, 21 (1960): 110–16. A more theoretical explanation of Jefferson's debt to Locke is set forth by Sanford Kessler in "Locke's
Influence on Jefferson's 'Bill for Establishing Religious Freedom,'" *Journal of Church and
State* 25 (1983): 231–52.

tion, Locke contends, "It is only Light and Evidence that can work a change in Men[']s Opinions; which light can in no manner proceed from corporal Sufferings, or any other outward Penalties."[9] Accepting Locke's claim that evidence alone can persuade the mind, Jefferson recognizes that the mind cannot be compelled to belief: "All attempts to influence it [the mind] by temporal punishments, or burthens, or by civil incapacitations tend only to beget habits of hypocrisy and meanness." Coercive force can lead a man to profess disingenuously a belief or an opinion, but it cannot create inner conviction. The mind's insusceptibility to restraint and compulsion secures its freedom even under duress.[10]

Not only is the human mind impervious to force; it cannot reject evidence it finds persuasive. Jefferson states, "The opinions and belief of men depend not on their own will, but follow involuntarily the evidence proposed to their minds." Here he adopts a teaching articulated by Locke in *An Essay Concerning Human Understanding.* "Our will hath no power to determine the knowledge of the mind one way or another, that is done only by the objects themselves, as far as they are clearly discovered," Locke says.[11] This aspect of the mind's freedom implies that in one sense, the mind is radically determined. Individuals do not willfully choose or select their own opinions; rather, opinions are the involuntary conclusions drawn from an individual's perception of evidence.[12]

9. John Locke, *A Letter Concerning Toleration,* ed. James H. Tully (Indianapolis, IN: Hackett, 1983), 27.

10. Numerous scholars have noted the weakness of Locke's argument about the futility of force. For a thoughtful recent discussion of this point, see Giorgi Areshidze, *Democratic Religion from Locke to Obama: Faith and the Civic Life of Democracy* (Lawrence: University Press of Kansas, 2016), 54–57; Jeremy Waldron, "Locke: Toleration and the Rationality of Persecution," in *Justifying Toleration: Conceptual and Historical Perspectives,* ed. Susan Mendus (Cambridge: Cambridge University Press, 1988): 61–86.

11. John Locke, *An Essay Concerning Human Understanding* (New York: Dover Publications, 1959 [orig. pub. 1689]), book 4, chapter 13, section 2, 358. See also book 4, chapter 20, section 16, 455:

> As knowledge is no more arbitrary than perception; so, I think, assent is not more in our power than knowledge. When the agreement of any two ideas appears to our minds, whether immediately or by the assistance of reason, I can no more refuse to perceive, no more avoid knowing it, than I can avoid seeing those objects which I turn my eyes to, and look on in daylight; and what upon full examination I find the most probable, I cannot deny my assent to.

12. The Virginia assembly eliminated Jefferson's phrase "and manifested his supreme will that free it shall remain by making it altogether insusceptible of restraint," thus eliminating

From these two philosophical observations establishing the mind's freedom—its insusceptibility to coercion and its involuntary subjection to persuasive evidence—Jefferson establishes the natural right of religious freedom.[13] Political authorities that exercise coercive authority over opinions, especially religious opinion, act irrationally and illegitimately. They act irrationally because attempts to influence the mind by force necessarily must fail. Lawmakers who legislate beliefs thus attempt to do what cannot be done. Jefferson goes so far as to denounce the "impious presumption" of rulers who assume "dominion over the faith of others." Such rulers act foolishly, Jefferson continues, because "the holy author of our religion" uses "reason alone" to influence the human mind.[14]

The exercise of coercive authority over religious opinions is illegitimate because individuals cannot and thus do not cede such authority to the state. Jefferson makes this point most definitively in his *Notes on the State of Virginia*, wherein he states that civil government cannot exercise jurisdiction over the opinions of men because "our rulers can have authority over such natural rights only as we have submitted to them." "The rights of conscience we never submitted," Jefferson continues, "we could not submit." Returning to the Virginia Statute, the rights of conscience cannot be submitted because men themselves lack sovereignty over their own beliefs and opinions.[15] Opinions are not subject to the will, and, therefore, individuals can-

Jefferson's statement about the mind's determinism from the bill's adopted text. See Carl H. Esbeck, "Virginia," in *Disestablishment and Religious Dissent: Church-State Relations in the New American States, 1776–1833*, ed. Carl H. Esbeck and Jonathan J. Den Hartog (Columbia: University of Missouri Press, 2019), 161–63.

13. These two epistemological observations also serve as the basis for Jefferson's theological assertions that "Almighty God hath created the mind free," and "all attempts to influence it by temporal punishments, or burthens [sic], or by civil incapacitations . . . are a departure from the plan of the holy author of our religion. . . ." See Muñoz, *God and the Founders*, 86–87.

14. Jefferson equates divine intention with the operations of nature, which implies that piety requires men to respect the mind's natural operations. Impiety and irrationality are synonymous terms for Jefferson. For a discussion of how the laws of nature are identical to the laws of "nature's God" in Jefferson's thought, see Michael P. Zuckert, "Thomas Jefferson on Nature and Natural Rights," in *The Framers and Fundamental Rights*, ed. Robert A. Licht (Washington: American Enterprise Institute Press, 1991), 139–47. See also Kody W. Cooper and Justin Buckley Dyer, "Thomas Jefferson, Nature's God, and the Theological Foundations of Natural-Rights Republicanism," *Politics and Religion* 10 (2017): 662–88.

15. Jefferson, *Notes of the State of Virginia,* query 17, "Religion," in *Portable Thomas Jefferson*, ed. Merrill D. Peterson (New York: Penguin Books 1977), 210. In query 17, Jefferson states that we do not submit our rights of conscience to state authorities because "we are answerable for them to our God."

not grant the state jurisdiction over them.[16] Men cannot relinquish what they do not control.

According to Jefferson's account of the mind, what makes governmental authority over opinions irrational and illegitimate is that individuals do not govern their minds as they govern their bodies. Individuals cannot grant the state authority over their opinions, which means that "the rightful purposes of civil government" must be limited to those occasions "when principles break out into overt acts against peace and good order." The individual's lack of sovereignty over his own beliefs leads Jefferson to draw a categorical distinction between beliefs and opinions, on the one hand, and conduct, on the other. Government has legitimate jurisdiction over actions; over beliefs and opinions, it has not.[17]

Jefferson contends both that direct coercion of religious opinions is impermissible and that restricting or granting civil rights based on religious beliefs is illegitimate. "Our civil rights have no dependance [*sic*] on our religious opinions," he declares, "any more than our opinions in physics or geometry." Emoluments and religious tests for public offices, accordingly, deprive an individual "injuriously of those privileges and advantages to which, in common with his fellow citizens, he has a natural right." As I shall discuss in chapter 4, not all the Founding-era states agreed that the natural right of religious liberty required nondiscrimination in political and civil rights. But that conclusion follows from the premises of Jefferson's argument.

The statute enacts legal protections that are derived from and designed to protect the epistemologically grounded natural right of religious liberty:

> *We the General Assembly of Virginia do enact* that no man shall be compelled to frequent or support any religious worship, place, or ministry whatsoever, nor shall be enforced, restrained, molested, or burthened in his body or goods, nor shall

16. As far as I know, Locke never uses the term "inalienable" rights; but in the following passage from *A Letter Concerning Toleration*, 26, he anticipates the concept:

> Nor can such power [care of souls] be vested in the Magistrate by the *consent of the People*; because no man can so far abandon the care of his own Salvation, as blindly to leave it to the choice of any other. . . . For no Man can, if he would, conform his Faith or Worship to the Dictates of another.

17. The belief-action distinction does not imply that Jefferson believes that government can legitimately prohibit *any* action. Rather, as he states in *Notes on the State of Virginia*, "the legitimate powers of government extend to such acts only as are injurious to others." Thomas Jefferson, *Notes on the State of Virginia*, query 17, in *Portable Thomas Jefferson*, 210.

otherwise suffer, on account of his religious opinions or belief; but that all men shall be free to profess, and by argument to maintain, their opinions in matters of religion, and that the same shall in no wise diminish, enlarge, or affect their civil capacities.

As I discuss in *God and the Founders*, the prohibitions against compelled attendance and compelled support of worship do not follow from the freedom of the mind alone. They depend on prudential considerations the statute adopts.[18] But Jefferson's account of the mind's freedom allows him to reason that individuals should not be punished on account of their religious opinions, or have their civil privileges indexed to those opinions.

James Madison's Natural Theology of Religious Freedom

Jefferson's statute was adopted after years of sharp debate and political wrangling. Among the documents drafted during that contest was "Memorial and Remonstrance against Religious Assessments," a pamphlet published anonymously by James Madison. Madison's immediate target was a church-state bill advanced by Patrick Henry that would have imposed a property tax to fund religious ministers. The Memorial may or may not have decisively influenced the defeat of Henry's legislation, but it has become extraordinarily influential in modern church-state jurisprudence, in no small part because it contains Madison's most thorough account of the natural right to religious liberty—an account that Noah Feldman identifies as "the most important systematic defense of equal religious liberty that had ever been written."[19]

Understanding the philosophical basis of Madison's Memorial is not simple. The Memorial's fifteen articles contain a number of different arguments, and Madison employs modes of reasoning—natural theology and

18. See Muñoz, *God and the Founders*, 92–97.

19. Noah Feldman, *The Three Lives of James Madison: Genius, Partisan, President* (New York: Random House, 2017), 66. For a discussion of the relative influence of the Memorial and Remonstrance in Virginia in 1785 and in Supreme Court jurisprudence, see Donald L. Drakeman, "Which Original Meaning of the Establishment Clause Is the Right One?" in *The Cambridge Companion to the First Amendment and Religious Liberty*, ed. Michael D. Breidenbach and Owen Anderson (New York: Cambridge University Press, 2020), 371; Mark David Hall, "Madison's Memorial and Remonstrance, Jefferson's Statute for Religious Liberty, and the Creation of the First Amendment," *American Political Thought* 3 (2014): 32–63.

social compact theory—that are not well understood today.[20] He relies, moreover, on a number of unstated premises. In what follows, I will attempt to explain the Memorial's philosophical and theological derivation of the "unalienable natural right" to religious freedom, and uncover those unstated propositions. I will omit a discussion of the Memorial's prudential arguments.[21]

Madison's position is often lumped together with Jefferson's because the two Virginians were close political allies. Their church-state thought certainly converges at points—the Memorial makes the same epistemological argument that Jefferson does in the Virginia Statute. But Madison places Jefferson's (and Locke's) philosophical considerations in the context of man's religious duties. Indeed, Madison's emphasis on religious obligation is the most distinctive element of his church-state thinking.[22]

20. For discussion of social compact theory and our contemporary lack of understanding, see Harry V. Jaffa, "Too Good to Be True?" in *Crisis of the Strauss Divided: Essays on Leo Strauss and Straussianism, East and West* (Lanham, MD: Rowman and Littlefield, 2012), esp. 226–27, 234–38. For an especially thoughtful recent account that both uses Madison and imitates his type of reasoning, see Kathleen Brady, *The Distinctiveness of Religion in American Law: Rethinking Religion Clause Jurisprudence* (New York: Cambridge University Press, 2015), 80–99.

21. For thoughtful discussions of Madison's Memorial and Remonstrance, including its prudential arguments, see Eva Brann, "Madison's 'Memorial and Remonstrance,'" in *The Past-Present: Selected Writings of Eva Brann*, ed. Pamela Kraus (Annapolis, MD: St. John's College Press, 1997): 209–49; Paul Weber, "James Madison and Religious Equality: The Perfect Separation," *Review of Politics* 44 (1982): 163–86; Jeffrey Sikkenga, "Government Has No 'Religious Agency': James Madison's Fundamental Principle of Religious Liberty," *American Journal of Political Science* 56 (2012): 745–56.

22. Madison did not monopolize the connection between rights and duties, however. In his *Lectures on Law*, James Wilson also connects natural rights to natural duties:

> In his unrelated state, man has a natural right to his property, to his character, to liberty, and to safety. From his peculiar relations, as a husband, as a father, as a son, he is entitled to the enjoyment of peculiar rights, and obliged to the performance of peculiar duties. These will be specified in their due course. From his general relations, he is entitled to other rights, simple in their principle, but, in their operation, fruitful and extensive. His duties, in their principle and in their operation, may be characterized in the same manner as his rights. In these general relations, his rights are, to be free from injury, and to receive the fulfilment of the engagements, which are made to him: his duties are, to do no injury, and to fulfil the engagements, which he has made. On these two pillars principally and respectively rest the criminal and the civil codes of the municipal law. These are the pillars of justice.

James Wilson, *Collected Works of James Wilson*, ed. Kermit L. Hall and Mark David Hall (Indianapolis, IN: Liberty Fund, 2007), 2:1062.

The Memorial's first article begins with a "fundamental and undeniable truth" about man's obligations to God, which Madison quotes from Article 16 of the 1776 Virginia Declaration of Rights:

> 1. Because we hold it for a fundamental and undeniable truth, "that religion or the duty which we owe to our Creator and the manner of discharging it, can be directed only by reason and conviction, not by force or violence," ... [23]

The Virginia Statute also discusses God—Jefferson derives the natural right to religious freedom from the fact that "Almighty God hath created the mind free"—but omits discussion of duties to him. Jefferson emphasizes the autonomy that man enjoys on account of his created nature; the mind's freedom is the crucial fact in Jefferson's account of religious liberty. Madison, on the other hand, emphasizes what we *owe* to God.

Madison contends that our duties to God and the manner in which we discharge them must be directed by reason and conviction, not force or violence. But how, one might ask, does Madison know the content of our duties to God? Is his contention about the nature of religious obligation itself a matter of reason, or does Madison simply consult his own creedal convictions? Madison cites as his authority Article 16 of the 1776 Virginia Declaration of Rights, but this just pushes the same questions back one level: What are the grounds of the "fundamental and undeniable truth" stated in Article 16?

Many commentators maintain that the Memorial assumes a Protestant account of religious belief.[24] This position is not unreasonable, since Madison was an Episcopalian and his argument certainly resonates with some Protestant theology. But Madison does not cite the New Testament or any religious authority in this context. Madison, moreover, almost never invokes religious authority or relies upon sectarian theological beliefs to reach conclusions about political matters. Madison's own account of his reasoning

---

23. James Madison, "Memorial and Remonstrance Against Religious Assessments," 1785, in Vincent Phillip Muñoz, *Religious Liberty and the American Supreme Court: The Essential Cases and Documents*, updated edition (Lanham, MD: Rowman and Littlefield, 2015), 606.

24. For interpretations that emphasize the Protestant character of Madison's argument, see Lance Banning, *The Sacred Fire of Liberty: James Madison and the Founding of the Federal Republic* (Ithaca, NY: Cornell University Press, 1995), 436n68; Gary Rosen, *American Compact: James Madison and the Problem of Founding* (Lawrence: University Press of Kansas, 1999), 23; Nicholas P. Miller, *The Religious Roots of the First Amendment: Dissenting Protestants and the Separation of Church and State* (New York: Oxford University Press, 2012), 141–48. Cf. Muñoz, *God and the Founders*, 29–32.

about religion, furthermore, counsels against presuming that he simply relied upon his own beliefs or those of his immediate audience. Later in his life, in a response to a request for his opinion about a pamphlet claiming to prove a priori the existence of God, Madison wrote the following:

> ... the belief in a God All Powerful, wise and good, is so essential to the moral order of the World and to the happiness of man, that arguments which enforce it cannot be drawn from too many sources. ...
>
> But whatever effect may be produced on some minds by the more abstract train of ideas which you so strongly support, it will probably always be found that the course of reasoning from the effect to the cause, "from Nature to Nature's God," will be the more universal and more persuasive application. The finiteness of the human understanding betrays itself on all subjects, but more especially when it contemplates such as involve infinity.[25]

One private letter, of course, cannot be regarded as definitive, but Madison scholar Ralph Ketcham identifies this passage as "perhaps his [Madison's] most significant comment" on the subject of theological speculation.[26]

With that in mind, let me suggest an answer to this question: How does Madison know "that the duty which we owe to our Creator and the manner of discharging it, can be directed only by reason and conviction, not by force or violence"?[27] The Memorial contains a specific metaphysical anthropology from which Madison derives his theological conclusions. The quotation from the Virginia Declaration of Rights implicitly recognizes man's capacities of reason and free will. Individuals can discharge religious duties according to reason because they possess the capacity to reason. They can worship with conviction because they possess the faculties of considering, evaluating, and deciding—which, taken together, one can call free will. Article 1 asserts that men's opinions are insulated from others—they depend "only on the evidence contemplated by their own minds," and not on "the dictates of other men." Even if another person wills me to believe

25. James Madison, Letter to Frederick Beasley, November 20, 1825, in *Selected Writings of James Madison*, ed. Ralph Ketcham (Indianapolis, IN: Hackett, 2006), 303.

26. See Ketcham's introduction to Madison's Beasley letter, *Selected Writings of James Madison*, 303.

27. A version of this and the next several paragraphs initially appeared in Vincent Phillip Muñoz, "Two Concepts of Religious Liberty: The Natural Rights and Moral Autonomy Approaches to the Free Exercise of Religion," *American Political Science Review* 110 (2016): 369–81.

something—and is willing to use force to "persuade" me—the human mind is structured in such a way that "evidence" rather than "the dictates of other men" form and maintain my convictions.

Taken together, these capacities for reason and freedom allow men to be self-directed moral agents, not unreflective slaves of instinct or passion. Our capacities enable us to apprehend moral principles and norms (including those believed to be divinely revealed) and choose to follow them (or not). These capacities for moral apprehension and choice, in turn, make possible a distinctly human manner of worship: individuals can worship God freely according to conviction and conscience.[28]

From the worship that man's natural capacities make possible, Madison derives a conclusion about the kind of worship that God must find favorable. In his second official presidential proclamation calling for a national day of "public humiliation and prayer," Madison proclaimed:

> If the public homage of a people can ever be worthy [of] the favorable regard of the Holy and Omniscient Being to whom it is addressed, it must be that, in which those who join in it are guided only by their free choice, by the impulse of their hearts and the dictates of their consciences. . . . [29]

28. In his *Lectures on Law*, James Wilson, *Collected Works of James Wilson*, 1:504–5, employs the same sort of reasoning to infer the existence of the natural moral law and the propriety of man's subjection to it:

> To be without law is not agreeable to our nature; because, if we were without law, we should find many of our talents and powers hanging upon us like useless incumbrances [*sic*]. Why should we be illuminated by reason, were we only made to obey the impulse of irrational instinct? Why should we have the power of deliberating, and of balancing our determinations, if we were made to yield implicitly and unavoidably to the influence of the first impressions? Of what service to us would reflection be, if, after reflection, we were to be carried away irresistibly by the force of blind and impetuous appetites?

29. Presidential Proclamation, July 23, 1813, in *The Papers of James Madison: Presidential Series*, ed. J. C. A. Stagg et al. (Charlottesville: University of Virginia Press, 1984–), 6:458–59. As president, Madison issued four religious proclamations.

Robert Louis Wilken, *Liberty in the Things of God: The Christian Origins of Religious Freedom* (New Haven, CT: Yale University Press, 2019), 13, offers an account by the early Christian father Tertullian that is similar to the account of Madison presented here. Wilken translates a key passage from Tertullian's *Ad Scapulam* as follows:

> It is only just and a privilege inherent in human nature that every person should be able to worship according to his own convictions; the religious practice of one person neither harms nor helps another. It is not part of religion to coerce religious practice, for it is by choice not coercion that we are led to religion.

Madison reasons that man's capacity to worship freely—which includes, again, the freedom to choose not to worship—means that his *duty* to worship can only be discharged through worship directed by his own conscientious conviction. Worship lacking conviction, whether coerced or otherwise prompted, would not be true worship. As such it would not be fitting homage to a God that created mankind with freedom and reason. A God that creates us with the ability to freely worship deserves free worship in return.

Madison's account of man's religious duties rests on a number of suppositions about God and man: that a Creator exists; that God's creation is good; that God is omniscient and can know the "impulses of [individuals'] hearts"; and that man's created nature (as both free and rational) reflects and reveals both divine attributes and a divine order.[30] Because a chain of reason stretches "from Nature to Nature's God," human beings can reflect on our natural capacities and discover how we ought to worship. We can determine that the God who creates man capable of the exercise of freedom governed by reason would settle for nothing less than freely given worship reflective of each man's conscientious convictions. As Madison states at the conclusion of his presidential proclamation, only religion "freed from all coercive edicts," religion consisting of "free-will offerings

---

For Wilken's account of Thomas Jefferson's encounter with Tertullian's writings, see pp. 189–91.

30. On the reasonableness of the existence of a Creator, Madison wrote the following to Frederick Beasley, November 20, 1825, in *Selected Writings of James Madison*, 303–4:

> The finiteness of the human understanding betrays itself on all subjects, but more especially when it contemplates such as involve infinity. What may safely be said seems to be, that the infinity of time & space forces itself on our conception, a limitation of either being inconceivable; that the mind prefers at once the idea of a self-existing cause to that of an infinite series of cause & effect, which augments, instead of avoiding the difficulty; and that it finds more facility in assenting to the self-existence of an invisible cause possessing infinite power, wisdom & goodness, than to the self-existence of the universe, visibly destitute of those attributes, and which may be the effect of them. In this comparative facility of conception & belief, all philosophical Reasoning on the subject must perhaps terminate.

Madison's letter to Beasley, and his metaphysical anthropology that I have sketched, offer his response to contemporary scholars that are skeptical of any attempt to ground religious freedom on universal and timeless truths. Nelson Tebbe, in *Religious Freedom in an Egalitarian Age* (Cambridge, MA: Harvard University Press, 2017), 39, offers an example of this view when he asserts, "There simply is no authority that is available or accessible to ground judgments about the meaning of the First Amendment in this way."

of humble supplication, thanksgiving and praise . . . can be acceptable to Him whom no hypocrisy can deceive, and no forced sacrifices propitiate."[31]

I said above that the foundation of Madison's argument for religious freedom is the duty man owes to God. With his natural theology of proper religious worship established, I can now explain how Madison reasons from *duty* to the natural *right* of religious liberty. The argument operates from the propositions that men are obligated to worship God and that this worship can only be discharged when performed in accordance with each individual's reason and conviction. Given this "fundamental and undeniable truth," Madison presents two complementary arguments that lead to the conclusion that the exercise of religion according to conviction and conscience is an "unalienable right."

First, he repeats Jefferson's (and Locke's) epistemological argument that force simply cannot produce belief. Because force cannot produce conviction, law (of which coercion is a necessary component) cannot lead men to salvation.[32] Moreover, men could not grant authority over their religious opinions to the state even if they wanted to, for opinions follow evidence alone. As I stated above when discussing Jefferson's statute, the fact that men do not and cannot govern their minds as they govern their bodies limits governmental authority over religious beliefs.

Second, men possess an "unalienable right" to religious liberty because of the type of worship we owe to God—worship according to each man's conviction and conscience. This duty to worship God freely, Madison says, "is precedent, both in order of time and degree of obligation, to the claims of Civil Society."[33] Religious obligations are precedent in time in the sense that they exist in the "state of nature"—that is, the pre- or non-political condition that exists before civil society and government are created. More importantly, an individual's religious duties are precedent in "degree of obligation" in two related ways. Our obligations to God take priority over our obligations to other men on account of the justice due to God: God is superior to our fellow men, and therefore we ought to arrange our duties to other men so that they do not interfere with our duties to God. Our obligations to God also take priority over obligations to other men on ac-

---

31. Presidential Proclamation, July 23, 1813, in *The Papers of James Madison*, 6:458–59.

32. In his "Vices of the Political System of the United States," 1787, *Selected Writings of James Madison*, 37, Madison writes: "A sanction is essential to the idea of law, as coercion is to that of Government."

33. Madison, "Memorial and Remonstrance," in *Religious Liberty and the American Supreme Court*, 606.

count of the justice we owe ourselves. God's superior ability to reward and punish means it is never in an individual's interest to place his obligations to his fellow man above his obligations to God.[34] To say the same thing differently, our duties to the Creator are both prepolitical (they exist before a polity is established) and transpolitical (they go beyond and are superior to the purposes and authority of the polity). Their fundamental and authoritative character requires that we recognize them as rights vis-à-vis other men—in Madison's words, "What is here a right towards men, is a duty toward the Creator."[35]

Both of Madison's arguments assume the social compact theory of government I discussed in chapter 2. The nature of belief formation entails that we cannot give the state authority over our religious opinions. Similarly, the

34. In *A Man for All Seasons*, when asked by the Duke of Norfolk, ". . . I don't know whether the marriage was lawful or not. But damn it, Thomas, look at these names . . . You know these men! Can't you do as I did, and come with us, for fellowship?" Thomas More replies: "And when we stand before God, and you are sent to Paradise for doing according to your conscience, and I am damned for not doing according to mine, will you come along with me, for fellowship?" Robert Bolt, *A Man for All Seasons* (New York: Vintage International, 1990 [originally published 1960]), 132.

35. Madison, "Memorial and Remonstrance," in *Religious Liberty and the American Supreme Court*, 607. Madison was not the only Founder to derive and defend the inalienable natural right of religious free exercise from our duties to the Creator. Take the following statement from *The Essex Result*, likely written in 1778 by Theophilus Parsons:

> All men are born equally free. The rights they possess at their births are equal, and of the same kind. Some of those rights are alienable, and may be parted with for an equivalent. Others are unalienable and inherent, and of that importance, that no equivalent can be received in exchange. Sometimes we shall mention the surrendering of a power to controul our natural rights, which perhaps is speaking with more precision, than when we use the expression of parting with natural rights—but the same thing is intended. Those rights which are unalienable, and of that importance, are called the rights of conscience. We have duties, for the discharge of which we are accountable to our Creator and benefactor, which no human power can cancel. What those duties are, is determinable by right reason, which may be, and is called, a well informed conscience. What this conscience dictates as our duty, is so; and that power which assumes a controul over it, is an usurper; for no consent can be pleaded to justify the controul, as any consent in this case is void. The alienation of some rights, in themselves alienable, may be also void, if the bargain is of that nature, that no equivalent can be received. Thus, if a man surrender all his alienable rights, without reserving a controul over the supreme power, or a right to resume in certain cases, the surrender is void, for he becomes a slave; and a slave can receive no equivalent. Common equity would set aside this bargain.

Theophilus Parsons, "The Essex Result," in *American Political Writings During the Founding Era, 1760–1805*, ed. Charles S. Hyneman and Donald S. Lutz (Indianapolis, IN: Liberty Fund, 1983), 1:487.

transpolitical character of our religious obligations means it would never be just to God or to ourselves to grant the state sovereign authority over our religious exercises. These two related reasons lead Madison to conclude that the exercise of religion according to conviction and conscience is an "unalienable natural right."

As I discuss in *God and the Founders*, and as will be discussed in chapter 4, Madison advances a somewhat idiosyncratic constitutional rule of state noncognizance of religion.[36] But insofar as the "Memorial and Remonstrance" concludes that religious liberty is a natural right, it reflects the Founders' shared understanding. Two features of his argument distinguish Madison's contribution: the depth of his explanation that the unalienable character of religious liberty follows from our duties to the Creator, and his derivation of the character of those duties through reflection upon "Nature and Nature's God."

Madison's argument for religious freedom supposes a creator God and the authoritative status of nature. Given these suppositions—that God created nature (including human nature), and that this created nature establishes normative guides for human behavior—he philosophically deduces that man can only fulfill his religious duties according to his conviction and conscience. He therefore reasons that all men have an inalienable natural right to religious freedom.

Isaac Backus and the Christian Theology of the Natural Right to Religious Liberty

On matters of religious liberty, Jefferson and Madison are rightfully recognized as the two preeminent philosophical statesmen of the American Founding. Because of their historical roles and their continued prominence in Supreme Court church-state opinions, legal scholars (and the judges who rely upon them) are prone to overlook other Founding-era contributors to and arguments for religious liberty.[37] Lest we make the same mistake, I note that the period was awash with political sermons and pamphlets that

36. Muñoz, *God and the Founders*, 220–21.

37. For a discussion of the role of Jefferson and Madison in First Amendment Supreme Court jurisprudence, see Mark David Hall, "Jeffersonian Walls and Madisonian Lines: The Supreme Court's Use of History in Religion Clause Cases," *Oregon Law Review* 85 (2006): 563–614.

grounded the natural right to religious liberty in the Bible and Christian doctrine.[38]

In New England, the Reverend Isaac Backus, whom one commentator has recently labeled the "most prominent public face of Baptists in New England in the 1770s and 1780s," preached an evangelical Christian theory of church-state separation that culminated politically in the recognition of the natural right to religious freedom.[39] Backus's theology was rooted in Calvinist notions of the individual's election by God's mysterious grace.[40] Only the individual who had experienced the "internal call" of the Holy Spirit, Backus wrote, could be a true "ambassador of the Lord of Hosts."[41] From this, Backus concluded that "Christ will have no pressed soldiers in his army,"[42] and that "true religion is a voluntary obedience unto God."[43] Doctrinally, Backus's theology entailed an emphatic rejection of infant baptism; politically, it demanded fierce opposition to all forms of state authority over religion.

The most succinct statement of Backus's church-state position is found in his 1779 draft of a declaration of rights for the state of Massachusetts. The first two articles he proposed are as follows:

38. For an extensive investigation of eighteenth-century election sermons in Congregational New England, see Philip Hamburger, "Natural Rights, Natural Law, and American Constitutions," *Yale Law Journal* 102 (1993): 907–60. For a recent discussion of the Bible in the Founders' political discourse, see Daniel L. Dreisbach, *Reading the Bible with the Founding Fathers* (New York: Oxford University Press, 2016).

39. Joe L. Coker, "Isaac Backus and John Leland: Baptist Contributions to Religious Liberty in the Founding Era," in *Faith and the Founders of the American Republic*, ed. Daniel L. Dreisbach and Mark David Hall (New York: Oxford University Press, 2014), 306. Noah Feldman offers a helpful account of the Founding-era Baptist position in "The Intellectual Origins of the Establishment Clause," *New York University Law Review* 77 (2002): 386–90. For a discussion of the political theology and political influence of the Baptists and other religious dissenters in Founding-era Virginia, see Esbeck, "Virginia," in *Disestablishment and Religious Dissent*, 157–61.

40. For a brief and helpful overview of the Reformed tradition and an argument about its influence on the American Founding, see, Mark David Hall, "Vindiciae, Contra Tyrannos: The Influence of the Reformed Tradition in the American Founding," in *Faith and the Founders of the American Republic*, 34–62.

41. Isaac Backus, "A Discourse Showing the Nature and Necessity of an Internal Call to Preach the Everlasting Gospel" (1754), in *Isaac Backus on Church, State, and Calvinism: Pamphlets, 1754–1789*, ed. William G. McLoughlin (Cambridge, MA: Harvard University Press, 1968), 78.

42. Backus, "A Fish Caught in His Own Net" (1768), in *Isaac Backus on Church, State, and Calvinism*, 198.

43. "Government and Liberty Described" (1778), in *Isaac Backus on Church, State, and Calvinism*, 351.

1. All men are born equally free and independent, and have certain natural, inherent and unalienable rights, among which are the enjoying and defending life
and liberty, acquiring, possessing, and protecting property, and pursuing and
obtaining happiness and safety.   :

2. As God is the only worthy object of all religious worship, and nothing
can be true religion but a voluntary obedience unto his revealed will, of which
each rational soul has an equal right to judge for itself, every person has an unalienable right to act in all religious affairs according to the full persuasion of
his own mind, where others are not injured thereby. And civil rulers are so far
from having any right to empower any person or persons, to judge for others
in such affairs, and to enforce their judgments with the sword, that their power
ought to be exerted to protect all persons and societies, within their jurisdiction
from being injured or interrupted in the free enjoyment of this right, under any
pretense whatsoever.[44]

Men, who are born equally free and independent, Backus says, have an "unalienable right to act in all religious affairs according to the full persuasion
of [their] own mind[s]," because authentic religious commitment requires
"voluntary obedience" to God's revealed will. As Judd Owen summarizes,
"Backus's theology led to a doctrine of religious freedom, because it mis-
trusted all attempts by man to direct Christ's church or otherwise lead human beings to God."[45]

I have shown that Madison employed natural theology to reach the conclusion that God demands worship according to reason and conviction.
Backus arrived at the same conclusion through the Reformed tradition's
interpretation of sacred scripture. Both affirmed that the nature of true religious worship is, in Backus's words, that "each rational soul has an equal
right to judge for itself, [and] every person has an unalienable right to act
in all religious affairs according to the full persuasion of his own mind."

Backus was the most influential Baptist in New England at the time of
the American Founding, but his account of the natural right to religious
liberty was neither novel nor idiosyncratic.[46] The American tradition of theologically grounded arguments for the separation of church and state ex-

44. In *Isaac Backus on Church, State, and Calvinism*, 487–88.
45. J. Judd Owen, "The Struggle between 'Religion and Nonreligion': Jefferson, Backus,
and the Dissonance of America's Founding Principles," *American Political Science Review* 101
(2007): 495.
46. It was also not exclusively Baptist. Consider the following paragraph from a petition
submitted by Presbyterians during the 1785 church-state conflict in Virginia:

tends back to Roger Williams, the seventeenth-century founder of Rhode
Island. Versions of Backus's theological adaptation of natural rights political philosophy were articulated by earlier eighteenth-century Protestant
theologians.[47] The major themes of Backus's specific church-state political
theology are present, notably, in the writings of Elisha Williams, a mid-
eighteenth-century Congregational theologian and rector of Yale College.
Anticipating Backus, Williams grounded religious freedom in the voluntary nature of authentic religious practice. It is a "self-evident maxim," he
wrote, "*that a Christian is to receive his Christianity from CHRIST alone,*"
and not, as he emphasized in the same sermon, from "the pope, by a council, by a convocation or a parliament, from writings of fathers, or any doc-
tors of learning and reputation." Christ was only to be followed after a
direct personal encounter with the scriptures. ". . . The sacred scriptures are
the rule of faith and practice to a Christian," and therefore "*every Christian has a right of judging for himself* what he is to believe and practice in
religion according to that rule." At the heart of Williams's political theology was this "right of private judgment," which in the same sermon he explained as follows:

> Every man has an equal right to follow the dictates of his own conscience in the
> affairs of religion. Every one is under an indispensable obligation to search the
> scripture for himself (which contains the whole of it) and to make the best use
> of it he can for his own information in the will of GOD, the nature and duties of

---

The end of civil government is security to the temporal liberty and property of mankind, and to protect them in the free exercise of religion. Legislators are invested with
powers from their constituents for these purposes only, and their duty extends no
further. Religion is altogether personal, and the right of exercising it unalienable; and
it is not, cannot, and ought not to be, resigned to the will of the society at large; and
much less to the legislature, which derives its authority wholly from the consent of the
people, and is limited by the original intention of civil associations.

Memorial of the Presbyterians of Virginia to the General Assembly (August 13, 1785), in
American State Papers Bearing on Sunday Legislation, ed. William A. Blakely (Washington:
Religious Liberty Association, 1911), 113–14.

47. Thomas West suggests that the first appearances of social compact / natural rights
political theory in American Protestant theological and political thought occur in John Wise's
book *A Vindication of the Government of New-England Churches* (1717) and a 1725 article by
John Buckley. See Thomas G. West, "The Transformation of Protestant Theology as a Condition of the American Revolution," in *Protestantism and the American Founding*, ed. Thomas S.
Engeman and Michael P. Zuckert (Notre Dame, IN: University of Notre Dame Press, 2004),
204–5. See also Feldman, "Intellectual Origins of the Establishment Clause," 372–98.

Christianity. And as every Christian is so bound; so he has an unalienable right to judge of the sense and meaning of it, and to follow his judgment wherever it leads him; even an equal right with any rulers be they civil or ecclesiastical.[48]

Anticipating Backus's argument, Williams seamlessly wove his scriptural defense of private judgment together with social compact theory. When entering a civil state, he explained, individuals alienate the executive power they possess in the state of nature to protect their life and property, but not their sovereignty over their religious beliefs. Anticipating Jefferson's and Madison's conclusions, Williams held that "the members of a civil state *do retain their natural liberty or right of judging for themselves in matters of religion.*"[49]

The same teachings were preached by Backus's contemporary and fellow Baptist minister Dr. Samuel Stillman. In his May 26, 1779, election-day sermon on Matthew 22:21, Stillman endeavored "to draw the line between the things that belong to Caesar and those that belong to God." He did so first by quoting Locke's *Second Treatise* and repeating its teachings concerning natural human equality, the state of nature, and legitimate government's institution via consent. The "great end for which men enter into a state of civil society," Stillman explained, "is their *own advantage*," including, fundamentally, the protection of their natural rights. To explicate the specific Gospel injunction to "render therefore to Caesar the things that are Caesar's, and unto God the things that are God's," Stillman quoted at length from Locke's *Letter Concerning Toleration*, concluding that the power of a magistrate "is wholly confined to the things of this world." This limitation, Stillman explained, "secure[s] to every man the inestimable right of private judgment."[50]

*   *   *

48. Elisha Williams, "The Essential Rights and Liberties of Protestants: A Seasonable Plea for the Liberty of Conscience and the Right of Private Judgment in Matters of Religion," (1744) in *Political Sermons of the Founding Era: 1730–1805*, ed. Ellis Sandoz (Indianapolis, IN: Liberty Fund, 1990), 64, 55, 61. Of course, not all Protestant theologians agreed that the "right of private judgment" was theologically sound. For a discussion of the eighteenth-century theological debate among Protestants on the matter, see Miller, *The Religious Roots of the First Amendment*, 91–95.

49. Emphasis in the original. Williams, "The Essential Rights and Liberties of Protestants," 61.

50. Samuel Stillman, *A Sermon Preached Before the Honorable Council, and the Honorable House of Representatives of the State of Massachusetts-Bay in New England at Boston* (Boston: T. and J. Fleet, 1779), 7–9, 25.

The right of private judgment connected moral theology to natural rights social compact constitutionalism. Many devout Americans did not ground their commitment to religious freedom in Jefferson's epistemology or Madison's natural theology; prominent preachers of the time offered a Christian account of the natural right of religious liberty. The Founding generation's diverse understandings of the grounds for natural rights, moreover, were thought to be mutually supportive. Reason and revelation were understood to be complementary sources of knowledge, including of the truth of natural rights political principles.

This discussion of Backus, Williams, and Stillman also shows that the idea of the natural right to religious free exercise was not recognized only in late-eighteenth-century Virginia, nor even first discussed there.[51] The natural right to religious freedom was acknowledged throughout the new nation. It was defended philosophically and theologically. Conceptualizing religious liberty as a natural right was the common understanding of the American mind at the time of the nation's founding.

In the previous three chapters I have set forth the Founders' shared understanding of religious freedom as an "unalienable" natural right, and illuminated the philosophical and theological foundations on which that agreement was built. The Founders agreed on the principle that all individuals possess an inalienable right to religious freedom, and that the core of this right protects the freedom to worship according to conscience. On other related topics, however, they disagreed. In the next chapter, I address how the Founders disagreed about the separation of church and state.

51. In Virginia, Presbyterians were particularly articulate and influential in arguments about religious freedom. See Carl H. Esbeck, "Protestant Dissent and the Virginia Disestablishment, 1776–1786," *Georgetown Journal of Law and Public Policy* 7 (2009): 92–98.

CHAPTER FOUR

The Founders' Disagreement

Natural Rights and the Separation of Church from State

A rguably the most significant battle for religious freedom in early America occurred in mid-1780s Virginia.[1] The debate has played and continues to play a prominent role in the Supreme Court's Establishment Clause
jurisprudence, in part because it produced James Madison's "Memorial and
Remonstrance" and culminated in the adoption of Thomas Jefferson's Virginia Statute for Religious Liberty.[2] We often forget, however, those who
opposed Madison and Jefferson: Patrick Henry and, at least initially, George
Washington.[3] Jefferson and Madison are usually portrayed as the champions of religious freedom, but Henry and Washington were no less supportive of our "first freedom." Properly understood, the Virginia "battle" was
not a fight between proponents of freedom and proponents of religious

---

1. The best account of the Virginia battle over religious freedom remains Thomas E. Buck-
ley, S.J., *Church and State in Revolutionary Virginia, 1776–1787* (Charlottesville: University
Press of Virginia, 1977). See also Carl H. Esbeck, "Protestant Dissent and the Virginia Dis-
establishment, 1776–1786," *Georgetown Journal of Law and Public Policy* 7 (2009): 51–103;
John A. Ragosta, *Wellspring of Liberty: How Virginia's Dissenters Helped Win the American
Revolution and Secured Religious Liberty* (New York: Oxford University Press, 2010).

2. See, in particular, *Everson v. Board of Education*, 330 U.S. 1 (1947); *Town of Greece v.
Galloway*, 572 U.S. 565 (2014); *Trinity Lutheran Church of Columbia, Inc. v. Comer*, 582 U.S. __
(2017).

3. George Washington to George Mason, October 3, 1785, in *The Writings of George Washington*, ed. John C. Fitzpatrick (Washington: US Government Printing Office, 1938), 28:285; Vincent Phillip Muñoz, *God and the Founders: Madison, Washington, and Jefferson* (New York:
Cambridge University Press, 2009), 50–51.

oppression, but rather a disagreement among patriots about what natural rights principles demanded when applied to public policies regarding what we now call "the separation of church and state."

Thus far, I have attempted to articulate the Founders' shared principle of religious freedom. Agreement on fundamentals, however, did not yield agreement on all matters of public policy. This chapter attempts to show that, while the Founders agreed that religious liberty is an inalienable natural right, they began to disagree when they moved beyond the core right to worship according to conscience.[4] This chapter begins by documenting the two most significant areas of church-state policy disagreements: taxpayer funding of religious ministers and religious qualifications on political and civil rights, including religious tests for office. It then presents the conceptual framework that explains those disagreements. To summarize the chapter's main conclusions: on matters of church-state policy beyond the right to worship, the Founders divided into what we might call "expansive liberals" and "narrow republicans."[5] The more classically liberal Founders on church-state matters held a more expansive view of religious freedom that broadly limited the scope of legitimate state action, thereby proscribing religious taxes to support ministers and the state's use of religion as a criterion for conferring political and civil rights. The more republican Founders on church-state matters, by contrast, held a narrower view of religious liberty that provided more constitutional space for the adoption of majoritarian church-state public policies. Both "expansive liberals" and "narrow republicans" understood their positions to be compatible with the natural right of religious freedom; they disagreed about the extent to which that

---

4. Jud Campbell, "Natural Rights and the First Amendment," *Yale Law Journal* 127 (2017): 254, reaches a similar conclusion regarding freedom of speech and freedom of the press:

> ... [Founding-era] Americans who shared an understanding of speech and press freedoms as natural rights often profoundly disagreed about the legal implications of the First Amendment. Federalists in the late 1790s, for instance, typically invoked the English common law to defend the constitutionality of sedition prosecutions, while many Republicans appealed to practical experience and common sense to reach the opposite conclusion. Yet this virulent disagreement among contending elites began with a shared recognition of expressive freedom as a natural right.

5. I use "liberal" is the sense of "classical liberal," not in the sense of modern progressivism. For a synopsis of "the 'classical liberal' synthesis," see Richard A. Epstein, *The Classical Liberal Constitution: The Uncertain Quest for Limited Government* (Cambridge, MA: Harvard University Press, 2014), 17–33. The nomenclature "expansive liberals" and "narrow republicans" applies only to church-state matters. It should not be read to suggest that church-state "expansive liberals" necessarily would have espoused classical liberal principles or policies on all other political matters.

right limited democratic governance and whether it was politically prudent for government to support religion directly.

Taxpayer Support of Religion

The Founders' most significant church-state disagreement involved the propriety of taxation specifically to support religious ministers, church buildings, and ministries.[6] In the pre-1787 state declarations of rights and constitutions, three states (Maryland, Massachusetts, New Hampshire) explicitly authorized such taxes. Six states (New Jersey, Delaware, Pennsylvania, North Carolina, Georgia, South Carolina) and Vermont (which became a state in 1791 but adopted a constitution in 1777) prohibited compelled financial support of ministers or ministries without consent or contrary to conscience. Of the four states that did not include specific provisions in their founding charters or new constitutions, Connecticut taxed citizens for the support of religion, while Virginia, New York, and Rhode Island did not. One should note that language pertaining to the (im)propriety of tax support of religion was distinct from language pertaining to religious establishments—a point to which I will return.

The three states that explicitly authorized tax support of religion (Maryland, Massachusetts, New Hampshire) also protected the freedom to worship according to conscience. These states did not understand the freedom of conscientious worship to preclude compelled financial support of religion.[7] The basic New England system required the inhabitants of a

6. An earlier version of this section appeared in Vincent Phillip Muñoz, "Church and State in the Founding-Era State Constitutions," *American Political Thought* 4 (2015): 1–38. Other parts of this chapter initially appeared in Vincent Phillip Muñoz and Kevin Vance, "How the Founders Agreed about Religious Freedom but Disagreed about the Separation of Church and State," in *The Wiley Blackwell Companion to Religion and Politics in the U.S.*, ed. Barbara A. McGraw (West Sussex, UK: John Wiley and Sons, 2016), 85–97.

7. Connecticut, which did not adopt a post–Revolutionary War state constitution until 1818, also taxed residents to support minister salaries and house of worship, but its statutory religious freedom guarantees were limited to those persons "professing the Christian Religion." The same 1784 statute provided dissenting Protestants an exemption from ministerial taxes upon demonstration of attendance and support of their own church; exemptions, however, were not extended to those who did not attend or support a church. The law was explicit on this point, as table 5 shows. For discussions of Connecticut's church-state arrangements, see Gerard V. Bradley, *Church-State Relationships in America* (Westport, CT: Greenwood Press, 1987), 22–24; Thomas J. Curry, *The First Freedoms: Church and State in America to the Passage of the First Amendment* (New York: Oxford University Press, 1986), 178–84; Anson Phelps Stokes, *Church and States in the United States*, with introduction by Ralph Henry Gabriel

TABLE 4. **Tax support of religious ministers vs. establishment language: State declarations of rights and constitutions, 1777–86***

State	Explicit legislative authorizations for tax support for religion and religious ministers	Establishment language	Taxes legislated
MD 1776 DoR	XXXIII: . . . nor ought any person to be compelled to frequent or maintain, or contribute, unless on contract, to maintain any particular place of worship, or any particular ministry; yet the Legislature may, in their discretion, lay a general and equal tax, for the support of the Christian religion; leaving to each individual the power of appointing the payment over of [*sic*] the money, collected from him, to the support of any particular place of worship or minister, or for the benefit of the poor of his own denomination, or the poor in general of any particular county: . . .	None	No
MA 1780 DoR	III: . . . the legislature shall, from time to time, authorize and require, the several towns, parishes, precincts, and other bodies-politic or religious societies to make suitable provision, at their own expense, for the institution of the public worship of God and for the support and maintenance of public Protestant teachers of piety, religion, and morality in all cases where such provision shall not be made voluntarily. . . . *Provided, notwithstanding,* That the several towns, parishes, precincts, and other bodies-politic, or religious societies, shall at all times have the exclusive right of electing their public teachers and of contracting with them for their support and maintenance. And all moneys paid by the subject to the support of public worship and of the public teachers aforesaid shall, if he require it, be uniformly applied to the support of the public teacher or teachers of his own religious sect or denomination, provided there be any on whose instructions he attends; otherwise it may be paid toward the support of the teacher or teachers of the parish or precinct in which the said moneys are raised.	III: . . . no subordination of any sect or denomination to another shall ever be established by law.	Yes
NH 1784 DoR	VI: . . . the people of this state . . . do hereby fully impower [*sic*] the legislature to authorize from time to time, the several towns, parishes, bodies-corporate, or religious societies within this state, to make adequate provision at their own expence [*sic*], for the support and maintenance of public protestant teachers of piety, religion and morality: *Provided notwithstanding,* That the several towns, parishes, bodies-corporate, or religious societies, shall at all times have the exclusive right of electing their own public teachers, and of contracting with them for their support and maintenance. And no portion of any one particular religious sect or denomination, shall ever be compelled to pay towards the support of the teacher or teachers of another persuasion, sect or denomination.	VI: . . . no subordination of any one sect or denomination to another, shall ever be established by law.	Yes

continues

TABLE 4. (*continued*)

State	Explicit legislative authorizations for tax support for religion and religious ministers	Establishment language	Taxes legislated
NJ 1776 Const.	XVIII: . . . nor shall any person, . . . ever be obliged to pay tithes, taxes, or any other rates, for the purpose of building or repairing any other church or churches, place or places of worship, or for the maintenance of any minister or ministry, contrary to what he believes to be right, or has deliberately or voluntarily engaged himself to perform.	XIX. That there shall be no establishment of any one religious sect in this Province, in preference to another; . . .	No
DE 1776	DoR Sect. 2: . . . and that no man ought or of right can be compelled to attend any religious worship or maintain any ministry contrary to or against his own free will and consent, . . .	Const. ART. 29. There shall be no establishment of any one religious sect in this State in preference to another; . . .	No
PA 1776 DoR	II: . . . no man ought or of right can be compelled to attend any religious worship, or erect or support any place of worship, or maintain any ministry, contrary to, or against, his own free will and consent: . . .	None	No
NC 1776 Const.	XXXIV: . . . nor be obliged to pay, for the purchase of any glebe, or the building of any house of worship, or for the maintenance of any minister or ministry, contrary to what he believes right, or has voluntarily and personally engaged to perform; . . .	XXXIV: That there shall be no establishment of any one religious church or denomination in this State, in preference to any other; . . .	No
GA 1777 Const.	LVI: [All persons whatever] shall not, unless by consent, support any teacher or teachers except those of their own profession.	None	Yes
VT 1777/ 1786 DoR	III. . . . no man ought, or of right can be compelled to attend any religious worship, or erect or support any place of worship, or maintain any minister, contrary to the dictates of his conscience; . . .	None	Yes
SC 1778 Const.	XXXVIII: No person shall, by law, be obliged to pay towards the maintenance and support of a religious worship that he does not freely join in, or has not voluntarily engaged to support.	XXXVIII: The Christian Protestant religion shall be deemed, and is hereby constituted and declared to be, the established religion of this State. [Specific articles of faith and rules for internal church organization specified.]	No

TABLE 4. (*continued*)

State	Explicit legislative authorizations for tax support for religion and religious ministers	Establishment language	Taxes legislated
NY 1777 Const.	XXXV: That all such parts of the said common law, and all such of the said statutes and acts aforesaid, or parts thereof, as may be construed to establish or maintain any particular denomination of Christians or their ministers . . . are repugnant to this constitution, be, and they hereby are, abrogated and rejected.	See same section	No

*With the exception of the text from the 1776 Delaware Declaration of Rights, texts in this table can be found in *The Federal and State Constitutions, Colonial Charters, and Other Organic Laws of the United States*, 2nd edition, ed. Ben Perley Poore (Washington: Government Printing Office, 1878): 1:819 (MD); 1:957–58 (MA); 2:1281 (NH); 2:1313 (NJ), 1:277 (DE); 2:1541 (PA); 2:1413–14 (NC); 1:383 (GA); 2:1868 (VT); 2:1626–27 (SC); 2:1338 (NY). Text of the 1776 Delaware Declaration of Rights can be found in *The Founders' Constitution*, ed. Philip B. Kurland and Ralph Lerner (Indianapolis: Liberty Fund, n.d.; originally published Chicago: University of Chicago Press, 1987), 5:5.

TABLE 5. **Tax support of religious ministers: Significant legislation in states without clear rules in constitutional documents, 1784–86***

State		Taxes legislated?
CT 1784	"An Act Securing the Rights of Conscience in Matters of Religion, to Christians of every Denomination in this State": As the happiness of the People, and the good Order of Civil Society, essentially depend upon Piety, Religion, and Morality, it is the Duty of the Civil Authority to provide for the Support and Encouragement thereof; . . . And all Persons shall be taxed for the Support of the Ministry and other Charges of the Society wherein they dwell, who do not attend and help Support any other public Worship; . . .	Yes
VA 1786	"A Bill Establishing Religious Freedom": . . . no man shall be compelled to frequent or support any religious worship, place, or ministry whatsoever, . . .	No

*"An Act Securing the Rights of Conscience in Matters of Religion, to Christians of every Denomination in this State," in *Acts and Laws of the State of Connecticut, in America* (New London, CT: Timothy Green, 1784), 21–22; "A Bill Establishing Religious Freedom" in Vincent Phillip Muñoz, *Religious Liberty and the American Supreme Court*, updated edition (Lanham, MD: Rowman and Littlefield, 2015), 604–5.

geographically defined town, parish, or society to elect a minister who would then receive that locality's religious taxes. A town might have more than one tax-supported minister if local legislation allowed. Taxes were collected and

(New York: Harper and Brothers, 1950), 1:408–14; Paul Wakeman Coons, *The Achievement of Religious Liberty in Connecticut* (New Haven, CT: Yale University Press, 1936).

For a recent discussion that finds the Maryland, Massachusetts, and New Hampshire position to be incoherent, see Edward J. Erler, *Property and the Pursuit of Happiness: Locke, the Declaration of Independence, Madison, and the Challenge of the Administrative State* (Lanham, MD: Rowman and Littlefield, 2019), 217–26.

administered locally, as were exemptions for dissenters, which varied from place to place.[8] Maryland's 1776 Declaration of Rights specifically left "to each individual the power of appointing the payment over the money, collected from him, to the support of any particular place of worship or minister," and provided, additionally, that the taxpayer could direct his religious taxes to benefit "the poor of his own denomination." The state, however, did not enact religious-tax legislation. Attempts to pass a "clergy bill" in the early to mid-1780s failed, and the system was never actually implemented.[9]

As noted, six states (New Jersey, Delaware, Pennsylvania, North Carolina, Georgia, South Carolina) and Vermont prohibited compelled support without consent or contrary to conscience. Some of these states legislated religious taxes; others did not. Georgia's 1777 Constitution, for example, stated that all persons "shall not, unless by consent, support any teacher or teachers except those of their own profession."[10] In 1785, the Georgia legislature adopted a property tax "for the regular establishment and support of the public duties of religion."[11] The legislation provided that each county with at least thirty heads of family was to select a minister of a church of its choosing to whom state tax dollars would flow. When the population

8. For discussions of New England's system of religious taxes, see Bradley, *Church-State Relationships in America*, 22–24; Chester James Antieau, Arthur T. Downey, and Edward C. Roberts, *Freedom from Federal Establishment: Formation and Early History of The First Amendment Religion Clauses* (Milwaukee, WI: Bruce Publishing, 1964), 38–41; Leonard W. Levy, *The Establishment Clause: Religion and the First Amendment*, 2nd ed. (Chapel Hill: University of North Carolina Press, 1994), 30–49; Mark Douglas McGarvie, *One Nation under Law: America's Early Struggles to Separate Church and State*, (DeKalb, IL: Northern Illinois University Press, 2005), 154–56; John Witte Jr., "'A Mild and Most Equitable Establishment of Religion': John Adams and the Massachusetts Experiment," *Journal of Church and State* 41 (1999): 213–52. Also see the chapters in *Disestablishment and Religious Dissent: Church-State Relations in the New American States, 1776–1783*, ed. Carl H. Esbeck and Jonathan J. Den Hartog (Columbia: University of Missouri Press, 2019): Massachusetts by John Witte, Jr. and Justin Latterell, New Hampshire by Brian Franklin, Connecticut by Robert J. Imholt, Vermont by Shelby M. Balik, and Maine by Marc M. Arkin.

9. For a discussion of the ultimately futile attempts to legislate church taxes in Maryland, see Antieau, Downey, and Roberts, *Freedom from Federal Establishment*, 67–68; Michael D. Breidenbach, "Maryland," in *Disestablishment and Religious Dissent*, 317–20; Ellis M. West, *The Free Exercise of Religion in America: Its Original Meaning* (Cham, Switzerland: Palgrave Macmillan, 2019), 99–109.

10. Constitution of Georgia, 1777, Article 56. The 1789 Georgia Constitution, Section 5, stated more clearly that "all persons shall have the free exercise of religion, without being obliged to contribute to the support of any religious profession but their own." See *Federal and State Constitutions*, 1:383, 386.

11. *The Colonial Records of the State of Georgia*, ed. Allen D. Candler (Atlanta: Chas P. Byrd, 1911), 19(2): 395–98.

grew sufficiently large to warrant another church, at least twenty heads of
family could petition to be recognized as a separate church and have their
minister receive a proportionate share of tax dollars.[12] Vermont adopted a
similar system of religious taxation with local control in 1783.[13] Delaware
considered but did not adopt such a system in 1786.[14] The practices of these

12. Joel A. Nichols, "Georgia: The Thirteenth Colony," in *Disestablishment and Religious
Dissent*, 236.

13. Article 3 of Vermont's 1777 Declaration of the Rights of the Inhabitants of Vermont,
like Delaware's 1776 Declaration of Rights, recognized that "all men have a natural and unalienable right to worship ALMIGHTY GOD, according to the dictates of their own consciences and understanding" and "that no man ought, or of right can be compelled to attend
any religious worship, or erect, or support any place of worship, or maintain any minister,
contrary to the dictates of his conscience." In 1783, Vermont legislated a series of Parish and
Ministry Acts that included systems of religious taxation and exemptions to support religious
ministers and meetinghouses at the town level. As the historian Shelby Balik explains, the acts
required that two-thirds of voters in each town agree on a place of worship and a minister.
Dissenters could obtain exemptions with certificates signed by church officials representing
their congregations. By default, each adult was assumed to be "of Opinion with the major
part of the Inhabitants within such Town or Parish where he[,] she or they shall dwell" until
producing an exemption certificate. See *Journals and Proceedings of the General Assembly of
the State of Vermont, Part II, State Papers of Vermont* (Bellows Falls: P. H. Gobie Press, 1925),
3:189; "An Act to Enable Towns and Parishes to Erect Proper Houses for Public Worship and
Support Ministers of the Gospel, 1783," in John A. Williams, ed., *Laws of Vermont, 1781-1784,
State Papers of Vermont* (Montpelier, 1965), 13:195; "An Act for Supporting Ministers of the
Gospel, 1787," in *Laws of Vermont, 1785-1791*, 14:348-50. For a discussion of these provisions,
see Shelby M. Balik, "Disestablishment in Vermont," in *Disestablishment and Religious Dis-
sent*, 293-308; Shelby M. Balik, "Equal Right and Equal Privilege: Separating Church and
State in Vermont," *Journal of Church and State* 50 (2008): 23-48.

14. Section 2 of Delaware's 1776 Declaration of Rights provided "that no man ought or of
right can be compelled to attend any religious worship or maintain any ministry contrary to
or against his own free will and consent, . . ." Article 30 of the state constitution (*Federal and
State Constitutions*, 1:278) made the provision binding as a matter of constitutional law. The
provision was understood, at least by some, to allow religious taxes as long as the taxpayer
exercised some control over the direction of his tax dollars. According to the historian Evan
Haefeli ("Delaware," in *Disestablishment and Religious Dissent*, 45), George Read drafted a
"plan for education" for Delaware that, had it passed, would have required a general assessment to the benefit of clergy maintenance reminiscent of Patrick Henry's plan for Virginia.
The effort, which took place in 1786, was ultimately unsuccessful, and Haefeli reports that
Read's specific plan has been lost. It had notable supporters, however, including John Dicken-
son, who in a letter to Read wrote the following:

> It is the duty of government, with the utmost attention and caution, to promote and
> enforce the sublime and beneficial morality, as well as theology, of Christianity; and,
> considering them as connected with government, how can this be done better than
> by employing men of wisdom, piety, and learning to teach it, and how can they be so
> employed unless they are properly supported, and how can they be supported but by
> the government that employs them? Let impositions be laid for this purpose. If any
> man conscientiously scruples their lawfulness, let him be permitted to appropriate his

states indicate that prohibitions against compelled financial support of religion without "consent" or "contrary to the dictates of conscience" were thought compatible, at least by some, with religious taxes that afforded taxpayers some control over their tax dollars.[15]

Virginia legislated a complete ban of taxpayer support of religion. Jefferson's 1786 Virginia Statute for Religious Liberty declared that "the natural rights of mankind" included that "no man shall be compelled to frequent or support any religious worship, place, or ministry whatsoever." It more comprehensively prohibited tax support of religious ministers and

---

share to the use of the poor, or any other public service. Thus government would strenuously carry on the grand work of teaching virtue and religion, without offering the least violence to the conscience of any individual. . . .

John Dickinson to George Read, April 28, 1786, in William Thompson Read, *Life and Correspondence of George Read, a signer of the Declaration of Independence: With Some Notices of Some of His Contemporaries* (Philadelphia, 1870), 412–13.

Note that I rescind my previously published interpretation (Muñoz, "Church and State in the Founding-Era State Constitutions," 21–22) regarding the permissibility of religious taxes consistent with the Delaware and Vermont declarations of rights.

15. Cf. West, *The Free Exercise of Religion in America*, 202–3. The existence of Georgia's 1785 church tax, Vermont's 1783 church tax, and efforts to legislate a similar tax in Delaware in 1786 refute West's contention that "there is no external evidence to support" my interpretation that constitutional language such as Georgia's was understood to be compatible with some forms of religious taxation. For West's discussion of the Georgia law, see pp. 113–15; for the Vermont law, pp. 160–62; West does not discuss the legislation proposed in Delaware. For similar reasons, Thomas J. Curry, *The First Freedoms*, 220, incorrectly concludes:

Of the eleven states that ratified the First Amendment, nine (counting Maryland) adhered to the viewpoint that support of religion and churches should be voluntary, that any governmental financial assistance to religion constituted an establishment of religion and violated its free exercise.

Noah Feldman, in "Intellectual Origins of the Establishment Clause," *New York University Law Review* 77 (2002): 341, writes:

Establishment of religion, the Framers' generation thought, often had the effect of compelling conscience. Going beyond compulsory church attendance or required forms of worship, the Framers' generation worried that conscience would be violated if citizens were required to pay taxes to support religious institutions with whose beliefs they disagreed.

Feldman is correct that some members of the Framers' generation held this position, as I will discuss later in this chapter, but it was not as universal as his comment suggests. For a thoughtful response to Feldman, see Steven D. Smith, "Taxes, Conscience, and the Constitution," *Constitutional Commentary* 23 (2006): 365–80. For a discussion of noncoercive establishments in the context of contemporary political theory, see Daniel Brudney, "On Noncoercive Establishment," *Political Theory* 33 (2005): 812–39.

ministries than those state provisions that prohibited support only "contrary to or against his own free will or support," to use language from Delaware's 1776 Declaration of Rights. New York's 1777 constitution "abrogated and rejected" those parts of the common law of England and other colonial statutes that could be "construed to establish or maintain any particular denominations of Christians or their ministers." Precisely what types of state funding this provision prohibited is not clear, although after its adoption no group attempted to persuade the state legislature to adopt a system of taxpayer support of churches.[16] Rhode Island, which until 1843 was governed under its colonial charter of 1663, did not have a tradition of imposing religious taxes.[17]

Both the Founding-era state charters and actual state practices from 1776 to 1787 reveal divergent approaches to religious taxes.[18] In Massachusetts and New Hampshire, government support for religion was constitutionally prescribed, and a system of local taxation and minister appointments was legislated. In several states, religious taxes were constitutionally permissible with some taxpayer direction. When such taxes were legislated, states adopted practices similar to New England's system of local administration. In some states, religious taxes were constitutionally permissible but never enacted. In Virginia, taxation for the support of religious ministers was said to be a violation of natural rights.

The reader may have noticed that I have discussed state religious taxation without reference to state establishment clause provisions. The reason for doing so is relatively simple: in the Founding-era state declarations of rights and constitutions, text concerning limitations on compelled financial support was distinct from text pertaining to religious establishments.[19] Pennsylvania's 1776 Declaration of Rights, for example, prohibited compelled

16. For a discussion of the adoption of the church-state provisions of New York's 1777 Constitution, see John Webb Pratt, *Religion, Politics, and Diversity: The Church-State Theme in New York History* (Ithaca, NY: Cornell University Press, 1967), 81–97; Kyle T. Bulthuis, "Religious Disestablishment in the State of New York," in *Disestablishment and Religious Dissent,* 127–31. Regarding the absence of religious taxes in New York, see Pratt, *Religion, Politics, and Diversity,* 115; Curry, *The First Freedoms,* 161–62; McGarvie, *One Nation under Law,* 111.

17. Levy, *Establishment Clause,* 27. See also James S. Kabala, "Church and State in Rhode Island," in *Disestablishment and Religious Dissent,* 55–57.

18. For a helpful overview of legal and constitutional issues surrounding tax exemptions for religion, including during the Founding era, see John Witte Jr., "Tax Exemption of Church Property: Historical Anomaly or Valid Constitutional Practice? *Southern California Law Review* 64 (1991): 363–415.

19. New York, I should note, is a possible exception.

financial support of "any place of worship, or . . . ministry, contrary to, or against, . . . free will and consent," but its charters included no language pertaining to religious establishments. Massachusetts's and New Hampshire's declarations of rights authorized religious taxes and also declared that "no subordination" of any "sect or denomination to another shall ever be established by law." The term "establishment" seems not to have been used in state charters to refer to constitutional rules pertaining to taxpayer funding of religion.

Comparing the religious establishment and no-coercive-support provisions of the North and South Carolina constitutions shows further that taxpayer funding of religion was not necessarily viewed as an establishment. Article 34 of North Carolina's 1776 Constitution provided

> That there shall be no establishment of any one religious church or denomination in this State, in preference to any other.

The same article then immediately included additional language prohibiting nonvoluntary support of religion:

> neither shall any person . . . be obliged to pay, for the purchase of any glebe, or the building of any house of worship, or for the maintenance of any minister or ministry, contrary to what he believes right, or has voluntarily and personally engaged to perform. . . .

South Carolina's 1778 Constitution, by contrast, declared,

> The Christian Protestant religion shall be deemed, and is hereby constituted and declared to be, the established religion of this State.

But it also included language similar to North Carolina's prohibition of nonvoluntary support of religion:

> No person shall, by law, be obliged to pay towards the maintenance and support of a religious worship that he does not freely join in, or has not voluntarily engaged to support.

North Carolina and South Carolina both prohibited forms of compelled support of religion, but the former prohibited "the establishment of any one religious church or denomination" whereas the latter declared that "the Christian Protestant religion shall be . . . the established religion of this State."

The Supreme Court has long associated the First Amendment's prohibition against religious establishments with prohibitions against taxpayer funding of religion, but that connection is not immediately evident from the texts of the Founding-era state declaration of rights and constitutions. Whatever an "establishment" of religion was, the Founding-era state constitutions did not use the term synonymously or interchangeably with religious taxes or compelled financial support of religion. Accordingly, to understand the difference among the Founding-era states regarding tax support of religion, I have focused on what the state charters actually stated about such support, not on their texts pertaining to religious establishments. This finding also means that Founding-era state charters do *not* support the widespread assumption that taxpayer support of religion alone constitutes the Founders' understanding of a religious establishment.[20]

I will address the possible meanings of religious "establishment" in chapter 7. Later in this chapter, I will return to the issue of taxpayer support of religion and the different arguments the Founders gave to support their competing positions. But before doing so, I will document the Founders' other area of church-state disagreement: religious limitations on political and civil rights.

---

20. For a relatively recent example of a scholar who adopts this widespread but mistaken assumption, see Sarah Barringer Gordon, who writes in *The Spirit of the Law: Religious Voices and the Constitution in Modern America* (Cambridge, MA: Belknap Press of Harvard University Press, 2010), 5:

> When the Constitution was drafted in 1787, six of the original thirteen states had religious establishments. That is, these states had a variety of means for imparting religion to their inhabitants, usually though a tax-supported system of church support.

Gordon, like many scholars, assumes a particular construction of what constitutes a religious "establishment" and then imposes that construction to categorize Founding-era state practices. See also Muñoz, "Church and State in the Founding-Era State Constitutions," 24, where I explain:

> Given modern constitutional law's association of establishments with taxpaying funding of religion, it is also surprising that, in the founding-era declarations of rights and constitutions, official text concerning religious establishments was distinct from text pertaining to limitations on compelled financial support. Six states (NJ, DE, NC, SC, MA, NH) included both text about religious establishments and text regarding compelled support of religion. If "establishment" and taxpayer support were synonymous, this duplication would make no sense. Moreover, no systematic relationship existed between prohibitions against compelled support and limitations on establishments, . . .

Religious Tests for Political Office and Civil Rights

The second area of church-state disagreement during the Founding era involved the propriety of using religious criteria for the enjoyment or protection of political and civil rights. The most significant disagreement here involved religious tests for office holding, though there was near unanimity in state-level practices.[21] States also used religious criteria as the qualifying basis for "equal protection" of nonnatural civil rights, the enjoyment of specified rights, and the enjoyment of or exclusion from some legal privileges.

Religious tests for state-level offices were typically imposed through constitutionally specified eligibility qualifications and/or sectarian oaths of office. The Massachusetts Constitution of 1780, for example, employed both. Chapter 2 specified that only Christians were eligible to hold the offices of governor and lieutenant governor; Chapter 4 then provided the following oath (or, for Quakers, affirmation) for any person elected governor, lieutenant governor, councillor, senator, or representative:

> I, A. B., do declare, that I believe the Christian religion, and have a firm persuasion of its truth; and that I am seised [sic] and possessed, in my own right, of the property required by the constitution, as one qualification or place to which I am elected.[22]

Every state constitution except those of Virginia and New York imposed religious tests for office through either an express restriction or a religious oath. New York's liberality, moreover, was more apparent than real; in 1788 it adopted legislation that effectively prohibited conscientious Catholics from holding office.[23]

As table 6 shows, some states limited their guarantees of the equal enjoyment of civil rights to Protestants or, in the case of Pennsylvania, to

21. For excellent discussions of religious tests for office during the Founding era, see Daniel L. Dreisbach, "The Constitution's Forgotten Religion Clause: Reflections on the Article VI Religious Test Ban," *Journal of Church and State* 38 (1996): 261–95; Gerard V. Bradley, "The No Religious Test Clause and the Constitution of Religious Liberty: A Machine that Has Gone of Itself," *Case Western Reserve Law Review* 37 (1987): 674–747.

22. Massachusetts Constitution of 1780, Chapter 2, Section 1, Article 2 (governor); Chapter 2, Section 2, Article 1 (lieutenant governor); Chapter 6, Article 1 (oath); *Federal and State Constitutions*, 1:964, 967, 969.

23. Article 42 of the New York 1777 Constitution required all foreigners seeking naturalization to "abjure and renounce all allegiance and subjection to all and every foreign king,

TABLE 6. **Religious tests for political office and civil rights: State declarations of rights, constitutions, 1777–84***

	Nondeprivation/ equal protection for civil rights limited to	**Religious tests and oaths/ affirmations for office**[†]	**Exclusions of ministers from officeholding**	**Exemptions from bearing of arms**
VA 1776				
NJ 1776	Protestants demeaning themselves peacefully	Protestants demeaning themselves peacefully		
DE 1776	*Christians who do not disturb the peace, happiness or safety of society*[‡]	"I, A B. do profess faith in God the Father, and in Jesus Christ His only Son, and in the Holy Ghost, one God, blessed for evermore; and I do acknowledge the holy scriptures of the Old and New Testament to be given by divine inspiration."	Yes	*Yes*
PA 1776	*Men who acknowledge the being of a God*	"I do believe in one God, the creator and governor of the universe, the rewarder of the good and the punisher of the wicked. And I do acknowledge the Scriptures of the Old and New Testament to be given by Divine inspiration."		*Yes*
MD 1776		*Declaration of a belief in the Christian religion* "That every person, appointed to any office of profit or trust, shall ... subscribe a declaration of his belief in the Christian religion."	Yes	
NC 1776		"That no person, who shall deny the being of God or the truth of the Protestant religion, or the divine authority either of the Old or New Testaments, or who shall hold religious principles incompatible with the freedom and safety of the State, shall be capable of holding any office or place of trust or profit in the civil department within this State."	Yes	
GA 1777		Protestants	Yes	
NY 1777			Yes	Quakers only

continues

TABLE 6. (*continued*)

	Nondeprivation/ equal protection for civil rights limited to	Religious tests and oaths/ affirmations for office[†]	Exclusions of ministers from officeholding	Exemptions from bearing of arms
SC 1778	Christian Protestants demeaning themselves peacefully and faithfully	Protestants	Yes	
MA 1780	*Christians demeaning themselves peacefully*	Christians "I, A.B., do declare that I believe the Christian religion, and have a firm persuasion of its truth...."		
NH 1784	*Christians demeaning themselves quietly, and as good subjects of the state*	Protestants		Yes
VT 1777/1786	*Protestants/ none*[§]	"You do believe in one God, the Creator and Governor of the Universe, the rewarded [*sic*] of the good, and punisher of the wicked. And you do acknowledge the scriptures of the Old and New Testament to be given by divine inspiration; and own and profess the Prot-estant religion." (1786)**		Yes

*With the exception of the 1776 Delaware Declaration of Rights, all volume and page citations in parentheses are to Poore's *Federal and State Constitutions*: New Jersey Constitution, 1776, Article 19 (2:1313); Delaware Declaration of Rights, 1776, Sections 3, 10 (*Founders' Constitution* 5:5–6), Delaware Constitution, 1776, Articles. 22, 29 (1:276–78); Pennsylvania Declaration of Rights, 1776, II, VIII (2:1541), Pennsylvania Constitution, 1776, Section 10 (2:1543); Maryland Declaration of Rights, 1776, Article 35 (1:820), Maryland Constitution, 1776, Articles 37, 55 (1:828, 825); North Carolina Constitution, 1776, Articles 31, 32 (2:1413); Georgia Constitution, 1777, Articles 6, 57 (1:379, 383); New York Constitution, 1777, Artciles 39, 40 (2:1338–39); South Carolina Constitution, 1778, Articles 3, 12, 21, 38 (2:1626, 1621–24); Massachusetts Declaration of Rights, 1780, Article 3 (1:957–58), Massachusetts Constitution, 1780 (Test: Chapter 2, Section 1, Article 2) (Oath: Chapter 6, Article 1) (1:964, 970); New Hampshire Bill of Rights, 1784, Article 6 (2:1281); New Hampshire Constitution, 1784, (2:1286–87); Vermont Declaration of Rights, 1777, 1786, Article 3 (2:1859, 1868); Vermont Constitution of 1786, Articles 10, 12 (2:1871, 1868).

[†]Delaware, Pennsylvania, Vermont, South Carolina, Massachusetts, and New Hampshire required those about to take an office to swear or affirm the oath of office. Maryland and Georgia made no provisions for affirmations or oaths of office. The absence in Georgia's constitution of an affirmation alternative is notable in part because the constitution required every person entitled to vote to take an oath or affirm allegiance to the state and its constitution.

[§]Section 3 of the 1776 Delaware Declaration of Rights (*Founders' Constitution* 5:5) stated that "all persons professing the Christian religion ought forever to enjoy equal rights and privileges in this state, unless, under colour of religion, any man disturb the peace, the happiness or safety of society."

[¶]The 1777 Vermont Declaration of Rights, Article III, stated, "nor can any man who professes the protestant [sic] religion, be justly deprived or abridged of any civil right, as a citizen, on account of his religious sentiment, or peculiar mode of religious worship:..." The 1786 Vermont Declaration of Rights, Article III, stated, "nor can any man be justly deprived or abridged of any civil right as a citizen, on account of his religious sentiments, or peculiar mode of religious worship;..." *Federal and State Constitutions*, 2:1859, 1868.

**The oath in the 1786 Vermont Constitution slightly altered the language of the oath in the 1777 Constitution. Italicization indicates that the text appears in a declaration of rights.

those who believed in God. Six states prohibited religious ministers from holding office. While religious affiliation or profession was often made a ground of civil disability, some states also extended civil privileges on account of religious affiliation. Five states exempted individuals conscientiously scrupulous of bearing arms from being forced to do so (New York limited its exemption to Quakers alone). To receive these exemptions, however, the individual had to pay for a substitute to take his place. Six of the eight states that required an oath to take a public office allowed individuals to affirm rather than swear the oaths, a provision that relieved Quaker officeholders in particular from a conflict with their religious precepts.

Explaining the Founders' Disagreement

The foregoing discussion shows that, beyond protections securing the right to worship as such, the Founders disagreed about the implications of the natural right to religious liberty. Guided by Madison and Jefferson, Virginia adopted what we have labeled "expansive liberalism." The 1786 Virginia Statute declared it to be "of the natural rights of mankind" that

> no man shall be compelled to . . . support any religious worship, place, or ministry whatsoever . . . nor shall otherwise suffer, on account of his religious opinions or beliefs; . . . and that the same shall in no wise diminish, enlarge, or affect their civil capacities.

Virginia, more comprehensively than any other state, prohibited religious taxes and religion-based qualifications on civil and political rights. Virginia, however, was something of an outlier.[24] More common among the

---

prince, potentate, and State in all matters, ecclesiastical as well as civil." This language was adopted by the New York State Assembly in 1788 as an oath of office required for anyone elected governor, to the state legislature or to Congress, or appointed to a state civil or military office. For a discussion of the adoption of the 1788 legislation, see Jason K. Duncan, *Citizens or Papists? The Politics of Anti-Catholicism in New York, 1625–1821* (New York: Fordham University Press, 2005), 71–72. See also Pratt, *Religion, Politics, and Diversity*, 107. According to Antieau, Downey, and Roberts, *Freedom from Federal Establishment*, 94, Francis Cooper in 1806 became the first Catholic to take a seat in the New York Assembly.

24. Carl H. Esbeck, "Virginia," in *Disestablishment and Religious Dissent*, 169–71. Jack N. Rakove, "Once More into the Breach: Reflections on Jefferson, Madison, and the Religion Problem," in *Making Good Citizens: Education and Civil Society*, ed. Diane Ravitch and Joseph P. Viteritti (New Haven, CT: Yale University Press, 2001), 245.

Founding-era states was the practice of what I have called "narrow republicanism," an approach that held state tax support of religion and the use
of religion to accomplish civic ends to be compatible with natural rights
principles of religious freedom.

The differences among the Founding-era states reflect a constitutional
disagreement over the scope of the inalienable natural right of religious liberty and a political disagreement over the prudence of governmental utili-
zation of religion. Regarding the constitutional disagreement, "expansive
liberalism" holds that religion itself, not just religious worship, lies beyond
the legitimate jurisdiction of government. It is classically liberal in the sense
that it imposes an across-the-board limitation on governmental authority.
"Narrow republicanism," as the name suggests, adopts a narrower view of
the domain of conduct protected by the right of religious liberty. It holds
that only worship as such lies beyond the jurisdiction of government. Both
positions agree that the state lacks legitimate authority to pursue the salvation of citizens' souls or piety for its own sake, but "narrow republicanism" allows the state to employ religion to achieve otherwise legitimate civic
ends. The view is "republican" insofar as it permits the public to deliberate
about the political usefulness of religion and to employ religion (or exclude
religion) for civic purposes. "Narrow republicanism" allows the public to
support, advance, limit, and exempt religion and religious individuals in the
pursuit of otherwise valid policies; it does not demand such policies, but it
permits them. "Expansive liberalism," by contrast, holds that government
classifications on the basis of religion (for civil privileges or penalties) are
impermissible. Although I discuss "expansive liberalism" and "narrow republicanism" as fixed and separate positions, they are most accurately understood as positions on a continuum.

Narrow Republicanism

We can begin our discussion of "narrow republicanism" by returning to Virginia and Patrick Henry's proposed 1784 legislation, "Establishing a Provision for Teachers of the Christian Religion." Henry sought to impose a
tax assessment to fund religious ministers in the state of Virginia. The bill
specified that the taxpayer could direct his taxes to support the Christian
society of his choosing. If no such society were specified, collected taxes
would be used "for the encouragement of seminaries of learning within
the Counties whence such sums shall arise, and to no other use or purpose
whatsoever." The bill began as follows:

Whereas the general diffusion of Christian knowledge hath a natural tendency to correct the morals of men, restrain their vices, and preserve the peace of society, which cannot be effected without a competent provision for learned teachers, who may be thereby enabled to devote their time and attention to the duty of instructing such citizens, as from their circumstances and want of education, cannot otherwise attain such knowledge; and it is judged that such provision may be made by the Legislature, without counteracting the liberal principle heretofore adopted and intended to be preserved by abolishing all distinctions of preeminence amongst the different societies or communities of Christians.[25]

Henry framed the bill to emphasize its civic purposes: correcting morals, restraining vices, and preserving peace. Religious teachers ought to be supported because "Christian knowledge" helps foster among the people the virtues that republican government requires. In emphasizing the cultivation of civic virtue, Henry adopted a rationale similar to that offered by Jefferson to support his own contemporaneous bill for taxpayer support of public education. In his proposed "Bill for the More General Diffusion of Knowledge," Jefferson advocated taxpayer funding of education because wise officeholders and knowledgeable citizens (who elect and then hold those officeholders accountable) are necessary to safeguard natural rights within a republican regime.[26] Henry's bill states that tax support of Christian ministers will further the same ends. Such taxes, moreover, do not "counteract the liberal principle" because the bill "abolish[es] all distinctions of preeminence amongst the different societies or communities of Christians." Relatedly, note what the bill does not say. It does not advocate support of Christian ministers because they teach the true religion, or because they are necessary for the salvation of citizens' souls. The bill, in other words, does not claim to advance religion or religious truth for their own sake. The bill's title, in fact, was revised to omit language relating to worship and to emphasize the bill's educational purposes.[27]

25. Henry's 1784 proposed legislation, "Establishing a Provision for Teachers of the Christian Religion," can be found in Muñoz, *God and the Founders*, 229–30.

26. The bill's preamble can be found in *Founders' Constitution*, 1:672.

27. Thomas Buckley suggests that Henry reframed the bill to make it more politically palatable, which is surely true; but Buckley omits that it was more palatable as rewritten because it was made more civic, which made it more compatible with what I am calling the "narrow republicanism" understanding of the natural right to religious freedom. Buckley, *Church and State in Revolutionary Virginia*, 105. See also Eva T. H. Brann, "Madison's 'Memorial and Remonstrance,'" in *The Past-Present: Selected Writings of Eva Brann*, ed. Pamela Kraus (Annapolis, MD: St. John's College Press, 1997), 210.

Henry's general assessment bill reflects a syllogism that lies at the heart of "narrow republicanism's" political science: Republican government requires a virtuous citizenry; the cultivation of virtue depends on religion; republican governments, therefore, ought to support religion. These ideas were advanced most famously by President George Washington in his Farewell Address. " 'Tis substantially true," Washington stated, "that virtue or morality is a necessary spring of popular government." But virtue and morality, he warned, require religion: "And let us with caution indulge the supposition, that morality can be maintained without religion. Whatever may be conceded to the influence of refined education on minds of peculiar structure, reason and experience both forbid us to expect that National morality can prevail in exclusion of religious principle." Therefore, "of all the dispositions and habits which lead to political prosperity, Religion and morality are indispensable supports. In vain would that man claim the tribute of Patriotism, who should labour to subvert these great Pillars of human happiness, these firmest props of the duties of Men and citizens."[28]

Because religion, particularly Protestant Christianity, was believed to be essential to the development of republican citizenship, "narrow republican" constitutions authorized taxpayer support of religion, including the direct subsidization of religious ministers, as I have documented above.[29] This approach most clearly animated the drafting of the Founding-era constitutions of Maryland, Massachusetts, and New Hampshire, all of which authorized tax support of religion and religious ministers. And this approach guided the political practice of Georgia, Vermont, and Connecticut, all of which allowed religious taxes with a degree of taxpayer direction. It is worth repeating that all these states (except Connecticut) also provided guarantees for the right of religious liberty to "person[s]" (Maryland), [all] subject[s]" (Massachusetts), "every individual" (New Hampshire), "all persons" (Georgia), and "all men" (Vermont).[30] In the "narrow republican" understanding, religious freedom did not include freedom from religious taxation.

28. George Washington, Farewell Address, September 19, 1796, in *George Washington: A Collection*, ed. W. B. Allen (Indianapolis, IN: Liberty Fund, 1988), 521. It should be noted that George Washington did not directly call for the tax support of religion in his Farewell Address. During the dispute in Virginia over Patrick Henry's proposed general assessment, however, Washington said he was not opposed in principle to religious taxes. See Muñoz, *God and the Founders*, 50–51.

29. For a broader discussion of the other ways the Founders cultivated morality, see part 2 of Thomas West, *The Political Theory of the American Founding: Natural Rights, Public Policy, and the Moral Conditions of Freedom* (New York: Cambridge University Press, 2017), 163–306.

30. See table 1 in chapter 1.

We can return to the 1784 New Hampshire Bill of Rights to illustrate further the "narrow republican" position. As discussed in chapter 2, Article 4 recognized the "unalienable" character of the "rights of conscience," and Article 5 stated that "every individual has a natural and unalienable right to worship GOD according to the dictates of his own conscience. . . ." Article 6 then declared:

As morality and piety, rightly grounded on evangelical principles, will give the best and greatest security to government, and will lay in the hearts of men the strongest obligations to due subjection; and as the knowledge of these, is most likely to be propagated through a society by the institution of the public worship of the DEITY, and of public instruction in morality and religion; therefore, to promote those important purposes, the people of this state have a right to impower, and do hereby fully impower the legislature to authorize from time to time, the several towns, parishes, bodies corporate, or religious societies within this state, to make adequate provision at their own expence, for the support and maintenance of public protestant teachers of piety, religion and morality. *Provided notwithstanding*, That the several towns, parishes, bodies-corporate, or religious societies, shall at all times have the exclusive right of electing their own public teachers, and of contracting with them for their support and maintenance. And no portion of any one particular religious sect or denomination, shall ever be compelled to pay towards the support of the teacher or teachers of another persuasion, sect or denomination.[31]

Much like Patrick Henry's proposed bill, New Hampshire's Bill of Rights offers civic, not sectarian, reasons for government support of religion. The "important purposes" of funding religion, Article 6 states, are to help provide "the best and greatest security to government" and "due subjection" to it in the hearts of citizens. New Hampshire did not justify support for religion in order to "do service to the Lord" or to "increase the body of Christ," the ends of the community stipulated by John Winthrop in "A Model of Christian Charity."[32] Rather, government should support religion

---

31. The same pattern of recognition of the right to worship and of the propriety of government financial support of religion is apparent in the 1776 Maryland Declaration of Rights (Article 33) and the 1780 Massachusetts Declaration of Rights (Articles 2 and 3).

32. John Winthrop, "A Modell of Christian Charitie," (1630) in *The Sacred Rights of Conscience: Selected Writings on Religious Liberty and Church-State Relations in the American Founding*, ed. Daniel Dreisbach and Mark David Hall (Indianapolis, IN: Liberty Fund, 2010), 129. Note that I have modernized Winthrop's spelling.

because religious belief and practice help secure good civic character, including respect for and obedience to government. New Hampshire's Bill of Rights also provided taxpayers a degree of control over religious taxes through local selection of tax-funded minsters.

All the states that adopted or practiced the "narrow republican" framework, in fact, allowed some degree of local control over religious taxes, which suggests that the ideal was for taxpayers to fund religious ministers of their own denomination, at least if they were Protestant. It is a step too far, however, to suggest that the "narrow republican" states held that the right of religious liberty itself mandated that the individual taxpayer had a *right* to direct his tax dollars. This point was made definitively by Theophilus Parsons, chief justice of the Supreme Judicial Court of Massachusetts, in the state case *Barnes v. Falmouth* (1810). Those who object to state funding of religion, Parsons explained, "mistake a man's conscience for his money." Their great error, he continued, "lies in not distinguishing between liberty of conscience in religious opinions and worship, and the right to appropriating money by the state. The former is an unalienable right; the latter is surrendered to the state, as the price of protection." It is reasonable and legitimate for the state to support religion with tax dollars, Parsons further explained, because religion supports the common good of society. He wrote:

> The object of public religious instruction is to teach, and to enforce by suitable arguments, the practice of a system of correct morals among the people, and to form and cultivate reasonable and just habits and manners; by which every man's person and property are protected from outrage, and his personal and social enjoyments promoted and multiplied. From these effects every man derives the most important benefits; and whether he be, or be not, an auditor of any public teacher, he receives more solid and permanent advantages from this public instruction, than the administration of justice in courts of law can give him. The like objection may be made by any man to the support of public schools, if he have no family who attend; and any man, who has no lawsuit, may object to the support of judges and jurors on the same ground; when, if there were no courts of law, he would unfortunately find that causes for lawsuits would sufficiently abound.[33]

33. *Thomas Barnes v. The Inhabitants of the First Parish in Falmouth*, 6 Mass. 401, 408–10 (1810). The relevant passages of Parson's opinion are reproduced in *Church and State in American History: Key Documents, Decisions, and Commentary from Five Centuries*, 4th ed., ed. John F. Wilson and Donald L. Drakeman (New York: Routledge, 2020), 71–74.

Parsons provides a concise summary of the "narrow republican" justification for state support of religion: such support redounds to public benefits (virtuous conduct, in this case religiously inspired) while still respecting the rights of conscience.[34]

Similar arguments were used to justify religious tests for holding political office. As discussed above, prior to 1787, every state but Virginia
adopted some form of religious test for state officeholders. The federal
Constitution of 1787 left state office restrictions untouched, but prohibited
religious tests for national offices. The "narrow republican" arguments in
favor of religious tests for office were articulated most clearly by those who
criticized the federal prohibition.[35] "It may be said that the meaning [of the
absence of religious tests for federal office] is not to discard it [religion],
but only to shew that there is no need of it in public officers; they may be
as faithful without as with," wrote the New Hampshire Anti-Federalist "A
Friend to the Rights of the People." He continued:

> This is a mistake—when a man has no regard to God and his laws nor any be-
> lief of a future state he will have less regard to the laws of men, or to the most
> solemn oaths or affirmations; it is acknowledged by all that civil governments
> can't well be supported without the assistance of religion; I think therefore that
> so much deference ought to be paid to it, as to acknowledge it in our civil es-
> tablishment; and that no man is fit to be a ruler of protestants, without he can
> honestly profess to be of the protestant religion.[36]

The Massachusetts writer "David" explicitly connected religious tests for
office to the preservation of political liberty:

---

34. For a contemporaneous defense of the "narrow republicanism," see Worcestriensis,
number IV, *Massachusetts Spy*, September 4, 1776, reprinted in *American Political Writing
during the Founding Era: 1760–1805*, ed. Charles S. Hyneman and Donald S. Lutz (Indianapolis, IN: Liberty Fund, 1983), 1:449–54. Worcestriensis compares citizens who pay taxes to
support religions they do not favor to citizens who pay taxes to support wars they believe
unnecessary or imprudent. Disagreement alone, he suggests, does not exempt one from supporting public policy made by legitimate authorities.

35. For a discussion of New England Anti-Federalists' criticism of the Constitution's lack
of religious tests for federal office holding, see Jean Yarbrough, "New Hampshire: Puritanism
and the Moral Foundations of America," in *Ratifying the Constitution*, ed. Michael Allen Gillespie and Michael Lienesch (Lawrence: University Press of Kansas, 1989), 240–41.

36. A Friend to the Rights of the People, "Anti-Federalist, No. 1," (February 8, 1788) in *The
Complete Anti-Federalist*, ed. Herbert J. Storing (Chicago: University of Chicago Press, 1981),
4:242.

Never did any people possess a more ardent love of liberty than the people of this state; yet that very love of liberty has induced them to adopt a religious test, which requires all publick officers to be of some Christian, protestant persuasion, and to abjure all foreign authority. Thus religion secures our independence as a nation, and attaches the citizens to our own government.

"David," like "A Friend to the Rights of the People," held that the Protestant character of officeholders was essential. Atheists had to be excluded because "they have no principles of virtue"; papists, "because they acknowledge a foreign head, who can relieve them from the obligation of an oath."[37]

We might suspect that such arguments are pretextual—that what "David" and "A Friend of the Rights of the People" really wanted was to privilege Protestantism. That may be; it is not easy to measure or know actual motivations. As I will discuss in chapter 8, my construction of the First Amendment's Religion Clauses will require a mechanism to "smoke out" pretextual civic claims that actually aim to advance sectarian religious ends. But simply to dismiss "narrow republican" arguments as covert arguments for theocracy or for privileging Protestantism is to fail to understand one of the leading positions articulated during the Founding era, a position that was dominant in New England and championed by leading statesmen throughout the nation. To take one final example, consider Richard Henry Lee, the Virginian who served as president of the Continental Congress. Lee wrote the following in a 1784 letter:

Refiners may weave as fine a web of reason as they please, but the experience of all times shews [sic] Religion to be the guardian of morals—And he must be a very inattentive observer in our Country, who does not see that avarice is accomplishing the destruction of religion, for want of a legal obligation to contribute something to its support.[38]

Even if the underlying motivations of "narrow republicans" included the advancement of Protestantism, they consistently presented their position

37. "Letter by David," (March 7, 1788), in *Complete Anti-Federalist*, 4:247–48. For a particularly colorful and satirical criticism of the federal Constitution's absence of religious tests for office, see "Aristocrotis," in *Complete Anti-Federalist*, 3:205–06. Also, see "Essay by Samuel," *Independent Chronicle and Universal Advertiser* (Boston), (January 10, 1788) in *Complete Anti-Federalist*, 4:195–96.

38. Richard Henry Lee, letter to James Madison, November 26, 1784, in *The Letters of Richard Henry Lee*, ed. James Curtis Ballagh (New York: Macmillan, 1914), 2:304.

in terms of the common good of society. Religion helps nurture the civic character necessary for republican self-government; therefore, narrow republicans reason, government legitimately can and prudentially should support religion.

Expansive Liberalism

The recipient of Lee's 1784 letter was James Madison, the most forceful advocate of what I have labeled "expansive liberalism," the leading church-state alternative to "narrow republicanism" at the time of the Founding. To repeat a point made already, I use "liberal" here in the sense of classical liberalism, not modern progressivism. The core of "expansive liberalism" is the proposition that the inalienable right of religious liberty places not only worship but religion itself beyond the jurisdiction of government.[39]

In Madison's 1785 "Memorial and Remonstrance against Religious Assessments," published in opposition to Patrick Henry's proposed assessment bill, we see a philosophical defense of the position's most distinctive political manifestation, namely belief in the impropriety of government funding of religion as such. "Religion," Madison writes, is "exempt from the authority of the Society at large," and therefore cannot be subject to the jurisdiction of the legislative body. Lacking such authority, the legislature cannot legitimately pass religious taxes to support religious ministers exclusively. "Who does not see," Madison asks, ". . . that the same authority which can force a citizen to contribute three pence only of his property for the support of any one establishment, may force him to conform to any other establishment in all cases whatsoever?" Madison encourages Virginia's citizens "to take alarm at the first experiment on our liberties," because Henry's bill transgresses the state's legitimate authority.

Madison's primary and principled argument is that Henry's bill assumes an authority that government does not and cannot have. If the legislature is permitted to violate the "sacred" and inalienable rights of conscience, Madison contends, it can do anything. "Either then," he concludes,

we must say, that the will of the Legislature is the only measure of their authority; and that in the plentitude of this authority, they may sweep away all

39. While I emphasize Madison and Jefferson in my explanation of "expansive liberalism," a more thorough historical account would also include discussion of their alliance with dissenting Protestants. For such an account, see Esbeck, "Protestant Dissent and the Virginia Disestablishment."

our fundamental rights; or, that they are bound to leave this particular right untouched and sacred....[40]

Madison's rhetoric may seem excessive, but what he sees to be at stake is not just an imprudent and unnecessary tax, but the fundamental principles of American constitutionalism. Legitimate government, his argument presumes, is established via a social compact that both confers and limits governmental authority. If government is allowed to trespass the terms of the compact—and especially if government is allowed to trespass the sacred and inalienable rights of conscience—then the very idea of limited government is obliterated.

The impropriety of religious taxes is the most significant, but not the only, implication of "expansive liberalism's" understanding of the inalienable natural right of religious liberty. The exclusion of religion from government's cognizance also means that government cannot legitimately use religious affiliation as a criterion for civil rights, including the right to hold public office. Jefferson employs this reasoning in his draft of the Virginia Statute:

> that our civil rights have no dependance [sic] on our religious opinions, any more than [on] our opinions in physics or geometry; that therefore the proscribing any citizen as unworthy [of] the public confidence by laying upon him an incapacity of being called to offices of trust and emolument, unless he profess or renounce this or that religious opinion, is depriving him injuriously of those privileges and advantages to which, in common with his fellow citizens, he has a natural right....[41]

In response to Anti-Federalists' critique of the federal Constitution's prohibition of religious tests for officeholding, Federalists adopted the "ex-

40. James Madison, "Memorial and Remonstrance against Religious Assessments," 1785, in *Religious Liberty and the American Supreme Court*, 610.

41. "A Bill for Establishing Religious Freedom in Virginia," in *Religious Liberty and the American Supreme Court*, 604–5. Madison employed this nondiscrimination principle against Jefferson in a private letter criticizing Jefferson's draft constitution for the state of Virginia. Jefferson had included a provision excluding "Minsters of the Gospel" from eligibility to serve in the state's general assembly. See Madison, letter to John Brown (ca. October 15, 1788), in *The Writings of James Madison*, ed. Gaillard Hunt (New York: GP Putnam's Sons, 1900–1910), 5:288. The relevant passages of Jefferson's draft of a constitution can be found in *The Writings of Thomas Jefferson*, ed. Andrew A. Lipscomb (Washington: Thomas Jefferson Memorial Association, 1904), 2:286–87. See, also, Muñoz, *God and the Founders*, 40.

pansive liberal" arguments that such tests were an "impious deprivation of the rights of men,"[42] and that the "civil government has no business to meddle with the private opinions of the people."[43] Madison himself sought to insert an "expansive liberal" provision into what would become the First Amendment when he proposed the First Congress adopt the text, "The civil rights of none shall be abridged on account of religious belief or worship. . . ."[44]

Madison and Jefferson championed "expansive liberalism" as a matter of principle, but they also thought it politically wise. Madison in particular believed that religious belief and practice could sustain itself without government support. Even if republican government required a citizenry possessed of the sort of moral character that only religion could nurture, religion did not need government. Government, therefore, did not need to support religion to enjoy religion's benefits. "We are teaching the world the great truth," Madison wrote to Edward Livingston in 1822, "that [governments] do better without Kings [and] Nobles than with them. The merit will be doubled by the other lesson that Religion flourishes in greater purity, without than with the aid of [government]."[45] A year earlier, Madison had written to F. L. Schaeffer: "The experience of the United States is happy disproof of the error so long rooted in the unenlightened minds of well meaning Christians, as well as in the corrupt hearts of persecuting usurpers, that without a legal incorporation of religious and civil polity, neither could be supported."[46] Government support of religion, in fact, tended to corrupt. "During almost fifteen centuries has the legal establishment of Christianity been on trial. What have been its fruits?" Madison asked rhetorically in his "Memorial and Remonstrance." His answer: "More or less in all places,

42. Tench Coxe, "An Examination of the Constitution," 1787, in *Founders' Constitution*, 4:639.

43. Oliver Ellsworth, "Landholder, no. 7," December 17, 1787, in *Founders' Constitution*, 4:640.

44. As I shall discuss in the next chapter, the First Congress rejected this part of Madison's proposed text. It should be noted that in the First Congress, Madison did not attempt to impose the rule that an individual could not be privileged on account of religion—a position he had advanced during the drafting of the Virginia Declaration of Rights in 1776 and argued for in his "Memorial and Remonstrance" (article 4) in 1785. For further discussion of how Madison's proposed text departed from his principle of religious noncognizance, see Muñoz, *God and the Founders*, 34–39.

45. Letter from James Madison to Edward Livingston, July 10, 1822, in *Writings of James Madison*, 9:98, 102–3.

46. Letter from James Madison to F. L. Schaeffer, Dec. 3, 1821, in *Letters and Other Writings of James Madison: 1816–1828* (New York: R. Worthington, 1884), 3:242–43.

pride and indolence in the Clergy, ignorance and servility in the laity, in both, superstition, bigotry and persecution." The effect of ecclesiastical establishments on civil society was similarly baneful: "In some instances [ecclesiastical establishments] have been seen to erect a spiritual tyranny on the ruins of the Civil authority; in many instances they have been seen upholding the thrones of political tyranny: in no instances have they been seen the guardians of the liberties of the people."

As already discussed, Virginia adopted "expansive liberalism" when it adopted Jefferson's Statute for Religious Freedom in 1786. Because the statute was passed as an ordinary piece of legislation, the bill's last sentence called attention to its fundamental character:

> the rights hereby asserted are of the natural rights of mankind, and that if any act shall be hereafter passed to repeal the present or to narrow its operation, such act will be an infringement of natural right.

*　　*　　*

While the Founders in general shared a commitment to natural rights, not all would have agreed that the specific church-state policies adopted in Virginia were, in fact, "of the natural rights of mankind." Religious freedom, like most foundational principles of politics, is not fully self-defining or self-executing. Advocates of a shared principle can disagree when confronted with the exigency of pressing it into political practice. Such disagreements emerged among the Founders regarding the scope and political meaning of the principle of religious liberty when they moved beyond protection of worship according to conscience. We can summarize that disagreement, which this chapter has attempted to elucidate, by specifying the principle of religious liberty and the attendant doctrinal rules and prudential judgments of the two leading positions during the Founding era. (The italicized text below indicates how "expansive liberalism" offers a more expansive conception of the rights of religious liberty and, correspondingly, a narrower scope for democratic political action.)

"Narrow Republicanism": Principle and Doctrine of Religious Liberty. Individuals possess an inalienable natural right to religious liberty and therefore the state may not exercise jurisdiction over religious worship as such. The state, accordingly, may not penalize, prohibit, or mandate religious worship as such and it may not pursue the end of saving citizens' souls.

"Narrow Republicanism": Politics of Church and State. The state may employ religion as a means to accomplish otherwise legitimate civic ends. Since morality is essential to republican citizenship, and religion is essential to morality, government should promote the religious character of the citizenry.

"Expansive Liberalism": Principle and Doctrine of Religious Liberty. Individuals possess an inalienable natural right to religious liberty and therefore the state may not exercise jurisdiction over religious worship as such *or over an individual's religious beliefs, affiliations, or practices.* The state, accordingly, may not penalize, prohibit, or mandate religious worship as such, and it may not pursue the end of saving citizens' souls; *it also may not impose religious taxes for the exclusive support of religion, or affect an individual's civil rights on account of his or her religious beliefs or affiliation.*

"Expansive Liberalism": Politics of Church and State. The state may *not* employ religion as a means to accomplish otherwise legitimate civic ends. *Even if* morality is essential to republican citizenship and religion is essential to morality, *religion does not need governmental support and therefore government ought not directly support religion.*

The Founders debated these matters as vigorously as we debate them today, perhaps even more so. Adjudicating the merits of that debate, however, is not necessary for the next part of this book, the goal of which is to articulate what we can know about the original meaning of the First Amendment's Religion Clauses. That task requires us only to understand both that the Founders agreed that all individuals have an inalienable right to conscientious religious worship, and that they disagreed over whether religious liberty carved out a larger domain of conduct immune from lawful governmental action. Having the Founders' agreement and disagreements before us will place us in a better position to investigate the Religion Clauses' original meaning.

PART 2

Constitutional Originalism: The Original Meanings of the Religion Clauses

In part 1, I attempted to set forth how the Founders agreed about religious liberty but disagreed about the separation of church and state. From reviewing what we might call the "Founding Constitutions"—the declarations of rights and constitutions adopted at the state level between 1776 and 1791—I concluded that the Founders agreed that religious liberty is an inalienable natural right that protects the freedom for individuals to worship according to conscience and, accordingly, that the state lacks legitimate authority to coerce worship or punish nonworship. Beyond freedom of worship, the Founders disagreed. "Expansive liberals," as I have called them, held a more expansive understanding of religious liberty and, correspondingly, advanced more capacious restrictions on state authority. They contended that respect for religious freedom prohibits the state from imposing religious taxes or using religious affiliation to deprive individuals of civil or political rights. "Narrow republicans," as the name suggests, took a narrower view of the scope of religious liberty and thus a more republican approach to church-state matters. They contended that the state legitimately could employ religion and religious affiliation to foster otherwise legitimate civic ends, including direct tax support for religious ministers and ministries for the civic purpose of fostering moral character. Apprehending the Founders' church-state agreements and disagreements will help us better understand the original meaning of the First Amendment's Religion Clauses. This is the topic of part 2.

In the next two chapters, I advance a relatively straightforward thesis: that the original meanings of the Religion Clauses reflect the Founders' agreements and disagreements.[1] The Founders agreed that religious liberty is a natural and inalienable right that all legitimate governments must respect. The text of the Free Exercise Clause reflects this broad agreement by recognizing the principle of religious freedom. The Founders disagreed about what the principle of religious liberty meant for a number of important church-state policy questions. That disagreement is acknowledged in the text of the Establishment Clause, which originally communicated two rules: (1) that the *national* government shall not make a religious establishment, and (2) that the national government shall make no law concerning *state* establishments. The Establishment Clause was drafted to affirm that the national government lacked authority over religious establishments and that most church-state policy issues would remain within the states. By recognizing, first, the right of religious free exercise at a more general or abstract level and, second, the national government's lack of authority over religious establishments (thereby confirming that state church-state arrangements would be free from national interference), the First Congress proposed text that was consistent with the Founders' agreements about religious liberty, while respecting their state-level disagreements about the proper separation of church from state.

Doing Originalism: A Note on Method

The next two chapters attempt to present a good-faith and historically accurate originalist account of the First Amendment's Religion Clauses. Of course, what originalism is or should be are much discussed and debated questions.[2] Before proceeding, let me discuss the interpretive framework that guides the next two chapters.

---

1. For thoughtful reflections on the meaning of "meaning" in the context of constitutional originalism, see Solum's discussion in Robert W. Bennett and Lawrence B. Solum, *Constitutional Originalism: A Debate* (Ithaca, NY: Cornell University Press, 2011), 54–58.

2. There is no shortage of works on originalism. A slightly dated but still helpful overview is offered by Johnathan O'Neill, *Originalism in American Law and Politics: A Constitutional History* (Baltimore: Johns Hopkins University Press, 2005). Other studies, including more recent ones, include Keith Whittington, "The New Originalism," *Georgetown Journal of Law and Public Policy* 22 (2004): 599–613; Keith Whittington, "Originalism: A Critical Introduction," *Fordham Law Review* 82 (2013): 375–409; Ilan Wurman, *A Debt against the Living: An Introduction to Originalism* (New York: Cambridge University Press, 2017); Lee J. Strang,

Broadly speaking, the inquiry that follows falls within what is called "the new originalism," but does not dismiss insights offered by proponents of other originalist methods, including the relevance of the drafters' intentions. As explained by Keith Whittington, one of originalism's leading contemporary theorists,

> At its most basic, originalism argues that the discoverable public meaning of the Constitution at the time of its initial adoption should be regarded as authoritative for purposes of later constitutional interpretation.[3]

The focus on the text's public meaning is a somewhat recent development.[4] The first wave of originalist scholarship, developed in the late 1970s and 1980s, focused on discerning the original intentions of the drafters of the Constitution's text. This approach, now labeled "original intentions originalism," was met by numerous critics including, notably, Paul Brest, who argued, among other things, that it was impossible to find a single intention animating texts that had many authors.[5] Partially in response to Brest and other critics, originalists shifted their focus from identifying the original intentions of the Framers to uncovering the original understandings of the text's ratifiers. Since it was the ratifiers of the Constitution who acted with sovereign authority, it was argued that their understanding of the text is what is legally binding. Of course, there were more ratifiers than framers, and the ratifiers were dispersed throughout the country. Critics therefore contended that it was doubtful, if not impossible, that one could

---

Originalism's Promise: A Natural Law Account of the American Constitution (New York: Cambridge University Press, 2019), 7–42. One might also consult the many scholarly works on the subject by Lawrence B. Solum, including "Originalist Methodology," *University of Chicago Law Review* 84 (2017): 269–95; Bennett and Solum, *Constitutional Originalism*, 1–36.

3. Whittington, "Originalism: A Critical Introduction," 377. For a discussion of what is new in the "new originalism," see Mitchell N. Berman and Kevin Toh, "On What Distinguishes New Originalism from Old: A Jurisprudential Take," *Fordham Law Review* 82 (2013): 545–76.

4. For a discussion of this point, see Randy E. Barnett and Evan D. Bernick, "The Letter and the Spirit: A Unified Theory of Originalism," *Georgetown Law Journal* 107 (2018), 7–18.

5. Paul Brest, "The Misconceived Quest for the Original Understanding," *Boston University Law Review* 60 (1980): 204–38. In "The Original Understanding of Original Intent," *Harvard Law Review* 98 (1985): 885–948, H. Jefferson Powell, another notable critic of original intentions originalism, argued that the Framers themselves did not believe that their intentions should be regarded as a binding source for constitutional meaning. For a helpful recent discussion of original intent originalism, including the difficulties it faces in the face of multiple legislators or drafters, see John O. McGinnis and Michael B. Rappaport, *Originalism and the Good Constitution* (Cambridge, MA: Harvard University Press, 2013), 121–23.

ascertain their understandings and identify some unitary understanding of the Constitution's various provisions.[6] Led by Justice Antonin Scalia, originalists then turned their focus to ascertaining the original public meaning of the text.[7] Textualism holds that it is the Constitution's text that is binding, and that the meaning of the text is to be found by ascertaining the public meaning of the words and phrases as they were ordinarily used and understood at the time.

This study accepts Whittington's conclusion that "originalist theory has now largely coalesced around original public meaning as the proper interpretive inquiry."[8] The next two chapters attempt to uncover, respectively, what we can know about the original meaning of the text of the Establishment and Free Exercise Clauses. Focusing on the text's original public meaning, however, does not preclude looking for the drafters' intentions.[9] I shall attempt to show, in fact, that appreciating the various concerns of the First Amendment's drafters helps to make sense of the text's meaning.[10] While the meaning of the text may not be exactly the same as the intentions that animated it, understanding the text's original purpose and design is conducive to apprehending its original meaning.

Two other scholarly developments within the orbit of "new originalism" also inform the next two chapters and part 3 of this study. Constitutional theorists have identified a distinction between constitutional *interpretation* and constitutional *construction*.[11] To simplify, constitutional

6. Solum, *Constitutional Originalism*, 9.

7. Antonin Scalia, *A Matter of Interpretation: Federal Courts and the Law* (Princeton, NJ: Princeton University Press, 1997), 23–25. On Scalia's jurisprudence, see Ralph A. Rossum, *Antonin Scalia's Jurisprudence: Text and Tradition* (Lawrence: University Press of Kansas, 2006).

8. Whittington, "Originalism: A Critical Introduction," 380.

9. Whittington, "Originalism: A Critical Introduction," 382. On the relevance of intentions for the originalist inquiry, see Larry Alexander and Saikrishna Prakash, "'Is that English You're Speaking?' Why Intention Free Interpretation Is an Impossibility," *San Diego Law Review* 41 (2004): 967–95.

10. Donald L. Drakeman, *The Hollow Core of Constitutional Theory: Why We Need the Framers* (New York: Cambridge University Press, 2020), 15–16, helpfully captures the relevance of the drafting record for this inquiry:

> The constitutional record can provide meaningful and even definitive evidence of the original meaning in at least two ways. It can identify a specific understanding of provisions that otherwise appear vague or ambiguous either from a nineteenth-century or a twenty-first century perspective, and it can provide evidence of the Framers' rationale for adopting the provision, which will be necessary when interpreters need to apply the provision, especially (but not exclusively) to new and different circumstances.

11. For discussions of the interpretation-construction distinction, see Barnett and Bernick, "Letter and Spirit"; Lawrence B. Solum, "The Interpretation-Construction Distinction," *Constitutional Commentary* 27 (2010): 95–118. For a concise overview, see Amy Barrett, "The

interpretation involves the act of divining or uncovering the meaning of a constitutional text. This often involves investigating contemporaneous understandings and uses of the provision's words. Lawrence Solum defines interpretation as the activity that "aims at the recovery of the communicative content of the constitutional text."[12] Interpretation finds the meaning of a text within the text itself. Constitutional *construction*, at least as I am using the term, becomes necessary when the ability to find the meaning of a text through constitutional interpretation runs out. As described by Whittington, constitutional constructions

> elucidate the text in the interstices of discoverable, interpretive meaning, where the text is so broad or so underdetermined as to be incapable of faithful but exhaustive reduction to legal rules."[13]

Constitutional constructions bring something external to the text in order to give it meaning when the process of interpretation cannot, by itself, determine meaning and derive a straightforward legal rule from it. "Unlike jurisprudential interpretation," Whittington explains, "construction provides for an element of creativity in construing constitutional meaning."[14]

Cognate to the distinction between interpretation and construction is another distinction, recently recovered by Jack Balkin, concerning the three basic types of constitutional language: rules, standards, and principles. Balkin writes:

Interpretation/Construction Distinction in Constitutional Law," *Constitutional Commentary* 27 (2010): 1–8. Cf. Sotirios A. Barber and James E. Fleming, *Constitutional Interpretation: The Basic Questions* (New York: Oxford University Press, 2007), 91–97, in which the authors express reservations about the distinction.

12. Lawrence B. Solum, "Originalism and Constitutional Construction," *Fordham Law Review* 82 (2013): 474.

13. Keith Whittington, *Constitutional Construction: Divided Powers and Constitutional Meaning* (Cambridge, MA: Harvard University Press, 1999), 5. Solum's account of constitutional construction differs slightly from the one I am presenting. Solum, in *Constitutional Originalism*, 2–4, writes: "Constitutional practice includes two distinct activities: (1) constitutional interpretation, which discerns the linguistic meaning of the text, and (2) constitutional construction, which determines the legal effect of the text." I am using the concept of constitutional construction more in line with Whittington's original employment of the term—as the process by which constitutional meaning is elaborated when constitutional interpretation (in Solum's sense of the term) cannot determine the linguistic meaning of the text. For a discussion of the difference between Whittington's and Solum's constructions of "construction," see Berman and Toh, "On What Distinguishes New Originalism from Old." See also Strang, *Originalism's Promise*, 311n149.

14. Whittington, *Constitutional Construction*, 5.

Balkin

> The text of our Constitution contains different kinds of language. It contains
> determinate rules (the president must be thirty-five, there are two houses of
> Congress). It contains standards (no "unreasonable searches and seizures," a
> right to a "speedy" trial). And it contains principles (no prohibitions of the free
> exercise of religion, no abridgements of the freedom of speech, no denials of
> equal protection).[15]

Before one can interpret or construct a particular constitutional text, one
has to determine what kind of legal norm it expresses; that is, both interpretation and construction require ascertaining whether a provision articulates a rule, adopts a standard, or declares a principle.[16] Constitutional
rules tend to be amenable to straightforward constitutional interpretation; standards and principles often require constitutional construction.

15. Jack M. Balkin, *Living Originalism* (Cambridge, MA: Harvard University Press, 2011), 6.

16. Constitutional theorists refer to this inquiry as a search for the proper level of generality of a given provision. For a brief but helpful discussion of the issue, including citations to
the relevant scholarly literature, see Thomas Colby, "The Sacrifice of the New Originalism,"
Georgetown Law Journal 99 (2011): 726–27.

This book presumes that fidelity to the Constitution requires, first and foremost, fidelity to
the type of language a constitutional provision embodies. I do not presume, as Justice Scalia
does in *A Matter of Interpretation*, 134–35, that "the operative provisions of the document [the
Constitution and the Bill of Rights] ... abound in concrete and specific dispositions." Scalia's
conclusion is obviously true of some provisions, but not necessarily true of all provisions. Scalia contends that "it would be most peculiar for aspirational provisions to be interspersed ran-
domly among the very concrete and hence obviously nonaspirational prescriptions that the
Bill of Rights contains. . . . It is more reasonable to think that the provisions are all of a sort."
It seems even more reasonable to investigate the drafting of a specific provision to ascertain
the type of text a provision embodies. For different though compatible responses to Scalia
on this point, see Lawrence Tribe's and Ronald Dworkin's responses to Scalia in *A Matter of
Interpretation*, 68–74, 87–94, 124. See also Whittington, "Originalism: A Critical Introduction,"
386–87. Also see chapter 7, note 26, discussing Calabresi and Lawson's criticism of Scalia.

James Fleming's constitutional constructivism "conceives our Constitution as a scheme of
abstract aspirational principles and ends, not a code of detailed rules." That is certainly true of
some of the Constitution's provisions, but it is not true of all of them. Where it is true, I mostly
agree with Fleming's contention that "interpreting the Constitution with fidelity requires
judgments of moral and political theory about how those principles are best understood." I
would add, however, that faithfully interpreting the Founders' Constitution requires understanding the Founders' political theory and constructing the Constitution's abstract principles
in light of it. See James E. Fleming, *Fidelity to Our Imperfect Constitution: For Moral Readings
and against Originalisms* (New York: Oxford University Press, 2015), 20–21. For a somewhat
dated but still helpful discussion of the relationship between rules and standards to different
methods of constitutional interpretation, see Pierre Schlag, "Rules and Standards," *UCLA
Law Review* 33 (1985): 390–98. For an account skeptical of the existence of "legal principles,"
see Larry Alexander, "The Objectivity of Morality, Rules, and Law: A Conceptual Map," *Alabama Law Review* 65 (2013): 501–17.

Professor Balkin labels his "living originalism" approach "text and principle." The approach nicely captures what I shall attempt to do in the next two chapters, although I prefer the label "text and design" or "design originalism."[17] Design originalism recognizes that, at least for some constitutional provisions, to understand the meaning of the text one also has to comprehend what purposes or ends the text was designed to achieve. I prefer "text and design" over "text and principle" because not all texts encode principles; some texts express rules or standards. "Text and design" also attempts to capture what Randy Barnett and Evan Bernick call "good-faith constitutional construction," which they describe as follows: "Good-faith constitutional construction seeks to implement the Constitution *faithfully* by ascertaining and adhering to the original functions of the constitutional text—its 'spirit.' "[18]

As part of the effort to uncover the original public meanings of the First Amendment Religion Clauses, the next two chapters attempt to determine whether the Establishment and Free Exercise Clauses articulate rules, standards, or principles. This inquiry will allow us to determine both to what extent the First Amendment's Religion Clauses must be constructed and, to the extent that they must be constructed, whether the respective text should be approached as a rule, standard, or principle. I shall show that the Establishment Clause contains two rules that the Framers

17. I note one difference between Balkin's understanding of the Constitution's principles and my own. Balkin, in *Living Originalism*, 350n12, writes: "I agree with Dworkin that principles have an indeterminate scope and jurisdiction, and that principles are not conclusive, so that decisionmakers must balance principles against other considerations." In my account, whether a principle can or should be balanced against other considerations depends in large part on the nature of the principle itself. Some principles, including the jurisdictional principle of religious free exercise, resist balancing.

18. Randy E. Barnett and Evan Bernick, "Letter and Spirit," 5. Note that some originalists, including Barnett himself at one time, denied that constitutional constructions could be a part of originalism. For a discussion of this point, including the reasons Barnett changed his position, see pp. 14–18 of the aforementioned article.

For a discussion of the similarities between "living originalists," such as Jack Balkin, and "new originalists" who defend constitutional constructions, see Eric J. Segall, *Originalism as Faith* (New York: Cambridge University Press, 2018), 90–102. While I agree with many of Segall's observations, part 3 of this study aims to show that it is not uniformly true, as Segall contends, that "the construction zone that the New Originalists advocate is a place where the original meaning and historical evidence play at most limited roles" (p. 98).

Some notable originalists reject the possibility of "constructionist originalism." See, in particular, John O. McGinnis and Michael Rappaport, "Original Methods Originalism: A New Theory of Interpretation and the Case Against Construction," *Northwestern University Law Review* 103 (2009): 751–802.

left underdetermined, and that the Free Exercise Clause articulates a principle that also requires construction.

One further methodological point. In part 2 I will show that, despite the limits of the available drafting record, we can offer a more-than-probable account of the Religion Clauses' original design. I use the phrase "more-than-probable" intentionally. Every scholar writing on this subject would like to offer the "definitive account" of the text. The paucity of the drafting record and the inescapable difficulties associated with interpreting it, however, make it difficult to reach sure conclusions.[19] I shall attempt to offer an account that faithfully makes sense of what the drafting record yields. But that record demands scholarly humility. Any scholar working in this area must acknowledge that the drafting records available to us yield some insights but also contain gaps that no amount of careful reviewing can fill or erase.

19. For discussions of the documentary record and its integrity, see Marion Tinling, "Thomas Lloyd's Reports of the First Federal Congress," *William and Mary Quarterly*, 3rd series, 18 (1961): 519–45; James H. Hutson, "The Creation of the Constitution: The Integrity of the Documentary Record," *Texas Law Review* 65 (1986), 35–38.

CHAPTER FIVE

The Original Meaning of the Establishment Clause

This chapter argues that the Framers adopted the First Amendment's Establishment Clause to recognize

1. the new national legislature's lack of authority to establish a religion.
2. that church-state affairs would remain primarily at the state level.

Corresponding to the Founders' overarching design, the Establishment Clause imposes two constitutional rules:

A. Congress shall make no law erecting a religious establishment.
B. Congress shall make no law concerning state-level religious establishments.

The chapter also argues

3. that Founding-era records pertaining to the constitutional ratification debates, the drafting of the Establishment Clause in the First Congress, and other church-state documents fail to yield a definite or precise meaning of what constitutes "an establishment of religion."

The Founders accomplished 1 and 2 and adopted constitutional rules A and B while nevertheless doing 3. That is, they drafted text prohibiting a national establishment and national interference with state establishments without precisely defining what constitutes an establishment of religion. That the Founders did not resolve what constitutes a religious establishment means that the original meaning of the Establishment Clause is partially underdetermined. Given the underdetermined character of the text, I shall argue in part 3 that the Establishment Clause cannot simply be interpreted; it must be constructed.

The Establishment Clause's original design is reflected in the final adopted and ratified text, but it is most clearly revealed by the drafting debates in the First Congress. This chapter, accordingly, focuses on the drafting record.[1] Understanding that record requires us to consider why the First Congress was debating a church-state provision in the first place. The chapter therefore begins with a discussion of the historical context in which the First Amendment emerged and the particular circumstances that led to its drafting and adoption. After discussing the Anti-Federalists' criticism of the proposed Constitution, and their proposed religion amendments, the chapter examines Madison's original proposal and the subsequent debates and textual revisions. The aim of the chapter is to uncover what we can and cannot know about the original meaning of the text of the Establishment Clause, including what kind of text (rule, standard, or principle) it is.

The Historical Context of the Drafting of the First Amendment: Anti-Federalist Opposition to the Constitution

Because of the prominence of the Bill of Rights in contemporary political life, we might assume that the First Congress extensively deliberated about what we now consider to be our fundamental freedoms, including

1. I refer to the drafting record in the First Congress, at least initially, for the same reasons Justice Scalia justified consulting *The Federalist Papers*: not primarily to ascertain the Framers' original intentions, but to attempt to uncover the text's original meaning. See Antonin Scalia, *A Matter of Interpretation: Federal Courts and the Law* (Princeton, NJ: Princeton University Press, 1997), 38. Although Jack M. Balkin, in "The New Originalism and the Uses of History," *Fordham Law Review* 82 (2013): 655, turns to historical records for somewhat different reasons than I do, I share his conclusions that, "in constitutional construction, adoption history is a valuable resource available to originalists and nonoriginalists alike" and that "refusing to employ adoption history serves no important theoretical principle. . . ."

Parts of this chapter first appeared in Vincent Phillip Muñoz, "The Original Meaning of the Establishment Clause and the Impossibility of Its Incorporation," *University of Pennsylvania Journal of Constitutional Law* 8 (2006): 585–639. This chapter is significantly and substantively different from that article.

religious freedom. The truth is a bit less exalted.[2] The First Amendment in particular, and the Bill of Rights as a whole, were adopted by the Constitution's champions to address an immediate political problem—Anti-Federalist opposition to the new government.[3] This is not to say that the Framers were completely unconcerned with protecting religious liberty, but understanding the meaning of the text they adopted and the reasons why they adopted that text requires us to understand the Framers within their own immediate historical and political context. A leading concern of the First Congress was to assuage fears expressed by the Constitution's critics. A discussion of those criticisms, therefore, must precede our investigation of the Establishment Clause's original meaning.[4]

Perhaps most significantly, Anti-Federalists contended that the proposed federal constitution failed to recognize or protect essential personal rights, including the right of religious liberty. The Framers who assembled in Philadelphia during the summer of 1787 had spent almost no time discussing religious freedom. With little recorded deliberation, the delegates prohibited religious tests or qualifications for any federal office.[5] Toward

2. Donald L. Drakeman, in *Church, State, and Original Intent* (New York: Cambridge University Press, 2010), 196–97, writes, "The First Congress had a number of important things to do, and sorting out the proper relationship between church and state was nowhere on that list."

3. For an excellent history of the creation of the Bill of Rights, see Robert A. Goldwin, *From Parchment to Power: How James Madison Used the Bill of Rights to Save the Constitution* (Washington: AEI Press, 1997). For a helpful discussion of Madison's reasons for championing the Bill of Rights, see Jeremy D. Bailey, *James Madison and Constitutional Imperfection* (New York: Cambridge University Press, 2015), 70–80.

4. Gary D. Glenn, "Forgotten Purposes of the First Amendment Religion Clauses," *Review of Politics* 49 (1987): 341, argues "that if the Bill of Rights were adopted primarily at the behest of anti-Federalists, then the meaning of the religion clauses must be sought, at least initially, in what they had to say about religion during the ratification debates." See also Robert Natelson, "The Original Meaning of the Establishment Clause," *William and Mary Bill of Rights Journal* 14 (2005): 79, which notes that many commentators fail to consider the reasons why the Establishment Clause was adopted when they attempt to ascertain its original meaning. For an account of the Anti-Federalists that makes an argument somewhat different from mine, see Donald L. Drakeman, "The Anti-Federalists and Religion," in *Faith and the Founders of the American Republic*, ed. Daniel L. Dreisbach and Mark David Hall (New York: Oxford University Press, 2014), 120–43.

5. Charles Pinckney first proposed the ban on August 20, 1787. It was referred to the committee of five, and then, on August 30, 1787, a slightly modified version of Pinckney's proposal passed unanimously. See *The Records of the Federal Convention of 1787*, ed. Max Farrand (New Haven, CT: Yale University Press; rev. ed. 1966), 2:342, 457, 461. James E. Wood Jr., in "No Religious Test Shall Ever Be Required: Reflections on the Bicentennial of the U.S. Constitution," *Journal of Church and State* 29 (1987): 201, claims that the religious test ban was without historical precedent and was "at variance with the prevailing patterns and practices in all of the original colonies, and during their early years of statehood." It should be noted, though, that Virginia's 1776 Constitution did not include religious restrictions on officeholding. For

the end of the convention, the delegates rejected James Madison's and Charles Pinckney's proposal to grant Congress power to establish a university "in which no preference or distinctions should be allowed on account of religion." The religion provision, however, does not appear to have played a part in their proposal's defeat.[6] The Constitution's near silence regarding religion allowed Anti-Federalists to play to fears of the unknown and parade the possibility of potential abuses of power by the federal government.[7]

Calls for amendments, including a declaration of rights, appeared immediately after the Philadelphia Convention transmitted the proposed constitution to the Confederation Congress. At the end of September 1787, Richard Henry Lee from Virginia drafted a set of proposals that he sought to add to the constitution before it was transmitted to the states for ratification. Lee's document began:

> It having been found from universal experience that the most express declarations and reservations are necessary to protect the just rights and liberty of mankind from the silent, powerful, and ever active conspiracy of those who govern.

It then listed a number of rights, the very first one of which was:

> That the rights of Conscience in matters of Religion shall not be violated.[8]

---

discussions of the federal ban on religious tests for office, see Chester James Antieau, Arthur T. Downey, and Edward C. Roberts, *Freedom from Federal Establishment: Formation and Early History of the First Amendment Religion Clauses* (Milwaukee: Bruce Publishing, 1964), 92–97; Gerard V. Bradley, "The No Religious Test Clause and the Constitution of Religious Liberty: A Machine That Has Gone of Itself," *Case Western Reserve Law Review* 37 (1987): 674–747; Daniel L. Dreisbach, "The Constitution's Forgotten Religion Clause: Reflections on the Article VI Religious Test Ban," *Journal of Church and State* 38 (1996): 261–95.

6. Madison (September 14, 1787), in *Records of The Federal Convention of 1787*, 2:612, 616. The only recorded debate on the matter includes two sentences in opposition by New York delegate Gouverneur Morris, who claimed such a university was unnecessary. For a discussion of the proposal for a national university during the Constitutional Convention, see George Thomas, *The Founders and the Idea of a National University: Constituting the American Mind* (New York: Cambridge University Press, 2015), 63–64.

7. Glenn, in "Forgotten Purposes of the First Amendment Religion Clauses," 342, helpfully notes that "there was not one neatly defined anti-Federalist position [regarding religion] but rather a cluster of arguments." See also Robert Allen Rutland, *The Birth of the Bill of Rights 1776–1791*, revised edition (Boston: Northeastern University Press, 1983 (first published University of North Carolina Press, 1955), 127–28.

8. Richard Henry Lee, "Proposed Amendments to the Constitution," ca. September 27 or 28, 1787, in *Letters of Members of the Continental Congress*, ed. Edmund Burnett (Washington:

The demand for a declaration of rights that included the right of religious liberty would be repeated by the proposed constitution's leading critics. "The Federal Farmer," one of the most able Anti-Federalist essayists, argued,

> It is true, we [the people of the United States] are not disposed to differ much, at present, about religion; but when we are making a constitution, it is to be hoped, for ages and millions yet unborn, why not establish the free exercise of religion, as a part of the national compact. There are other essential rights, which we have justly understood to be the rights of freemen; as freedom from hasty and unreasonable search warrants, warrants not founded on oath, and not issued with due caution, for searching and seizing men's papers, property, and persons.[9]

The Philadelphian "Centinel" paraphrased the 1776 Pennsylvania Declaration of Rights to make the same point:

> The new plan, it is true, does propose to secure the people of the benefit of personal liberty by the *habeas corpus*; and trial by jury for all crimes, except in case of impeachment: but there is no declaration, that all men have a natural and unalienable right to worship Almighty God, according to the dictates of their own consciences and understanding; and that no man ought, or of right can be compelled to attend any religious worship, or erect or support any place of worship, or maintain any ministry, contrary to, or against his own free will and consent; and that no authority can or ought to be vested in, or assumed by any power whatever, that shall in any case interfere with, or in any manner controul, the right of conscience in the free exercise of religious worship. . . .[10]

Carnegie Institute, 1936), 8:648. For a discussion of Lee's efforts, see Rutland, *The Birth of the Bill of Rights*, 120–25. As noted in chapter 4, Lee advocated government funding of religion.

   9. "Letters from the Federal Farmer IV," October 12, 1787, in *The Complete Anti-Federalist*, ed. Herbert J. Storing (Chicago: University of Chicago Press, 1981), 2:245, 249. See, generally, Herbert J. Storing, "Introduction to Letters from the Federal Farmer," in *The Complete Anti-Federalist*, 2:214–17. Robert Rutland, in *The Birth of the Bill of Rights*, 139, identified "The Federal Farmer" as Richard Henry Lee, a claim that is disputed by Michael Zuckert and Derick Webb in *The Anti-Federalist Writings of the Melancton Smith Circle* (Indianapolis, IN: Liberty Fund Press, 2009), 418–19, who identify "The Federal Farmer" as Melancton Smith.

   10. "Letters of Centinel," October 24, 1787, in *Complete Anti-Federalist*, 2:152. "An Old Whig," n.d., *Complete Anti-Federalist*, 3:34, also used language consistent with the inalienable natural rights conception of religious freedom:

> The first of these [liberties], which it is of the utmost importance for the people to retain to themselves, which indeed they have not even the right to surrender, and

Anti-Federalists did not define with precision what they meant by the
"right of conscience" or "free exercise of religion,"[11] but together with freedom from unreasonable searches and seizures and trial by jury, they repeatedly identified the right to religious freedom as deserving express
constitutional protection.[12]

Some Anti-Federalists suggested that one specific way the proposed
new national government might threaten the free exercise of religion was
through the erection of a national religious establishment. According to
"Deliberator," a Pennsylvania Anti-Federalist,

> Congress may, if they shall think it for the "general welfare," establish an unifor-
> mity in religion throughout the United States. Such establishments have been
> thought necessary, and have accordingly taken place in almost all the other
> countries in the world, and will, no doubt, be thought equally necessary in this.[13]

"A Countryman" contended that a national religious establishment would
"make every body worship God in a certain way, whether the people thought

---

which at the same time it is of no kind of advantage to government to strip them of, is
LIBERTY OF CONSCIENCE.

11. The interrelatedness of the terms predates the founding period. William Penn, for example, defined "liberty of conscience" in 1670 as follows:

By Liberty of Conscience, we understand not only a meer [sic] Liberty of the Mind,
in believing or disbelieving this or that Principle or Doctrine, but the Exercise of our
selves in a visible Way of Worship, upon our believing it to be indispensibly [sic] required at our Hands, that if we neglect it for Fear or Favour of any Mortal Man, we
Sin, and incur Divine Wrath....

William Penn, "The Great Case of Liberty of Conscience" (1670), in *The Political Writings of
William Penn*, ed. Andrew R. Murphy (Indianapolis, IN: Liberty Fund, 2002), 85–86.

12. See, for example, Richard Henry Lee's widely circulated October 16, 1787, letter to
Edmund Randolph and his accompanying call for amendments, in *The Documentary History
of the Ratification of the Constitution*, ed. John P. Kaminski and Gaspare J. Saladino (Madison:
State Historical Society of Wisconsin, 1988), 8:62, 65. See also "Essays of an Old Whig," n.d.,
in *Complete Anti-Federalist*, 3:37; "Essays by Cincinnatus," November 15, 1787, in *Complete
Anti-Federalist*, 6:14; "The Address and Reasons of Dissent of the Minority of the Convention
of the Pennsylvania to their Constituents," December 18, 1787, in *Complete Anti-Federalist*,
3:157. For lists of Anti-Federalist demands for an amendment protecting religious free exercise, see Natelson, "The Original Meaning of the Establishment Clause," 96n127; Ellis M.
West, *The Free Exercise of Religion in America: Its Original Constitutional Meaning* (Cham,
Switzerland: Palgrave Macmillan, 2019), 244n45.

13. "Essay by Deliberator," *Freeman's Journal* (Philadelphia), February 20, 1788, in *Complete Anti-Federalist*, 3:179.

it right or no, and punish them severely, if they would not."[14] During the
New York Ratifying Convention, Thomas Tredwell contended that the
proposed national government would not remain limited to those powers
expressly given to it and, therefore, he said,

> I could have wished also that sufficient caution had been used to secure to us
> our religious liberties, and to have prevented the general government from tyr-
> annizing over our consciences by a religious establishment—a tyranny of all
> others most dreadful, and which will assuredly be exercised whenever it shall be
> thought necessary for the promotion and support of their political measures.[15]

The fear of a national establishment was part of the Anti-Federalists'
more general concern that a country as large as the proposed United States
could not remain free under a set of uniform laws. Inspired by Montesquieu's maxim that republican government could encompass only a small
territory and that rule in large territories necessarily tends towards tyranny, some Anti-Federalists saw a national religious establishment as a
leading example of how the new constitution would result in centraliza-
tion, consolidation, and—through enforced uniformity of religious practice—oppression.[16] "Agrippa," one of the most articulate of Massachusetts's
Anti-Federalists, summarized the matter as follows:

14. "Letters from a Countryman V," *New York Journal*, January 17, 1788, in *Complete Anti-
Federalist*, 6:87.
15. Thomas Tredwell, New York Ratifying Convention, July 2, 1788, in *The Founders' Constitution*, ed. Kurland and Lerner (Indianapolis, IN: Liberty Fund, n.d.; originally published
Chicago: University of Chicago Press, 1987), 1:475.
16. "Deliberator" articulated his fear of the establishment of uniformity in religion in
an essay on the subject of how the proposed constitution would lead to consolidation. For
Montesquieu's discussion of the connection between size and despotic rule, see Charles De
Secondat, Baron De Montesquieu, *The Spirit of the Laws*, book 8, chapter 20. Whether the
Anti-Federalists interpreted Montesquieu properly is an altogether separate question. For a
discussion of the Anti-Federalist concern with unlimited (in their view) powers of the national
government and the consolidation that such powers would bring, see Herbert J. Storing, *What
the Anti-Federalists Were For: The Political Thought of the Opponents of the Constitution* (Chicago: University of Chicago Press, 1981), 15–37.
    Steven K. Green, "Federalism and the Establishment Clause: A Reassessment," *Creighton
Law Review* 38 (2005), 781–85, argues that during the ratification debates, very few Anti-
Federalists sought to protect then-existing state religious establishments from federal encroachment. Green fails to consider how the Anti-Federalists' concern with consolidation was
related to their attempt to retain state authority over church-state matters. See also Drakeman, "The Anti-Federalists and Religion," 132–35.

Attention to religion and good morals is a distinguishing trait in our [Massachu-
setts] character. It is plain, therefore, that we require for our regulation laws,
which will not suit the circumstances of our southern brethren, and the laws
made for them would not apply to us. Unhappiness would be the uniform product of such laws; for no state can be happy, when the laws contradict the general
habits of the people, nor can any state retain its freedom, while there is a power
to make and enforce such laws. We may go further, and say, that it is impossible
for any single legislature so fully to comprehend the circumstances of the different parts of a very extensive dominion, as to make laws adapted to those
circumstances.[17]

Anti-Federalists' fear of a national establishment did not necessarily
mean they opposed governmental support for religion at the local level.[18]
Agrippa's comment reflects beliefs shared by many New England Anti-
Federalists and other "narrow republicans": that democratic government
requires a moral people, that morality requires religion, and therefore that
religion ought to be supported by the government. Indeed, New England
Anti-Federalists also criticized the proposed constitution for the absence
of religious tests for office.[19] Many Anti-Federalists held that the states, on

17. "Letters of Agrippa XII," *Massachusetts Gazette*, January 11, 1788, in *Complete Anti-
Federalist*, 4:94.

18. Henry Abbot's comments during the debates in the North Carolina Ratifying Convention reflect the ambivalent thinking of many Anti-Federalists about religious establishments:

Some are afraid, Mr. Chairman, that, should the Constitution be received, they would
be deprived of the privilege of worshipping God according to their consciences, which
would be taking from them a benefit they enjoy under the present constitution. They
wish to know if their religious and civil liberties be secured under this system, or
whether the general government may not make laws infringing their religious liberties. . . . Many wish to know what *religion* shall be established. I believe a majority of
the community are Presbyterians. I am, for my part, against any exclusive establishment; but if there were any, I would prefer the Episcopal. The exclusion of religious
tests is by many thought dangerous and impolitic.

Debate of the North Carolina Ratifying Convention, July 30, 1788, in *The Sacred Rights of
Conscience,* ed. Daniel L. Dreisbach and Mark David Hall (Indianapolis, IN: Liberty Fund,
2009), 394.

19. See, for example: "Essay by Samuel," January 10, 1788, in *Complete Anti-Federalist*,
4:196 ("If civil rulers won't acknowledge God, he won't acknowledge them"); "Address by A
Watchman," February 1788, in *Complete Anti-Federalist*, 4:232 ("There is a door opened for
the Jews, Turks, and Heathen to enter into publick office, and be seated at the head of the government of the United States"); Pauline Maier, *Ratification: The People Debate the Constitution, 1787–1788* (New York: Simon and Schuster, 2010), 152, 176–77, 191, 220. For the debates

account of their smaller size and greater homogeneity, were the natural home for republican moral education, and thus that the states could cultivate civic virtue in ways that would be oppressive if undertaken by the national government.[20] Akhil Amar nicely captures this Anti-Federalist view:

> The possibility of national control over a powerful intermediate association [churches] self-consciously trying to influence citizens' worldviews, shape their behavior, and cultivate their habits obviously struck fear in the hearts of Anti-Federalists. Yet local control over such intermediate organizations seemed far less threatening, less distant, less aristocratic, less monopolistic—just as local banks were far less threatening than a national one, and local militias far less dangerous than a national standing army. Given the religious diversity of the continent—with Congregationalists dominating New England, Anglicans down south, Quakers in Pennsylvania, Catholics huddling together in Maryland, Baptists seeking refuge in Rhode Island, and so on—a single national religious regime would have been horribly oppressive to many men and women of faith; local control, by contrast, would allow dissenters in any place to vote with their feet and find a community with the right religious tone.[21]

The Anti-Federalist concern regarding a national religious establishment was not animated by a general principle of opposition to government support of religion or by antiestablishmentarianism. Some Anti-Federalists did argue that a national establishment could force a citizen to practice a religion not his own and thereby violate the right of religious liberty, but they did not champion the right of a citizen to live in a republic without an established religion. Most Anti-Federalists were not against religious establishments per se; they were for republican localism. No one asserted nonestablishment to be an individual right, and no Anti-Federalists called for an amendment to restrict the states from supporting or establishing religions. Many Anti-Federalists did not consider nonestablishment to be

---

in the state ratifying conventions pertaining to religious tests for office, see *Sacred Rights of Conscience*, 388–400. See also Dreisbach, "The Constitution's Forgotten Religion Clause."

20. Storing, *What the Anti-Federalists Were For*, 22–23. For a discussion of Samuel Adams' understanding of the cultivation of civic virtue through the support of moral education at the state level, see Michael Allen Gillespie, "Massachusetts: Creating Consensus," in *Ratifying the Constitution*, ed. Michael Allen Gillespie and Michael Lienesch (Lawrence: University Press of Kansas, 1989), 140–41.

21. Akhil Reed Amar, *The Bill of Rights: Creation and Reconstruction* (New Haven, CT: Yale University Press, 1998), 45.

consistent with good government at the state level.[22] The Anti-Federalist fear of a national establishment, to repeat, was connected to the size of the nation, the nation's regional religious diversity, and the distance between federal power and local interests. Anti-Federalists, especially those in New England, only feared a national religious establishment.[23]

Proposed Amendments to the Constitution

Anti-Federalist criticisms led seven states to draft recommended amendments in the process of ratifying the Constitution.[24] Five of the seven included provisions pertaining to religion.[25] Led by Patrick Henry, Virginia submitted the following as part of its recommended bill of rights:

22. Carl H. Esbeck, in "The Uses and Abuses of Textualism and Originalism in Establishment Clause Interpretation," *Utah Law Review* 2011 (2011): 512n81, helpfully explains,

> While favoring the protection of religious conscience, many Antifederalists were establishmentarians. They reasoned in a circular fashion that saw republican self-government as possible only if there is a virtuous citizenry, that public virtue is largely learned by properly constituted religion, and that therefore religion should be actively aided and supported by the government.

Cf. West, *The Free Exercise of Religion in America*, 245n49.

23. Esbeck, in "Uses and Abuses of Textualism and Originalism," 513, reaches a similar conclusion:

> the overriding concern of the Antifederalists with respect to religion . . . had to do with wanting to explicitly preserve jurisdiction over church-government relations as a power vested in the states, as well as to disable any implied national power to invade religion conscience.

24. For an excellent discussion of this point, see Goldwin, *From Parchment to Power*, 36–48. For discussions of the constitutional ratification debate that focuses on religion, see Antieau, Downey, and Roberts, *Freedom from Federal Establishment*, 111–22; Esbeck, "Uses and Abuses of Textualism and Originalism," 508–25. For a discussion of the politics in Virginia surrounding amendments and Madison's election to the Virginia Ratifying Convention in 1788, see Gregory C. Downs, "Religious Liberty That Almost Wasn't: On the Origins of the Establishment Clause of the First Amendment," *University of Arkansas Little Rock Law Review* 30 (2007): 19–29. For a helpful list of drafts of potential federal religion clause amendments, see John Witte Jr. and Joel A. Nichols, *Religion and the American Constitutional Experiment*, 4th ed. (New York: Oxford University Press, 2016), 295–96.

25. I omit from discussion South Carolina's proposal that sought to amend the Religious Test Clause in Article 6 to read, "no *other* religious test shall ever be required." For a discussion of this point, see Witte and Nichols, *Religion and the American Constitutional Experiment*, 353n41. Massachusetts was the other state whose proposals did not include a religion amendment. According to Antieau, Downey, and Roberts, *Freedom from Federal Establish-*

That religion, or the duty which we owe to our Creator, and the manner of discharging it, can be directed only by reason and conviction, not by force or violence; and therefore all men have an equal, natural, and unalienable right to the free exercise of religion, according to the dictates of conscience, and that no particular religious sect or society ought to be favored or established, by law, in preference to others.[26]

Rhode Island repeated and submitted Virginia's language in its recommended "declarations of rights."[27] North Carolina's list of rights and amendments also used Virginia's language, though because its initial convention voted neither to reject nor to ratify the Constitution, it did not submit its draft to Congress.[28] New York's ratifying convention submitted text similar to Virginia's:

That the people have an equal, natural, and unalienable right freely and peaceably to exercise their religion, according to the dictates of conscience; and that no religious sect or society ought to be favored or established by law in preference to others.[29]

---

ment, 114, evidence from the Massachusetts ratification debate "indicates that the people of Massachusetts failed to propose a religious liberty and antiestablishment amendment because it was their understanding that the Congress simply had no such power, and that their right to religious freedom was adequately protected by the state constitution."

26. *The Debates in the Several State Conventions on the Adoption of the Federal Constitution, as Recommended by the General Convention at Philadelphia, in 1787*, 2nd ed., ed. Jonathan Elliot (Philadelphia: J. B. Lippincott and Co., 1861), 3:659 (hereafter *Elliot's Debates*). The preamble of Virginia's declaration of ratification also said "that among other essential rights, the liberty of conscience and of the press cannot be cancelled, abridged, restrained or modified by any authority of the United States." *Elliot's Debates*, 3:653.

27. *Elliot's Debates*, 1:334. Rhode Island's ratifying convention did not convene until March 1790. It submitted its ratification along with its declaration of rights and proposed amendments on May 29, 1790. Every state that proposed amendments—except for New Hampshire, the first state to submit amendments—divided its proposals into two distinct lists, labeling those pertaining to structure "amendments," and labeling those pertaining to individual rights, "declaration of rights."

28. *Elliot's Debates*, 4:244, 1:333. For a discussion of North Carolina's two ratifying conventions, see Albert Ray Newsome, "North Carolina's Ratification of the Federal Constitution," *North Carolina Historical Review* 17 (1940): 287–301.

29. *Elliot's Debates*, 1:328. Gerard V. Bradley, in *Church-State Relationships in America* (Westport, CT: Greenwood Press, 1987), 78, contends that Governor George Clinton was the animating force behind New York's amendment, and that Clinton's record as governor "reveals a decided preference for state aid to religion within the confines of a nonestablishment constitution."

New Hampshire proposed the following:

> Congress shall make no laws touching religion, or to infringe the rights of
> conscience.[30]

Additionally, the minorities that lost the ratification fights in Pennsylvania and Maryland recommended a religion amendment, although these
lacked the states' official sanction.[31] The Pennsylvania "Minority Dissent,"
which was signed by twenty-one of the twenty-three delegates that voted
against ratification, offered:

> The right of conscience shall be held inviolable, and neither the legislative, ex-
> ecutive nor judicial powers of the United States shall have authority to alter,
> abrogate, or infringe any part of the constitution of the several states, which
> provide for the preservation of liberty in matters of religion.[32]

A group of Maryland's Anti-Federalists proposed:

> that there be no National Religion established by Law; but that all Persons be
> equally entitled to protection in their religious Liberty.[33]

By employing phrases like "the free exercise of religion," "the rights of
conscience," or other equivalent language, all the recommended amendments reflected or responded to the Anti-Federalists' concern that the
proposed national constitution failed to protect adequately the religious
free exercise rights of individuals. I will discuss in the next chapter how
these concerns were translated into what became the Free Exercise Clause.
Beyond this agreement, however, an important difference can be de-
tected. The "Minority Dissent" in Pennsylvania and New Hampshire emphasized the absence of national power over religion, whereas the other

---

30. *Elliot's Debates*, 1:326. It is worth noting that whereas several states proposed two
distinct lists—one of structural amendments, the other pertaining to individual rights—New
Hampshire proposed just one list of constitutional amendments.

31. *Religious Liberty in A Pluralistic Society*, 2nd edition, ed. Michael S. Ariens and Robert A. Destro (Durham, NC: Carolina Academic Press, 2002), 79.

32. "The Address and Reasons of Dissent of the Minority of the Convention of Pennsylvania to Their Constituents," *Pennsylvania Packet and Daily Advisor*, December 18, 1787, in
Complete Anti-Federalist, 3:150–51.

33. "Address of a Minority of the Maryland Ratifying Convention," *Maryland Gazette*
(Baltimore), May 6, 1788, in *Complete Anti-Federalist*, 5:97.

states sought to regulate how national power might be used if or when the national government enacted laws that favored or established religion.

The text from Pennsylvania puts this difference in focus. It explicitly protected state constitutional authority from national interference by denying all three branches of the national government "authority to alter, abrogate or infringe on any part of the constitution of the several states" regarding "the preservation of liberty in matters of religion." Pennsylvania's proposed amendment sought to protect state sovereignty. Similarly, New Hampshire, by prohibiting Congress from making "laws touching religion," appears to have aimed at walling off the entire subject matter of religion from national legislation.[34] Anti-Federalists in these states adopted an approach that may have been initially advanced by Charles Pinckney of South Carolina early in the Philadelphia Convention. In May 1787, as part of the "Pinckney Plan," Pinckney is recorded as including the following text:

> The Legislature of the United States shall pass no Law on the subject of Religion. . . . [35]

Restricting national authority over religion would have had the dual effect of protecting religious liberty against national violation and affirming state authority over the subject matter. The latter was especially important to those Anti-Federalists who believed that concurrent national and state authority would necessarily and inevitably favor the national

34. Though Stephen K. Green, in *The Second Disestablishment* (New York: Oxford University Press, 2010), 64, disputes the conclusion that the original meaning of the Establishment Clause was designed to protect the authority of state governments over religious establishments, he recognizes that the proposed amendment by New Hampshire "can arguably be interpreted as expressing a desire to protect existing religious establishments from the federal government." Green finds the Pennsylvania dissenters' proposal to contain "the clearest states' rights motivation." Cf. West, *Free Exercise of Religion in America*, 256–57.

35. *Elliot's Debates*, 5:131 (May 29, 1787). For discussions about the controversy and speculation surrounding the "Pinckney Plan," see Marty D. Matthews, *Forgotten Founder: The Life and Times of Charles Pinckney* (Columbia: University of South Carolina Press, 2004), 40–45; Dreisbach, "The Constitution's Forgotten Religion Clause," 270n47; Leonard W. Levy, *The Establishment Clause: Religion and the First Amendment*, 2nd ed. (Chapel Hill: University of North Carolina Press, 1994), 80n1; Charles Warren, *The Making of the Constitution* (New York: Barnes and Noble, 1928), 142–43n3. According to Levy (p. 57), Pinckney introduced the plan for an establishment of all Protestant churches that became part of the South Carolina's 1778 constitution.

government and extinguish state power. The "Impartial Examiner" stated the matter as follows:

> The idea of two sovereignties existing within the same community is a perfect solecism. If they be supposed equal, their operations must be commensurate, and like two mechanical powers of equal *momenta* counteracting each other; — here the force of one will be destroyed by the force of the other: and so there will be no efficiency in either. If one be greater than the other, they will be similar to two unequal bodies in motion with a given degree of velocity, and imping- ing each other from opposite points; — the motion of the lesser in this case will necessarily be destroyed by that of the greater: and so there will be efficiency only in the greater.[36]

Some Anti-Federalists were convinced that to protect state sovereignty over any given subject matter, an express denial of national authority was required.[37] In Pennsylvania and New Hampshire, proposals similar to the "Pinckney Plan" affirmed the national government's lack of authority over the subject matter of religion.[38]

Anti-Federalists in Virginia, North Carolina, Rhode Island, and New York took a different approach. Their amendments sought to regulate how Congress might exercise potential authority over religion by requir-

36. The Impartial Examiner I, *Virginia Independent Chronicles,* February 20, 1787, in *Documentary History of the Ratification of the Constitution,* 8:392. For a discussion of the Anti-Federalists' objections to the Supremacy Clause, see Christopher R. Drahozal, *The Su- premacy Clause: A Reference Guide to the United States Constitution,* foreword by Carter G. Phillips (Westport, CT: Prager, 2004), 25–30.

37. The Pennsylvanian "An Old Whig," in *Complete Anti-Federalist,* 3:36–37, made this argument specifically with regard to religious establishments:

> I hope and trust that there are few persons at present hardy enough to entertain thoughts of creating any religious establishment for this country . . . , but if a majority of the continental legislature should at any time think fit to establish a form of religion, for the good people of this continent, with all the pains and penalties which in other coun- tries are annexed to the establishment of a natural church, what is there in the proposed constitution to hinder their doing so? Nothing: for we have no bill of rights, and every thing therefore is in their power and at their discretion. And at whose discretion? We know not any more than we know the fates of these generations which are yet unborn.

For a discussion of this argument as it unfolded in Pennsylvania, see Michael J. Faber, *An Anti- Federalist Constitution: The Development of Dissent in the Ratification Debates* (Lawrence: Uni- versity Press of Kansas, 2019), 61–62, 68–69.

38. As discussed below, Federalists also embraced this position throughout the ratification debates.

ing that no religious sect or society "ought to be favored or established, by law, in preference to others." These states sought to prevent favoritism of one sect over others in the event that the new national government was to legislate on religious matters. A guarantee of sect nonpreferentialism would minimize the perceived dangers associated with the uniformity of law across a large and diverse nation.

The difference between New Hampshire's and Pennsylvania's recommended amendments, on the one hand, and those of Virginia and the other states, on the other, can be traced in part to Patrick Henry. A vehement critic of the proposed federal constitution, Henry played a dominant role in the Virginia ratifying convention, where he championed the Anti-Federalist call for a bill of rights. During that convention, Virginia's Federalists had argued that no amendment relating to religion was necessary because, as James Madison contended, "there is not a shadow of right in the general government to intermeddle with religion. Its least interference with it would be a most flagrant usurpation."[39] Henry thought

---

39. James Madison, Statement at the Virginia Ratifying Convention (June 12, 1788), in *Elliot's Debates*, 3:330. During the ratification debates, Federalists repeatedly argued that the proposed federal government possessed only delegated powers, and that no power was delegated concerning religion. James Iredell, in North Carolina's ratifying convention on July 30, 1788, offered the standard Federalist argument:

> [Congress] certainly ha[s] no authority to interfere in the establishment of any religion whatsoever; and I am astonished that any gentleman should conceive they have. Is there any power given to Congress in matters of religion? Can they pass a single act to impair our religious liberties? If they could, it would be a just cause of alarm.... If any future Congress should pass an act concerning the religion of the country, it would be an act which they are not authorized to pass, by the Constitution, and which the people would not obey. Every one would ask, "Who authorized the government to pass such an act? It is not warranted by the Constitution, and is barefaced usurpation."

As his remarks continued, Iredell offered a second response characteristic of the Federalist argument, contrasting the Constitution's guarantee of a republican form of government with its absence of a guarantee of religious freedom:

> It has been asked by that respectable gentleman (Mr. Abbot) what is the meaning of that part, where it is said that the United States shall *guaranty* to every state in the Union a republican form of government, and why a *guaranty* of religious freedom was not included. The meaning of the guaranty provided was this: There being thirteen governments confederated upon a republican principle, it was essential to the existence and harmony of the confederacy that each should be a republican government, and that no state should have a right to establish an aristocracy or monarchy. That clause was therefore inserted to prevent any state from establishing any government but a republican one. Every one must be convinced of the mischief that would ensue, if any state had a right to change its government to a monarchy. If a monarchy was

such assurances were woefully insufficient. To rebut the Federalists' delegated powers argument, he highlighted the explicit limitations on national power listed in Article 1, Section 9 of the Constitution. Those reservations, Henry said, were like a bill of rights. That the Philadelphia Convention thought it necessary to explicitly protect some rights belied the Federalist contention that a bill of rights was not necessary. It "reverses the position of the friends of this Constitution, that every thing is retained which is not given up" and, instead, reveals that "every thing which is not negatived [sic] shall remain with Congress." The inclusion of express reservations in Article 1, Section 9, Henry concluded, "destroys [the Federal-

---

established in any one state, it would endeavor to subvert the freedom of the others, and would, probably, by degrees succeed in it. . . . It is, then, necessary that the members of a confederacy should have similar governments. But consistently with this restriction, the states may make what change in their own governments they think proper. Had Congress undertaken to guaranty religious freedom, or any particular species of it, they would then have had a pretence to interfere in a subject they have nothing to do with. Each state, so far as the clause in question does not interfere, must be left to the operation of its own principles.

James Iredell, Statement at the North Carolina Ratifying Convention (July 30, 1788), in *Elliot's Debates*, 4:192, 194–95. For further examples of the Federalists' argument made at the state conventions, see Edmund Randolph, Statement at the Virginia Ratifying Convention (June 10, 1788), in *Elliot's Debates*, 3:194, 204 (arguing that "no power is given expressly to Congress over religion," and rather that the "exclusion of religious tests is an exception from this general provision, with respect to oaths or affirmations"); Edmund Randolph, Statement at the Virginia Ratifying Convention (June 15, 1788), in *Elliot's Debates*, 3:463, 469 (asserting that religious freedom is protected by the omission of additional provisions in the Constitution); James Bowdoin, Statement at the Massachusetts Ratifying Convention (January 23, 1788), in *Elliot's Debates*, 2:81, 87 ("It would require a volume to describe [the rights of particular states], as they extend to every subject of legislation, not included in the powers vested in Congress"); James Madison, Statement at the Virginia Ratifying Convention (June 12, 1788), in *Elliot's Debates*, 3:328, 330 (citing the plurality of religions in the United States as a safeguard against religious tyranny, as part of a larger argument against a bill of rights); Theophilus Parsons, Statement at the Massachusetts Ratifying Convention (January 23, 1788), in *Elliot's Debates*, 2:88, 90 ("It has been objected that the Constitution provides no religious test by oath, and we may have in power unprincipled men, atheists and pagans. No man can wish more ardently . . . that all our public offices may be filled by men who fear God and hate wickedness; but it must be filled with the electors to give the government this security").

For further discussion of the Federalist response in the state ratifying conventions, see Joseph M. Snee, "Religious Disestablishment and the Fourteenth Amendment," *Washington University Law Quarterly* (1954): 373–77. The most well-known Federalist explanation of the Constitution's lack of a bill of rights, of course, is offered by Alexander Hamilton in *The Federalist* 84. See also James Wilson, Statement at the Pennsylvania Ratifying Convention (November 28, 1787), in *Elliot's Debates*, 2:434–37, asserting that a bill of rights would interfere with the reservation of personal powers that ensures protection of rights, and Wilson's October 6, 1787, "State House Speech" (in *Founders' Constitution*, 1:449).

ists'] doctrine."[40] Disbelieving that the new national government's powers would remain limited, Henry concluded that a bill of rights was absolutely necessary to protect essential rights, including religious freedom. And if the new national government was inevitably going to exercise power over religion, Henry was determined to ensure that that power would be exercised in a nonpreferential manner.[41]

At the end of the 1788 Virginia ratifying convention, accordingly, Henry helped draft several constitutional amendments, including a twenty-article declaration of rights. For his religion amendment, Henry modified Article 16 of Virginia's 1776 Declaration of Rights as follows (Henry's additions are in italics):

> That Religion or the Duty which we owe to our Creator, and the Manner of discharging it, can be directed only by Reason and Conviction, not by Force or Violence; and therefore all Men ~~are equally entitled~~ *have an equal, natural, and unalienable Right* to the free Exercise of Religion, according to the Dictates of Conscience; and that ~~it is the mutual duty of all to practice Christian forbearance, love, and charity toward each other~~ *no particular Religious Sect or Society of Christians ought to be favored or established by Law in preference to others.*[42]

40. Patrick Henry, Statement at the Virginia Ratifying Convention (June 15, 1788), in *Elliot's Debates*, 3:461–62. On the same day, Governor Edmund Randolph offered the Federalist response to Henry's criticism, namely that "every exception [Article 1, Section 9] mentioned is an exception, not from general powers, but from the particular powers therein vested." Randolph, Statement at the Virginia Ratifying Convention (June 15, 1788), in *Elliot's Debates*, 3:464. Thomas Tredwell would repeat Henry's criticism in the New York Ratifying Convention a few weeks later on July 2, 1788, in *Founders' Constitution*, 1:474–75.

41. Cf. Levy, *Establishment Clause*, 93. Levy, I believe, fails to distinguish the different approaches advanced by Pennsylvania and New Hampshire on the one hand, and Virginia on the other, because he fails to integrate into his analysis Patrick Henry's skepticism that the new national government would not exercise authority over religion.

42. In his *Debates on the Adoption of the Ratification of the Federal Constitution*, Elliot reproduces only the declaration of rights that was adopted by the convention on June 27, 1788 (see 3:657–59), which he notes was "nearly the same" as that proposed by Henry on June 24. Elliot does not reproduce the actual text of the declaration of rights Henry proposed on June 24. On June 9, Henry had sent to John Lamb a copy of the declaration of rights and amendments he said he intended to introduce. It is reasonable to assume that Henry submitted to the Virginia convention on June 24 the same text he sent to Lamb on June 9. This assumption is supported by that fact that it is known that, following the vote for ratification on June 26, the committee that prepared the final set of recommended amendments deleted the words "of Christians" from the final clause of Henry's June 24 proposal. For a discussion of this point, see Jeff Broadwater, *George Mason, Forgotten Founder* (Chapel Hill: University of North Carolina Press, 2006), 236. The text of the amendments that Henry sent to Lamb on June 9

The explicit reference to Christianity would be removed by Virginia's ratifying convention, but the added "no preference" language would remain
and be sent to Congress.

Henry's strategy, to repeat, appears to have differed significantly from
Pennsylvania's and New Hampshire's. Whereas those states proposed an
amendment that would have explicitly prevented Congress from "touching religion" (in New Hampshire's formulation), Henry sought to ensure
that, were the national government to exercise authority over religion, it
would do so in a nonpreferential manner. Henry's skepticism about the
allegedly limited authority of the proposed federal government seems to
have led him to seek to regulate national power over religion, not prevent
it altogether.[43]

---

and, we assume, introduced on the convention floor on June 24 can be found in *Documentary
History of the Ratification of the Constitution*, 18:41–45.

It may be impossible to know with certainty, but Henry is most likely the individual re-
sponsible for the changes made to Article 16 of the Declaration of Rights. The month before
the convention began, Virginia's leading Anti-Federalists had caucused and made George
Mason chair of a committee whose task was to draw up a list of amendments to be proposed
at the convention. According to Mason's biographer Jeff Broadwater, by June 8 Mason had
prepared a list of thirteen structural amendments, but had not completed a declaration of
personal rights. On June 9, Mason sent a copy of the aforementioned twenty-article declaration of rights to Lamb, a New York Anti-Federalist. On June 9 Patrick Henry also wrote to
Lamb, referencing the list of structural amendments and the declaration of rights. Mason and
Henry were both part of the leadership of Virginia's Anti-Federalists, and both may have
contributed to the drafting of the twenty-article declaration of rights. But given that we know
that Mason had not completed a declaration of rights by June 8 and that it was completed by
June 9, it seems unlikely that Mason drafted the declaration of rights alone. Moreover, the
changes made to Article 16 reflect the position that Henry championed in 1784 during the
state legislature's general assessment debate. In that debate, Mason stood opposed to Henry's
proposed bill to aid religion and aligned himself with Jefferson and Madison. See Broadwater,
George Mason, 147–50, 234–36. Henry's June 9 letter to Lamb can be found in *Documentary
History of the Ratification of the Constitution*, 18:39–40.

43. Henry's skepticism about the proposed national government's lack of power over
religion, and his significant political skill in making the point, is reflected in Madison's correspondence about Henry during the Virginia ratification convention. In a letter dated June 12,
1788, John Blair Smith wrote to Madison, "He [Henry] has found means to make some of the
best people here believe, that a religious establisht. [*sic*] was in Contemplation under the new
govt." John Blair Smith to James Madison, in *The Papers of James Madison*, Congressional
Series, ed. J. C. A. Stagg et al. (Charlottesville: University Press of Virginia, 2010), 11:120. On
Henry's intention—and how his proposed non-preference language might contradict it—see
Esbeck, "Virginia," in *Disestablishment and Religious Dissent: Church-State Relations in the
New American States, 1776–1783*, ed. Carl H. Esbeck and Jonathan J. Den Hartog (Columbia:
University of Missouri Press, 2019), 167.

The Drafting of the Establishment Clause

When James Madison collected the various states' proposals for amendments to begin working on what would become the Bill of Rights, he must have noticed the tension that existed between New Hampshire's and Virginia's official recommended amendments. The former specified limits on federal authority; the latter might be read to expand it. One can imagine the frustration Madison might have felt with Henry in particular. Disregarding the Federalist argument that restrictions on nonexistent powers might be construed to create powers not actually granted, Henry had engineered an amendment that might create the very federal power over religion that many of his own New England Anti-Federalist allies feared.[44] Perhaps the Anti-Federalists could have hashed out their differences in a second constitutional convention—which is how they sought to amend the Constitution.[45]

That second constitutional convention never took place because Madison took charge of the amendment process in the First Federal Congress. During the state ratifying conventions, Anti-Federalists exerted considerable influence. Recall that the vote in favor of the Constitution only narrowly passed in Virginia (89–79) and New York (30–27). If a second constitutional convention were called, Anti-Federalists might exert even more influence. But Federalists controlled the First Congress.[46] Madison

44. See Esbeck's helpful discussion of this point in "Uses and Abuses of Textualism and Originalism," 529.

45. Faber, *Anti-Federalist Constitution*, 312, reports that in late 1788 a second constitutional convention "looked entirely possible." Calls for a second constitutional convention had been issued even before the Philadelphia Convention finished its work. During the Philadelphia Convention, Edmund Randolph repeatedly proposed a motion for a second convention. On May 5, 1789, just four weeks into the first session of the First Congress, Theodorick Bland, a congressman from Virginia, introduced a motion calling for a convention pursuant to Article 5 of the Constitution. The next day, John Laurance of New York presented an application from the New York legislature for a second constitutional convention. See Goldwin, *From Parchment to Power*, 23–26, 76–77. Reflecting on the mixed legacy of the Bill of Rights from the Anti-Federalist view, Herbert Storing, in *What the Anti-Federalists Were For*, 65, writes, "In one sense, the success of the Bill of Rights reflects the failure of the Anti-Federalists."

46. According to Thornton Anderson, *Creating the Constitution: The Convention of 1787 and the First Congress* (University Park: Pennsylvania State University Press, 1993), 176, Anti-Federalists occupied only ten seats in the House and two seats in the Senate in the First Federal Congress. See also Faber, *Anti-Federalist Constitution*, 314–15; Goldwin, *From Parchment to Power*, 144; Esbeck, "Uses and Abuses of Textualism and Originalism," 525. On April 8, 1789, regarding amendments to the Constitution, Madison wrote to James Pendleton: "From appearances there will be no great difficulty of obtaining reasonable ones. It will depend

understood that if the First Congress drafted amendments, Federalists would dictate their content as well as consolidate their ratification victory. Proposing amendments thus became Madison's focus in the first months of the First Congress, much to the frustration of several of his colleagues who preferred to put off the subject. Like almost all Federalists, Madison did not think amendments were necessary to correct flaws in the Constitution itself, but he did see them as politically necessary to quell fears excited by the Anti-Federalists during the battle over ratification.[47]

The House of Representatives

Madison's Original Proposed Text

On June 8, 1789, Madison introduced in the House of Representatives the set of amendments that would eventually become the Bill of Rights.[48] For

---

however entirely on the temper of the federalists, who predominate as much in both branches, as could be wished." *Creating the Bill of Rights: The Documentary Record of the First Federal Congress*, ed. Veit, Bowling, and Bickford (Baltimore: Johns Hopkins University Press, 1991), 229. In their study of the Anti-Federalists and the First Congress, John H. Aldrich and Ruth W. Grant, in "The Antifederalists, the First Congress, and the First Parties," *Journal of Politics* 55 (1993): 296–97, write, "Even the final form of the Bill of Rights was less the product of continuing antifederalist influence than the result of clever maneuverings by James Madison to minimize the extent of compromise with them."

47. Regarding the propriety of amendments to the newly adopted Constitution, Madison wrote to Jefferson, October 17, 1788, in *Founders' Constitution*, 1:477:

My own opinion has always been in favor of a bill of rights; provided it be so framed as not to imply powers not meant to be included in the enumeration. At the same time I have never thought the omission a material defect, nor been anxious to supply it even by *subsequent* amendment, for any other reason than that it is anxiously desired by others. I have favored it because I supposed it might be of use, and if properly executed could not be of disservice.

For discussions of Madison's political and strategic thinking concerning the adoption of the Bill of Rights, see Herbert J. Storing, "The Constitution and the Bill of Rights," in *Toward a More Perfect Union: Writings of Herbert J. Storing*, ed. Joseph M. Bessette (Washington: AEI Press, 1995), esp. 111–12; Goldwin, *From Parchment to Power*, 75–82; James H. Hutson, *Church and State in America: The First Two Centuries* (New York: Cambridge University Press, 2008), 148–55; Faber, *Anti-Federalist Constitution*, 316–18.

48. A concise version of records of the debates in the First Congress pertaining to the drafting of the First Amendment Religion Clauses is available in *Religious Liberty and the American Supreme Court*, updated edition, ed. Vincent Phillip Muñoz (Lanham, MD: Rowman and Littlefield, 2015), 618–24.

what would become the First Amendment's Religion Clauses, Madison proposed:

> The civil rights of none shall be abridged on account of religious belief or worship, nor shall any national religion be established, nor shall the full and equal rights of conscience be in any manner, or on any pretext, infringed.[49]

Madison did not adopt any of the Anti-Federalists' proposed amendments.[50] He drafted his own unique text that responded to some but not all of the Anti-Federalists' concerns. Most clearly, Madison heeded the demand that the "rights of conscience" be explicitly protected. He also countenanced Anti-Federalist concerns about a national religious establishment. Here, though, his language did not clearly specify, as New Hampshire had proposed, that the national government could make no laws "touching religion," but instead used Maryland's formulation: that no "national religion" shall be established. Given that Madison had taken the New Hampshire position at the Virginia ratifying convention—contending that there was "not a shadow of right in the general government to intermeddle with religion," and that the national government's "least interference" with it "would be a most flagrant usurpation"[51]—it is somewhat surprising that he did not propose language more similar to New Hampshire's proposal.

Most notable about Madison's submitted text are his additions, omissions, and substitutions to what Anti-Federalists had proposed. Madison eschewed Henry's approach of imposing a nonpreferential regulation on national legislation favoring or establishing a religion. He added instead a provision that no state had recommended: "The civil rights of none shall

49. *Annals of Congress*, 1st Cong., 1st sess., 451.

50. Commenting on Madison's proposed amendments in the First Congress as a whole, Donald S. Lutz, in "The State Constitutional Pedigree of the U.S. Bill of Rights," *Publius* 22 (1992): 20, writes, "The forty-two distinct rights contained [in Madison's] nine proposed amendments . . . bear only a modest relation to what was proposed by the ratifying conventions." Lutz continues (p. 28):

> Madison apparently wished to avoid the amendments proposed by the ratifying conventions, but he needed to make some connection with the state interests to mollify the Antifederalists. The tactic he fasted upon was to exploit seams in the Antifederalist position on what amendments to make.

51. James Madison, Statement at the Virginia Ratifying Convention (June 12, 1788), *Elliot's Debates*, 3:330.

be abridged on account of religious belief or worship." The differences
between the two provisions are significant. Henry's nonpreferential language, as already discussed, could be read to suggest that the new national
government had the authority to favor or even establish a religion, as long
as it did so nonpreferentially. Madison's language did not support a reading that might augment national power. Moreover, Madison proposed a
new and additional restriction on national power. As noted, no state had
requested language protecting individuals' civil rights from abridgment
on account of religion; some New England Anti-Federalists, in fact, had
lamented the absence of religious tests for national offices. Madison, it appears, sought to take advantage of his position as draftsman to include an
"expansive liberal" provision.

It also should be noted that Madison distinguished nondeprivation-of-
civil-rights language from rights-of-conscience language: "The civil rights
of none shall be abridged on account of religious belief" is itemized separately from "nor shall the full and equal rights of conscience be in any
manner, or on any pretext, infringed." This presents something of a puzzle:
Did Madison not think the full and equal rights of conscience included the
nondeprivation of civil rights on account of religion? If so, why did he list
the provisions separately?

It may be impossible to know for certain, but one of Madison's chief
reservations about a bill of rights was that "a positive declaration of some
of the most essential rights could not be obtained in the requisite latitude."
As he explained to Jefferson in an October 1787 letter, he was particularly
concerned that the rights of conscience would be defined too narrowly:

> I am sure that the rights of Conscience in particular, if submitted to public
> definition would be narrowed much more than they are likely ever to be by an
> assumed power. One of the objections in New England was that the Constitu-
> tion by prohibiting religious tests opened a door for Jews Turks & infidels.[52]

Madison was aware that not everyone agreed with him that the non-
abridgment of civil rights on account of religion followed from the natural
and inalienable rights of conscience. He might have separated the two
provisions with the intention that the former be available regardless of
how the latter would be construed.

---

52. James Madison to Thomas Jefferson, October 17, 1787, in *Founders' Constitution*, 1:477.

Madison also went beyond Anti-Federalist demands by proposing an amendment to be applied against the states, though it omitted language pertaining to religious establishments and the deprivation of civil rights:

> No State shall violate the equal rights of conscience, or the freedom of the press, or the trial by jury in criminal cases.[53]

Regarding this proposed amendment, Madison said:

> Nothing can give a more sincere proof of the attachment of those who opposed this constitution to these great and important rights, than to see them join in obtaining the security I have now proposed; because it must be admitted, on all hands, that the state governments are as liable to attack these invaluable privileges as the general government is, and therefore ought to be as cautiously guarded against.[54]

The House responded to Madison's proposed amendments with irritation and opposition. Samuel Livermore of New Hampshire objected that "he could not say what amendments were requisite, until the [new national] Government was organized."[55] Roger Sherman from Connecticut said, "It seems to be the opinion of gentlemen generally, that this is not the time for entering upon the discussion of amendments: our only question therefore is, how to get rid of the subject."[56] John Vining from Delaware repeated the standard Federalist argument "that a bill of rights was unnecessary in a Government deriving all its powers from the people."[57]

---

53. *Annals of Congress*, 1st Cong., 1st sess., 452.

54. *Annals of Congress*, 1st Cong., 1st sess., 458. Snee, "Religious Disestablishment and the Fourteenth Amendment," 384, interprets the limited scope of the restriction on state governments as indicating that Madison did not regard the prohibition of an establishment to be necessary to protect the rights of conscience. Snee writes, "In his [Madison's] mind at least, the two were quite distinct and that the establishment of religion by law is not per se an infringement of the equal rights of conscience." I believe it would be more accurate to infer that Madison limited the scope of the state amendment because (1) he appreciated the difference of opinion among the Founders regarding the compatibility of religious establishments and freedom of conscience and, therefore, (2) a limited amendment was more likely to be adopted. For a different criticism of Snee on this point, see Green, *Second Disestablishment*, 65–66.

55. *Annals of Congress*, 1st Cong., 1st sess., 465.

56. *Annals of Congress*, 1st Cong., 1st sess., 466.

57. *Annals of Congress*, 1st Cong., 1st sess., 467.

Most members did not want to be bothered with something they thought unnecessary and, therefore, a waste of time.[58]

The Select Committee's Modifications

Sensing that he would get nowhere with the full House, Madison managed to have consideration of amendments moved to a select committee consisting of one member from each of the eleven states represented.[59] Over the course of the week, the committee modified Madison's original language as follows (words added are in italics):

> ~~The civil rights of none shall be abridged on account of religious belief or worship, nor shall any national~~ *no* religion *shall* be established *by law*, nor shall the ~~full and~~ equal rights of conscience be ~~in any manner, or on any pretext,~~ infringed.[60]

58. Bradley, *Church-State Relationships in America*, 88, describes the reception of Madison's efforts to pass amendments as follows:

> South Carolina Senator Ralph Izad wrote Jefferson that the amendments were a waste of time. Pierce Butler, the state's second senator, referred to them as a "few milk and water amendments," an epithet echoed by the powerful Virginia antifederalist George Mason. Pennsylvania Congressman George Clymer appropriately called them a "tub or a number of tubs to the whale." To Senator Robert Morris, they were "nonsense" and to Fisher Ames "trash." Fellow Virginia antifederalist Edmund Randolph described their effect as an "anodyne to the discontented." South Carolina's Aedanus Burke portrayed the select committee's version of Madison's amendments as "little better than whip-syllabus, frothy and full of wind, formed only to please the palate." Fisher Ames picked up Burke's epicurean metaphor: the proposals "will stimulate the stomach as hasty pudding ... rather food than physic. An immense mass of sweet and other herbs and roots for a diet drink."

59. The select committee, which consisted of one member from each state, was comprised of Baldwin, Benson, Boudinot, Burke, Clymer, Gale, Gilman, Goodhue, Madison, Sherman, and Vining. For a discussion of the committee membership, see Bradley, *Church-State Relationships*, 90–91.

60. *Annals of Congress*, 1st Cong., 1st sess., 757. According to Mark David Hall, the select committee of eleven produced a draft bill of rights that "follows Madison's draft, but ... [with] important differences." The committee's draft, which is in the handwriting of Roger Sherman, included the following in place of Madison's religion amendment:

> The people have certain natural rights which are retained by them when they enter into Society, Such are the Rights of Conscience in matters of religion....

The select committee's draft, which according to Hall was composed between July 21 and July 28, 1788, had no language pertaining to an establishment of religion. See Mark David Hall, *Roger Sherman and the Creation of the American Republic* (New York: Oxford University

Notably, the Select Committee of Eleven deleted Madison's nondeprivation-of-civil-rights provision.[61] The committee also removed the word "national," which, as I will discuss below, would become a point of contention. Madison had proposed that the amendment be inserted into Article 1, Section 9 of the Constitution, which would have indicated that it limited the authority of the national government. Given this proposed placement in the Constitution's text, it is possible that the select committee found the word "national" redundant.[62]

The Full House of Representatives Debate

After more pleading from Madison, the full House finally took up consideration of amendments on August 15, 1789. The select committee's text was met with immediate criticism. Congressman Peter Sylvester, from New York, feared that the text might be "liable to a construction different from what had been made by the committee," and misconstrued "to abolish religion altogether."[63] Since we lack knowledge of the committee's deliberations, it is hard to know precisely what Sylvester had in mind. Perhaps he feared that "established by law" would be interpreted as "recognized by law." If so, "no religion shall be established by law" could be interpreted to prohibit religions from legally incorporating or maintaining any standing in law; the amendment, so understood, would have eliminated religious societies' legal rights. Given that the committee had dropped the word "national," moreover, Sylvester might have thought the text was now ambiguous as to which level of government it applied to—state, national, or

---

Press, 2013), 135–36, 208n40, 216–17. See also Scott D. Gerber, "Roger Sherman and the Bill of Rights," *Polity* 28 (1996): 521–40.

61. Michael J. Malbin, *Religion and Politics: The Intentions of the Authors of the First Amendment* (Washington: American Enterprise Institute for Public Policy Research, 1978), 5, suggests that "a plausible reason" why the committee dropped the phrase "the Civil Rights of none shall be abridged on account of religious belief or worship" is that the phrase was redundant, protecting nothing not covered by the Constitution's Article 6 ban on religious tests for office or by the other clauses of the proposed amendment. Malbin fails to recognize that, as discussed in chapter 4, the Founders disagreed on whether the abridgment of civil rights on account of religion violated the rights of conscience, so it was unlikely to have been seen as redundant, at least by all. An alternative possibility is that the provision was controversial and was therefore dropped. As no records of the committee's deliberations exist, it is impossible to know for certain.

62. Esbeck, "Uses and Abuses of Textualism and Originalism," 537. See also Levy, *Establishment Clause*, 95.

63. *Annals of Congress*, 1st Cong., 1st sess., 757.

both.[64] Perhaps he thought that without the inclusion of the word "national" the text could be applied against the state governments and construed to interfere with their existing church-state arrangements.[65]

After a stylistic comment from John Vining, Elbridge Gerry spoke. An Anti-Federalist from Massachusetts, Gerry suggested that the text "would read better if it was no religious doctrine shall be established by law."[66] The New England states' systems of taxpayer funding of religion did not include specific doctrinal requirements, so if Gerry's language was applied against them it would have left those state arrangements unaffected. Gerry also might have thought that a prohibition against establishing religious doctrine would eliminate possible questions about the impropriety of taxpayer funding of religion—that is, he may have thought that a prohibition against establishing religious doctrines implicitly allowed taxpayer funding of religion. Or perhaps Gerry thought the establishment of religious doctrine itself was a substantive evil that deserved explicit textual prohibition. It ought to be recalled that the 1778 South Carolina Constitution officially established the Christian Protestant religion and prescribed five specific doctrinal tenets for any church that sought to be legally incorporated within the state. Gerry might have associated baneful religious establishments with state regulation of religious doctrine and sought, accordingly, to ensure that that would not occur under the new national constitution.[67]

Roger Sherman, from Connecticut, took a different tack. Speaking next, he repeated the argument he had made in June, that he "thought the amendment altogether unnecessary, inasmuch as Congress had no authority whatever delegated to them by the constitution to make religious establishments."[68] Speaking directly after and in response to Sherman, Daniel Carroll from

64. Marc M. Arkin, "Regionalism and the Religion Clauses: The Contribution of Fisher Ames," *Buffalo Law Review* 47 (1999): 787.

65. Cf. Malbin, *Religion and Politics*, 6–7; Derek Davis, *Original Intent: Chief Justice Rehnquist and the Course of American Church/State Relations* (Buffalo: Prometheus Books, 1991), 57; Hutson, *Church and State in America*, 156; Drakeman, *Church, State, and Original Intent*, 205; Esbeck, "Uses and Abuses of Textualism and Originalism," 539; West, *Free Exercise of Religion in America*, 264.

66. *Annals of Congress*, 1st Cong., 1st sess., 757.

67. See Thomas J. Curry, *The First Freedoms: Church and State in America to the Passage of the First Amendment* (New York: Oxford University Press, 1986), 133, 202. I discuss South Carolina's 1778 religious establishment in chapter 7.

68. *Annals of Congress*, 1st Cong., 1st sess., 757. For a thorough treatment of Roger Sherman's contribution to the Constitution, including what would become the Bill of Rights, see Hall, *Roger Sherman and the Creation of the American Republic*.

Maryland argued that some statement protecting the rights of conscience should be adopted because "many sects have concurred in opinion that they [the rights of conscience] are not well secured under the present constitution." Carroll said he was not concerned about the "phraseology" of an amendment, but rather that his "object" was to secure one that would "satisfy the wishes of the honest part of the community."[69] It seems that for Carroll, as was likely true for most of the Federalist members of the First Congress, it was more important to get an amendment drafted than to draft a precise amendment.

Madison is recorded as having spoken after Carroll. His response, which applied to all three concerns articulated, is recorded as follows:

> He apprehended the meaning of the words to be, that Congress should not establish a religion, and enforce the legal observation of it by law, nor compel men to worship God in any manner contrary to their conscience. Whether the words are necessary or not, he did not mean to say, but they had been required by some of the State Conventions, who seemed to entertain an opinion that under the clause of the constitution, which gave power to Congress to make all laws necessary and proper to carry into execution the constitution, and the laws under it, enabled them to make laws of such a nature as might infringe the rights of conscience and establish a religion.[70]

By using the word "Congress" and drawing attention to the Necessary and Proper Clause, Madison seems to have sought to remind his colleagues that the proposed amendment was designed only to recognize limitations on the national government, not the states, and that it therefore would not affect state church-state arrangements. He clarified the subject matter ("Congress should not establish a religion, and enforce the legal observation of it by law"), thereby reassuring Sylvester (and perhaps Gerry) that the text did not mean that religious societies were prohibited from obtaining standing in the law.[71] Madison all but conceded Sherman's point that,

69. *Annals of Congress*, 1st Cong., 1st sess., 757–58.

70. *Annals of Congress*, 1st Cong., 1st sess., 758.

71. Malbin, *Religion and Politics*, 8, contends that Madison's use of "*a* religion" and "*a* national religion" reveals that Madison intended only to prohibit nonpreferential aid to religion. For Douglas Laycock's response (which was used by Justice David Souter in *Lee v. Weisman*, 505 U.S. 507 (1992) at 614–16), see Douglas Laycock, "'Nonpreferential' Aid to Religion: A False Claim about Original Intent," *William and Mary Law Review* 27 (1986): 881–82. These scholars, I believe, overstate the importance of "*a* religion" and "*a* national religion," and

strictly speaking, the amendment was unnecessary. But echoing Carroll's statement, he reminded his Federalist colleagues that amendments had been demanded, and promised, in the deal for ratification.

Benjamin Huntington from Connecticut was not satisfied with Madison's response. He is recorded as responding as follows:

> Mr. HUNTINGTON said that he feared, with the gentleman first up on this subject [Sylvester], that the words might be taken in such latitude as to be extremely hurtful to the cause of religion. He understood the amendment to mean what had been expressed by the gentleman from Virginia [Madison]; but others might find it convenient to put another construction on it. The ministers of their congregations to the eastward were maintained by contributions of those who belong to their society; the expense of building meeting-houses was contributed in the same manner. These things were regulated by by-laws. If an action was brought before a federal court on any of these cases, the person who had neglected to perform his engagements could not be compelled to do it; for a support of ministers, or buildings of places of worship might be construed into a religious establishment.
>
> By the charter of Rhode Island, no religion could be established by law; he could give a history of the effects of such a regulation; indeed the people were now enjoying the blessed fruits of it. He hoped, therefore, the amendment would be made in such a way as to secure the rights of conscience, and the free exercise of religion, but not to patronize those who professed no religion at all.[72]

Congress at the time sat in New York, so Huntington's reference to "congregations to the eastward" likely referred to his home state of Connecticut. Like many of the New England states (but not Rhode Island), Connecticut taxed its residents to support Protestant ministers and houses of worship. As discussed in chapter 4, "ecclesiastical societies" were geographically defined in state law, and citizens in each locality elected the Protestant ministry to be supported. Taxes were then collected for minister salaries and to support church construction and maintenance. After

---

incorrectly assume that the House's deliberations at this point focused on preferential versus nonpreferential aid to religion.

72. *Annals of Congress*, 1st Cong., 1st sess., 758. According to Marc M. Arkin, the term "contribution" was frequently used to describe compulsory taxes for the support of religion. Arkin, "Regionalism and the Religion Clauses," 788n94, citing M. Louise Greene, *Development of Religious Liberty in Connecticut* (Cambridge, MA: Riverside Press, 1905), 372.

Connecticut's legal reform of 1784, dissenting Protestants could obtain an exemption from the religious assessment upon demonstration of their attendance and support of their own sect; no such exemptions, however, were available to those who did not attend or belong to a church. Religious freedom in Connecticut did not mean freedom from religious tax assessments.

Huntington appears to have been concerned that the committee's language—"no religion shall be established by law, nor shall the equal rights of conscience be infringed"—might lead federal courts to find Connecticut's systems of tax support of religion unconstitutional. Again, because the committee had dropped the word "national," the text under consideration did not specify which level of government it applied against. The text conceivably could have been taken to apply against the states, perhaps in light of the Supremacy Clause.[73] Huntington made clear that he thought it would be a misinterpretation of the text and of Madison's intent if his state's system were found to be an unconstitutional religious establishment. Why exactly Huntington thought this would be a misinterpretation is ambiguous. It might have been because he believed Madison's text only restricted the national government and, therefore, applying it against Connecticut would have been erroneous. Alternatively, it might have been because Huntington believed Connecticut's system of support of religious ministers and places of worship did not constitute an establishment. Whatever is the case, Huntington feared that the proposed language might be misconstrued and applied against the states. He therefore wanted it changed.[74]

73. Philip B. Kurland, "The Irrelevance of the Constitution: The Religion Clauses of the First Amendment and the Supreme Court," *Villanova Law Review* 24 (1978–79): 8; Esbeck, "Uses and Abuses of Textualism and Originalism," 543–45; Kurt T. Lash, "The Second Adoption of the Establishment Clause: The Rise of the Nonestablishment Principle," *Arizona State Law Journal* 27 (1995): 1090–91.

74. I believe Noah Feldman somewhat mischaracterizes the Madison-Huntington exchange in *Divided by God: America's Church-State Problem—and What We Should Do about It* (New York: Farrar, Straus and Giroux, 2005). Feldman contends that, "in principle, all [the Framers] condemned use of coercive taxes to support religious institutions with which the taxpayer might disagree" (p. 41), and that "the advocates of a constitutional ban on establishment were concerned about paying taxes to support religious purposes that their conscience told them not to support" (p. 48). Feldman further claims that the Framers intended to ban nonpreferential aid to religion in their prohibition against establishments. As evidence for this last point, he cites the Huntington-Madison exchange: "This exchange between Madison and the New Englander Huntington shows definitively that, despite what is sometimes claimed, the Framers understood perfectly well that nonpreferential support for religion could and probably would be understood as an establishment of religion" (p. 48).

Madison's response to Huntington is recorded as follows:

Mr. MADISON thought, if the word "National" was inserted before religion, it
would satisfy the minds of honorable gentlemen. He believed that the people

---

Feldman is correct to say that Huntington feared that the language under consideration—
"no religion shall be established by law"—might be interpreted to prohibit the New England
practice of taxing citizens to support religion. But Huntington's comments indicate that he
thought that this would be a *misinterpretation* of the proposed text and Madison's intentions
that animated it. In order to prevent such a *misinterpretation*—that is, in order to protect the
states from the exact interpretation suggested by Feldman—Huntington wanted the language
changed. Feldman's contention that the Huntington-Madison exchange indicates that the
Framers understood the Establishment Clause to ban all taxpayer support of religion distorts
Huntington's position and the nature of his exchange with Madison. To repeat, Huntington
wanted the language under consideration changed (as it subsequently was) in order to prevent the exact misinterpretation made by Feldman.

Feldman also fails to consider how Livermore's subsequent proposal sought to address
Huntington's concern. Feldman recognizes that "it is absolutely correct" to say that the First
Amendment "was drafted so that it would not apply to the states when it was enacted." Yet
he contends, "But that does not mean that the Establishment Clause (as it is now called)
of the Constitution was actually intended to protect state establishments of religion from
congressional interference. . . ." Feldman continues, "The framers would never have imagined
that *Congress* would possess power to change state arrangements with respect to religion"
(pp. 48–49). But Huntington, as we have just discussed, articulated this exact fear at least with
respect to the federal judiciary—that the language that would become the Establishment
Clause might be misinterpreted to allow the federal courts to obstruct state church-state arrangements. While it is true that the Federalists who dominated the First Congress denied
that Congress possessed power to interfere with state establishments, it is not true that federal
interference with state establishments was beyond the Framers' imagination. As discussed
above, this was also a concern articulated by Anti-Federalists such as "Agrippa."

Feldman's claim that, "in principle, all [the Framers] condemned use of coercive taxes to
support religious institutions with which the taxpayer might disagree" (p. 41), is also not cor-
rect, for reasons discussed in chapter 4. For a similar criticism of the accuracy of Feldman's
history, see Steven D. Smith, "The Jurisdictional Establishment Clause: A Reappraisal," *Notre
Dame Law Review* 81 (2006): 1867. See also Steven D. Smith, "Taxes, Conscience, and the
Constitution," *Constitutional Commentary* 23 (2006): 374–75; Hutson, *Church and State in
America*, 156–57. For a competing interpretation of Huntington's intentions, see Ellis M. West,
The Religion Clauses of the First Amendment: Guarantees of States Rights? (Lanham, MD:
Lexington Books, 2011), 93–96.

Carl Esbeck, "Uses and Abuses of Textualism and Originalism," 545, offers an interpretation of Huntington's comments different from my own. Esbeck agrees that Huntington was
concerned that the text under consideration would be interpreted to hinder Connecticut's
church-state arrangement. But Esbeck then concludes that Huntington "was confused," because Huntington did not understand that the proposed amendments would only apply
against the national government. Huntington's remarks, however, do not suggest that he was
confused; rather, they suggest that he understood that Madison intended the text under consideration to apply only to the national government, but also that he believed Madison's text
was insufficiently clear on this point. Because the text was liable to be *misconstrued* to apply
against the states, Huntington wanted it changed.

feared one sect might obtain a pre-eminence, or two combine together, and establish a religion, to which they would compel others to conform. He thought if the word "National" was introduced, it would point the amendment directly to the object it was intended to prevent.[75]

It appears that Madison understood Huntington to be concerned that the text under consideration might be applied against the states. By reintroducing "National"—the word had been in his original proposal—the amendment more clearly would be understood to apply to the national government alone and, thereby, unlikely to be applied against state church-state arrangements.[76]

The House as a whole appears to have taken Sylvester's and Huntington's concerns seriously and acted to alleviate them.[77] New Hampshire's Samuel Livermore, the first speaker recorded after the Huntington-Madison exchange, immediately moved that text nearly identical to his state's proposal be adopted. It will be recalled that New Hampshire's proposed amendment was more obviously federal than most of the other proposed amendments. Livermore's statement in full is recorded as follows:

Mr. LIVERMORE (N.H.) was not satisfied with the amendment; but he did not wish them to dwell long on the subject. He thought it would be better if it were

75. *Annals of Congress*, 1st Cong., 1st sess., 758–59. The meaning of Madison's statement that "he [Madison] believed that the people feared one sect might obtain a pre-eminence, or two combine together, and establish a religion, to which they would compel others to conform" is not without ambiguity. Madison's argument may have been that by reaffirming federalism, the national government would (still) lack power to make an establishment and, therefore, that individuals would not have to fear religious coercion by one or two sects if they gained significant national political power. Given that Madison was responding to Huntington and given his focus on the word "National," this interpretation seems more than plausible. Alternatively, Madison might have been proposing what Steven Green calls a "substantive interpretation of nonestablishment." In Green's view, Madison was not primarily concerned with federalism, but rather sought to prevent dominance by any one sect or a union of sects at the national level. Whichever is more accurate, both interpretations understand Madison's statement to reveal that he viewed the amendment as indicating that the national government lacked authority to establish a religion. By reinserting the word "National," Madison seems to have been seeking to appease Huntington's fear that the amendment would be misinterpreted and applied against state church-state arrangements. Scholars who address Madison's comments include Steven K. Green, "Federalism and the Establishment Clause," 790; Esbeck, "Uses and Abuses of Textualism and Originalism," 545; West, *The Religion Clauses of the First Amendment*, 96.

76. Cf. Feldman, *Divided by God*, 48.

77. Cf. West, *The Religion Clauses of the First Amendment*, 96.

altered, and made to read in this manner, that Congress shall make no laws touching religion, or infringing the rights of conscience.[78]

Livermore may have thought that because it began with the word "Congress," New Hampshire's proposed language more clearly acknowledged Congress's lack of power over religion than did the alternative phrase "no religion shall be established by law." Starting with "Congress" also would erase the fear that the amendment could be misinterpreted and applied against the states, which, to repeat, appears to have been Sylvester's—and, it seems, Huntington's—primary concern.[79] The tone of Livermore's prefatory comments—not wanting to "dwell long on the subject"—suggests that Livermore, like most of his Federalists colleagues in the First Congress, did not think such language was actually needed to restrict Congress's power, because Congress lacked authority over religion in the first place.[80]

After an Anti-Federalist rant by Elbridge Gerry,[81] New Hampshire's text was adopted. The August 15 change was as follows (added words in italics):

no religion shall be established by law, nor shall the equal rights of conscience be infringed

78. *Annals of Congress*, 1st Cong., 1st sess., 759. New Hampshire had proposed, "Congress shall make no laws touching religion, or to infringe the rights of conscience." Livermore replaced "to infringe" with "infringing."

79. Esbeck, "The Uses and Abuses of Textualism and Originalism," 547, 568, contends that, though Livermore's text "had the consequence of preventing Congress from enacting legislation to overturn state laws on religion," this was not his intention nor was such an intention "even remarked by anyone." Esbeck, I believe, misreads the exchange between Sylvester, Huntington, and Madison, and thus fails to comprehend how Livermore's proposed text specifically reflects the concerns and intentions that had just been articulated.

Drakeman, *Church, State, and Original Intent*, 234, contends that "we have no idea what Samuel Livermore or, more broadly, the New Hampshire ratifying convention, sought to achieve with the 'no touching' proposal." See also Philip Hamburger, *Separation of Church and State* (Cambridge, MA: Harvard University Press, 2002), 101–2.

80. It is not surprising that Livermore did not wish to dwell on the subject of amendments any longer, as he had spoken out against Madison's original motion on June 8 to consider amendments at that time. See *Annals of Congress*, 1st Cong., 1st sess., 464–65. For a somewhat different interpretation of Livermore's proposal, see Drakeman, *Church, State, and Original Intent*, 207. See also Laycock, "'Nonpreferential' Aid to Religion," 887.

81. Malbin, *Religion and Politics*, 10, suggests that Gerry opposed Madison's use of the word "national" because it implied that the Constitution created one nation instead of a union of states, and that Gerry did not want a word with such symbolic importance in the Constitution.

Congress shall make no laws touching religion, or infringing the rights of conscience[82]

The nature of Livermore's proposal and the meaning of the House's action at this point have been misunderstood, so it is worth emphasizing how the House of Representatives most likely understood what it had just done. According to Justice Souter in *Lee v. Weisman* (1992),

> Livermore's proposal would have forbidden laws having anything to do with religion and was thus not only far broader than Madison's version, but broader even than the scope of the Establishment Clause as we now understand it.[83]

Souter's statement is true, but misleading. It is true insofar as Livermore's text categorically limited Congress's power over religion ("no laws touching"). But it is misleading insofar as it fails to acknowledge that Livermore's proposal was introduced within the context of the House's concern with drafting a text *that would not be applied against the states*, whereas Souter presumes an incorporated Establishment Clause. Livermore's text would not have required a broad separation between church and state at every level of government; it left undisturbed state governmental authority to aid religion in the manner and to the extent that the states thought most consistent with their own constitutions. At the time, New Hampshire's Bill of Rights explicitly authorized state officials to support and maintain "public protestant teachers of piety, religion and morality," because "morality and piety, rightly grounded on evangelical principles, will give the best and greatest security to government."[84] For the New England states, whose delegates drove the House debates on August 15, Livermore's text would help keep their systems of taxpayer support of religion free from federal interference. Livermore's proposal was *not*, in fact, "broader . . . than the scope of the Establishment Clause as we [the Supreme Court in 1992] now understand it." Livermore's text would have left compelled religious taxation at the state level untouched, and constitutionally unproblematic.

82. *Annals of Congress*, 1st Cong., 1st sess., 759.
83. *Lee v. Weisman*, 505 U.S. 577, 612–13 (1992).
84. New Hampshire Constitution of 1784, Article 6, in *The Federal and State Constitutions, Colonial Charters, and Other Organic Laws of the United States*, 2nd edition, ed. Ben Perley Poore, (Washington: Government Printing Office, 1878), 2:1281.

Final Substantive Revisions in the House

After the House adopted New Hampshire's text on August 15, no substantive discussion is found in the House records regarding the language that would become the Establishment Clause. On August 19, the House decided to place amendments at the end of the Constitution, instead of interspersing them within the existing text.[85] On August 20, the House agreed to the following alterations in response to a motion by Fisher Ames of Massachusetts:

> Congress shall make no laws ~~touching~~ *establishing* religion, or *to prevent the free exercise thereof,* or ~~infringing~~ *to infringe* the rights of conscience.[86]

The extant record does not reveal with clarity why the House replaced "laws touching" with "law establishing." The substance of the House's deliberations between August 15 and August 20, however, suggests a possible explanation. On August 17, the House debated the following text, which would eventually become the Second Amendment:

> A well regulated militia, composed of the body of the people, being the best security of a free state, the right of the people to keep and bear arms shall not be infringed; but no person religiously scrupulous shall be compelled to bear arms.[87]

As we shall discuss in the next chapter, various House members argued for and against the exemption for persons religiously scrupulous of militia service. Those favoring exemptions may have feared that the text that had been adopted on August 15 would hinder subsequent Congressional efforts to legislate religion-based exemptions from generally applicable laws. Moreover, those opposed to a constitutional right to religious exemptions from militia service had argued that such exemptions could and should be granted by the legislature. If Congress could "make no laws touching religion," then it might have lacked the authority to grant religious exemptions from generally applicable laws.[88] Whether the House

85. *Annals of Congress*, 1st Cong., 1st sess., 796.
86. *Annals of Congress*, 1st Cong., 1st sess., 796.
87. *Annals of Congress*, 1st Cong., 1st sess., 778.
88. Presumably, Congress would have had the implied power to exempt religious objectors from military service under its delegated power to raise and support armed forces.

became cognizant of this is a matter of speculation. But given that Congress debated this exact issue between its change from "Congress shall make no laws touching religion" to "Congress shall make no law establishing religion," it seems plausible that some members of Congress became aware that "no laws touching religion" would have imposed a new substantive restriction on congressional power—a restriction that would have limited Congress's ability to adopt laws touching religion, such as religious-based exemptions from military service.[89]

This reasoning is also supported by what we know about Fisher Ames, the congressman who proposed the August 20 text. According to Marc A. Arkin, author of the most complete account of Ames's contribution to the development of the First Amendment, Ames was an "ultra-Federalist" whose primary goal was to ensure that amendments did not weaken the national government.[90] Ames may have seen the change from "no laws touching" to "no law establishing" as necessary to retain the federal government's extant power over religion.[91]

Some scholars have contended that Ames's language ("no law establishing") was not really different in substance from Livermore's ("no laws

89. Cf. Kurt T. Lash, "Power and the Subject of Religion," *Ohio State Law Journal* 59 (1998): 1090n81. Lash contends that "there is no evidence that the adoption or rejection of any draft was motivated by a desire to retain some degree of federal power, and the historical context in which the drafts were considered makes such a proposition extremely unlikely." Lash, I believe, fails to adequately consider the House debates on August 17 and how they likely made the House aware of the propriety of retaining some degree of federal power to make laws touching religion.

90. Arkin, "Regionalism and the Religion Clauses," 767, 779.

91. The August 20 modification does not mean that the House dropped its concern about the amendment being misinterpreted and applied against the states. The House retained the phrasing, "Congress shall make no . . . ," which was originally employed to allay the concerns of Sylvester and Huntington. Unlike the select committee's proposal, "No religion shall be established," which conceivably could have been (mistakenly) applied against the states, the use of the word "Congress" removed the states from the amendment's reach. Again, what we know about Fisher Ames is likely revealing. Ames was also an ardent supporter of New England's system of tax support for religion and a critic of Madison's efforts to end such support in Virginia. He thought that tax support for "learned clergy" in every "small district" lay at the heart of New England's stable social order and successful culture. Given Ames's views about the propriety of tax support for religion and its essential role in the maintenance of New England's culture and social happiness, it is improbable that he was any less concerned than Livermore with protecting states from national interference in church-state matters. See Fisher Ames, "Phocion VII," (originally published in 1801) in *Works of Fisher Ames*, ed. W. B. Allen (Indianapolis, IN: Liberty Classics, 1983), 1:296. For Arkin's discussion of this point, see "Regionalism and the Religion Clauses," 791. For a different interpretation of this point in the House record, see West, *Religion Clauses of the First Amendment*, 99–103.

touching"). The historian Thomas Curry writes that "Ames's proposal did not differ in substance from what Madison wanted or from Livermore's previously accepted one," because the deliberations in Congress were "a discussion about how to state the common agreement that the new government had no authority whatsoever in religious matters."[92] The truth may be, as Steven Smith hypothesizes, that the Framers never focused on the difference between "no laws touching religion" and "no law establishing religion."[93] Or perhaps, as James Hutson suggests, Madison may have known that the Anti-Federalists would not be satisfied with a short general statement, and therefore knew it was important to be more specific and to include the term "establishment."[94] But, given that the House had just discussed legislative exemptions for conscientious objection to militia service, it is reasonable to infer that the House intentionally decided not to adopt a categorical ban on laws touching religion.[95] Even though the

92. Curry, *First Freedoms*, 214–15. Gerard Bradley, *Church-State Relationships*, 92, suggests that the two texts were "indistinguishable," in part because "in passing Ames's proposal instead of Livermore's without extended debate, the motivation of Livermore's proposal to leave state regimes undisturbed no doubt underlay the Ames language." While Bradley is likely right that the texts are similar relative to the Framers' motivations for leaving the states undisturbed, it does not follow that the texts are indistinguishable.

93. Smith, "The Jurisdictional Establishment Clause," 1862.

94. James Hutson, *Church and State in America*, 159. Leonard W. Levy, *Establishment Clause*, 101–2, makes the same claim, stating, "Apparently the House believed that the draft of the clause based on Livermore's motion might not satisfy the demand of those who wanted something said specifically against establishments of religion." Neither Hutson nor Levy provide any evidence to document this claim.

95. Regarding the House's change in language from "no laws touching religion" to "no laws establishing religion," Steven Smith, "Jurisdictional Establishment Clause," 1854, writes:

We might expect that the shift to what seems a much narrower version must have been the result of considerable debate, and that it should have provoked much disagreement. But in fact there is no evidence of such debate or disagreement, and no indication that anyone in Congress cared much about the change. For that matter, there was virtually no debate before the approval of Livermore's apparently far-reaching measure; even in offering it Livermore emphasized that it probably had the same meaning as other versions and that "he did not wish them to dwell long on the subject."

So, what should we make of this complacency? My suggestion is that this aspect of the legislative history, which might seem deeply puzzling or distressing, becomes quite understandable once we recognize that the Framers did not see themselves as doing the sort of thing we suppose they did or should have done—that is, as formulating for adoption into the Constitution some particular right or principle of religious freedom. That task would indeed have required more deliberation and debate, and it almost certainly would have provoked much greater controversy (as it did when it came up on the state level). But if the Framers saw themselves as merely putting into writing a jurisdictional allocation on which virtually everyone agreed anyway (and that was

Federalists had argued during the ratification debates that the new national government possessed no authority over religion, some members of the First Congress may have realized that this was not completely true.[96] As Carl Esbeck remarks, the broad scope of Livermore's "no laws touching religion" "surely would have caused someone in the House to think about congressional legislation's consequential effects on religion, not just about ultra vires actions clearly outside of Congress's enumerated powers." Esbeck continues:

> No one can say for certain, but likely the House had come to realize over the last five days [from August 15 to August 20] that the scope of the amendment's restraint needed to be narrowed lest countless and unavoidable effects of general legislation unintentionally impacting religion were to be within the negation of congressional power."[97]

In the end, it may not matter whether or not some members of the House concluded that Livermore's language was too broad. Regardless of the reasons, the House replaced "no laws touching" with "no law establishing religion," and the two texts clearly have different meanings. The alterations — "laws" to "law" and "touching" to "establishing" — significantly changed the prohibition. The adopted text prohibits one specific type of legislation (that which establishes religion) and it uses the singular "law," presumably because a religious establishment could be made with a law. The rejected text, by contrast, would have imposed an across-the-board prohibition that potentially reached every field of Congress's lawmaking power — hence, the use of the plural "laws." Even if, as some scholars have suggested, the House of Representatives intended or expected "no law establishing

---

already implicit, most of them believed, in the original Constitution), then it is understandable that they did not see the need to waste words or thought on the measure.

Even if what Smith says is true, more needs to be said. Even if Congress understood itself only to be reaffirming a preexisting jurisdictional line, it had good reason to be careful not to draw that line in a way that unnecessarily or accidentally circumscribed its own power. Moreover, the fact that the text was altered suggests, at minimum, that at least a majority of the House thought it was sufficiently important to make the change. Cf. Steven D. Smith, *Foreordained Failure: The Quest for a Constitutional Principle of Religious Freedom* (New York: Oxford University Press, 1995), 31.

96. Bradley, *Church-State Relationships in America*, 96. Hamburger, *Separation of Church and State*, 101–7.
97. Esbeck, "Uses and Abuses of Textualism and Originalism," 547, 552.

religion" to have the same meaning as "no laws touching religion," the adopted text is not as broad as the text it replaced.[98]

One further alteration was made before the House sent its adopted language to the Senate. The *Journal of the House of Representatives* records that the following changes were made on August 21 to the text adopted the previous day:

> Congress shall make no law establishing religion, or *prohibiting* ~~to prevent~~ the free exercise thereof, ~~or to infringe~~ *nor shall* the rights of €onscience *be infringed*.[99]

The reasons for the changes, including the change from "to prevent" to "prohibiting," are unclear. Possibilities include an unrecorded amendment or mistranscriptions in either the *Annals* or the final copy of the engrossed bill.[100] On August 24, the House sent the following to the Senate:

> Congress shall make no law establishing religion, or prohibiting the free exercise thereof, nor shall the rights of conscience be infringed.[101]

The House Proceedings in Summary

Before proceeding to the Senate's drafting records, we can pause to summarize the House debate and what it appears to reveal. The House, which was dominated by Federalists, took up amendments not because its members believed the Constitution was deficient or because they sought to articulate the "true" principles of religious liberty and church-state separation, but rather because ratification politics necessitated doing so. Anti-Federalists had expressed concerns that the new national government insufficiently protected essential personal rights, including the right to religious liberty, and, relatedly, that the new national government might erect a religious establishment. Madison's original proposal included lan-

---

98. Philip Hamburger, "Separation and Interpretation," *Journal of Law and Politics* 18 (2002): 56–59, reaches a similar conclusion through textual analysis alone.

99. Journal of the House of Representatives, August 21, 1789, in *The Documentary History of the First Federal Congress of the United States of America, 1789–1791*, ed. Linda Grant De Pauw (Baltimore: Johns Hopkins University Press, 1972), 3:159.

100. Michael W. McConnell, "The Origins and Historical Understanding of Free Exercise of Religion," *Harvard Law Review* 103 (1990): 1483.

101. Senate Journal, 1st Cong., 1st Sess., August 25, 1789, 63. On August 25, the Senate read the August 24 House resolution proposing articles of amendment to the Constitution.

guage that protected "the full and equal rights of conscience," which would become the Free Exercise Clause; language pertaining to religious establishment — "nor shall any national religion be established" — which would become the Establishment Clause; a provision prohibiting deprivation of civil rights on account of religion, which the House dropped; and a freedom of conscience provision intended to apply against the states. When the full House finally discussed a modified version of Madison's original proposal, the debate was driven primarily by New England congressmen, not by Madison himself. These congressmen were concerned that the text, intended to apply only to the national government, might be misconstrued to interfere with state-level arrangements. Specifically, concerns articulated by Connecticut Congressman Benjamin Huntington (who elaborated a point initially made by Peter Sylvester of New York) appear to have led Samuel Livermore of New Hampshire to introduce the following language from his state's proposed amendment: "Congress shall make no laws touching religion. . . ." "No laws touching religion" would have excluded Congress from the whole subject of religion, thereby affirming the national government's absence of power and leaving to the states exclusive jurisdiction over the subject matter of religion. During the ratification debates, some Federalists had argued that this is how the matter stood without an amendment, but, at most, this was only partially true. While no power enumerated in Article 1, Section 8 expressly granted Congress authority over religion as such, Congress could make laws touching religion through the exercise of its other delegated powers.[102] Some members of the House may have become aware that Congressional power could touch religion by legislating religious exemption from military service, for the First Congress addressed this very point in the days before replacing "no laws touching religion" with "no law establishing religion." The House ultimately adopted text that retained the structure of New Hampshire's proposal — beginning with the word "Congress" — yet it retreated from declaring comprehensively that Congress could not pass laws "touching religion." Instead, it declared that "Congress shall make no law establishing religion."

From the account of the drafting record presented above, we can state two conclusions about what the House sought to achieve:

---

102. Esbeck, "Uses and Abuses of Textualism and Originalism," 547, provides the example of congressional power to create federal bankruptcy courts that could discharge the debts of financially distressed churches.

1. The House aimed to adopt text specifying that Congress lacked power to make a religious establishment;
2. The House sought to adopt religious establishment language that would not mistakenly be applied against the states and interfere with state religious taxation policies.

It merits repeating that, in view of the limits of the documentary record, these conclusions are more "likely" than "definite." It is also worth noting that, apparently, at no point during its debates did the House discuss preferential versus nonpreferential aid to religion. Madison effectively tabled that issue in the House by omitting Patrick Henry's nonpreferential language from the beginning. Finally, and perhaps most importantly, at no point did the House identify with any sort of precision what an "establishment" of religion was. Congressman Huntington connected establishments to taxpayer funding of religion, albeit in an effort to shield his own state's system from any possible constitutional impingements. Congressman Gerry sought to link establishment to religious doctrine. Madison's most revealing comment—"He believed that the people feared one sect might obtain a pre-eminence, or two combine together, and establish a religion, to which they would compel others to conform"—connected establishments to legal compulsion, but without specifying what sort of legal compulsion he sought to prevent.

The Senate

On September 3, 1789, the Senate began considering the text adopted by the House. No record exists of the comments made by individual senators. All we have are the Senate votes on the various textual formulations proposed.[103] Given the paucity of the record, inferences about the Senate's intentions must remain tentative.

103. The journal of William Maclay, one of the first two Senators from Pennsylvania, provides one of the few accounts of the floor activity in the First Senate. Unfortunately, Maclay was ill during the time the Senate discussed what would become the First Amendment, and his diary is without helpful information. For Maclay's entries on the relevant days, see William Maclay, *Journal of William Maclay, United States Senator from Pennsylvania, 1789–1791*, ed. Edgar S. Maclay (New York: D. A. Appleton, 1890). For a discussion of the church-state views of several of the men in the First Senate, see Bradley, *Church-State Relationships in America*, 89–90.

On September 3, the Senate considered but rejected the following three alterations (proposed additions in italics):

Congress shall make no law establishing ~~religion~~ *one religious sect or society in preference to others*, or prohibiting the free exercise thereof, nor shall the rights of conscience be infringed

Congress shall ~~make no law establishing religion, or prohibiting the free exercise thereof, nor shall the rights of conscience be infringed~~ *not make any law, infringing the rights of conscience or establishing any religious sect or society*

Congress shall make no law establishing ~~religion~~ *any particular denomination of religion in preference to another*, or prohibiting the free exercise thereof, nor shall the rights of conscience be infringed

The Senate also rejected a motion to strike out the amendment in its entirety. In the last pertinent vote on September 3, the Senate adopted the House's text, minus the last clause:

Congress shall make no law establishing religion, or prohibiting the free exercise thereof, ~~nor shall the rights of conscience be infringed~~[104]

Six days later, the Senate revisited the subject, making the following changes:

Congress shall make no law establishing ~~religion~~ *articles of faith, or a mode of worship*, or prohibiting the free exercise ~~thereof~~ *of religion*[105]

It sent this language back to the House.

It appears that the Senate engaged in substantive deliberations about how to limit Congress's power. At least two of the rejected proposals ("no law establishing one religious sect or society" and "no law establishing any particular denomination of religion in preference to another") were similar to Patrick Henry's proposed nonpreferential amendment ("no particular religious sect or society ought to be favored or established, by law, in preference to others"), which suggests that the Senate considered

104. Senate Journal. 1st Cong., 1st sess., September 3, 1789, 70.
105. Senate Journal. 1st Cong., 1st sess., September 9, 1789, 77.

nonpreferentialism in a way the House did not.[106] Why the Senate rejected the nonpreferential formulations, however, is not clear. Perhaps principled objections to government-sponsored nonpreferential aid to religion were made. Alternatively, the Senate may have thought it improper for Congress to aid religion because of the states' authority over the subject matter. That the Senate considered rejecting the amendment entirely may indicate that some senators adopted the Federalist view that an amendment was unnecessary because the national government lacked jurisdiction over religion.

It is unclear how best to understand the text the Senate adopted on September 9—"Congress shall make no law establishing articles of faith or a mode of worship. . . ." Perhaps the Senate sought to avoid the question of financial support to religion, given that it was divisive in at least two different ways—whether such aid should be given and, if so, by what level of government. Alternatively, the textual move to "articles of faith" might have been advanced for the same reasons Elbridge Gerry proposed "no religious doctrine shall be established by law" in the House on August 15: no one favored the national government establishing articles of faith. Perhaps the Senate sought to prevent only this type of doctrinal establishment. All of these inferences are speculative.

The Senate also rejected the proposed amendment that would have been applied against the states. The record gives no indication as to why.[107]

---

106. Describing the composition of the Senate, Madison biographer Irving Brant, in *James Madison: Father of the Constitution* (New York: Bobbs-Merrill, 1950), 271, says Senator Richard Henry Lee of Virginia was "leagued" with New England supporters of established churches. Lee had supported Patrick Henry's 1784 general assessment proposal in Virginia. Brant suggests that Lee and the New England senators favored an amendment that would have allowed the national government to extend financial aid to religion. Lee's own description of his efforts in the Senate concerning amendments does not confirm Brant's speculations. See the letter from Richard Henry Lee and William Grayson to the Honorable Speaker of the House of Delegates, Virginia (September 28, 1789) in Richard H. Lee, *Memoir of the Life of Richard Henry Lee* (Philadelphia: Carey and Lea, 1825), 2:99–100.

107. Esbeck, "Uses and Abuses of Textualism and Originalism," 558, is probably correct in reasoning that "the probable rationale is that the Senate did not want . . . to disturb the varied state arrangements with respect to even the matter of liberty of conscience, a question on which there was some agreement among Americans at the time."

On August 17, when the House briefly debated Madison's provision that applied against the states, Thomas Tucker from South Carolina spoke against it on federalism grounds, stating:

This is offered, I presume, as an amendment to the Constitution of the United States, but it goes only to the alteration of the constitutions of particular States. It will be much better, I apprehend, to leave the State Governments to themselves, and not to

The House-Senate Conference Committee

When the House received the Senate's version, it called for a conference committee to resolve the differences between the two texts. The six-member committee consisted of Congressmen Madison (Virginia), Sherman (Connecticut), and Vining (Delaware), and Senators Oliver Ellsworth (Connecticut), William Paterson (New Jersey), and Charles Carroll (Maryland).[108] No record exists of the committee's deliberations. Before they met, the texts read thus:

House text: Congress shall make no law establishing Religion, or prohibiting the free exercise thereof, nor shall the rights of conscience be infringed

Senate text: Congress shall make no law establishing articles of faith or a mode of worship, or prohibiting the free exercise of religion

The committee would adopt the familiar words of our First Amendment:

Adopted text: Congress shall make no law respecting an establishment of religion, or prohibiting the free exercise thereof

---

interfere with them more than we already do; and that is thought by many to be rather too much. I therefore move, sir, to strike out these words.

Madison spoke next. His comments are recorded as follows:

Mr. Madison conceived this to be the most valuable amendment in the whole list. If there was any reason to restrain the Government of the United States from infringing upon these essential rights, it was equally necessary that they should be secured against the State Governments. He thought that if they provided against the one, it was as necessary to provide against the other, and was satisfied that it would be equally grateful to the people.

Annals of Congress, 1st Cong., 1st sess., 755.

108. *Annals of Congress*, 1st Cong., 1st sess., 939; *Senate Journal*. 1st Cong., 1st Sess., September 21, 1789, 84. According to Gerard Bradley, Vining, Paterson, and Carroll were all publicly committed to government aid to religion at some level of government, Sherman was "strictly New England orthodox," and Ellsworth was committed to the public enforcement of the truth of Christianity. See Bradley, *Church-State Relationships in America*, 89, 95. Sherman, it will be recalled, had argued in the House debates that an amendment was unnecessary. For further discussion of the views of the members of the conference committee and a hypothetical reconstruction of its possible deliberations, see Drakeman, *Church, State, and Original Intent*, 236–40. For a discussion of Sherman's church-state views and his participation in the drafting of the Religion Clauses, see Hall, *Roger Sherman and the Creation of the American Republic*, 6–7, 134–45, 152.

The words "respecting an" had not previously been considered in either the House or the Senate. These words also had not appeared in any existing state constitution. The reasons for the insertion of "respecting an" would seem to be particularly revealing of the joint committee's intentions and the original meaning of the adopted text.

Then, as now, the present participle "respecting" meant: "to look at, regard, or consider"; "to heed or pay attention to"; "to regard with deference, esteem, or honor"; to "expect, anticipate, look toward"; "with reference to, [or] with regard to."[109] The most straightforward reading of the final text is that Congress is prohibited from passing laws regarding an establishment—that is, Congress cannot (1) erect any type of religious establishment itself, or (2) make any laws concerning existing or potential (including state-level) establishments. "Respecting an establishment" imposes an explicit substantive limitation on Congress's power—it cannot establish a religion—and recognizes a jurisdictional limitation on Congressional power—it cannot make laws interfering with state establishments.[110]

109. See entries under "respect" and "respecting" in John Andrews, *A Complete Dictionary of the English Language*, 4th ed. (Philadelphia: William Young, 1789); John Ash, *The New and Complete Dictionary of the English Language* (London: E. and C. Dilly, 1775); Samuel Johnson, *A Dictionary of the English Language*, 4th ed. (London: W. Strahan, 1773); William Perry, *The Royal Standard English Dictionary*, 1st Am. ed. (Worcester: n.p., 1788); Thomas Sheridan, *A Complete Dictionary of the English Language*, 5th ed. (Philadelphia: William Young, 1789). All the above are cited in John Witte Jr., *God's Joust, God's Justice: Law and Religion in the Western Tradition* (Grand Rapids, MI: William B. Eerdmans, 2006), 196–97n96. See also *New Shorter Oxford English Dictionary,* 4th ed. (1993), 2:2565.

William C. Porth and Robert P. George, "Trimming the Ivy: A Bicentennial Re-Examination of the Establishment Clause," *West Virginia Law Review* 90 (1987): 136–37, contend:

> The obvious meaning of "respecting an" establishment of religion, then as now, is "regarding," or "having to do with," or "in reference to" such an establishment. And these words are broad enough to cover both a possible national establishment and actual (and potential) state establishments. They call particular attention to the constitutional disentitlement of the federal government to make any law setting up an established church at the federal level or interfering with established churches (and the right of the people to opt to establish churches) at the state level.

110. See Kent Greenawalt, *Religion and the Constitution* (Princeton, NJ: Princeton University Press, 2006), 2:29; Bradley, *Church-State Relationships in America,* 95; Lash, "The Second Adoption of the Establishment Clause," 1091. Cf. Drakeman, *Church, State, and Original Intent,* 210–11, 236–45, suggesting that "respecting an" should be read in the "institutional light" of the First Congress' intention to prohibit the institution of a single national church; and Drakeman, "Which Original Meaning of the Establishment Clause Is the Right One?" in *The Cambridge Companion to the First Amendment and Religious Liberty,* ed. Michael D. Breidenbach and Owen Anderson (New York: Cambridge University Press, 2020), 391, contending that "although the federalism approach is a reasonable candidate for being *an* ob-

Regarding the substantive restriction, "respecting an establishment" would seem to encompass all types of religious establishments—that is, both a "law establishing Religion" (the House's final text) and a "law establishing articles of faith or a mode of worship" (the Senate's final text).[111] "Respecting an" does not specify what an "establishment" is, but it does mean that whatever constitutes "an establishment of religion," Congress cannot erect one through its lawmaking power.

The jurisdictional aspect of "respecting an" is supported by the concerns articulated in the House debates that the text not be liable to a misconstruction that would lead it to restrict state-level church-state policies. A jurisdictional reading is also supported by how the word "respecting" is used elsewhere in the Constitution. Article 4, Section 3 of the Constitution declares, "The Congress shall have Power to dispose of and make all needful Rules and Regulations respecting the Territory or other Property belonging to the United States." This text grants Congress authority (thereby preempting state authority) over a particular jurisdiction—the territories and other property belonging to the United States. The text of the Establishment Clause would seem to do the opposite: to deny Congress jurisdiction (thereby recognizing the authority of the states) over

---

jective meaning of the text, it is unlikely to be *the* objective *public* meaning" (emphasis in original). For a separationist reading of "respecting an," see Laycock, "'Nonpreferential' Aid to Religion," 881. For a helpful account of the "three plausible readings" of "respecting an establishment of religion," see Witte and Nichols, *Religion and the American Constitutional Experiment*, 86–89.

111. Cf. Drakeman, *Church, State, and Original Intent*, 244–45, which contends that "respecting" narrowed the Establishment Clause's reach and focused the prohibition against an institutional church-state arrangement more clearly than either the House's or the Senate's final version. Although Drakeman does not place the same weight or meaning on the addition of the word "respecting" as I do, I agree with his conclusion that

> the federalism interpretation [of the Establishment Clause] is almost certainly the modern approach that most closely tracks the constitutional outcome anticipated by the framers and understood by the public.... States were the locus of church-state interactions, and even the citizens of the New England states that had ecclesiastical taxes expected that even more localized governments—individual cites and towns—would allocate those taxes based on the communities' desires. Freeing those community-based decisions from the complications and competition that would result from a national church was one of the underlying premises of the establishment clause. The clause was designed to ensure that a national church would not be superimposed on whatever other church-state choices might be made by states, cities, and towns.

Drakeman, "Which Original Meaning of the Establishment Clause Is the Right One?" 393.

laws regarding any establishment of religion.[112] Akhil Amar also notes that the beginning of the First Amendment, "Congress shall make no law," precisely tracks and inverts the Necessary and Proper Clause, "Congress shall have power . . . to make all laws which shall be necessary and proper. . . ."[113] By adding the word "respecting" to the phrase "Congress shall make no law," the conference committee appears to have reverse-engineered words already present in the Constitution to make clear that the national government lacked, and the states retained, jurisdiction over religious establishments.[114]

That the conference committee might have sought to more clearly reinforce federalism in church-state matters tracks with the tenor and direction of the House debates. Recall that, in response to criticisms that the text under consideration might interfere with state religious establishments, Samuel Livermore proposed, and the House adopted, New Hampshire's recommended text, "Congress shall make no law touching religion." This language would have removed religion as an object of national legislation and left the states exclusive jurisdiction over it, including over all issues pertaining to establishments. But the House retreated from this categorical ban when it adopted and sent to the Senate the language, "Congress shall make no law establishing religion." This final House text did not protect state authority as comprehensively as "no laws touching religion." The conference committee's "respecting an" filled the gap between the concerns articulated in the House debates and the language the House ultimately sent to the Senate, by adding a jurisdictional component (no interference with the state establishments) to the substantive restriction (no national establishment).[115] "Respecting an establishment" more

112. Kent Greenawalt, "Common Sense about the Original and Subsequent Understandings of the Religion Clauses," *University of Pennsylvania Journal of Constitutional Law* 8 (2006): 484–85.

113. Amar, *Bill of Rights*, 39. Amar also notes that the proposed placement of what would become the First Amendment in Article 1, Section 9, reveals the intention to limit the powers granted in Article I, Section 8.

114. Drakeman offers one of the more thorough and thoughtful accounts of the Establishment Clause's drafting. In *Church, State, and Original Intent*, 236–40, he considers the interpretation I here defend to be "possible" but to lack sufficient affirmative evidence to be "plausible." Also, compare to West, *The Religion Clauses of the First Amendment*, 104–7, who in my opinion fails to consider sufficiently how the word "respecting" was used in Article 4 of the Constitution; and to Noah Feldman, "The Intellectual Origins of the Establishment Clause," *New York University Law Review* 77 (2002): 407.

115. Cf. Esbeck, "Uses and Abuses of Textualism and Originalism," 567–75. Esbeck recognizes that on "a first reading," the addition of "respecting an" seemingly broadens the disempowerment of Congress from laws establishing religion to laws both establishing or disestablishing religion (p. 567). A few pages later, he recognizes: "True, the participle 'respecting'

meant that Congress was prohibited from interfering with laws 'respecting an establishment' of religion at the state level via laws" (p. 570). Yet, despite acknowledging the meaning of the participle "respecting," he finds the addition of "respecting an" to be merely stylistic.

Esbeck and I reach a similar conclusion regarding the Establishment Clause: that it is "jurisdictional" in the sense that it restrains Congress from making its own establishment or interfering with state authority over religious establishments. Nonetheless, we disagree on why the words "respecting an" were added to what became the Establishment Clause. One source of our difference is that Esbeck holds (pp. 555, 571) that Huntington's concern with federalism was satisfied by Livermore's proposal on August 15 and, therefore, that this concern could not have influenced the conference committee's action. But even if Huntington was satisfied by the text the House adopted on August 15 (how satisfied he might have been, we have no way of knowing), it does not mean that he and others might not have been more satisfied with text that more completely met their concerns. Esbeck fails to consider that "respecting an" more precisely addressed Huntington's concern.

As noted, Esbeck contends (pp. 568–69) that the addition of "respecting an" was "a mere stylistic change to the House version." This stylistic interpretation is doubtful for at least four reasons. First, Esbeck bases his interpretation on the assumption that the conference committee edited the text in a specific order—that the conference committee first dropped "rights of conscience." No evidence validates this assumption. Second, Esbeck assumes that the "drafters did not want the focus on 'religion' but on 'establishment.'" This assumption also cannot be verified by the available records. Third, and relatedly, Esbeck contends that the phrase "Congress shall make no law respecting an establishment of religion," emphasizes the "no-establishment" aspect of religious freedom more than the phrase "Congress shall make no law establishing religion." But the reverse is true: "make no law establishing religion" is more vigorously anti-establishmentarian than "make no law respecting an establishment," especially given the contemporaneous meaning of "respecting" and its jurisdictional connotation. Finally, if the conference committee wanted to achieve the end specified by Esbeck—to sharpen the anti-establishment text—they could have simply adopted the text "Congress shall not make a religious establishment. . . ." There was no need for the conference committee to introduce "respecting an" to achieve what Esbeck claims they sought to achieve.

An additional and even more fundamental difficulty with Esbeck's "merely stylistic" interpretation is that the changes made were not merely stylistic. "Congress shall make no law respecting an establishment" has a different meaning than "Congress shall not make a religious establishment."

Also, cf. West, *Free Exercise of Religion in America*, 266–74. West recognizes, correctly in my view, that Huntington thought that the proposed text might harm religion because it "did not explicitly identify the national government as its 'target,'" and therefore "might be used by the federal courts to limit state and local governments." Yet West then concludes, a few pages later, "that not a single member of Congress is recorded as having said anything at that time to indicate that the religion clauses were needed or meant to protect state establishments of religion from federal laws. . . ." Huntington may not have thought that an amendment was needed to protect state establishments, but if an amendment was adopted, Huntington wanted to be sure that it would not interfere with state church-state arrangements. West recognizes Huntington's concern with federalism. But he fails to see how this concern helps shed light on the subsequent addition of "respecting an" to the final version on the Establishment Clause, and he offers no compelling explanation as to why these words were added to the final text. West embraces, instead, the aggressive separationist construction that "'respecting an establishment of religion' was agreed on as a way of prohibiting not just a law establishing one national religion, but any and all laws that are characteristic of such an establishment—that is, laws that discriminate in any way for or against certain religious beliefs, practices, or groups"

precisely reflected the concerns articulated during the House debates than did the House's own adopted text.[116]

Additionally, an intention to more clearly shield state authority from Congressional interference is suggested by the conference committee's changes to the House's final text:

> Congress shall make no law ~~establishing~~ *respecting an establishment of* ~~R~~religion, or prohibiting the free exercise thereof~~, nor shall the rights of conscience be infringed~~

The House's final text included a substantive restriction on Congressional power—"Congress shall make no law establishing Religion"—but it did not so clearly limit Congress's power to interfere with state establishments. The members of the conference committee might have come to appreciate that, under the House's final text, Congress might have authority to regulate or interfere with state church-state arrangements through an artful construction of its implied powers—perhaps the Republican Guarantee Clause, the Commerce Clause, or, as the Anti-Federalists most feared, the Necessary and Proper Clause.[117] It ought to be recalled that in the House on August 15, Madison had cited fears of implied powers under the Necessary and Proper Clause as the reason why a religion amendment was necessary. The addition of "respecting an" more clearly limited Congress's powers vis-à-vis state authority regarding church-state arrangements, and thereby directly addressed a leading Anti-Federalist concern.

Unfortunately, we lack records from the joint House-Senate committee that might directly confirm or refute these inferences. The historical record offers no clear statement about what the conference committee intended by changing "no law establishing" to "no law respecting an establishment." We do know, however, that the committee members modified the text, and it is clear that the plain meaning of the adopted text is more

(p. 273), a construction that echoes Justice Wiley Rutledge in *Everson v. Board of Education*, 330 U.S. 1, 31 (1947).

116. Cf. Drakeman, *Church, State, and Original Intent*, 241–43; Drakeman, "Which Original Meaning of the Establishment Clause is the Right One?" 385–92.

117. Kurt Lash, "Power and the Subject of Religion," 1082, suggests that under its original Commerce Clause power, it was textually plausible that Congress had power to prohibit state religious establishments if those establishments interfered with the free flow of commerce. For citations to Anti-Federalist arguments focusing on the Necessary and Proper Clause, see West, *Free Exercise of Religion in America*, 250n61.

robust than the text it replaced. Whereas the House's text prohibited Congress only from establishing religion (whatever that might mean), the conference committee's text prohibited Congress from establishing religion *and* from making laws with regard to state religious establishments.

What We Know and Do Not Know from the Drafting Record about the Establishment Clause's Original Meaning

The Establishment Clause's Original Meaning Pertains to Federalism, but It Is Not a "Pure Federalism" Provision

The Establishment Clause imposes a substantive limitation on Congressional power that did not exist prior to the adoption of the First Amendment.[118] Article 4, Section 3 of the Constitution grants to Congress "Power to dispose of and make all needful Rules and Regulations respecting the Territory or other Property belonging to the United States." This endows Congress with the same plenary power that a state legislature has over its land,[119] which means that prior to the adoption of the First Amendment, Congress had the power to erect a religious establishment within a federal territory.[120] The Establishment Clause foreclosed this possibility.

No evidence exists to suggest that any member of the First Congress specifically intended the Establishment Clause to limit Congress's power over federally controlled areas such as the territories or the District of Columbia. This absence of evidence leads Akhil Amar to conclude that the Establishment Clause should be understood as a "pure federalism provision." He contends that it originally lacked "bite" regarding Congress's power over the territories, because the text was intended only to restrict the federal government from making laws with regard to state establishment policy.[121] Amar effectively interprets the text as if it reads, "Congress shall make no law respecting the state establishments of religion."[122]

118. See Greenawalt, "Common Sense about the Original and Subsequent Understandings of the Religion Clauses," 486–91.

119. Akhil Reed Amar, *America's Constitution: A Biography* (New York: Random House, 2005), 264. Smith, "The Jurisdictional Establishment Clause," 1859.

120. Article I, Section 8, of the Constitution grants Congress power "to exercise exclusive Legislation in all Cases whatsoever" over the territorial district that houses the national seat of government.

121. Amar, *Bill of Rights*, 45, 246.

122. Amar, *Bill of Rights*, 246.

Even if Amar correctly identifies the intentions and expectations of some of the First Amendment's drafters, his construction does not adequately reflect the adopted text.[123] The actual text prohibits Congress from making laws with regard to state establishments, and from making its own establishment. The latter prohibition restricts Congress's power over the territories, even if that was not part of the drafters' intentions. It may not have occurred to the Framers that the Establishment Clause would restrict Congress's power in the federal territories, but the text does so.[124] Its plain meaning does not lend itself to a "pure federalism" construction akin to the Tenth Amendment.[125]

123. See Witte, *God's Joust, God's Justice*, 197; Frederick Mark Gedicks, "Incorporation of the Establishment Clause Against the States: A Logical, Textual, and Historical Account," *Indiana Law Journal* 88 (2013): 700.

Amar implicitly assumes that the meaning of the text should be limited to the Framers' intentions and how they expected it to be applied. For a thoughtful discussion of both sides of this point, see Smith, "Jurisdictional Establishment Clause," 1859–61. See also Greenawalt, "Common Sense about Original and Subsequent Understandings of the Religion Clauses," 487–91.

124. Esbeck and Den Hartog, *Disestablishment and Religious Dissent*, 9. Amar, in *Bill of Rights*, 247–48, constructs his interpretation in part on the fact that New Hampshire's proposed amendment was not adopted by the First Congress. To recall, that proposal would have prohibited Congress from making laws "touching religion." Such broad language, according to Amar, would have imposed a substantive restriction on the national government. For example, he says that under it, Congress would not have been able to pass proreligion legislation for the federal territories. Amar correctly points out that New Hampshire's proposed text was modified and that Congress did retain some power over religion in the territories. But that does not mean, as he concludes, that the final text was "purely" jurisdictional in the sense of being concerned only with congressional legislation that directly regulated the state establishments. Amar, as noted, seems to elevate how the Framers expected the text to be applied over the plain meaning of the text they adopted.

125. It should be noted that, as Steven Smith has argued, what I have called the Establishment Clause's substantive and jurisdictional components are not wholly distinct. The substantive component can itself be considered a means to protect the authority of the states. To illustrate this point, Smith uses the following example: suppose *Roe v. Wade* was overturned, and then, to preempt Congress from passing either pro-life or pro-choice legislation, a constitutional amendment were adopted that declared, "Abortion being a subject within the proper jurisdiction of the states, Congress shall make no law respecting a right to abortion." The amendment would place a substantive restriction on Congress (that body could make no laws concerning a right to an abortion) in order to maintain a jurisdictional boundary—namely, to keep the question of abortion rights at the state level. Smith suggests the addition of "respecting an" to the Establishment Clause functions similarly. The prohibition on Congress from legislating an establishment leaves the subject matter exclusively to the states. Smith, "Jurisdictional Establishment Clause," 1878–79.

The Original Meaning of the Establishment Clause Limits the Power of the National Government Regarding Religious Establishments, Not Religion in General

The Establishment Clause's limitation on Congress's power does not amount to a blanket prohibition against legislation pertaining to religion. The Establishment Clause does not mean, as some commentators have suggested, that "religion was to be no business of the national government."[126] The House considered but rejected New Hampshire's categorical prohibition of federal laws "touching" the subject of religion. "Respecting an establishment of religion" appears to reflect the intention to recognize Congress's lack of power regarding religious establishments without declaring that Congress lacked authority to pass legislation that in any way touched religion.[127]

The Establishment Clause Imposes Two Constitutional Rules

As I discussed above, constitutional provisions can be classified as rules, standards, or principles. I have concluded that the text of the Establishment Clause contains two constitutional rules:

(A) Congress shall make no law erecting a religious establishment.

(B) Congress shall make no law concerning state-level religious establishments.

In pinpointing why the Establishment Clause's exact text was adopted, one sees that those words convey rules, not standards or principles. "Congress" was adopted to indicate that the amendment applied to the national government, not the states. "Establishment of religion" was adopted in place of "laws touching religion" to narrow the focus of the prohibition, allowing Congress to make laws that might affect or touch religion but that did not establish one—for example, conscientious exemptions from

126. Kurland, "The Irrelevance of the Constitution," 9. See also Lash, "Power and the Subject of Religion," 1088–93; Levy, *Establishment Clause*, 105. Lash contends that in conjunction with the Tenth Amendment, the Establishment Clause denied the federal government all power over the subject of religion. Lash's argument would be persuasive if the text adopted had been "Congress shall make no law regarding religion." Cf. Smith, "The Jurisdictional Establishment Clause," 1861–63.

127. This is not to say that the adopted text specified what legislation touching religion Congress might legitimately pass; it did not. Whatever power Congress possessed regarding religion was presumably incidental to a delegated power.

military service. "Respecting an" conveys that all types of religious establishments are prohibited, and that Congress may not pass legislation concerning state-level religious establishments.

The Drafting Record Does Not Yield a Clear or Definitive Meaning of What Constitutes "an Establishment of Religion"

If the above analysis is correct, we are left with one final extraordinarily
important question: what, precisely, is the substance of the Establishment
Clause's two rules? If Congress is prohibited from making an establishment, what exactly can it not do? And if Congress cannot make laws concerning state establishments, what range of church-state arrangements
are immune from federal legislative interference? What did the Framers
of the First Amendment understand to constitute an establishment of
religion?

As regrettable as it might be for originalists and originalism, the re-
cords pertaining to the drafting of the Establishment Clause in the First
Congress do not furnish a clear answer to these questions. Neither the
Anti-Federalists, in their call for amendments, nor the members of the
First Congress defined with precision what constituted "an establishment"
of religion.[128] The House records offer the most extensive documentation

128. Recognizing that no attempt was made to define the meaning of the Establishment
Clause, James Hutson, in *Church and State in America*, 158–59, "guesses" that the First Congress may have left the text deliberately ambiguous in reference to religious taxation, so as to
permit the members to interpret it as best suited their personal and religious interests.

Malbin, *Religion and Politics*, 14, argues that through their choice of "*an* establishment"
over "*the* establishment," the House-Senate conference committee indicated their intention
to allow nondiscriminatory aid to religion. Malbin contends that "*the* establishment of religion" would have emphasized the generic word "religion." If the First Congress prohibited
laws respecting "*the* establishment of religion," then it might be plausible to conclude that
it intended to prohibit all official preferences for religion over irreligion. But "*an* establishment," according to Malbin, "seems to ensure the legality of nondiscriminatory religious aid."
See also Robert Cord, *Separation of Church and State: Historical Reality and Current Fiction*
(New York: Lambeth Press, 1982), 11–12. As Laycock, in "'Nonpreferential' Aid to Religion,"
884–85, has pointed out, however, it is not clear that "*the* establishment of religion" emphasizes the word "religion" any more than "*an* establishment of religion." Moreover, Malbin un-
deremphasizes the importance of the conference committee's addition of the word "respecting" and how its concern with federalism might have dictated the choice of "an" over "the." If,
as I have suggested, the conference committee was concerned with protecting the authority of
the states, then the choice of "an" over "the" might make sense. If anything, "an establishment
of religion" would seem to be more generic than "the establishment of religion." As Laycock
also points out, "*the* establishment of religion" might suggest that there is only one kind of
establishment, whereas "an establishment of religion" could indicate the possibility of various

of the creation of the First Amendment, but they do not reveal a substantive discussion about what constituted an establishment of religion. On August 15, when the House was discussing the proposed text, "no religion shall be established by law, nor shall the equal rights of conscience be infringed," Madison is recorded as saying,

> he apprehended the meaning of the words to be, that Congress should not establish a religion, and enforce the legal observation of it by law, nor compel men to worship God in any manner contrary to their conscience.

Even if we take "and enforce the legal observation of it by law" to clarify what Madison meant by an established religion—the words, alternatively, could be understood to clarify what he meant by "equal rights of conscience"—this clarification is hardly more precise than the original, since what constitutes "enforc[ing] the legal observation" of religion is no more definite than what constitutes an establishment of religion.[129]

As I have discussed repeatedly, Congressman Huntington echoed Sylvester's concern that the text might be misinterpreted in such a way as to interfere with existing state practices. That concern for federalism, I have suggested, was addressed by the move to start the amendment with the word "Congress" and then, further, by including "respecting an" in the adopted text. But neither this general intention nor the specific textual protection for state authority clarifies what exactly remains exclusively within the states' domain.

It may be that the First Congress did not define the meaning of "establishment" because the term had a commonly accepted and understood meaning—that is, "establishment" did not need to be defined because all the drafters were working from a common public understanding of the term.[130] I will return to this possibility momentarily, but let me first suggest

---

kinds of establishments. Given that the states at the time legislated a variety of church-state arrangements, the use of the more generic "an" would make sense. "*An* establishment" would more obviously countenance this variety at the state level. Regardless, the significance of the Framers' use of "an" and not "the" seems questionable.

129. Cf. Michael W. McConnell, "Coercion: The Lost Element of Establishment," *William and Mary Law Review* 27 (1986): 937, which contends that Madison's comments indicate that "compulsion is not just an element, it is the essence of an establishment."

130. For example, Bradley, *Church-State Relationships in America*, 55, contends that "No sect preference was, by the time the First Amendment was debated, drafted, and ratified, the settled meaning of nonestablishment." For a different though equally self-assured account of the settled meaning of a religious establishment at the time of the Founding, see Justice Rutledge's

another. The First Congress likely felt no pressing need to define with precision what the Establishment Clause prevented Congress from doing. Many (perhaps most) of the Federalists in the First Congress originally thought that amendments were not necessary to limit Congress's power. Madison was able to convince enough of them that amendments were necessary to fulfill the promises made to the Constitution's critics, in order to assuage (and thereby defeat) them. When the House actually came around to drafting a religion amendment, members from New England sought language that clearly protected the authority of the states. This was hardly controversial, since the Federalists (and it should be remembered that most of the members of the First Congress were Federalists) had long argued that the national government lacked delegated authority over religion. Because most Federalists likely believed their own argument, they probably thought they were making explicit the nonexistence of power, not regulating a potential power that required specific limitations.[131] Even if the more attentive members of the House came to see that the national government possessed some power to make laws that touched religion, they were not primarily concerned about limiting the new national government's power. Moreover, they certainly had no incentive to draw attention to the fact that Congress actually did possess some authority to make laws that touched religion, given that leading Federalists had repeatedly denied this position during the ratification debates. Even though the Anti-Federalists had been right that the national government possessed power that reached religion, once the New England House members' concern with protecting state authority was assuaged, no constituency existed in the House to demand that the limitations placed on Congress be precisely defined. The Federalists could accomplish their

opinion in *Everson v. Board of Education*, 330 U.S. 1, 42–43 (1947). Compare both to Smith, "The Jurisdictional Establishment Clause," 1868, which contends that "the term 'establishment' has, and had, no single or fixed meaning." Michael W. McConnell, "Establishment and Disestablishment at the Founding, Part 1: Establishment of Religion," *William and Mary Law Review* 44 (2003): 2105–2208, offers perhaps the most historically thorough discussion of the subject.

131. Curry, *First Freedoms*, 216. Smith "The Jurisdictional Establishment Clause," 1852–56, argues that the "profoundly apathetic" tenor of the First Congress's "lackluster discussions," and the complacent manner with which the House altered and amended the particular words of what would become the Establishment Clause, suggest that the Framers sought to affirm that religion was within the jurisdiction of the states, an arrangement on which "everyone agreed."

aims by drafting an amendment without clarifying what constituted an impermissible establishment of religion. As Don Drakeman concludes,

> we need to realize that the circumstances giving rise to the Bill of Rights did not require James Madison or any of his congressional compatriots either to define the terms or to agree on any substantive church-state policy.[132]

The historical and political context of the development of the First Amendment allowed the Establishment Clause to be drafted without the drafters clearly defining what constituted "an establishment" of religion.[133]

Evidence beyond the Drafting Record

Even if the preceding analysis is correct, a common public understanding of what constitutes an "establishment" of religion might be found beyond the drafting record. Carl Esbeck has performed the most thorough review of the records surrounding the ratification of the Bill of Rights. He concludes:

> In summary, so far as indicated from the sparse convention records, state ratification of the Third Article [the First Amendment] generated no opposition, indeed no debate, except in Massachusetts and Virginia. In Massachusetts, the Antifederalists in the state senate were able to forestall ratification for reasons other than opposition to the Third Article. In Virginia, the opposition was by eight Antifederalists who held a slim majority in the state senate. Although it took almost two years, popular support for the Third Article eventually broke

---

132. Drakeman, *Church, State, and Original Intent*, 213–14. One should also keep in mind the relative importance the First Congress placed on drafting what became the Establishment Clause. As Drakeman (p.196–97) comments:

> The First Congress had a number of important things to do, and sorting out the proper relationship between church and state was nowhere on that list. . . . What eventually drove the consideration of the religion clauses was a different task from laying a foundation for modern civil liberties or delicately balancing secular and religious interests; rather, the Congress grudgingly took up the issue of a Bill of Rights simply to pass whatever amendments were necessary to appease the states that required or requested them so as to avoid calling the entire constitutional enterprise into question.

133. Levy, *Establishment Clause*, 105, reaches the same conclusion: "The history of the drafting of the establishment clause does not provide us with an understanding of what was meant by 'an establishment of religion.'"

The point of reviewing all these various and often inconsistent uses of the term "establishment" is not so much to add to our knowledge of the First Amendment, but, if anything, to subtract from it — or, perhaps, more accurately, to argue that those commentators who have asserted that there was a clear and widely shared understanding of the term "establishment" during the Founding Era may be overconfident. . . . All of the evidence most clearly shows that word was susceptible of being understood in various ways. . . . [136]

If we turn our focus to the state declarations of rights and state constitutions adopted before 1787, we also fail to find a clear meaning of the

134. Esbeck, "Uses and Abuses of Textualism and Originalism," 582–83.

135. Drakeman, *Church, State, and Original Intent*, 214–15. See also Antieau, Downey, and Roberts, *Freedom from Federal Establishment*, 143–58. After surveying the available evidence state by state, Antieau, Downey, and Roberts conclude (p. 157):

From the foregoing discussion of the ratification of the First Amendment, two basic historical facts stand out strongly: first, the necessary states ratified the amendments within a relatively short period of twenty-six months; second, there was notable lack of protest over or even comment on the content of the amendment as it was submitted to the states.

136. Drakeman, *Church, State, and Original Intent*, 224–25. A recent corpus linguistics analysis also found multiple meanings of uses of "establishment" of religion during the Founding era (broadly defined), though the authors are a bit more sanguine than Drakeman on eliminating some possible originalist constructions of the term. See Barclay, Earley, and Boone, "Original Meaning and the Establishment Clause: A Corpus Linguistics Analysis," *Arizona Law Review* 61 (2019): 505–60.

term "establishment" in the context of church-state relations. As discussed in chapter 4, and as I have documented elsewhere, four states (Virginia, Pennsylvania, Maryland, Georgia) and Vermont adopted no official language concerning religious establishments.[137] Three states (New Jersey, Delaware, North Carolina) declared that there was to be no establishment of one religious sect within the state in preference to any other. New York abrogated and rejected any aspect of English common law or existing statutes that established "any particular denomination of Christians or their ministers." The declaration of rights of two New England states (Massachusetts, New Hampshire) stated that "no subordination of any sect or denomination to another shall ever be established by law." South Carolina's 1778 Constitution established "the Christian Protestant religion." Much like the First Amendment, these provisions are not self-defining, and their immediate context does not yield a clear, definite, shared public meaning. Moreover, the various official state provisions do not neatly map onto the states' various practices in such a way that we can infer a clear meaning of how "establishment" was understood. I do not mean to suggest that these various provisions tell us nothing about what an "establishment" of religion might mean—indeed, in part 3 I will use South Carolina's constitution to help construct a meaning of "establishment"—but they do not yield a clear public meaning such that we can confidently conclude that the Framers and ratifiers of the Establishment Clause possessed a shared, common, public understanding of what constituted an "establishment" of religion.

*　　*　　*

Our lengthy review of why the religious freedom amendments were demanded and of the subsequent drafting of the Establishment Clause, coupled with a brief review of what scholars have discovered (or, more accurately, failed to discover) about the public meaning of "establishment" of religion, has failed to yield a definitive, contemporaneous public meaning of "Congress shall make no law respecting an establishment of religion." We have determined that the text conveys two rules, not a broad principle or standard—but those rules were left underdetermined by the

137. See Vincent Phillip Muñoz, "Church and State in the Founding-Era State Constitutions," *American Political Thought* 4 (2015): 24–27.

Establishment Clause's authors.[138] If the text is going to be enforced, it has to be constructed. I will offer an originalist construction of the Establishment Clause in part 3 of this study. But before doing so, I turn to the First Amendment's other religious freedom provision, the Free Exercise Clause.

---

138. Cf. Andrew P. Koppelman in "Phony Originalism and the Establishment Clause," *Northwestern University Law Review* 103 (2009): 740, who, like most separationists, holds that the Establishment Clause conveys a principle of nonestablishment. Koppelman goes on to argue (pp. 741–43) that even if the original meaning of the Establishment Clause pertained to a rule of federalism, the framers of the Fourteenth Amendment imposed the principle of nonestablishment on the states.

The Original Meaning of the Free Exercise Clause

Neither the First Congress nor the ratifying state legislatures debated the question of religious freedom in much detail, nor did they directly consider the scope of the First Amendment's free exercise protection. . . . As is the case for a number of the terms used in the Bill of Rights, it is not exactly clear what the Framers thought the phrase signified. — Justice Sandra Day O'Connor

dissenting in *City of Boerne v. Flores* (1997)[1]

The previous chapter examined the creation of the First Amendment in an attempt to set forth what can be determined about the original meaning of the Establishment Clause. In this chapter, I address some of the same material to determine what can be known about the original meaning of the Free Exercise Clause.[2] The chapter attempts to demonstrate how Justice Sandra Day O'Connor's statement above — that "it is not exactly clear what the Framers thought the phrase [free exercise] signified" — is

1. *City of Boerne v. Flores*, 521 U.S. 507, 550 (1997), citing Leonard W. Levy, *Judgments: Essays on American Constitutional History* (Chicago: Quadrangle Books, 1972), 173.
2. Parts of this chapter, now significantly revised, first appeared in Vincent Phillip Muñoz, "The Original Meaning of the Free Exercise Clause: The Evidence from the First Congress," *Harvard Journal of Law and Public Policy* 31 (2008): 1083–1120.

true but not exhaustive. The drafting records in the First Congress do not
yield a clear original meaning of what constitutes the "free exercise" of
religion. Those records do suggest, however, that the Free Exercise Clause
states a principle, as opposed to a rule or standard. The drafting records
of what would become the Second Amendment, moreover, directly address the question of religious exemptions from generally applicable laws,
and those records indicate that the First Congress did not understand
the meaning of free exercise to include religious exemptions from otherwise legitimate generally applicable laws. Even if the Framers of the First
Amendment left the Free Exercise Clause underdetermined, they provided some guidance for how we might construct an originalist approach
to religious free exercise that is consistent with the American Founding's
natural rights principles.

Like chapter 5, this chapter begins by reviewing the Anti-Federalists'
criticisms of the proposed constitution and their call for amendments to
protect religious freedom. I then review the drafting of the Free Exercise
Clause and the Second Amendment in the First Congress to gather what
can and cannot be known about the meaning of religious "free exercise."
My review of this evidence leads me to the following conclusions:

1. The Free Exercise Clause likely was not understood to include a right for the
   religious to receive exemptions from burdensome laws.
2. Religious free exercise was understood to be an individual right.
3. The available records do not offer a clear or precise understanding as to what,
   specifically, the Framers understood the Free Exercise Clause to mean.

I conclude that the Framers of the First Amendment left the Free Exercise
Clause underdetermined and, therefore, like the Establishment Clause,
the Free Exercise Clause must be constructed.

The Historical Context of the Drafting of the
Free Exercise Clause

As discussed in the previous chapter, the genesis of the Bill of Rights
as a whole, and the Free Exercise Clause in particular, lies in the Anti-
Federalists' criticisms of the proposed Constitution. Anti-Federalists claimed
that the Constitution failed to protect the right of religious "free exercise" and the right to worship according to the dictates of "conscience,"

terms they appear to have used interchangeably.[3] In his list of the rights "which ought to be established as a fundamental part of the national system," "The Federal Farmer," one of the most articulate Anti-Federalists, declared:

> It is true, we [the people of the United States] are not disposed to differ much, at present, about religion; but when we are making a constitution, it is to be hoped, for ages and millions yet unborn, why not establish the free exercise of religion, as a part of the national compact. There are other essential rights, which we have justly understood to be the rights of freemen; as freedom from hasty and unreasonable search warrants, warrants not founded on oath, and not issued with due caution, for searching and seizing men's papers, property, and persons.[4]

Anti-Federalists clearly conceived religious free exercise as an individual right, but most did not define with precision what they meant by that right.[5] A possible exception was penned by the Philadelphian "Centinel," who employed text from the 1776 Pennsylvania Declaration of Rights in his criticism of the proposed constitution:

> The new plan, it is true, does propose to secure the people of the benefit of personal liberty by the *habeas corpus*; and trial by jury for all crimes, except in case of impeachment: but there is no declaration, that all men have a natural and unalienable right to worship Almighty God, according to the dictates of their own consciences and understanding; and that no man ought, or of right can be compelled to attend any religious worship, or erect or support any place of worship, or maintain any ministry, contrary to, or against his own free will and consent; and that no authority can or ought to be vested in, or assumed by any

3. Michael W. McConnell, "The Origins and Historical Understanding of Free Exercise of Religion," *Harvard Law Review* 103 (1990): 1488.

4. "Letters from The Federal Farmer, #4," October 12, 1787, in *The Complete Anti-Federalist*, ed. Herbert J. Storing (Chicago: University of Chicago Press, 1981), 2:249.

5. I disagree with Steven D. Smith's argument in *Foreordained Failure: The Quest for a Constitutional Principle of Religious Freedom* (New York: Oxford University Press, 1995), 35–43, that the original meaning of the Free Exercise Clause primarily involves a concern with federalism. Smith does not consider the Anti-Federalists and how their concerns led to the adoption of the Bill of Rights. Ignoring the Anti-Federalists, I believe, leads Smith to overlook how the terms "free exercise" and "liberty of conscience" were used to refer to the individual right of religious freedom.

power whatever, that shall in any case interfere with, or in any manner controul, the right of conscience in the free exercise of religious worship. . . . [6]

Submitted Free Exercise Amendments

The amendments that emerged from the Constitution's ratification debates do not reflect "Centinel's" specificity. Five of the seven states that generated amendments included a provision related to the right of religious liberty.[7] None of these states offered precise measures. Virginia proposed:

> That religion, or the duty which we owe to our Creator, and the manner of discharging it, can be directed only by reason and conviction, not by force or violence; and therefore all men have an equal, natural, and unalienable right to the free exercise of religion, according to the dictates of conscience, and that no particular religious sect or society ought to be favored or established, by law, in preference to others.[8]

As I noted in the previous chapter, Rhode Island used Virginia's language in its recommended "declaration of rights."[9] North Carolina's list of rights and amendments also used Virginia's language, though its initial convention voted neither to reject nor to ratify the Constitution, and so did not submit its draft to Congress.[10] New York proposed:

6. "Letters of Centinel," October 24, 1787, in *Complete Anti-Federalist*, 2:152.

7. As discussed below, the seven states that generated amendments were Massachusetts, South Carolina, New Hampshire, Virginia, New York, North Carolina, and, belatedly, Rhode Island. Massachusetts's proposed amendments did not address religion. I omit from discussion South Carolina's proposal, which sought to amend the no-religious-test clause in Article 6 to read, "no *other* religious test shall ever be required." For a statement on the irrelevance of South Carolina's proposal, see John Witte, Jr., *Religion and the American Constitutional Experiment: Essential Rights and Liberties* (Boulder, CO: Westview Press, 2000), 303n29.

8. *The Debates in the Several State Conventions on the Adoption of the Federal Constitution, as Recommended by the General Convention at Philadelphia, in 1787*, 2nd ed., ed. Jonathan Elliot (Philadelphia: J. B. Lippincott and Co., 1861), 3:659 (hereafter *Elliot's Debates*). The preamble of Virginia's declaration of ratification also said, "that among other essential rights, the liberty of conscience and of the press cannot be cancelled, abridged, restrained or modified by any authority of the United States." *Elliot's Debates*, 3:653.

9. *Elliot's Debates*, 1:334.

10. *Elliot's Debates*, 4:244, 1:333.

That the people have an equal, natural, and unalienable right freely and peaceably to exercise their religion, according to the dictates of conscience; and that
no religious sect or society ought to be favored by law in preference to others.[11]

New Hampshire proposed the most succinct amendment:

Congress shall make no laws touching Religion, or to infringe the rights of
conscience.[12]

Additionally, the minorities who lost the ratification battle in Pennsylvania and Maryland circulated proposed amendments. The Pennsylvania
minority suggested:

The right of conscience shall be held inviolable; and neither the legislative, executive nor judicial powers of the United States shall have authority to alter,
abrogate, or infringe any part of the Constitution of the several states, which
provide for the preservation of liberty in matters of religion.[13]

The Maryland minority offered

that there be no national religion established by law, but that all persons be
equally entitled to protection in their religious liberty.[14]

Two related but different explanations might account for the proposed
amendments' failure to specify the meaning of "free exercise of religion,"
"rights [or right] of conscience," and "religious liberty." First, as I documented and discussed in part I, the Founders agreed about the core meaning of religious freedom. They conceived of religious free exercise (or "the
rights of conscience") as an inalienable natural right, possessed by all individuals, to worship according to conscience. That core meaning is reflected
in the four states' (Virginia, North Carolina, Rhode Island, New York)
proposed amendments that used the words "natural" and "unalienable" to

11. *Elliot's Debates*, 1:328.
12. *Elliot's Debates*, 1: 326.
13. "The Address and Reasons of Dissent of the Minority of the Convention of Pennsylvania to Their Constituents," *Pennsylvania Packet and Daily Advisor*, December 18, 1787, in
Complete Anti-Federalist, 3:150–51.
14. "Address of a Minority of the Maryland Ratifying Convention," *Maryland Gazette*
(Baltimore), May 6, 1788, in *Complete Anti-Federalist*, 5:97.

describe the right of religious free exercise, and also in the Pennsylvania minority proposal, which used the term "inviolable." Second, to the extent that disagreement existed beyond this commonly accepted core meaning, Anti-Federalists did not have an incentive or interest in drawing attention to it. To repeat a point made in the last chapter, the Anti-Federalists conceived of amendments as part of their larger strategy to make significant revisions to the Constitution through a constitutional convention. This is not to suggest that the Anti-Federalists did not seek protections for the rights of conscience. It is merely to say that their immediate goal and primary focus in proposing amendments was *not* to craft precise text with a definite meaning that would protect a clearly specified right. At least in 1787–88, Anti-Federalists believed that the politics of the Constitution's ratification demanded only that they make the case that amendments were needed—not that they draft them with particular care or specificity.[15]

The Drafting of the Free Exercise Clause in the First Congress

As I discussed in the previous chapter, Madison's deft political maneuver to draft amendments in the First Congress allowed Federalists to control the amendment process and arrest momentum for a second constitutional convention.[16] This led to a deeply ironic and still underappreciated situation: the Bill of Rights was drafted by partisans who thought amendments were unnecessary.[17] It also led to relatively sparse debates in the First Congress. As this chapter will show, the drafting record of the Free Exercise Clause itself provides little guidance for determining its original public meaning.

The House Debates

On June 8, 1789, James Madison introduced the following texts related to religious free exercise on the House floor:

15. See J. Gordon Hylton, "Virginia and the Ratification of the Bill of Rights, 1789–1791," *Virginia Law Review* 25 (1991): 436–37, 441–46, discussing the Virginia Anti-Federalists' strategy to call for a second constitutional convention. Also see the discussion and citations regarding this point in the previous chapter.

16. See Robert A. Goldwin, *From Parchment to Power: How James Madison Used the Bill of Rights to Save the Constitution* (Washington: AEI Press, 1997).

17. Hylton, "Virginia and the Ratification of the Bill of Rights," 434.

The civil rights of none shall be abridged on account of religious belief or worship, nor shall any national religion be established, nor shall the full and equal rights of conscience be in any manner, or on any pretext, infringed.[18]

No State shall violate the equal rights of conscience, or the freedom of the press, or the trial by jury in criminal cases.[19]

As I shall discuss later in this chapter, Madison also introduced a separate provision related to religiously based conscientious objection to military service.

In his free exercise text, Madison did not copy any of the amendments proposed by the various states. Moreover, he proposed an amendment directed against the states, something that no state had suggested or probably even contemplated.[20] Regarding the national government, Madison offered two separate provisions aside from his nonestablishment text: no abridgment of civil and political rights on account of religion, and no infringement of the "full and equal rights of conscience." For the states, he proposed only the nonviolation of the "equal rights of conscience."

As discussed in the previous chapter, juxtaposing the two proposed restrictions on the national government brings forth an interesting question: Did Madison not believe that the "full and equal rights of conscience" prevented the government from abridging civil and political rights on account of religion? Madison himself stated that the exclusion of religious ministers from eligibility for elected office was a violation of "a fundamental principle of religious liberty by punishing a religious profession with the privation of a civil right."[21] This was also the position legislated in Virginia's Statute for Religious Liberty, which held that the profession of religious opinions "shall in no wise diminish, enlarge, or affect [an

18. *Annals of Congress*, 1st Cong., 1st sess., 451.

19. *Annals of Congress*, 1st Cong., 1st sess., 452.

20. Most Anti-Federalists were concerned about potential encroachments on individual rights by the new national government and, accordingly, did not seek amendments to the Constitution to protect individuals from state governments. For discussions of this point, see Herbert J. Storing, *What the Anti-Federalists Were For: The Political Thought of the Opponents of the Constitution* (Chicago: University of Chicago Press, 1981), 69; McConnell, "The Origins and Historical Understanding of Free Exercise of Religion," 1484n381.

21. James Madison, ca. October 15, 1788, *The Writings of James Madison*, ed. Gaillard Hunt (New York: G. P. Putnam's Sons, 1900–10), 5:288.

individual's] civil capacities."[22] Why would Madison include nondeprivation of civil rights as a provision distinct from protection from the rights
conscience, if he thought the former was included within the latter?

I am aware of no evidence that conclusively answers this question, but
an obvious strategic consideration suggests itself. Madison was clearly
aware that not everyone agreed with his "expansive liberal" understanding of religious liberty. As discussed in chapter 4, "narrow republicans"
held a less capacious view of the limitations that religious liberty imposed
on state action, a view that allowed democratic majorities to attach civil
rights and privileges to religious affiliation and practice. By distinguishing
nondeprivation-of-civil-rights language from the "full and equal rights of
conscience," Madison might have been guarding against a narrow interpretation of the latter clause. Even if the "rights of conscience" provision was not construed as capaciously as Madison might have constructed
it, separate nondeprivation-of-civil-rights language could still protect
that aspect of Madison's understanding of religious liberty. We know that
Madison feared that any religious freedom amendment might be narrowly
constructed. Corresponding with Jefferson in 1788 about his reservations
about adding a bill of rights to the Constitution, he wrote,

> There is great reason to fear that a positive declaration of some of the most
> essential rights could not be obtained in the requisite latitude. I am sure that
> the rights of Conscience in particular, if submitted to public definition would
> be narrowed much more than they are likely ever to be by an assumed power.[23]

Madison's proposed amendments were sent to a committee consisting
of one representative from each of the eleven states represented in the

22. "A Bill for Establishing Religious Freedom in Virginia," in Vincent Phillip Muñoz,
Religious Liberty and the American Supreme Court: The Essential Cases and Documents, updated edition (Lanham, MD: Rowman and Littlefield, 2015), 605.

23. James Madison, letter to Thomas Jefferson, October 17, 1788 in *The Founders' Constitution*, ed. Philip Kurland and Ralph Lerner (Indianapolis, IN: Liberty Fund, n.d.; originally
published Chicago: University of Chicago Press, 1987), 1:477. James H. Hutson, *Church and
State in America: The First Two Centuries* (New York: Cambridge University Press, 2008), 155,
suggests that the expansive adjective "full" in Madison's phrase "the full and equal rights of
conscience" would have been universally understood to prohibit Congress from laying religious taxes, including those of the nonpreferential kind. I find this suggestion doubtful, since
it lacks support in the immediate context and does not comport with the understanding of
"rights of conscience" held by several of the Founding-era states.

First Congress. The committee, which included Madison, made the following changes to Madison's original drafts (additions in italics):

The civil rights of none shall be abridged on account of religious belief or worship, nor *no* shall any national religion *shall* be established *by law*, nor shall the full and equal rights of conscience be in any manner, or on any pretext, infringed.[24]

No State shall *infringe* violate the equal rights of conscience. . . .[25]

No records of the committee's proceedings exist, so we can only speculate as to why the committee made the revisions it did. It eliminated the nonabridgement-of-civil-rights provision, perhaps because not all agreed with it or, possibly, because it was thought to be redundant. The committee also eliminated the seemingly unnecessary words "full and" before "equal rights of conscience" in the amendment directed toward the national government, and replaced "violate" with "infringe" in the state amendment, making the language of the national and state amendments parallel to one another.[26]

On August 15, 1789, the full House considered the amended text:

No religion shall be established by law, nor shall the equal rights of conscience be infringed.[27]

As discussed in the previous chapter, the ensuing debate centered on the text that would become the Establishment Clause; nothing of substance

24. *Annals of Congress*, 1st Cong., 1st sess., 757.
25. *Annals of Congress*, 1st Cong., 1st sess., 783.
26. Cf. McConnell, "The Origins and Historical Understanding of Free Exercise of Religion," 1481, which interprets "full and equal rights of conscience" to imply that "the liberty of conscience is entitled not only to equal protection, but also to some absolute measure of protection apart from mere governmental neutrality"—that is, exemptions. If McConnell is correct, then the subsequent elimination of "full" by the First Congress could also be interpreted to imply the elimination of exemptions, an extrapolation that McConnell resists (at 1482). McConnell's attempt to draw a meaningful implication from the initial inclusion of the word "full" and then his denial that the word's subsequent exclusion has a meaningful implication seems to be a stretch. It appears to me that McConnell overinterprets the implications of the initial inclusion of "full," and that little can be drawn from the word's original inclusion or its subsequent elimination.
27. *Annals of Congress*, 1st Cong., 1st sess., 757.

was said about what would become the Free Exercise Clause. The House
made the following changes:

> *Congress shall make no laws touching* ~~no~~ religion *or infringing* ~~shall be estab-~~
> ~~lished by law, nor shall~~ the equal rights of conscience ~~be infringed.~~[28]

Two days later, on August 17, the House considered the amendment
directed at the states. Thomas Tudor Tucker of South Carolina objected
on the grounds that "it will be much better . . . to leave the State Governments to themselves, and not to interfere with them more than we already
do. . . ."[29] Madison responded that he conceived the state amendment to be

> the most valuable amendment in the whole list. If there was any reason to re-
> strain the Government of the United States from infringing upon these essen-
> tial rights, it was equally necessary that they should be secured against the State
> Governments. He thought that if they provided against the one, it was as nec-
> essary to provide against the other, and was satisfied that it would be equally
> grateful to the people.[30]

Samuel Livermore of New Hampshire suggested making the amendment
an "affirmative proposition,"[31] which was agreed to by the House, result-
ing in the following changes:

> ~~No State shall infringe~~ the equal rights of conscience, ~~nor~~ the freedom of speech;
> or of the press, ~~nor of~~ *and* the right of trial by jury in criminal cases, *shall not*
> *be infringed by any State.*[32]

In the final wording of the amendments sent to the Senate, this transposi-
tion was not made. No reason for the mistake is recorded.

28. *Annals of Congress*, 1st Cong., 1st sess., 759.

29. *Annals of Congress*, 1st Cong., 1st sess., 783.

30. *Annals of Congress*, 1st Cong., 1st sess., 784. Madison's proposed protection for the
"right of conscience" against state governments might be considered as evidence against Steven Smith's position in *Foreordained Failure*, 35–43, that the original meaning of the Free
Exercise Clause pertains to federalism. Madison's proposal, which the House voted to adopt,
only makes sense if the "right of conscience" belongs to individuals and, accordingly, could be
protected from state encroachment.

31. *Annals of Congress*, 1st Cong., 1st sess., 784.

32. *Annals of Congress*, 1st Cong., 1st sess., 784.

On August 20, Fisher Ames of Massachusetts proposed, and the House accepted, the following revisions to the amendment directed at the national government:

> Congress shall make no laws *establishing* ~~touching~~ religion, or *to prevent the free exercise thereof,* ~~infringing~~ *or to infringe* the rights of conscience.[33]

The reasons for the inclusion of "free exercise" in addition to "rights of conscience" is not clear, as no discussion of the matter exists in the House records. Immediately after the adoption of "free exercise," debate ensued over a proposed religious exemption from military service included with what would become the Second Amendment. As I shall discuss later in this chapter, no evidence exists to suggest that any delegate connected an argument for or against exemptions to the just-adopted language of "free exercise."

On August 21, the House resumed its consideration of amendments. In the *Journal of the House of Representatives*, the text of the national amendment is different from that adopted the previous day, with the following changes reflected in the record:

> Congress shall make no law establishing religion, or *prohibiting* ~~to prevent~~ the free exercise thereof, ~~or to infringe~~ *nor shall* the rights of ~~C~~conscience *be infringed*.[34]

The reasons for the changes, including the change from "to prevent" to "prohibiting," are unclear. Possibilities include an unrecorded amendment or mistranscriptions in either the *Annals* or the final copy of the engrossed bill.[35]

On August 24, the House sent the following to the Senate:

> Congress shall make no law establishing religion, or prohibiting the free exercise thereof, nor shall the rights of conscience be infringed.[36]

---

33. *Annals of Congress*, 1st Cong., 1st sess., 796.

34. *Journal of the House of Representatives*, August 21, 1789, in *The Documentary History of the First Federal Congress of the United States of America, 1789–1791*, ed. Linda Grant De Pauw (Baltimore: Johns Hopkins University Press, 1972), 3:159.

35. McConnell, "The Origins and Historical Understanding of Free Exercise of Religion," 1483.

36. *Senate Journal*, 1st Cong., 1st sess., August 25, 1789, 63. On August 25, the Senate read the August 24 House resolution proposing articles of amendment to the Constitution.

No State shall infringe the right of trial by Jury in criminal cases, nor the rights of conscience, nor the freedom of speech, or of the press.[37]

The Senate Record

On September 3, 1789, the Senate took up what would become the First Amendment. The following three motions to amend the House's language were considered and defeated (proposed additions in italics):

> Congress shall make no law establishing *one religious sect or society in preference to others* ~~religion, or prohibiting the free exercise thereof~~; nor shall the rights of conscience be infringed

> Congress shall *not make any law, infringing* ~~make no law establishing religion, or prohibiting the free exercise thereof; nor shall~~ the rights of conscience ~~be infringed~~ *or establishing any religious sect or society*

> Congress shall make no law establishing *any particular denomination of* religion *in preference to another*, or prohibiting the free exercise thereof; nor shall the rights of conscience be infringed

The Senate then adopted the following change:

> Congress shall make no law establishing religion or prohibiting the free exercise thereof, ~~nor shall the rights of Conscience be infringed~~.[38]

Three of the four motions considered on September 3, including the one that was adopted, moved to eliminate either "free exercise" or "rights of conscience." This may indicate that the Senate thought "free exercise" and "right of conscience" redundant, but why the Senate ultimately voted to keep "free exercise" and not "rights of conscience" is unclear. Neither the House nor the Senate debates suggest that the phrases were understood to express different meanings. The Senate may have kept "free exercise" for no better reason than that "rights of conscience" came at the end

---

37. *Senate Journal*, 1st Cong., 1st sess., August 25, 1789, 64.
38. *Senate Journal*, 1st Cong., 1st sess., September 3, 1789, 70.

of the amendment and thus was more convenient to remove.[39] No further changes to what would become the Free Exercise Clause are recorded in the Senate's deliberations.

On September 7, the Senate eliminated the amendment directed at the states.[40] No reason is recorded, though, given that senators at the time were elected by state legislatures, they may have thought it improper to adopt an amendment that restricted the states.[41] On September 9, the Senate adopted the following text:

> Congress shall make no law establishing articles of faith or a mode of worship, or prohibiting the free exercise of religion, or abridging the freedom of speech, or the press, or the right of the people peaceably to assemble, and petition to the government for the redress of grievances.[42]

The House-Senate Conference Committee and the Final Adopted Text

On September 24, 1789, a joint congressional committee reconciled the differences between the House and Senate versions and crafted what would become the First Amendment. The six-member committee consisted of Congressmen Madison (Virginia), Sherman (Connecticut), and Vining (Delaware), and Senators Charles Carroll (Maryland), Oliver Ellsworth

---

39. Cf. McConnell, "The Origins and Historical Understanding of Free Exercise of Religion," 1488–91. Despite repeatedly recognizing that the terms "liberty of conscience" and "free exercise of religion" were used interchangeably at the time (see pp. 1482–83, 1488, 1495) and therefore that the adoption of the latter instead of the former may have been "without substantive meaning" (p. 1488), McConnell claims that the adoption of "free exercise" instead of "rights of conscience" is "of utmost importance" (at 1489). McConnell's own evidence seems to belie that conclusion. Moreover, even if McConnell is right that "free exercise" protects religiously motivated conduct whereas "conscience" only protects beliefs (1488–89), his conclusion—that "free exercise" demands exemptions (at 1490)—does not necessarily follow. "Free exercise" could be understood to protect religiously motivated actions without requiring exemptions. For example, free exercise might be understood to prohibit state action that directly outlaws specific religious practices, such as a law outlawing the saying of the Catholic Mass.

Carl H. Esbeck, "The Uses and Abuses of Textualism and Originalism in Establishment Clause Interpretation," *Utah Law Review* 2011 (2011), 535, 539, 563, contends that some member of Congress did not want to protect atheists and that this concern may explain the elimination of "rights of conscience."

40. *Senate Journal*, 1st Cong., 1st sess., September 7, 1789, 72.

41. McConnell, "The Origins and Historical Understanding of Free Exercise of Religion," 1484.

42. *Senate Journal*, 1st Cong., 1st sess., September 9, 1789, 77.

(Connecticut), and William Paterson (New Jersey).[43] No record exists of the committee's deliberations. Before they met, the texts read:

> House Text: Congress shall make no law establishing Religion, or prohibiting the free exercise thereof, nor shall the rights of conscience be infringed

> Senate Text: Congress shall make no law establishing articles of faith or a mode of worship, or prohibiting the free exercise of religion

The committee would adopt the familiar words of the First Amendment:

> Adopted text: Congress shall make no law respecting an establishment of religion or prohibiting the free exercise thereof[44]

As discussed in the previous chapter, the conference committee's most significant action was to introduce the words "respecting an" prior to "establishment of religion." Regarding what became the Free Exercise Clause, the conference committee eliminated from the House text "nor shall the rights of conscience be infringed," following the Senate's actions on September 3. It also eliminated words that the Senate had added on September 3: "articles of faith or a mode of worship." Most significantly, the conference committee retained the language common to both the House and Senate texts: "prohibiting the free exercise thereof." The words "free exercise" originally appeared in the amendment proposed by the state of Virginia—"all men have an equal, natural, and unalienable right to the free exercise of religion"—and "free exercise thereof" was first introduced into the drafting debate by Fisher Ames in the House on August

---

43. *Annals of Congress*, 1st Cong., 1st sess., 939; *Senate Journal*, 1st Cong., 1st sess., September 21, 1789, 84. For further discussion of the views of the members of the conference committee and a hypothetical reconstruction of its possible deliberations, see Donald L. Drakeman, *Church, State, and Original Intent* (New York: Cambridge University Press, 2010), 236–40.

44. A slight discrepancy exists between the *Journal of the House of Representatives*, the *Senate Journal*, and the September 24, 1789, Conference Committee Report, on the one hand, and the *Annals of Congress* on the other. The first three sources report the final language of the Free Exercise Clause to be, ". . . or prohibiting *the* free exercise thereof . . . ," whereas the *Annals* reports, ". . . or prohibiting *a* free exercise thereof. . . ." See *Journal of the House of Representatives*, September 24, 1789, reprinted in *The Documentary History of the First Federal Congress*, 3:228; *Senate Journal*, 1st Cong., 1st sess., September 24, 1789, 76; Conference Committee Report, September 24, 1789, reprinted in *The Documentary History of the First Federal Congress*, 4:47; *Annals of Congress*, 1st Cong., 1st sess., 948.

20. The conference committee's textual modification fails to reveal any clear insight into the text's original meaning.

What Can Be Ascertained from the Drafting of the Free Exercise Clause?

What is true of the conference committee is also true of the drafting record as a whole: the drafting history furnishes little insight into the original meaning of the Free Exercise Clause. No member of Congress articulated what he understood by "free exercise" or "rights of conscience." Fisher Ames and some members of the House, who included both phrases in their proposed amendments, might have thought that they conferred different types of protection. Even supposing this, they offered no explanation of the difference; the available records from August 20, when Ames introduced the phrase "free exercise" in the House, do not mention any relevant discussion. Similarly, the records say nothing about the Senate's September 3 elimination of "rights of conscience" and retention of "free exercise." It may be that the Senate simply thought the phrases redundant. In short, the records do not reveal a clear and precise legal rule for the meaning of the "free exercise" of religion.

Religious Exemptions and the Drafting of the Second Amendment

The drafting record of the First Amendment may not be illuminating. But House members directly addressed the issue of religious exemptions from generally applicable laws during debates over what would become the Second Amendment. That debate suggests that the First Congress did *not* understand religious free exercise to include a right to religious exemptions from generally applicable laws. Ironically, the Second Amendment's drafting record is more revealing than that of the First regarding how the drafters understood the Free Exercise Clause's original meaning.

In addition to denouncing the Constitution's lack of protection for religious "free exercise," Anti-Federalists also decried the absence of conscientious exemptions from military service.[45] The criticism was expressed

45. Storing, *What the Anti-Federalists Were For*, 97n2.

with particular vigor in Pennsylvania, perhaps most colorfully by "Centinel." In response to Article 1, Section 8's provision of power to call forth the militia, "Centinel" remonstrated:

> This section will subject the citizens of these States to the most arbitrary military discipline, even death may be inflicted on the disobedient; in the character of militia, you may be dragged from your families and homes to any part of the continent, and for any length of time, at the discretion of the future Congress . . . ; there is no exemption upon account of conscientious scruples of bearing arms; no equivalent to be received in lieu of personal services. The militia of Pennsylvania may be marched to Georgia or New-Hampshire, however incompatible with their interests or consciences;—in short, they may be made as mere machines as Prussian soldiers.[46]

The criticism was sufficiently powerful that, as further discussed below, Virginia proposed and North Carolina and Rhode Island discussed an amendment exempting conscientious objectors from bearing arms along with ratification of the Constitution.

Recognition of the unique burden that military service placed on some religious believers was not unusual in the Founding period.[47] Delaware, Pennsylvania, New Hampshire, New York (for Quakers only), and Vermont included conscientious objection provisions in their declarations of rights or constitutions.[48] The provisions were not exemptions per se, because an equivalent payment was required in lieu of military service. Nonetheless, they reveal that it was within the Founders' legal horizon to

46. "Letters of Centinel," November 14, 1787, in *Complete Anti-Federalist*, 2:159–60. For other Pennsylvania Anti-Federalist criticisms, see "Letter by an Officer of the Late Continental Army," November 6, 1787, in *Complete Anti-Federalist*, 3:94; "Philadelphiensis," in *Complete Anti-Federalist*, 3:107; "The Address and Reasons of the Dissent of the Minority of the Convention of Pennsylvania to Their Constituents," December 18, 1787, in *Complete Anti-Federalist*, 3:164. Similar objections were made by Anti-Federalists in Maryland and New York. See Samuel Chase, "Notes of Speeches Delivered to the Maryland Ratifying Convention," in *Complete Anti-Federalist*, 5:86; "Address of a Minority of the Maryland Ratifying Convention," May 6, 1788, in *Complete Anti-Federalist*, 5:74; "Address of the Albany Antifederal Committee," April 26, 1788, in *Complete Anti-Federalist*, 6:123.

47. For a discussion of the history of religious exemptions from military conscription in America prior to the Founding period, see McConnell, "The Origins and Historical Understanding of Free Exercise of Religion," 1468–71.

48. See table 6 in chapter 4. See also Vincent Phillip Muñoz, "Church and State in the Founding-Era State Constitutions," *American Political Thought* 4 (2015): 27–30.

extend accommodations to individuals on account of the conscientious demands of religion.[49]

Virginia proposed the following text, which was also advanced in North Carolina and Rhode Island:

That any person religiously scrupulous of bearing arms ought to be exempted, upon payment of an equivalent to employ another to bear arms in his stead.[50]

Minorities from the Pennsylvania and Maryland ratifying conventions also proposed amendments related to conscientious objection from military service. The minority in Pennsylvania proposed the following:

The right of conscience shall be held inviolable; and neither the legislative, executive nor judicial powers of the United States shall have authority to alter, abrogate, or infringe any part of the constitution of the several states, which provide for the preservation of liberty in matters of religion.[51]

Pennsylvania's constitution at the time included a provision exempting men "conscientiously scrupulous of bearing arms" from being compelled

---

49. Recognition of the unique burden that military service placed on some religious believers was also made at the national level. In 1775, shortly before the outbreak of the Revolution, the Continental Congress included the following paragraph in its call for soldiers:

As there are some people, who, from religious principles, cannot bear arms in any case, this Congress intend no violence to their consciences, but earnestly recommend it to them, to contribute liberally in this time of universal calamity, to the relief of their distressed brethren in the several colonies, and to do all other services to their oppressed Country, which they can consistently with their religious principles.

Resolution of July 18, 1775, in *Journals of the Continental Congress, 1774–1789*, ed. Worthington C. Ford et al. (Washington, 1904–37), 2:187–89.

50. *Founders' Constitution*, 5:16 (Virginia); *Elliot's Debates*, 1:331–32, 4:244 (North Carolina), 1:335 (Rhode Island). As noted in chapter 5, North Carolina's initial convention voted neither to reject nor to ratify the Constitution, and so did not submit its draft amendments to Congress. Rhode Island's ratifying convention did not convene until March 1790. It submitted its ratification along with its declaration of rights and proposed amendments on May 29, 1790, nearly a year after the drafting of the First Amendment in the First Congress.

51. "The Address and Reasons of Dissent of the Minority of the Convention of Pennsylvania to Their Constituents," *Pennsylvania Packet and Daily Advisor*, December 18, 1787, in *Complete Anti-Federalist*, 3:150–51. The minority report also argued (at 3:164) that "the rights of conscience may be violated, as there is no exemption of those persons who are conscientiously scrupulous of bearing arms."

to do so, provided they paid in lieu of service.[52] The proposed amendment attempted to safeguard its own state constitutional protections from federal interference. The minority in Maryland proposed text that was more direct:

> No person, conscientiously scrupulous of bearing arms in any case, shall be compelled personally to serve as a soldier.[53]

As mentioned previously, Madison proposed the following when he submitted amendments to the First Congress on June 8, 1789:

> The right of the people to keep and bear arms shall not be infringed; a well armed and well regulated militia being the best security of a free country: but no person religiously scrupulous of bearing arms shall be compelled to render military service in person.[54]

The House first debated Madison's proposal on August 17. By then, the text had been modified to read:

> A well regulated militia, composed of the body of the people, being the best security of a free state, the right of the people to keep and bear arms shall not be infringed; but no person religiously scrupulous shall be compelled to bear arms.[55]

The ardent Anti-Federalist Elbridge Gerry immediately took exception to the provision, interpreting the language to grant the national government discretionary power to "declare who are those religiously scrupulous and prevent them from bearing arms." "Now, if we give a discretionary power to exclude those from militia duty who have religious scruples," Gerry is recorded as saying,

52. Pennsylvania Declaration of Rights, 1776, Article 8, in *The Federal and State Constitutions, Colonial Charters, and Other Organic Laws of the United States*, 2nd edition, ed. Ben Perley Poore (Washington: Government Printing Office, 1878), 2:1541.

53. "Address of a Minority of the Maryland Ratification Convention," May 6, 1788, in *Complete Anti-Federalist*, 5:97.

54. *Annals of Congress*, 1st Cong., 1st sess., 451.

55. *Annals of Congress*, 1st Cong., 1st sess., 778.

we may as well make no provision on this head. For this reason he wished the words to be altered so as to be confined to persons belonging to a religious sect scrupulous of bearing arms.[56]

James Jackson, a Revolutionary War hero, objected to the provision as "unjust" because it did not specify that conscientious objectors were obligated to make an equivalent payment in lieu of military service. Madison's original June 8 language, by including the words "in person," had implicitly recognized the prerogative of the legislature to demand a payment in lieu of military service. But "in person" had been eliminated by August 17. William Smith of South Carolina immediately supported Jackson's position, suggesting that the House adopt the proposed language submitted by Virginia and North Carolina, which included an equivalent payment provision.[57]

Roger Sherman "conceived it difficult to modify the clause and make it better." He noted that those religiously scrupulous of bearing arms "are equally scrupulous of getting substitutes or paying an equivalent. Many of them would rather die than do either one or the other...."[58] He also noted that "there are men amongst the Quakers who will turn out [for militia service], notwithstanding the religious principles of the society, and defend the cause of their country." Sherman seems to have been concerned that Gerry's proposed language might actually prevent those willing to serve in the militia from doing so.

John Vining said he wished the text to remain as it stood, stating that "he saw no use in it if it was amended so as to compel a man to find a substitute, which, with respect to the Government, was the same as if the person himself turned out to fight."[59]

After a point of inquiry from Maryland's Michael Stone, Egbert Benson of New York moved to eliminate the conscientious objector provision altogether. He is recorded as saying:

Mr. Benson moved to have the words "but no person religiously scrupulous shall be compelled to bear arms," struck out. He would always leave it to the benevolence of the Legislature, for, modify it as you please, it will be impossible to express it in such a manner as to clear it from ambiguity. No man can claim

56. *Annals of Congress*, 1st Cong., 1st sess., 779–80.
57. *Annals of Congress*, 1st Cong., 1st sess., 778–79.
58. *Annals of Congress*, 1st Cong., 1st sess., 779.
59. *Annals of Congress*, 1st Cong., 1st sess., 779.

this indulgence of right. It may be a religious persuasion, but it is no natural right, and therefore ought to be left to the discretion of the Government. If this stands part of the constitution, it will be a question before the Judiciary on every regulation you make with respect to the organization of the militia, whether it comports with this declaration or not. It is extremely injudicious to intermix matters of doubt with fundamentals.[60]

Benson's statement addressed the two issues under discussion. Leaving exemptions to the legislature would allow the First Congress to avoid the difficult issues pertaining to eligibility and potential payments in lieu of service. More fundamentally, Benson argued that religious exemptions from militia service should not be a constitutional right because they are not a part of the natural right to religious liberty.[61] Benson seems to have supposed that, at least pertaining to religious liberty, specific textual protections should be limited to natural rights. His comment about "discretion" suggests that he anticipated constitutional rights to be categorical. If exemptions were recognized as a constitutional right, granting them could not be balanced in light of other competing governmental interests. Relatedly, Benson also feared that a constitutional right to conscientious objection would involve the judiciary "on every regulation ... with respect to the organization of the militia." Clearly anticipating judicial review, he seems to have believed that conscientious objectors' lawsuits would invite improper judicial oversight over the organization of the militia. Benson did acknowledge that the government could "indulge" conscientious objectors, but if such a privilege were to be extended, he said the matter properly belonged to the legislature. He appears not to have worried about the insufficiency of discretionary legislative exemptions, remarking that the legislature "will always possess humanity enough to indulge this class of citizens in a matter they are so desirous of."[62]

60. *Annals of Congress*, 1st Cong., 1st sess., 779–80.

61. For a discussion of how the Founders understood the protection of natural rights to be compatible with the imposition of civil obligations, including the duty of military service, see Philip Hamburger, "Equality and Diversity: The Eighteenth-Century Debate about Equal Protection and Equal Civil Rights," *Supreme Court Review* (1992): 305. Although he does not discuss Benson in particular, Hamburger's explanation of how eighteenth-century religious dissenters understood the right of religious liberty to be inalienable and limited seems to capture Benson's position. See Philip Hamburger, "More is Less," *Virginia Law Review* 90 (2004): 839–57.

62. *Annals of Congress*, 1st Cong., 1st sess., 780. Benson's explicit distinction between legislatively granted exemptions and judicially granted exemptions casts significant doubt on Mc-

Benson's comments appear to have garnered substantial, though not majority, support in the House. Immediately after his statement, a motion was made to strike out the exemption clause. It failed by a vote of twenty-two to twenty-four.[63]

Three days later, on August 20, the House again debated the provision. This time, Thomas Scott from Pennsylvania raised objections. He repeated Benson's criticism that the matter was "a legislative right altogether." And he added a second objection. If religious objectors could neither be called to service nor be made to pay an equivalent, "a militia can never be depended upon."[64] Recourse would then need to be made to a standing army, an institution thought by some to be inimical to liberty.[65] Scott seemed to be particularly vexed by the problem of draft-bed conversions. With uncompensated exemptions available, "the generality of persons will have recourse to these pretexts to get excused from bearing arms." Scott said he did not mean to deprive those who were religiously scrupulous from "any indulgence the law affords," but "to guard against those who are of no religion."[66]

Representative Elias Boudinot of New Jersey is the only person recorded as responding to Scott. A Presbyterian and future president of the American Bible Society, Boudinot said he hoped "that in establishing this Government, we may show the world that proper care is taken that the Government may not interfere with the religious sentiments of any person. . . . By striking out the clause," he continued, "people may be led to believe that there is an intention in the General Government to compel all its citizens to bear arms." Responding directly to Scott's concerns about the militia's dependability, Boudinot asked rhetorically, "Can any dependence . . . be placed in men who are conscientious in this respect?" Moreover, he continued, "What justice can there be in compelling them to bear arms, when, according to their religious principles, they would rather die than use them?" This latter point suggests that Boudinot thought that

---

Connell's supposal that "if legislatures conceived of exemptions as an appropriate response to conflicts between law and conscience, there is every reason to suppose that the framers and ratifiers of the federal Constitution would expect judicially enforceable constitutional protections for religious conscience to be interpreted in much the same manner." Michael W. McConnell, "Free Exercise Revisionism and the *Smith* Decision," *Chicago Law Review* 57 (1990): 1119.

63. *Annals of Congress*, 1st Cong., 1st sess., 780.
64. *Annals of Congress*, 1st Cong., 1st sess., 796.
65. Storing, *What the Anti-Federalists Were For*, 17.
66. *Annals of Congress*, 1st Cong., 1st sess., 796.

exemptions were not only prudent (given that conscientious objectors would likely make bad soldiers), but also necessary to meet the just demands of religious freedom. After Boudinot's comments, the record includes the following: "Some further desultory conversation arose, and it was agreed to insert the words 'in person' to the end of the clause; after which, it was adopted. . . ."[67]

The restoration of Madison's original "in person" is significant. The phrase "but no person religiously scrupulous shall be compelled to bear arms in person" suggests that the House viewed exemptions from military service more as a privilege than as a right. As Sherman and Vining recognized in the House debate on August 17, many of those who opposed bearing arms were equally scrupulous of obtaining substitutes or paying for an equivalent.[68] If religious individuals were understood to possess a right not to perform military service on account of conscientious objection, then, for the same reason, they would also seem to possess a right not to be legally compelled to find or pay for an equivalent. The reinsertion of "in person" therefore suggests that the House understood conscientious objection not to override all of a citizen's civil obligations. Stated differently, the inclusion of "in person" reflects the evident judgment by

67. *Annals of Congress*, 1st Cong., 1st sess., 796.

68. According to Ellis M. West, "The Right to Religion-Based Exemptions in Early America: The Case of Conscientious Objectors to Conscription," *Journal of Law and Religion* 10 (1993/1994): 381:

> The [military service] exemptions granted to conscientious objectors [in early America] were seldom, if ever, considered by them to be adequate or satisfactory because they were limited or conditional in nature. To avoid military service, the objectors had to secure a substitute or pay a fine or special tax. It is quite clear, moreover, that the lawmakers who imposed the fines or taxes considered them to be the equivalent to [*sic*] military service, and their amount was set accordingly. As a result, the exemptions were rejected by most Mennonites, Brethren, and Quakers, some of whom suffered imprisonment and loss of property for failure to serve, pay a fine/tax, *or* secure a substitute. Moreover, the lawmakers in the various states were quite aware that pacifists objected to paying a fine or tax in lieu of military service.

Emphasis in the original. Material cited by West includes Peter Brock, *Pacifism in the United States: From the Colonial Era to the First World War* (Princeton, NJ: Princeton University Press, 1968), 199–200; R. R. Russell, "Development of Conscientious Objector Recognition in the United States," *George Washington Law Review* 20 (1952): 409–48; Richard K. MacMaster, Samuel L. Horst, and Robert F. Ulle, *Conscience in Crisis: Mennonites and Other Peace Churches in America, 1739–1789* (Scottdale, PA: Herald Press, 1979), 62–63, 354–91, 523–25, 532; Richard K. MacMaster, *Land, Piety, Peoplehood* (Scottdale, PA: Herald Press, 1985), 256–57.

the House that the state can legitimately and knowingly prescribe conduct that burdens religious individuals' consciences. By restoring "in person," the House rejected Boudinot's hope that they "show the world that
proper care is taken that the Government may not interfere with the religious sentiments of any person."

More significantly, on September 9, 1789, the Senate eliminated the conscientious objector provision altogether.[69] No record exists of the Senate's
deliberations on this point.

The Senate's elimination of the conscientious objector provision would
seem to undermine pro-exemption scholar Michael McConnell's asser-
tion that "the significance of Boudinot's position . . . is that he, with a majority of the House, considered exemption from a generally applicable
legal duty to be 'necessary' to protect religious freedom."[70] McConnell
fails to acknowledge that Congress as a whole *rejected* Boudinot's position. The real significance of Boudinot's position, then, would seem to be
that the First Congress considered and ultimately rejected it—that is, that
the First Congress considered and rejected constitutional text that would
have provided a right to religious exemptions from burdensome laws.[71]

Several points can be gleaned from Congress's debates over the right
to conscientious objection from military service. Clearly, some members
of the First Congress understood the matter to be one of principle. A few
articulated the opinion that the right of religious freedom itself demanded
a constitutionally recognized provision for exemptions from military service. Other House members rejected that argument, claiming that the matter was not one of natural or constitutional right, but only of legislative
discretion. Congressman Egbert Benson spoke against conscientious exemptions, partly because they would necessarily lead to judicial review of
certain legislative and executive actions. A majority in the House voted to
allow conscientious objectors to abstain from military service in person,
but the majority did not recognize a more general right to be exempt from
civic obligations wherever they conflicted with one's religious beliefs.

69. *Senate Journal*, 1st Cong., 1st sess., September 9, 1789, 77.

70. McConnell, "The Origins and Historical Understanding of Free Exercise of Religion,"
1501.

71. In *Fulton v. City of Philadelphia*, 593 U.S. ___, slip op. 51 (2021), Justice Samuel Alito
repeats McConnell's argument on this point. Like McConnell, Justice Alito does not consider
the implications of the full Congress's rejection of constitutional text that would have provided religious exemptions from burdensome laws.

Finally, Congress considered and rejected a constitutional right to exemption based on religion.

Perhaps most importantly for the purposes of this chapter, no evidence exists to suggest that any member of the House connected the debate over conscientious objectors to the debate over the text that would become the Free Exercise Clause. Recall that the House's debate over religious exemptions occurred within the context of drafting what would become the Second Amendment, not the First. On August 20, immediately preceding the Scott-Boudinot exchange about the constitutional propriety of exemptions, the House adopted the following text:

> Congress shall make no law establishing religion, or to prevent the free exercise thereof, or to infringe the rights of conscience.[72]

No evidence exists to indicate that Boudinot, whom Michael McConnell calls the "most eloquent defender" of the right to conscientious objection, ever suggested that this free exercise text protected conscientious objectors.[73] The fact that the House continued to debate a conscientious objector provision *immediately after* it had adopted language protecting "free exercise" suggests that it did not consider "free exercise" to include the right to exemptions from generally applicable laws. If "free exercise" were commonly understood to include religious exemptions from burdensome generally applicable laws, then surely some member of Congress would have connected the two debates and suggested that the text prohibiting Congress from making a law "to prevent the free exercise" of religion also protected conscientious objectors. Or if, as Justice Alito speculates, some thought that a specific conscientious objector amendment was necessary "because they feared that exemptions from military service would be held to fall into the free-exercise right's carveout for conduct that threatens public safety,"[74] then we would expect at least one member of the House to make this point. But no member of the House connected the debate over conscientious exemptions from military service to the text protecting religious free exercise. Just as no one suggested that a separate conscientious objector provision was redundant because exemptions were already provided by the "free exercise" language, no one suggested that a sepa-

72. *Annals of Congress*, 1st Cong., 1st sess., 796.
73. McConnell, "The Origins and Historical Understanding of Free Exercise of Religion," 1500.
74. *Fulton v. City of Philadelphia*, 593 U.S. __, slip op. at 51 (2021) (Alito, J., concurring).

rate conscientious objector provision was needed because religious free exercise exemptions would not be sufficient. There simply is no evidence that anyone made any connection between the just-adopted language protecting religious "free exercise" and religious exemptions. The concurrent but separate discussions in the House on a right to religious free exercise, on the one hand, and on religious exemptions from military service, on the other, seem to indicate that the members of the House did not understand religious free exercise to include exemptions from generally applicable laws.[75]

This conclusion is also suggested by the Anti-Federalists' demand that a right to conscientious objection be recognized *in addition to* a right to religious free exercise. The states whose majorities proposed a conscientious objector amendment (Virginia, North Carolina, and Rhode Island) also proposed an amendment recognizing that "all men have an equal, natural, and unalienable right to the free exercise of religion, according to the dictates of conscience." If these states thought that this language granted religious exemptions from burdensome laws, then they would not have needed to propose an additional conscientious objector amendment.[76]

The Founding-era state charters that included explicit conscientious objector provisions reflect this same understanding. As discussed in chapter 4, the declarations of rights or constitutions of Delaware, Pennsylvania, Vermont, New Hampshire, and New York (for Quakers only) included specific provisions protecting conscientious objectors.[77] The state charters of Delaware, Pennsylvania, Vermont, and New York also separately protected the "free exercise" of religious worship, and New Hampshire's 1784 Bill of Rights protected every individual's "right to worship GOD according to the dictates of his own conscience."[78] The existence of separate texts protecting the right of conscientious objection to military service and the right of religious free exercise suggests that the latter right did not encompass the former. To take a specific example, Article 2 of the Declaration of Rights of Pennsylvania's Constitution of 1776 stated:

75. Cf. McConnell, "The Origins and Historical Understanding of Free Exercise of Religion," 1501. Also see West, "The Right to Religion-Based Exemptions in Early America," 398–400.

76. The minority in Maryland, similarly, proposed both an exemption from bearing arms for those "conscientiously scrupulous" of doing so, and a separate amendment stating that "all persons be equally entitled to protection in their religious liberty." "Address of a Minority of the Maryland Ratification Convention," May 6, 1788, in *Complete Anti-Federalist*, 5:97.

77. See table 6 in chapter 4.

78. See table 1 in chapter 1.

That all men have a natural and unalienable right to worship Almighty God according to the dictates of their own consciences and understanding. . . . And that no authority can or ought to be vested in, or assumed by any power whatever, that shall in any case interfere with, or in any manner controul, the right of conscience in the free exercise of religious worship.[79]

Article 8 of the same document stated:

Nor can any man who is conscientiously scrupulous of bearing arms, be justly compelled thereto, if he will pay such equivalent, nor are the people bound by any laws, but such as they have in like manner assented to, for their common good.[80]

Again, if Pennsylvania's Article 2's right of religious free exercise was understood to include exemptions from generally applicable but religiously burdensome laws, there would have been no need for Article 8's declaration concerning conscientious objectors.

The debates in the First Congress mirror the general understanding reflected in the Founding-era state declarations of rights: the right of religious "free exercise" was not understood to include the right to exemptions from generally applicable laws.

What We Know and Do Not Know from the Drafting Record about the Free Exercise Clause's Original Meaning

Our review of the call for and drafting of an amendment protecting the free exercise of religion leads to the following three conclusions.

"Free Exercise" Seems Not to Have Been Understood to Connote a Rule of Religious Exemption

At the beginning of this chapter, I noted Justice O'Connor's contention that the First Congress neither debated nor directly considered the scope of the First Amendment's free exercise provision. It is true that the drafting records pertaining to the Free Exercise Clause reveal little about the text's original meaning. But the records pertaining to the drafting of the

79. *Federal and State Constitutions,* 2:1541.
80. *Federal and State Constitutions,* 2:1541.

Second Amendment suggest that religious free exercise was not commonly understood to encompass a right to exemption from generally applicable laws. If "free exercise" had such a public meaning and understanding, it is practically certain that in debating religious conscientious exemption from militia service, some member of Congress would have invoked, or at least noted, that the language of "free exercise" already provided the protection that was under consideration. It seems more likely that "free exercise" in the First Amendment was not understood to encompass a right of exemption from generally applicable laws that burdened individuals' religious consciences. That would explain why the subsequent debate over Second Amendment exemptions took place.

The Drafting Records from the First Congress Suggest That the Free Exercise Clause Was Meant to Protect an Individual Right

Anti-Federalists pressed for an amendment because, they argued, the proposed national constitution did not protect individuals' rights to worship according to the dictates of conscience. Their proposed language reflects an understanding of religious liberty as a right belonging to individuals and groups of individuals. Virginia, North Carolina, and Rhode Island proposed, "all men have an equal, natural, and unalienable right to the free exercise of religion, according to the dictates of conscience." New York proposed, "that the people have an equal, natural, and unalienable right freely and peacefully to exercise their religion, according to the dictates of conscience." A minority of delegates from Maryland proposed, "all persons be equally entitled to protection in their religious liberty."

Madison's initial House proposal and its subsequent revisions in the First Congress are also consistent with the idea that "free exercise" was understood to be a right belonging to individuals and groups of individuals. Admittedly, the available records capture little substantive discussion. The texts themselves, however—including the final text that became the First Amendment—convey an individual rights understanding.

The Drafting Records in the First Congress Do Not Reveal a Clear Rule for the "Free Exercise" of Religion, Suggesting That the Text Instead Communicates a Principle

The precise meaning of the individual right of religious free exercise was not directly discussed during the First Amendment's drafting debates. Aside from our conclusions that "free exercise" likely does *not* mean exemptions and is an individual right, the available records do not reveal a commonly understood meaning of the final text.

From contemporaneous uses of the term, it is not clear that the specific words "free exercise" had one determinate meaning that was commonly understood at the time. The phrase "free exercise" was employed in a number of Founding-era charters.[81] As noted, Virginia used it in its proposed amendment, which itself was based on Article 16 of the 1776 Virginia Declaration of Rights. That declaration held, in part, that "all men are equally entitled to the free exercise of religion, according to the dictates of conscience." "Free exercise" appeared there because the young James Madison proposed it in place of George Mason's original proposed text, "that all men should enjoy the fullest toleration in the exercise of religion."[82] The best explanation for Madison's revision was offered by George Washington in his beautiful 1790 letter to the Hebrew Congregation at Newport, Rhode Island:

> All possess alike liberty of conscience and immunities of citizenship. It is now no more that toleration is spoken of, as if it was by the indulgence of one class of people, that another enjoyed the exercise of their inherent natural rights.

"Toleration" was no longer spoken of because the free exercise of religion is a natural right, and thus not an indulgence granted by the state.

Other Founding-era state charters also employed the words "free exercise." The declaration of rights prefacing the 1776 constitutions of Delaware and Pennsylvania and the 1786 Vermont Constitution included the phrasing:

> that no authority can or ought to be vested in, or assumed by any power whatever, that shall in any case interfere with, or in any manner controul, the right of conscience in the free exercise of religious worship.[83]

---

81. See table 1 in chapter 1. According to McConnell, "The Origins and Historical Understanding of Free Exercise of Religion," 1425, the term "free exercise" first appeared in an American legal document in 1648, when Lord Baltimore required Maryland's new Protestant governor and counselors not to disturb Christians (including Roman Catholics) in the "free exercise" of their religion.

82. Vincent Phillip Muñoz, *God and the Founders: Madison, Washington, and Jefferson* (New York: Cambridge University Press, 2009), 32–34.

83. See table 1 in chapter 1. *Founders' Constitution*, 5:5; *Federal and State Constitutions*, 2:1541 (PA), 2:1868 (VT). See also Muñoz, "Church and State in the Founding-Era State Constitutions," 18.

Article 56 of the 1777 Georgia Constitution provided,

> All persons whatever shall have the free exercise of their religion; provided it
> be not repugnant to the peace and safety of the State; and shall not, unless by
> consent, support any teacher or teachers except those of their own profession.[84]

The Founders used "free exercise" to refer to the principle of religious
freedom, but there is no single rulelike manner in which the words were
used. Moreover, these words were not always used. Some states, including
New Jersey, Massachusetts, and New Hampshire, did not include the words
"free exercise," but did use versions of the phrase "worship according to
conscience."[85] It is not clear that these states understood their religious
freedom protections to differ from those of the other states. Article 38
in New York's 1777 Constitution seems to use "free exercise" and "liberty
of conscience" synonymously:

> And whereas we are required, by the benevolent principles of rational liberty,
> not only to expel civil tyranny, but also to guard against that spiritual oppres-
> sion and intolerance wherewith the bigotry and ambition of weak and wicked
> priests and princes have scourged mankind, this convention doth further, in the
> name and by the authority of the good people of this State, ordain, determine,
> and declare, that the free exercise and enjoyment of religious profession and
> worship, without discrimination or preference, shall forever hereafter be al-
> lowed, within this State, to all mankind: *Provided*, That the liberty of conscience,
> hereby granted, shall not be so construed as to excuse acts of licentiousness, or
> justify practices inconsistent with the peace or safety of this State.[86]

From the repeated and various ways in which the words "free exercise" were employed in Founding-era charters, it appears that they were
used to communicate the principle that individuals possessed a right of
religious freedom, often in the context of discussion of natural rights. It
does not appear that the words were understood to convey a precise or
definite rule. This usage—to communicate a principle—is consistent with
how the words were used during the drafting of what became the First
Amendment.

84. *Federal and State Constitutions*, 1:383.
85. See table 1 in chapter 1.
86. *Federal and State Constitutions*, 2:1338.

The debates surrounding the ratification of the Bill of Rights also fail to shed light on what the ratifiers understood "free exercise" of religion to mean, if indeed such a concrete meaning even existed. Michael McConnell devotes one paragraph consisting of less than one page of his comprehensive 108-page historical account of the Free Exercise Clause's original meaning to the ratification debates. He summarizes the ratification records as "unilluminating."[87]

* * *

The Free Exercise Clause was drafted because Anti-Federalists such as the "Federal Farmer" had demanded that "the free exercise of religion" and other "essential rights" be established as part of the new national compact. As discussed in chapter 1, most of the Founding-era states recognized and protected religious freedom as a natural right. While some Federalists thought a bill of rights was unnecessary because of the limited and delegated character of national powers, no one at the time argued against religious freedom, or that individuals did not possess rights of religious freedom.

To meet the Anti-Federalists' demands for an amendment to protect religious freedom, it was not necessary for the First Congress to debate or define the amendment's terms with any precision. Indeed, many of those who drafted the text thought the amendments to be unnecessary. This explains why the drafting records read like a legislative markup session. Attention was focused on crafting text that was not redundant or stylistically awkward. Nothing suggests that the First Congress engaged in a substantive discussion of the meaning of "free exercise" in the context of drafting what would become the First Amendment's Free Exercise Clause.

This review of the drafting record for the First Amendment's Free Exercise Clause leads me to the following conclusions:

87. McConnell, "Origins and Historical Understanding of Free Exercise of Religion," 1485. Hylton, "Virginia and the Ratification of the Bill of Rights," 455–56, reports that Anti-Federalists in the Virginia state senate argued against ratification because the proposed religion amendments were not sufficient to protect the rights of conscience. He notes, however, that few participants in the Virginia ratification debate believed those arguments to be sincere; they were thought to be "a nakedly political attempt to win support for the antifederalist cause from Virginia's Baptists and members of other dissenting religious groups."

1. "Free Exercise" seems not to have been understood to connote a rule of religious exemption.
2. The drafting records in the First Congress suggest that the Free Exercise Clause was meant to protect an individual right.
3. The drafting records in the First Congress do not reveal a clear rule for the "Free Exercise" of religion. This suggests that the text instead communicates a principle.

These three findings drive a further conclusion: the Free Exercise Clause, like the Establishment Clause, must be constructed. We can know something about the Free Exercise Clause's original meaning, but that meaning is underdetermined.

How we might construct both the Free Exercise Clause and the Establishment Clause consistently with the Founders' political philosophy is the topic of part 3 of this study, to which I now turn.

PART 3

Constitutional Meaning:
Constructing the Religion Clauses

CHAPTER SEVEN

Natural Rights Constructions of the First Amendment Religion Clauses

[handwritten annotation: No look of liquidation/! /public's tradition . / views]

My investigation of the original meanings of the religion provisions of the First Amendment has led to the conclusion that they must be constructed. A good-faith effort to evaluate the available historical evidence led me to conclude in chapter 5 that the Framers did not specify what constitutes an "establishment" of religion. Similarly, I concluded in chapter 6 that the meaning of the "free exercise" of religion was also left underdetermined during the drafting and ratification of the First Amendment. Both the Establishment Clause and Free Exercise Clause lie within what constitutional theorists call "the construction zone."

Originalism and the Concept of Constitutional Constructions

As I have briefly discussed in the introduction and part 2, the idea of constitutional "construction" has been reintroduced recently into constitutional theory. Constitutional *interpretation* involves the act of divining or uncovering the meaning of a constitutional text; it finds the meaning of a text within the text itself. Constitutional *construction* is necessary when interpretation cannot yield meaning. Constitutional constructions, Keith Whittington explains, elucidate the text in the interstices of discoverable, interpretive meaning, where the text is so broad or so underdetermined as to be incapable of faithful but exhaustive reduction to legal rules.[1]

Constructions occur when the process of interpretation exhausts itself without yielding a sufficiently determinate legal meaning.

While the focus on constitutional construction is relatively recent in academic constitutional theory, the underlying idea is hardly new.[2] Randy Barnett and Evan Bernick find evidence of the interpretation-construction distinction in the legal writings of the nineteenth-century jurists Francis Lieber and Thomas Cooley.[3] Nonetheless, the concept and legitimacy of constitutional constructions are not universally accepted. Antonin Scalia, to take a noteworthy example, rejected the distinction between interpretation and construction.[4] Lawrence Solum, one of today's most prominent originalist scholars, has suggested that constitutional constructions are not within the province of originalism:

1. Keith Whittington, *Constitutional Construction: Divided Powers and Constitutional Meaning* (Cambridge, MA: Harvard University Press, 1999), 5. As I noted in chapter 5, footnote 13, Lawrence B. Solum, "The Interpretation-Construction Distinction," *Constitutional Commentary* 27 (2010): 95–96, offers a somewhat different framework for the interpretation-construction distinction than the one I am using. In Solum's account, "interpretation" refers to the process of determining a text's linguistic meaning; "construction" refers to the process of giving the text legal effect. I concur with both Whittington and Solum, however, that one enters the "construction zone" when "the text runs out"—i.e., when a legal provision is vague or underdetermined. See Lee J. Strang, *Originalism's Promise: A Natural Law Account of the American Constitution* (New York: Cambridge University Press, 2019), 31n149. See also Randy E. Barnett, "Interpretation and Construction," *Harvard Journal of Law and Public Policy* 34 (2011): 65–72.

2. The recent recovery of the idea of constitutional constructions is frequently associated with the publication of Whittington's *Constitutional Construction*.

3. Randy E. Barnett and Evan D. Bernick, "The Letter and the Spirit: A Unified Theory of Originalism," *Georgetown Law Journal* 107 (2018): 11–12. One might contend that Chief Justice John Marshall performed the Supreme Court's first constitutional construction in *Marbury v. Madison*, 5 U.S. 1 Cranch 137 (1803).

4. Antonin Scalia and Bryan A. Garner, *Reading Law: The Interpretation of Legal Texts* (St. Paul, MN: Thomson/West, 2012), 13–15. More recently, Ilan Wurman, in *A Debt against the Living: An Introduction to Originalism* (New York: Cambridge University Press, 2017), 86, has written that "it is not obvious . . . that there really is a difference between construction and interpretation even as defined by originalists." For a different sort of critique of the idea of "constructionist originalism," see John O. McGinnis and Michael B. Rappaport, *Originalism and the Good Constitution* (Cambridge, MA: Harvard University Press, 2013), 139–53.

What do originalists say about what we are calling the construction zone—the fields of constitutional doctrine that allow for the application of the general, abstract, and vague provisions of constitutional theory to particular cases? In a sense, originalism as a theory should be silent on this topic. It is a theory of constitutional interpretation, and when it offers an opinion on questions of constitutional construction (i.e., what should be done when the original meaning is underdeterminate), originalism exceeds its jurisdiction.[5]

Some critics of originalism concur. Thomas Colby offers an even more definitive rejection of originalist constructions:

> Originalism, by definition, does not and cannot dictate a "proper" constitutional construction.... When original interpretation produces a meaning that is not specific enough to resolve the issue at hand, we must go beyond originalism in order to decide the case. There can be no originalist answer to the question of which construction to apply; by definition, construction supplements interpretation and cannot be dictated by it.[6]

Colby's contention is shared by a number of leading originalist scholars who argue that when the Constitution's meaning is indeterminate, judges should not perform constructions but instead should defer to the political branches of government.[7]

5. Robert W. Bennett and Lawrence B. Solum, *Constitutional Originalism: A Debate* (Ithaca, NY: Cornell University Press, 2011), 69. See also John O. McGinnis and Michael Rappaport, "Original Methods Originalism: A New Theory of Interpretation and the Case against Construction," *Northwestern University Law Review* 103 (2009): 751–802. Randy Barnett, in "Interpretation and Construction," 69–70, one of the most prominent defenders of what I will call construction originalism, initially held this position.

6. Thomas B. Colby, "The Sacrifice of the New Originalism," *Georgetown Law Journal* 99 (2011): 734. In *Originalism as Faith* (New York: Cambridge University Press, 2018), 98, Eric J. Segall, another critic of originalism, offers a more moderate assessment, contending that "the construction zone that the New Originalists advocate is a place where the original meaning and historical evidence play at most limited roles." See, also, Wurman, *A Debt Against the Living*, 95.

7. See, e.g., Michael Stokes Paulsen, "How to Interpret the Constitution (and How Not to)," *Yale Law Journal* 115 (2006): 2057:

> Thus, if the Constitution supplies a rule, that rule prevails. But if the meaning of the Constitution's language fails to provide such a rule or standard—if it is actually indeterminate (or under-determinate) as to the specific question at hand—then a court has no basis for displacing the rule supplied by some other relevant source of law applicable to the case (typically, a rule supplied by political decisions made by an imperfect representative democracy).

If defined as narrowly as Solum and Colby insist, originalism may not be capable of guiding constitutional constructions. But originalism need not be so defined. And even if judges defer to the political branches, legislative and executive branch officials still need guidance on how to respect the Constitution's vague or underdetermined provisions. *Someone* will have to construct the text. Furthermore, the "presumption of constitutionality" decision-rule that some originalists favor—that when the Constitution's limitations are unclear, judges ought to presume an act is constitutional and thereby defer to the political branches—is not dictated by originalism but, rather, is itself a construction motivated by concerns about the role of judges and democratic legitimacy.[8] The history of church-state jurisprudence, furthermore, is a history of supposed originalist constructions.[9] Judges construct underdetermined constitutional texts. An originalism that ignores this fact and rejects the practice of construction necessarily must concede Ilan Wurman's conclusion that, when it comes to underdetermined text, a court's decision "will in some sense be an arbitrary choice among the competing plausible options."[10]

If it is to be an attractive jurisprudential methodology, originalism needs better alternatives than to "defer" or "act arbitrarily." Current originalist theory may not "entail any particular theory of constitutional construction," as Solum contends, but this study aims to exemplify how judges might perform good-faith originalist constitutional constructions.[11]

Text and Design: A Theory of Construction Originalism

Given that the theory of legitimate originalist constructions remains in its infancy, let me further explain the "text and design" approach—already

---

Keith Whittington initially held that constitutional construction was the province of the political branches. For his own description of his (somewhat) changed position, see Keith Whittington, "Constructing a New American Constitution," *Constitutional Commentary* 27 (2010): 125–29. For an approach to indeterminacy that is somewhat Thayerian but also integrates enforcement of limits on governmental powers through the Necessary and Proper Clause, see Gary Lawson, "Legal Indeterminacy: Its Cause and Cure," *Harvard Journal of Law and Public Policy* 19 (1996): 411–28.

8. For a short and simple account of "the presumption of constitutionality," see Wurman, *Debt against the Living*, 87–89. See also Barnett, "Interpretation and Construction," 70; Michael Stokes Paulsen, "The Most Dangerous Branch: Executive Power to Say What the Law Is," *Georgetown Law Journal* 83 (1994): 332–37.

9. This point will be discussed further in the next chapter.

10. Wurman, *Debt against the Living*, 95.

11. Bennett and Solum, *Constitutional Originalism*, 151.

briefly described in the introduction to part 2—that animates the constructions I will set forth. In those cases where a constitutional text provides an
indeterminate rule (such as the Establishment Clause) or an underdetermined abstract principle (such as the Free Exercise Clause), we necessarily
enter the construction zone. When the text articulates an abstract principle,
we necessarily must ask: Whose understanding of the principle ought to
guide a constitutional construction? Where should a judge turn to develop
his or her construction? If the judge is going to develop a construction herself and not simply defer to another branch of government, there are two
basic approaches she might take: (a) she can attempt to uncover how the
principle was understood at the time of its adoption, or (b) she can "think
for herself" and attempt to articulate the best possible understanding of
the principle.[12]

Ronald Dworkin's "moral reading" of the Constitution exemplifies the
latter approach. Dworkin contends that "we are governed by what our
lawmakers said—by the principle they laid down—not by any information
we might have about how they themselves would have interpreted those
principles or applied them in concrete cases."[13] A judge is not bound by
the drafters' expected application of a principle, in other words, but rather
by the principle itself. Even if the framers of the Fourteenth Amendment
expected its equality principle to be compatible with racial segregation,
Dworkin says that what is binding is the principle of equality itself. Segregation is unconstitutional, notwithstanding how equality was understood
in late-nineteenth-century America.[14]

Dworkin's distinction between a text's principle (what he calls the "semantic intentions") and the expected applications of the principle makes
sense as far as it goes, but that distinction itself does not clarify how we
ought to go about construing the principle embedded in the text, especially if that principle is indeterminate or underdetermined. And even if
we don't consider the drafters' or ratifiers' expected applications to be
binding, why not gain some clarity about how the principle itself was understood at the time of its adoption?

12. I adopt "think for herself" from the "philosophical approach" articulated by Sotirios A.
Barber and James E. Fleming, *Constitutional Interpretation: The Basic Questions* (New York:
Oxford University Press, 2007), 155.

13. Ronald Dworkin, *Freedom's Law: The Moral Reading of the American Constitution*
(Cambridge, MA: Harvard University Press, 1996), 10. For a discussion of Dworkin's evolving
disposition toward originalism, see Jeffrey Goldsworthy, "Dworkin as an Originalist," *Constitutional Commentary* 17 (2000): 49–78.

14. Ronald Dworkin, "Comment," in Antonin Scalia, *A Matter of Interpretation: Federal
Courts and the Law* (Princeton, NJ: Princeton University Press, 1997), 119.

For a Dworkinian such as James Fleming, original principles carry little authority or weight. Fleming contends that judges should embrace moral philosophy and construct the Constitution's principles to make the Constitution "the best it can be."[15] Constitutional fidelity means fidelity to the abstract aspirational commitments set forth in the Constitution's Preamble.[16] Fleming's "best it can be" approach does not necessarily dispense with history or depend on a progressive view of moral knowledge. It does, however, fit nicely with the progressive belief that our understanding of what morality requires improves over time, for the approach emancipates current judges (and the scholars that aspire to influence them) from past understandings of principles.[17]

15. James E. Fleming, in *Fidelity to Our Imperfect Constitution: For Moral Readings and against Originalisms* (New York: Oxford University Press, 2015), 60–61, nicely summarizes his position as follows:

> The commitment to fidelity is a commitment to honor our aspirations and framework for constitutional self-government: to build them out with integrity and responsibility, not to evade responsibility by claiming that we are just following the commands of the founding fathers and that they have already made our decisions for us. The former view also reflects an understanding of the Constitution itself as a framework for furthering the good things proclaimed in the Preamble—and an understanding that being faithful to the Constitution by honoring its aspirations will entail change as we confront new problems in new circumstances. We confront such problems with an attitude of integrity and responsibility, not an attitude of following commands that have already made our decisions for us. And not with an attitude of "updating" in the forward-looking, anti-fidelity sense of hackneyed versions of living constitutionalism. I do not call that "updating" the Constitution. I call it being faithful to the Constitution by honoring its promises, thereby interpreting it so as to make it the best it can be. In that sense, fidelity entails change.

See also Barber and Fleming, *Constitutional Interpretation: The Basic Questions.*
16. Fleming, *Fidelity to Our Imperfect Constitution*, 61–63.
17. The following captures Fleming's approach to history, in *Fidelity to Our Imperfect Constitution*, 78:

> In their willingness to reconsider the major and minor premises of past constitutional interpretations, practitioners of the philosophic approach are expected to think self-critically for themselves. They have to think self-critically about the best interpretation of our constitutional text, history, and structure. They have to reflect critically upon our aspirations in striving for the interpretation that makes the Constitution the best it can be. In doing this, they may well find themselves influenced by the great thinkers of the past or the present. After all, judges and others actively interested in the problems of constitutional meaning are usually educated people, with some exposure to the great thinkers—writers known to be such precisely because of the persuasive quality of their thought. But the goal of the philosophic approach is *truth* (or the best understanding of our Constitution) as distinguished from *opinion*—anyone's opinion,

The version of construction originalism advanced here attempts to construe the Constitution's abstract principles consistently with what can be determined about the principles' original meaning. It follows Dworkin's distinction between a text's principle and the original expected applications of that principle, and it concurs with Dworkin's statement that "we are governed by what our lawmakers said—by the principle they laid down."[18] But my approach to construction also contends that we ought to be governed by the original meanings of the Constitution's principles, at least insofar as those meanings can be determined. Construction originalism recognizes that lawmakers' principles might differ from their expected applications of them, and also that lawmakers might either mistakenly apply their principles or fail to fully appreciate their meaning. Evidence about the original expected applications, accordingly, may or may not help us uncover a principle's original meaning.[19] If it does prove helpful, it is because it helps us grasp the principle's meaning apart from a particular application of it—that is, we can apprehend the original meaning of the principle itself. If and when we can apprehend the original meaning of a constitutional principle, that understanding ought to be used to construct the text.

I will call the method of construction originalism advanced here "text and design" or "design originalism." Design originalism respects the fundamental originalist commitment to understanding and applying the meaning of the Constitution as originally embedded in its text, principles, and underlying purposes. It accepts both the "fixation thesis"—the idea that the linguistic meaning of the text was fixed at the time of each provision's adoption and ratification—and the "public meaning thesis"—the idea that meaning is best represented by the words, phrases, grammar, and syntax that characterized the linguistic practices of the contemporaneous public.[20] It recognizes, additionally, the necessity and legitimacy of constitutional constructions. Because the text of some constitutional provisions does not yield clear legal rules (for reasons of ambiguity, vagueness, indeterminacy, underdeterminacy, etc.), even after consulting how the words

---

including the opinions of great philosophers. The truly philosophic judge, therefore, would not apply the teachings of any of the great thinkers in a doctrinaire fashion.

18. Dworkin, *Freedom's Law*, 10.

19. For a helpful discussion of this point, see Keith Whittington, "Originalism: A Critical Introduction," *Fordham Law Review* 82 (2013): 382–86.

20. For a helpful account of the "fixation thesis" and "public meaning thesis," see Lawrence Solum's discussion of them in Bennett and Solum, *Constitutional Originalism*, 4.

were typically used at the time, the drafting record, and other resources, discovering textual meaning requires going beyond the text. Constructions consistent with an originalist approach must in these cases also consider the ends or purposes of the textual provision in question within their historical context. In short, design originalism looks at both the text's design and the principles that animate that design. While not using the label "design originalism," Barnett and Bernick offer a concise summary of it:

> The Constitution's provisions, like the Constitution as a whole, are calculated to perform particular functions, and they would be without value if they did not do so. Truly understanding and applying the text may *require* an understanding of those functions. Lacking certainty about how to resolve a given case on the basis of the Constitution's linguistic meaning alone, judges must make a decision on the basis of *some* reason. To formulate a rule with reference to the function—or functions—that a relevant provision is designed to perform is not a matter of making the law "the best it can be" but giving effect *to* the law as best one can. A judge who decided a case on the basis of a reason that cannot be grounded in original functions—however normatively appealing that might seem—would be departing from the law entirely.[21]

They conclude: "Judges should seek, identify, and use the *original* functions to guide their implementation of the original meaning of the text."[22]

Although John McGinnis and Michael Rappaport reject what they label "constructionist originalism," their "original methods originalism," as applied to resolving ambiguous and vague text, would seem to license my proposed method of construction originalism. They write:

> Under the original interpretive rules, we believe that interpreters were required to select the interpretation of ambiguous and vague terms that had the stronger evidence in its favor. When the interpretation of language was unclear, the interpreter would consider the relevant originalist evidence—evidence based

21. Emphasis in the original. Barnett and Bernick, "The Letter and Spirit," 32. For Barnett and Bernick's defense of construction originalism grounded on judges as fiduciaries and the judicial duty of good faith performance, see pp. 26–32.

22. Emphasis in the original. Barnett and Bernick, "The Letter and Spirit," 32n159. See also Lawrence B. Solum, "Communicative Content and Legal Content," *Notre Dame Law Review* 89 (2013): 500, explaining that "the public context may include facts about the general point or purpose of the provision (as opposed to the 'intention of the author'), and those facts may resolve [textual] ambiguities."

on text, structure, history, and intent—and select the interpretation that was supported more strongly by the evidence.[23]

The method of "design originalism" that I propose provides what McGinnis and Rappaport call for: a consideration of "the relevant originalist evidence—evidence based on text, structure, history, and intent" undertaken so as to "select the interpretation that [i]s supported more strongly by the evidence." Indeed, the method mirrors one of their specific "original methods," which is to "look to the reason and spirit of the law—'the cause which moved the legislator to enact the law.'"[24]

While these considerations will particularly interest originalists, nonoriginalists might also find value in articulating what an originalist constitutional construction would involve. Even James Fleming contends that the Constitution's original meaning at least should be treated as "one source of constitutional meaning."[25] For those who seek to offer a "moral" or "best it can be" reading of the Constitution, design originalism offers a starting point and one plausible reading of the text—perhaps even the "best" reading possible.

Design Originalism: Method

As I briefly discussed in part 2, the initial step of construing a constitutional provision requires determining the kind of text it is—that is, its genre as a rule, standard, or principle.[26] Rules are often, though not

23. McGinnis and Rappaport, "Original Methods Originalism," 774.

24. McGinnis and Rappaport, "Original Methods Originalism," 789. McGinnis and Rappaport's internal quotation is from Blackstone's *Commentaries*.

25. Fleming, *Fidelity to Our Imperfect Constitution*, 23. Justice William Brennan was even more open to originalist considerations in Establishment Clause cases. In the school prayer case *Abington School District v. Schempp*, Brennan wrote, "The line we must draw between the permissible and the impermissible is one which accords with history and faithfully reflects the understanding of the Founding Fathers." *Abington School District v. Schempp*, 374 U.S. 203, 294 (1963).

26. I do not mean to suggest that making this determination is always simple and straightforward. As Steven Calabresi and Gary Lawson explain in "The Rule of Law as a Law of Law," *Notre Dame Law Review* 90 (2014): 496:

There is no single, noncontroversial way to determine the extent to which a norm is rule-like. Rules, as distinct from standards or particularistic decisionmaking methods, have some significant degree of generality and definiteness, but there is no metric for measuring how general and/or definite something must be in order to be called a

always, amenable to straightforward interpretation—for example, the requirement stipulated in Article 2, Section 1 that those eligible to the office of president shall have attained the age of thirty-five years. Standards and principles are more likely to require constructions. For a constitutional provision that sets forth an indeterminate rule or standard, an originalist construction will first search for the reasons the rule or standard was adopted. For a constitutional provision that articulates an abstract principle, an originalist construction will attempt to determine the principle's original meaning.

For every kind of text (rules, standards, and principles), grasping the text's design—which includes, crucially, the mischief it was designed to address and the ends or purposes it was intended to realize—ought to guide an originalist construction. Regarding principles, the aim of the inquiry is to determine as much as possible about the original meaning of the principle itself, *not* any particular expected applications of it, since these may fall short of or even contradict the principle.[27] As we shall see, the

---

rule. . . . Notwithstanding these difficulties, people distinguish rules from standards all of the time, . . .

Later in the same article, pp. 502–3, the authors provide a response to those, including Justice Scalia, who contend that courts should only enforce constitutional rules:

The extensive role of standards in understanding the Constitution means that one cannot dismiss expressly standard-like provisions as constitutional anomalies, to be minimized or ignored for interpretive purposes. The Constitution uses rules when it means to use rules, and it uses standards when it means to use standards. It makes extensive use of both. To discover the meaning of the Constitution, one cannot start with a presumption in favor of one or the other kind of formulation. One finds what one finds. If Justice Scalia believes otherwise, he is simply wrong.

On this latter point, also see Randy E. Barnett, "Scalia's Infidelity: A Critique of 'Faint-Hearted' Originalism,'" *University of Cincinnati Law Review* 75 (2006): 11–12.

27. To anticipate an objection, let me offer a concrete example of how we might distinguish the meaning of a constitutional principle from its expected applications. The First Congress that drafted the Religion Clauses also passed legislation adopting an official legislative chaplain. In fact, the First Congress voted to appoint and pay for a chaplain for each house in the same week that it voted to approve the final draft of the First Amendment for submission to the states (See *Marsh v. Chambers*, 463 U.S. 783, 790 [1983]). We can infer that a significant number of the First Amendment's drafters believed that legislative chaplains were consistent with the First Amendment. The Founders' own principle of religious free exercise, however, forbids the state to exercise authority over religious worship as such. Insofar as the chaplain's official duties included presiding over acts of religious worship, the Founders' practice (which we take to reflect their expected applications of the First Amendment) contradicts their principle (which we use to construct the First Amendment). For reasons I will explain below and in chapter 8, official legislative chaplains also violate an originalist construction of

construction of the Free Exercise Clause's principle will direct us toward the Founders' political philosophy, whereas the construction of the Establishment Clause's rules will direct us toward the Founders' practices.

The basic method of design originalism can be outlined as follows:

1. Determine the kind of text at issue: a rule, standard, or principle.

2a. If a principle, determine what can be known about the original meaning of that principle.

2b. If a rule or standard, determine the underlying mischief to be addressed and purpose to be achieved by the rule or standard.

3a. Construct a doctrine in light of the principle's original meaning in a manner that is consistent with the text itself.

3b. Construct a doctrine in light of the rule's or standard's underlying mischief/purpose in a manner that is consistent with the text itself.

4. Construct the text in a manner that is consistent with other constitutional provisions.

An originalist construction must be consistent with the text and with what is known about its original meaning, even if what is known is merely a proposition about what the text did *not* originally mean. If the drafting record reveals that a provision was crafted to mean *not x*, it should not be constructed to mean *x*. Just because a provision requires construction does not mean we have no knowledge of what the provision does not mean. History still remains important. When constructing a text, a legal interpreter also will likely be concerned with precedent, but the role and relative weight of precedent, properly speaking, lies beyond construction originalism per se. Having reached an originalist construction, an interpreter may or may not want to mold it with precedent to various degrees. That judgment, however, is not dictated by the originalist construction method itself.[28]

---

the Establishment Clause. Because we can know and independently come to understand the Founders' principles apart from their practices, we can identify occasions when the Founders' practices violate their principles.

28. For thoughtful recent studies on the role of precedent, see Amy Coney Barrett, "Originalism and Stare Decisis," *Notre Dame Law Review* 92 (2017): 1921–43; Michael S. Paulsen, "Does the Supreme Court's Current Doctrine of *Stare Decisis* Require Adherence to the Supreme Court's Current Doctrine of *Stare Decisis*?" *North Carolina Law Review* 86 (2008): 1165–1212; Strang, *Originalism's Promise*, 91–141. See also Randy J. Kozel, *Settled versus Right: A Theory of Precedent* (New York: Cambridge University Press, 2017), and the symposium on the book in *Constitutional Commentary* 33 (2018).

The method outlined above offers a way to perform originalist constructions consistent with the Constitution's letter and spirit. As helpfully explained by Barnett and Bernick:

> Just as discovering the "spirit of the deal" requires an investigation into "the commercial context in which [a contract is] created," discovering the functions of the Constitution's various clauses and structural design entails investigation into the context in which they were enacted. This is a familiar task for originalists—the inquiry into the law's spirit is no less grounded in empirical facts than inquiry into the law's letter. Constitutions, statutes, and contracts are products of human design, and—as we will elaborate—one need not read minds to determine what they are designed to do. The Constitution was the result of a careful, if often contentious, "design process." Each provision and structural design element was crafted for a reason or reasons. We discover these reasons by examining how the Constitution's various components interact with one another, as well as by consulting what was said about them both in public and in private.[29]

Design Originalism: Constructing the Religion Clauses

Let me now attempt to use this "design originalism" methodology to construct the First Amendment's Religion Clauses. Step 1 is to determine what kind of provision is embedded in the text—a rule, standard, or principle. In chapters 5 and 6, I determined that the Establishment Clause contains two rules and the Free Exercise Clause sets forth a principle:

ESTABLISHMENT CLAUSE RULES
- Congress shall make no law erecting a religious establishment.
- Congress shall make no law concerning state-level religious establishments.

FREE EXERCISE CLAUSE PRINCIPLE
- Congress shall not violate the right of religious liberty.

---

29. Barnett and Bernick, "Letter and Spirit," 34, quoting Gary Lawson, "Reflections of an Empirical Reader (or: Could Fleming Be Right This Time?)," *Boston University Law Review* 96 (2016): 1472.

Step 2 requires that we attempt to determine the underlying reasons why these provisions were adopted, and what they were designed to do.

Constructing the First Amendment's Principle of Religious Free Exercise

I will start with the Free Exercise Clause. For now, I assume the provision's incorporation to apply against the states, though I will return to this point at the end of this section.

The evidence reviewed in chapter 6 led me to conclude that

1. "free exercise" seems not to have been understood to entail a rule of religious exemption.
2. the drafting records in the First Congress suggest that the Free Exercise Clause was meant to protect an individual right.
3. the drafting records in the First Congress do not reveal a clear rule for the "free exercise" of religion. This suggests that the text communicates a principle.

An originalist construction should aim to set forth a constitutional doctrine that reflects the principle of religious liberty that the Founders articulated. It should be consistent with the First Amendment's text, including our construction of the Establishment Clause.

As I discussed in part 1, the Founders most clearly articulated their shared common understanding of the right of religious liberty in the state declarations of rights adopted between 1776 and 1786. These documents can serve as the groundwork for an originalist construction. In these founding constitutions, the Founders declared religious liberty to be an inalienable natural right. As discussed in chapters 1 and 2, the concepts of "inalienability" and "natural rights" are only intelligible in light of the Founders' social compact theory of government. In chapter 3, I showed that the Founders reached their judgments concerning the natural right of religious liberty through Enlightenment reasoning (Jefferson), natural theology (Madison), and Christianity (Backus).

Natural rights exist prior to and independent of government; individuals possess them on account of their human nature. *Inalienable* natural rights are rights over which individuals retain sovereignty when they form and empower a government. The inalienable natural right of religious liberty is a jurisdictional concept. The Founders held that authority over religious exercises as such could not, and therefore had not, been granted to the government. This jurisdictional understanding is apparent in, among other places, the texts of the Pennsylvania (1776), Delaware (1776), and Vermont (1777) Declarations of Rights:

> no authority can or ought to be vested in, or assumed by any power whatever that shall in any case interfere with, or in any manner controul the right of conscience in the free exercise of religious worship.[30]

No authority over religious free exercise *can* be vested in government, due to its inalienable character. The nature of religious freedom itself does not allow individuals to give authority to government over it.

Because authority over religious exercise cannot be delegated, the state lacks jurisdiction over religious exercises as such. In chapter 2, I explained that the Founders declared two specific, reciprocal, core religious liberty immunities from state power: (a) No individual could be punished (in the Founders' language, "hurt, molested, or restrained")[31] on account of his religious opinions, profession, or observances as such; and (b) no individual could be compelled to embrace, profess, or observe religious beliefs or practices.

These immunities find collective expression in the following construction of the Free Exercise Clause:

> Congress and the states shall make no law that exercises jurisdiction over religious exercises as such.

Thus constructed, no government may

- punish religious beliefs or exercises as such.
- prohibit religious beliefs or exercises as such.
- mandate religious beliefs or exercises as such.
- regulate religious beliefs or exercises as such.

---

30. *The Founders' Constitution*, ed. Philip B. Kurland and Ralph Lerner (Indianapolis, IN: Liberty Fund, n.d.; originally published Chicago: University of Chicago Press, 1987), 5:5 (Delaware); *The Federal and State Constitutions, Colonial Charters, and Other Organic Laws of the United States*, 2nd edition, ed. Ben Perley Poore (Washington: Government Printing Office, 1878), 2:1541 (Pennsylvania), 2:1859 (Vermont). See also Muñoz, "Church and State in the Founding-Era State Constitutions," 14–15.

31. See MA and NH in table 1 in chapter 1.

I have used the modifier "as such" to indicate that the state is prohibited from regulating, punishing, prohibiting, or mandating religious beliefs or exercises *on account of* their religious character or *for* religious reasons. While the state may prohibit animal cruelty and regulate water quality, it cannot prohibit the "sacramental slaughter" of animals or specify that "holy water" must maintain a certain level of purity to be "holy."

Government's lack of authority over religious exercises does *not* mean that legislation cannot *incidentally* affect, burden, or even prohibit religious exercises when the state is pursuing otherwise legitimate ends. This conclusion follows from the premises that all natural rights have natural limits, and that government is instituted to protect natural rights and therefore is given authority to pursue certain limited ends.

As I discussed in chapter 2, the law of nature, which is the law of reason, sets the boundary or scope of every natural right. While this teaching may sound abstract, it is no more complicated than the common-sense maxim that one individual cannot legitimately use his freedom to take away or impair the legitimate freedom of others. Since all men and women are created equal and equally possess the same rights by nature, no individual may legitimately use his natural liberty to impinge the rights of others. My natural right to move my body as I like does not include the liberty to strike you in the face.

That natural rights are bounded means religious freedom in the state of nature does *not* encompass religiously motivated actions that trespass the law of nature. Religiously motivated actions that violate others' natural rights are not part of or protected by the natural right to religious liberty. The natural right of religious liberty does not protect the Aztec practice of child sacrifice; no person has the natural right to inflict unprovoked harm on another, especially an innocent child, even if that harm is motivated by sincere religious conviction.

This understanding of natural rights clearly informed Egbert Benson's comments in the First Congress when the House of Representatives debated, in the context of drafting the Second Amendment, a right to exemptions from military service for religious conscientious objectors. Conscientious objection "may be a religious persuasion," he said, "but it is no natural right, and therefore ought to be left to the discretion of the Government."[32] Religious motivation alone, Benson understood, does not qualify an action or activity for protection under the umbrella of the right of religious liberty. Conscientious objection, in particular, is not part of the

32. *Annals of Congress*, 1st Cong., 1st sess., 779–80.

natural right of religious liberty, because it is reasonable that members of a political community be called on to fight to defend the community. It is not contrary to the law of nature for a government to raise an army and to expect all who are protected by it to serve in it.

In the state of nature, individuals must themselves enforce the law of nature to secure their natural rights. Political communities are formed and governments are constituted in part to assume this role—in the words of the Declaration of Independence, "to secure these rights, governments are instituted among men." The people form a compact with one another to mutually surrender their natural executive powers to the community. The community, in turn, forms a government, which is given the power to make laws for the community. The basis of these laws is, or at least ought to be, the natural law. Put otherwise, the primary end of the legislative power is to transform the precepts of the reasonable uses of one's liberty (which, as discussed in chapter 2, are sometimes vague or ambiguous) into a code of positive law for the community. Government is not given authority to legislate on everything—the existence of inalienable rights means that the people limit government's legitimate authority—but when it acts within its sphere of authority, government can legitimately proscribe behavior.

If a positive law is reasonable—that is, if it is consistent with the law of nature and within the state's legitimate ends—an individual's nonalienated natural right of religious liberty is not implicated. In agreeing to be part of the social compact and the government formed under it, individuals consent to abide by the law; indeed, perhaps the most elementary aspect of citizenship is to follow the laws of the community.[33] It would be

---

33. In this light, consider the following sentence from George Washington's 1789 letter to the Quakers:

> While men perform their social Duties faithfully, they do all that Society or the State can with propriety demand or expect; and remain responsible only to their Maker for the Religion or modes of faith which they may prefer or profess.

Thomas Jefferson echoed Washington's statement in his 1802 letter to the Danbury Baptist Association:

> Adhering to this expression of the supreme will of the nation in behalf of the rights of conscience, I shall see with sincere satisfaction the progress of those sentiments which tend to restore to man all his natural rights, convinced he has no natural right in opposition to his social duties.

In *Religious Liberty and the American Supreme Court: The Essential Cases and Documents*, updated edition, ed. Vincent Phillip Muñoz (Lanham, MD: Rowman & Littlefield, 2015), 625, 627.

impossible for a political community to function if individuals retained the privilege of disregarding those laws with which they disagreed, regardless of the source of that disagreement.[34] The community *can* grant legal exemptions to religious and other citizens from burdensome laws; but this is a matter of discretionary civil rights, not natural rights. Within the state of nature, the natural right of religious liberty does not include the moral right to violate the law of nature. Likewise, within the social compact, the nonalienated natural right of religious liberty does not include the legal right to be exempt from otherwise valid laws.

I have assumed that the positive law furthers legitimate civic ends consistent with the constitution established by the political community. If the legislative power passes a law that exceeds its jurisdiction, the law is null and void and ought to be found so by the competent power. This is not true only for matters of religious liberty; it is a necessary consequence of any and all government failures to stay within its legitimate sphere of authority.[35] No exemptions from such laws should be needed, because no citizens ought to be required to follow a law that the government lacks legitimate authority to enact.

In America, the national political community has specified the power given to the federal government in the Constitution, and one of the Constitution's mechanisms to enforce limits on governmental power is judicial review. Regarding the Free Exercise Clause, this means that if the legislative power makes a law that assumes jurisdiction over religious exercises as such, then the judicial power is obligated to strike the law down as null and void because it exceeds Congress's constitutional authority.[36] So

34. The classic exposition of this point remains Abraham Lincoln's First Inaugural Address.

35. In this light, consider Article 15 of Madison's "Memorial and Remonstrance," in *Religious Liberty and the American Supreme Court*, 610. See also Vincent Phillip Muñoz, *God and the Founders: Madison, Washington, and Jefferson* (New York: Cambridge University Press, 2009), 29.

36. Alexander Hamilton offers the defense for the judiciary possessing this role in *Federalist 78*:

> The complete independence of the courts of justice is peculiarly essential in a limited Constitution. By a limited Constitution, I understand one which contains certain specified exceptions to the legislative authority; such, for instance, as that it shall pass no bills of attainder, no ex-post-facto laws, and the like. Limitations of this kind can be preserved in practice no other way than through the medium of courts of justice, whose duty it must be to declare all acts contrary to the manifest tenor of the Constitution void. Without this, all the reservations of particular rights or privileges would amount to nothing.

constructed, the Free Exercise Clause protects religious liberty by establishing a hard boundary on state action: government cannot exercise jurisdiction over religious exercises as such. Government can never punish,
prohibit, mandate, or regulate religious beliefs or exercises on account of
their religious character.

This construction of religious free exercise follows from the inalienable natural rights political philosophy that originally animated American
constitutionalism. As such, applying it to the states through any version of
the Fourteenth Amendment's incorporation of the Bill of Rights poses no
philosophical difficulties. Indeed, the construction itself is informed by the
principle of religious liberty most clearly articulated in the Founding-era
state declarations of rights. This is not to say that the original meaning of
the Fourteenth Amendment demands incorporation—that question lies
beyond this inquiry.[37] It is only to say that the incorporation of a natural
rights construction of the Free Exercise Clause could coherently extend the
Founders' political and constitutional philosophy of religious freedom to
the states.

The construction of the Free Exercise Clause I have set forth—
Congress and the states (assuming incorporation) shall make no law that
exercises jurisdiction over religious exercises as such—is derived from the
Founders' shared natural rights political theory. It polices jurisdictional
limits on government. It does not include a constitutional right to exemptions from otherwise valid but religiously burdensome laws, but it also
does not forbid legislative or executive action to provide such exemptions.

My construction captures the Founders' principle of religious liberty
and the understanding that was articulated during the text's drafting. It
is also confirmed by the text itself. The Free Exercise Clause imposes an
absolute ban: Congress (and the states) can "make *no law* . . . prohibiting
the free exercise" of religion. Its scope is different from that of the Fourth
Amendment's protection against "unreasonable" searches and seizures,
or the Fifth Amendment's protections against deprivations of life, liberty,
and property "without due process of law." The First Amendment affords

In Alexander Hamilton, James Madison, John Jay, *The Federalist Papers*, ed. Clinton Rossiter,
introduction by Charles R. Kesler (New York: Signet Classics, 2003), 465.

37. For a recent account of the Fourteenth Amendment's original meaning, see Kurt T.
Lash, *The Fourteenth Amendment and the Privileges and Immunities of American Citizenship*
(New York: Cambridge University Press, 2014). See also David R. Upham, "The Meaning of
the 'Privileges and Immunities of Citizens' on the Eve of the Civil War," *Notre Dame Law
Review* 91 (2016): 1117–66.

no constitutional space for "reasonable" prohibitions of religious free exercise if "due process" is afforded or if "compelling state interests" are pursued. The categorical character of the Free Exercise Clause comports with the idea that the state lacks jurisdiction over the nonalienated right to religious liberty.[38]

We can make the same point by comparing the exemptionist construction of the Free Exercise Clause to the First Amendment's actual text. The exemptionist reading effectively construes the text to state, "Congress shall make no law . . . prohibiting the free exercise of religion *unless it has a compelling reason to do so and it uses properly tailored means.*" As I shall discuss in the conclusion to this book, the exemptionist construction fundamentally transforms the text, allowing that which the text plainly prohibits.

Constructing the First Amendment's Rules of No Establishment

Constructing the Free Exercise Clause requires grasping the Founders' understanding of the principle of religious liberty, and drawing from that principle constitutional doctrines consistent with the First Amendment's text. Constructing the Establishment Clause is a bit more complex. I concluded in chapter 5 that the Establishment Clause articulates two rules:

- Congress shall make no law erecting a religious establishment.
- Congress shall make no law concerning a state-level religious establishment.

I also concluded that the First Amendment's drafting and ratification records do not evince what constitutes a religious "establishment." I have suggested that we should attempt to comprehend the rules' purposes, asking: What mischiefs are the rules designed to prevent, and what ends are they designed to secure?[39] We can then construct constitutional doctrines that advance those ends and are consistent both with the Establishment

---

38. Cf. John Witte Jr. and Joel A. Nichols, *Religion and the American Constitutional Experiment*, 4th ed. (New York: Oxford University Press, 2016), 84–86. In his concurring opinion in *Fulton v. City of Philadelphia*, 593 U.S. ___ (2021), Justice Alito never confronts the categorical character of the Free Exercise Clause, despite his attention to the First Amendment's text.

39. For an extraordinarily helpful account of the "mischief rule," see Samuel L. Bray, "The Mischief Rule," *Georgetown Law Journal* 109 (2021): 967–1013.

Clause's text and, importantly, with the construction of the Free Exercise Clause adopted above.

Constructing the Establishment Clause also involves another level of complexity, at least assuming that the Fourteenth Amendment incorporated it to apply against the states. In chapter 5, I showed that one of the two rules—Congress shall make no law concerning state-level religious establishments—reflected the drafters' concerns that the new restrictions on the *national* government ought not interfere with existing *state-level* church-state arrangements. Incorporation, however, imposes constitutional limits on state authority. It would be contradictory to apply against the states a constitutional provision that was drafted, at least in part, so as not to restrict state practices. I simply note for now that we must address how or even whether an originalist construction of the Establishment Clause can be squared with the doctrine of incorporation. Before taking up that question, I will proceed to conduct an originalist construction of "establishment."

The Establishment Clause's Original Design

We can begin to determine the underlying purposes of the Establishment Clause, including the mischiefs it was designed to prevent, by returning to the reasons why the text was drafted. Recall that during the ratification debates, Anti-Federalists charged that the national government under the proposed Constitution would inevitably violate fundamental liberties, including religious freedom. Some Anti-Federalists were particularly concerned that religious liberty would be threatened by a national religious establishment. In the New York ratifying convention, Thomas Tredwell stated:

> I could have wished also that sufficient caution had been used to secure to us our religious liberties, and to have prevented the general government from tyrannizing over our consciences by a religious establishment—a tyranny of all others most dreadful, and which will assuredly be exercised whenever it shall be thought necessary for the promotion and support of their political measures.[40]

---

40. Thomas Tredwell, Statement in the New York Ratifying Convention, July 2, 1788, in *Founders' Constitution*, 1:475.

The Anti-Federalist "A Countryman" said that a national religious establishment would "make every body [sic] worship God in a certain way, whether the people thought it right or no, and punish them severely, if they would not."[41] Anti-Federalists clearly and rightly associated a national religious establishment with religious coercion.

As I discussed in chapter 5, Anti-Federalists did not object to religious establishments per se. They feared national power far more than state power, especially in church-state matters. Local communities, especially compared to the nation as a whole, were more homogenous. To the extent that religious diversity existed within a state, state officials would be closer and more responsive to the local population. States, moreover, tended to implement church-state policies such as religious taxes and state-funded ministers at the town level. For all these reasons, state establishments were viewed as less dangerous than national establishments.

Such state practices might be interrupted or threatened by a remote and unaccountable national government that, Anti-Federalists said, would impose uniform laws throughout the nation. Recalling Montesquieu's doctrine that rule in large territories necessarily tends toward tyranny, they charged that "it is impossible for any single legislature so fully to comprehend the circumstances of the different parts of a very extensive dominion, as to make laws adapted to those circumstances."[42] Akhil Amar, as I discussed in chapter 5, nicely captures the Anti-Federalist view:

The possibility of national control over a powerful intermediate association [churches] self-consciously trying to influence citizens' worldviews, shape their behavior, and cultivate their habits obviously struck fear in the hearts of Anti-Federalists. Yet local control over such intermediate organizations seemed far less threatening, less distant, less aristocratic, less monopolistic—just as local banks were far less threatening than a national one, and local militias far less dangerous than a national standing army. Given the religious diversity of the continent—with Congregationalists dominating New England, Anglicans down south, Quakers in Pennsylvania, Catholics huddling together in Maryland, Baptists seeking refuge in Rhode Island, and so on—a single national religious regime would have been horribly oppressive to many men and women of faith;

41. "Letters from a Countryman V," *New York Journal*, January 17, 1788, in *The Complete Anti-Federalist*, ed. Herbert J. Storing (Chicago: University of Chicago Press, 1981), 6:87.

42. "Letters of Agrippa XII," *Massachusetts Gazette*, January 11, 1788, in *Complete Anti-Federalist*, 4:94.

local control, by contrast, would allow dissenters in any place to vote with their feet and find a community with the right religious tone.[43]

Those who demanded an amendment prohibiting a national religious establishment were motivated by an underlying concern to prevent the nationalization of church-state matters and the attendant religious coercion they feared would accompany it.

Federalists offered no principled objection by way of response. They certainly were not against religious liberty, nor did they favor the national government possessing authority to establish and coerce religion. Federalists contended that the national government lacked power to do what the Anti-Federalists feared, and thus they did not share the Anti-Federalists' anxieties. The records of the drafting of the Establishment Clause reflect the Federalists' indifference. Many in the First Congress—and it must be remembered that Federalists dominated the First Congress—simply wanted to draft an amendment that would enervate Anti-Federalist opposition without interfering with state-level church-state policies or, it appears, with the national government's otherwise legitimate authority to pass some legislation that touched upon religion (e.g., religious exemptions from military service).

James Madison, who did more than any other individual to usher amendments through the First Congress, made the most telling comment on the Establishment Clause's substantive purpose on August 15, 1789:

He [Madison] apprehended the meaning of the words to be, that Congress should not establish a religion, and enforce the legal observation of it by law, nor compel men to worship God in any manner contrary to their conscience. Whether the words are necessary or not, he did not mean to say, but they had been required by some of the State Conventions, who seemed to entertain an opinion that under the clause of the constitution, which gave power to Congress to make all laws necessary and proper to carry into execution the constitution, and the laws made under it, enabled them to make laws of such a nature as might infringe the rights of conscience and establish a national religion; to prevent these effects he presumed the amendment was intended, and he thought it as well expressed as the nature of the language would admit.[44]

43. Akhil Reed Amar, *The Bill of Rights: Creation and Reconstruction* (New Haven, CT: Yale University Press, 1998), 45.
44. *Annals of Congress*, 1st Cong., 1st sess., 758.

Madison's comment tracks the exact concerns articulated by the Anti-Federalists. They had claimed that the national government might contend that the demands of the "general welfare" made a national religious establishment necessary and proper.[45] Without conceding the validity of the Anti-Federalists' fears, Madison nonetheless sought to draft text that would allay their concerns that the national government "might infringe the rights of conscience" by legislating a religious establishment that compelled the observance of religion and worship contrary to conscience. The Establishment Clause was designed, in large measure, to remedy the mischief of possible abridgements of religious liberty by the national government through a national religious establishment.

Elucidating the Establishment Clause's Meaning in Light of Its Design, and Consistently with the First Amendment's Text

Given that religious establishments can generate unjust coercion of conscience, it might seem that we could construct "establishment of religion" simply to prohibit religious coercion: "Congress and the states (assuming incorporation) shall make no law coercing religion." The construction effectively would make the Establishment and Free Exercise Clauses redundant but, given the First Congress's apathy toward the amendment effort as a whole, perhaps it would not be altogether surprising that different provisions on the same subject overlap in their protections.

To read "shall make no law respecting an establishment" as "shall make no law coercing religion" might be a plausible construction, but it suffers shortcomings beyond redundancy with the Free Exercise Clause.[46] A "no-coercion" construction drops the text's original design of only restricting the national government, which, of course, might be a necessary consequence of the Fourteenth Amendment and the doctrine of incorporation. But there

---

45. According to "Deliberator," *Freeman's Journal* (Philadelphia), February 20, 1788, in *Complete Anti-Federalist*, 3:179:

> Congress may, if they shall think it for the "general welfare," establish an uniformity in religion throughout the United States. Such establishments have been thought necessary, and have accordingly taken place in almost all the other countries in the world, and will, no doubt, be thought equally necessary in this.

46. Regarding the interpretative rule that a reader should avoid interpretations that render words to be redundant or surplusage, see McGinnis and Rappaport, *Originalism and the Good Constitution*, 119.

exists an additional difficulty: a "no coercion" construction simply does not square with the text itself.

Chapter 5 documented that, even if many members of the First Congress thought amendments were unnecessary, when they drafted the Establishment Clause they deliberately adopted some words and excised others. Specifically, the drafters seem to have purposefully picked the word "establishment" to demarcate the prohibition on Congress. To review, on August 15, the House of Representatives adopted the following language:

Congress shall make no laws touching religion. . . . [47]

Five days later, the House edited the text as follows:

Congress shall make no laws touching *establishing* religion. . . . [48]

It may be true, as Carl Esbeck suggests, that "no one can say for certain" why the House changed the text from "no laws touching religion" to "no law establishing religion," but we can infer a good reason for the change. Esbeck explains:

Likely the House had come to realize over the last five days [from August 15 to August 20] that the scope of the amendment's restraint needed to be narrowed lest countless and unavoidable effects of general legislation unintentionally impacting religion were to be within the negation of congressional power. [49]

"No laws touching religion" would have imposed a categorical prohibition that potentially reached every aspect of Congress's lawmaking power, whereas "no law establishing religion" instead prohibited one specific type of legislation: a law establishing religion. The alterations—"laws" to "law" and "touching" to "establishing"—significantly narrowed the prohibition. If we are to construe the actual text, we have to elucidate the meaning of religious "establishment." It may be, as Justices Scalia and Thomas and other leading scholars have suggested, that a religious establishment is essentially coercive. Nonetheless, we would still need to specify in what particular ways

47. *Annals of Congress*, 1st Cong., 1st sess., 759.
48. *Annals of Congress*, 1st Cong., 1st sess., 796.
49. Carl H. Esbeck, "The Uses and Abuses of Textualism and Originalism in Establishment Clause Interpretation," *Utah Law Review* 2011 (2011): 547, 552.

establishments coerce.[50] The First Amendment does not use the word "coercion"; it uses the word "establishment." The words are not synonymous.

We also must account for the words "respecting an" and how they inform the Establishment Clause's design. These words also appear to have been deliberately adopted. As discussed in chapter 5, the joint House-Senate conference committee adopted the phrase "respecting an establishment" at the very end of the drafting process even though it had not been previously considered or used in the House or Senate and appears in no Founding-era state constitution. Congress is not merely prohibited from establishing a religion; Congress shall make no law "respecting an establishment."

Examining how the Framers used the term "establishment" suggests a more exact construction than "no coercion"—one that better reflects the actual text adopted (including "respecting an"), reflects the underlying concern with religious coercion, and develops the Establishment Clause to be complementary to (not redundant with) the Free Exercise Clause.

The drafting records reveal two common uses of "establishment" in the context of church-state relations. Some draft provisions sought to prohibit a "religion," "religious sect," or "religious society" from being established. The state of Virginia, for example, proposed that "no particular sect or society ought to be favored or established, by law. . . ."[51] Such proposals sought to prevent Congress from entering into a privileged relationship with an institutional church, a sect, or a religion. We can refer to such proposals as bans on "church establishments." Alternatively, some Framers sought to prevent Congress from establishing "religious doctrines," "articles of faith," or "modes of worship." On August 15, 1789, during the House of Representatives' drafting debates, Elbridge Gerry proposed the language, "no religious doctrine shall be established by law."[52] The Senate later adopted, "Congress shall make no law establishing articles of faith or

---

50. In his dissenting opinion in *Lee v. Weisman*, 505 U.S. 577, 640 (1992), which was joined by Chief Justice Rehnquist and Justices White and Thomas, Justice Scalia writes, "The coercion that was a hallmark of historical establishments of religion was coercion of religious orthodoxy and of financial support by force of law and threat of penalty." See also Michael W. McConnell, "Coercion: The Lost Element of Establishment," *William and Mary Law Review* 27 (1986): 933–41.

51. *The Debates in the Several State Conventions on the Adoption of the Federal Constitution, as Recommended by the General Convention at Philadelphia, in 1787*, 2nd ed., ed. Jonathan Elliot (Philadelphia: J. B. Lippincott, 1861), 3:659.

52. *Annals of Congress*, 1st Cong., 1st sess., 757.

a mode of worship. . . ."[53] We can call these proposals bans on "state establishments." Whereas language directed at "church establishments" sought to prevent Congress from entering into a privileged relationship with a church or churches, language directed at "state establishments" sought to prohibit government itself from functioning like an institutional church, and from directly legislating articles of faith or modes of worship. "Church establishments" and "state establishments" are complementary concepts; they are alternative methods of creating a relationship of privilege and control between the institutions of church and state.

That an "establishment" of religion might be construed to demarcate specific types of privileges and controls between government and churches is supported by considering the one Founding-era state that officially established a religion. Article 38 of the 1778 South Carolina Constitution provided:

> The Christian Protestant religion shall be deemed, and is hereby constituted and declared to be, the established religion of this State.[54]

South Carolina erected a "church establishment" insofar as it specified that the Protestant religion was established, granting privilege to that religion over all others. It was statist—a "state establishment"—inasmuch as Article 38 legislated specific articles of faith to be accepted by each established church:

1st. That there is one eternal God, and a future state of rewards and punishments.
2d. That God is publicly to be worshipped.
3d. That the Christian religion is the true religion.
4th. That the holy scriptures of the Old and New Testaments are of divine inspiration, and are the rule of faith and practice.
5th. That it is lawful and the duty of every man being thereunto called by those that govern, to bear witness to the truth.[55]

Established churches in South Carolina were eligible for two important privileges. First, they could apply for a charter of incorporation, which

---

53. *Senate Journal*, 1st Cong., 1st sess., September 9, 1789, 77.
54. *Federal and State Constitutions*, 2:1626.
55. *Federal and State Constitutions*, 2:1626.

allowed the church to own property as a corporate body.[56] Without corporate status, it was considerably more difficult to perpetuate a church; church property would have to be legally held by church leaders or a pastor, which increased the danger that it would be used for the holders' own purposes or passed to their own families upon death, rather than to those who would perpetuate the church itself. Corporate status also allowed a church to prosecute and protect its own rights in courts of law.[57] Second, a legally established church could use the state's coercive power to collect "pew assessments" and other financial obligations it imposed on its members. South Carolina's Article 38 held that "no person shall, by law, be obliged to pay towards the maintenance and support of a religious worship that he does not freely join in, or has not voluntarily engaged to support." While the provision forbade religious taxes collected from all the state's residents and distributed by government, it allowed for provisions (usually in a church's act of incorporation) that made church-imposed financial obligations legally enforceable by church officials against church members.[58] As South Carolina historian James Underwood has written,

> Even though the government did not impose the tax directly itself, it, in essence, delegated taxing authority to the incorporated, established churches when it permitted [in the particular act of incorporation], and made enforceable at law, assessments going beyond the terms of the pewholder agreement with the church.[59]

State-conferred privileges were only half of South Carolina's religious establishment. It also imposed a number of regulatory controls. In addition to requiring the aforementioned five articles of faith, Article 38 mandated the democratic election of clergy:

56. Kellen Funk, "Church Corporations and the Conflict of Laws in Antebellum America," *Journal of Law and Religion* 32 (2017): 268; James Lowell Underwood, *The Constitution of South Carolina* (Columbia: University of South Carolina Press, 1992), 3:66–67.

57. For a brief but helpful discussion of the advantages of corporate status for churches during the Founding era, see Douglas G. Smith, "The Establishment Clause: Corollary of Eighteenth-Century Corporate Law?" *Northwestern University Law Review* 98 (2003): 254–55.

58. See, for example, "An Act for Incorporating the Calvinist Church of French Protestants," act no. 1166 of 1783, sect. 9, in *The Statutes at Large of South Carolina*, ed. David J. McCord (Columbia, SC: A. S. Johnston, 1840), 8:123–24.

59. Underwood, *Constitution of South Carolina*, 3:70. Cf. Ellis West, *The Free Exercise of Religion in America: Its Original Meaning* (Cham, Switzerland: Palgrave Macmillan, 2019), 202–3.

And that the people of this State may forever enjoy the right of electing their
own pastors or clergy, and at the same time that the State may have sufficient
security for the due discharge of the pastoral office, by those who shall be ad-
mitted to be clergymen, no person shall officiate as minister of any established
church who shall not have been chosen by a majority of the society to which
he shall minister, or by persons appointed by the said majority, to choose and
procure a minister for them. . . . [60]

The same article also prescribed an oath-of-office-esque declaration for
all established ministers.[61] When a church became a part of the establishment, furthermore, the state could impose specific limitations on that
particular church through its act of incorporation. A 1783 statute incorporating a Calvinist church of French Protestants, for example, allowed
the church "to purchase, receive, have, hold, enjoy, possess and retain . . .
any estate or estates, real or personal, messuages, lands, tenements or her-
editaments, of what kind or nature soever, not exceeding in the whole
five hundred pounds sterling per annum."[62] For this particular church, the
legal privilege of establishment came at a cost: state-imposed limitation
on financial growth.

Given that South Carolina was the only Founding-era state that expressly established a religion, it is surprising that its 1778 Constitution has

60. *Federal and State Constitutions*, 2:1627.
61. *Federal and State Constitutions*, 2:1627. Article 38 provided:

No person shall officiate as minister of any established church who shall not . . . have
made and subscribed to the following declaration, over and above the aforesaid five
articles, viz: "That he is determined by God's grace out of the holy scriptures, to instruct the people committed to his charge, and to teach nothing as required of necessity to eternal salvation but that which he shall be persuaded may be concluded and
proved from the scripture; that he will use both public and private admonitions, as well
to the sick as to the whole within his cure, as need shall require and occasion shall be
given, and that he will be diligent in prayers, and in reading of the same; that he will
be diligent to frame and fashion his own self and his family according to the doctrine
of Christ, and to make both himself and them, as much as in him lieth, wholesome
examples and patterns to the flock of Christ; that he will maintain and set forwards,
as much as he can, quietness, peace, and love among all people, and especially among
those that are or shall be committed to his charge."

62. "An Act for Incorporating the Calvinist Church of French Protestants," act no. 1166
of 1783, sect. 4, in *Statutes at Large of South Carolina*, 8:123–24. James Underwood, "The
Dawn of Religious Freedom in South Carolina: The Journey from Limited Tolerance to Constitutional Right," in *The Dawn of Religious Freedom in South Carolina*, ed. Underwood and
Burke, introduction by Walter Edgar (Columbia: University of South Carolina Press, 2006),
33–34.

not played a more significant role in the Supreme Court's Establishment Clause jurisprudence. From it we see clearly that the one unambiguous example of a Founding-era religious establishment legislated relationships both of state privileges and of state controls. Privileges in South Carolina included the delegation of the state's coercive authority to established churches so that they could collect financial contributions from church members, as well as the legal right to own property as a corporate entity. Government controls included the specification of official articles of faith that a church had to adopt, regulations for the selection of ministers, and limitations on financial growth.

The same pattern of institutional privileges and controls can be observed in other states that authorized state funding of religious ministers and ministries, even if those states—including Massachusetts, New Hampshire, Georgia, and Vermont—didn't textually "establish" a religion.[63] Take Massachusetts, which according to John Adams erected a "most mild and equitable establishment."[64] The 1780 Massachusetts Declaration of Rights did not impose articles of faith or explicitly establish an official church, but it did erect key elements of what we have called a "church establishment." Specifically, the Declaration of Rights authorized a system of religious taxation for Protestant ministers and regulated their selection. As noted in chapter 4, Article 3 of the Declaration of Rights provided that "the people of this commonwealth have a right to invest their legislature with power to authorize and require" local political and religious communities "to make suitable provision, at their own expense, for the institution of the public worship of God and for the support and maintenance of public Protestant teachers of piety, religion, and morality in all cases where such provision shall not be made voluntarily." The same article also specified

63. See the discussion of these states' practices of religious taxation and regulation of minister selection in chapter 4.

64. See John Witte Jr., "'A Most Mild and Equitable Establishment of Religion': John Adams and the Massachusetts Experiment," *Journal of Church and State* 41 (1999): 214. Whether the Massachusetts Constitution of 1780 established a religion was a matter of dispute. In his opinion constitutionally defending Massachusetts's system of tax support for religion, Theophilus Parsons, chief justice of the Massachusetts Supreme Judicial Court, repeatedly refers to it as an "establishment." See *Barnes v. Falmouth*, 6 Mass. 401, 406, 408, 412 (1810). The historian John D. Cushing, in "Notes on Disestablishment in Massachusetts, 1870–1833," *William and Mary Quarterly* 26 (1969): 169, states that to call the early constitutional church-state Massachusetts system an "establishment" is "not altogether accurate [but] is useful." For a discussion of how the term "establishment" was used during the Founding era, see Donald L. Drakeman, *Church, State, and Original Intent* (New York: Cambridge University Press, 2010), 216–29.

"that the several towns, parishes, precincts, and other bodies-politic, or religious societies, shall at all times have the exclusive right of electing their public teachers and of contracting with them for their support and maintenance." It then went one step further than even South Carolina's establishment by declaring that

> the people of this commonwealth have also a right to, and do, invest their leg-
> islature with authority to enjoin upon all the subjects an attendance upon the
> instructions of the public teachers aforesaid, at stated times and seasons, if
> there be any on whose instructions they can conscientiously and conveniently
> attend.[65]

If we look to the practices of the one state that *did* officially establish a religion (South Carolina) and a state that some considered to have established a religion (Massachusetts), we can extrapolate that religious establishments in early America involved relationships of privilege and control between the state and religious institutions.[66] Privileges included special church taxes collected by the government and distributed solely to churches to support ministers and church facilities; the delegation of state authority to churches to enforce tithes from their members (and, in Massachusetts, church attendance); and particular legal privileges, such as corporate status, not available to nonestablished churches or nonestablished ministers.[67] State controls included (but were not necessarily limited to)

65. *Federal and State Constitutions*, 1:957.

66. My analysis agrees at least in part with that offered by Michael W. McConnell in "Establishment and Disestablishment at the Founding, Part I: Establishment of Religion," *William and Mary Law Review* 44 (2003): 2015–2208. McConnell's review of a much broader swath of history, including what constituted an establishment in England and the American colonies, leads him to conclude: "government *control* over religion . . . is arguably the most salient aspect of the historical establishment" (p. 2207, McConnell's emphasis).

67. I do not mean to suggest that the specific privileges and controls legislated in South Carolina and Massachusetts exhaust the elements of a religious establishment. The licensing of preachers and the ability to officiate legally recognized weddings, for example, were aspects of Virginia's colonial establishment. See Thomas E. Buckley, S.J., *Church and State in Revolutionary Virginia* (Charlottesville: University Press of Virginia, 1977), 4, 66–68. Regarding incorporation, Kellen Funk, in "Church Corporations and the Conflict of Laws in Antebellum America," 269, helpfully explains:

> Thus, while disestablishment certainly involved the abolition of privileges such as
> compulsory tithe assessments, a significant feature of disestablishment in many states
> was not the abolition of a privilege — incorporation — but rather its extension to many
> more candidates.

state regulation of articles of faith, rules for the selection of ministers, and financial limitations on church growth.[68]

These relationships of institutional privileges and controls offer a basis for a construction of the Establishment Clause that both corresponds to the actual text and captures the reasons for the text's adoption. We can construe the First Amendment's prohibition of laws "respecting an establishment of religion" to prohibit Congress from legislating specific relationships of privilege and control between governments and institutional churches. We can categorize the types of prohibited relationships as

- "state establishments": government itself exercising the functions of an institutional church, including the regulation of internal church matters such as the content of doctrine and the selection of ministers.
- "church establishments": delegation of government's coercive authority to churches, especially in matters of taxation and financial contribution.

This construction construes "respecting an" to signify that there is more than one kind of establishment; there are two broad kinds, and both are prohibited.

Constructing the First Amendment's Establishment Clause to prohibit Congress from legislating relationships of privilege and control between government and institutional churches coheres both with the underlying reasons why the Establishment Clause was adopted, and with the actual

---

68. In this regard, consider James Madison's presidential veto in 1811 of a congressional act incorporating a Protestant Episcopal church within the District of Columbia. Madison wrote:

> The Bill enacts into, and establishes by law, sundry rules and proceedings relative purely to the organization and polity of the Church incorporated, and comprehending even the election and removal of the Minister of the same, so that no change could be made therein, by the particular Society, or by the General Church of which it is a member, and whose authority it recognizes. This particular Church, therefore, would so far be a religious establishment by law, a legal force and sanction being given to certain articles in its constitution and administration. . . .

Madison also objected to special legal privileges that the incorporation act extended to the church. Madison's veto message can be found in *The Papers of James Madison,* Presidential Series, ed. J. C. A. Stagg et al., (Charlottesville: University of Virginia Press, 1984), 3:176. Congress first passed the bill on February 8, 1811. Following Madison's veto message dated February 21, 1811, the House of Representatives debated the constitutionality of the bill and the means of reconsidering it before voting against its passage on February 23, 1811. See *Annals of Congress,* 11th Congress, 3rd session, 129, 828, 983–85, 995–98.

text's original meaning as revealed by the drafting record. It prohibits specific types of religious coercion: state delegation of coercive power to churches, and state coercion of religious institutions, especially through direct regulation of religious doctrine and the selection of church leadership. The construction is informed by practices associated with religious establishment in the states at the time of the Founding. Moreover, it complements the natural rights construction of the Free Exercise Clause: whereas the Free Exercise Clause primarily protects individuals against governmental legislation concerning religious exercises as such, the Establishment Clause protects religious institutions from state control, and also individuals from the coercion that would result from delegation of the state's coercive authority to religious institutions.

Can the Establishment Clause Be Incorporated?

Earlier, I set aside the issue of the Establishment Clause's incorporation so that I could first develop an originalist construction. Having developed that construction, I now ask whether it can be incorporated to apply against the states. Let me state again that whether the Fourteenth Amendment was designed to incorporate any or all of the Bill of Rights lies beyond the scope of this study.[69] The questions before us are: (1) whether the construction I have just set forth can be coherently incorporated to apply against the states and, if it can, (2) whether doing so would contradict or undermine the text's original design.

The first question is easily answered. There is no reason why the Establishment Clause as constructed could not be applied against state governments. There is nothing inherently federal in the substantive limitations articulated. The incorporated Establishment Clause would prohibit Congress *and* state governments from legislating relationships of privileges and controls with institutional churches—that is, legislating exclusive legal privileges for churches, regulating church doctrines or selection of ministers, or delegating to churches the state's coercive authority.

The second question is more complicated. During the drafting of the Establishment Clause, various individuals clearly communicated that they did not want the text to interfere with extant state-level church-state

69. For a thoughtful study that addresses this question, see Kurt T. Lash, "The Second Adoption of the Establishment Clause: The Rise of the Nonestablishment Principle," *Arizona State Law Journal* 27 (1995): 1085–1154.

arrangements. Incorporating the Establishment Clause to restrict the states contradicts some of the First Congress members' expressly stated intentions.

Incorporation also clashes with the conclusion I reached about the text's original meaning. In chapter 5 I argued that the phrase "respecting an establishment" communicates that Congress is prohibited both from legislating a national religious establishment and from passing legislation concerning state establishments. The latter prohibition recognized state authority over public policies related to religious establishments. The Establishment Clause was designed to preclude two mischiefs: a national establishment of religion and national interference with state-level church-state arrangements. Incorporation is necessarily incompatible with this second purpose, regardless of what constitutes an establishment of religion. To the extent that the Establishment Clause was drafted to reaffirm federalism in church-state matters, incorporation undermines its original design.

I concluded in chapter 5 that the Establishment Clause contains two rules:

- Congress shall make no law erecting a religious establishment.
- Congress shall make no law concerning state-level religious establishments.

The first rule can be incorporated; the second rule cannot. It is therefore impossible to apply the full meaning of our originalist construction of the Establishment Clause against the states.

The constitutional legitimacy of incorporating the first rule and erasing the second depends not on the original meaning of the Establishment Clause, constructed or otherwise, but rather on the meaning of the Fourteenth Amendment. If the Fourteenth Amendment is understood to have suspended or overturned those aspects of the First Amendment that pertained to federalism, and to apply all the remaining provisions against the states, then incorporation of our constructed Establishment Clause can proceed consistently within the sanction of the Fourteenth Amendment. That would entail, properly speaking, an originalist construction of the Establishment Clause as constitutionally amended and applied to the states by the Fourteenth Amendment.

This study does not explore the meaning of the Fourteenth Amendment or competing theories of incorporation. It is at least conceivable that some theories of incorporation subsume the substantive aspect of the Establishment Clause—the first rule—and thus require a construction applicable to both national and state governments. And, of course, the Establishment Clause was incorporated in *Everson v. Board of Education* (1947). Without resolving whether the Fourteenth Amendment was designed to incorporate the Establishment Clause against the states, I will proceed to discuss in chapter 8 how an incorporated Establishment Clause, constructed in the manner set forth in this chapter, would adjudicate various cases.[70] I must emphasize, however, that applying the Establishment Clause against the states is not fully consistent with the text's original design.

The Relationship between the Constructed Clauses and Natural Rights

I have constructed the First Amendment's Religion Clauses as follows. The Free Exercise Clause prohibits Congress and the states from making any law that exercises jurisdiction over religious exercises as such. Neither Congress nor the states may make laws that punish, prohibit, mandate, or regulate religious beliefs or exercises as such. The Establishment Clause prohibits Congress and (supposing incorporation) the states from making any type of religious establishment—that is, a relationship of privilege and control between the institutions of church and state. Prohibited establishments include "state establishments" (state authorities exercising the functions of an institutional church, including the regulation of church doctrine and selection of leadership) and "church establishments" (state authorities delegating government's coercive authority to churches, especially in matters of taxation and financial contribution).

My construction of the Free Exercise Clause derives directly from the Founders' natural rights political philosophy. In part 1 of this study, I attempted to document that the Founders understood the principle of religious liberty in terms of inalienable natural rights. In part 2, I concluded that the Free Exercise Clause was designed to provide constitutional recognition of and protection for the principle of religious liberty. In this chapter, I translated the Founders' philosophical understanding into a legal doctrine.

70. In the conclusion, I further consider the legitimacy of the Establishment Clause's incorporation.

The relationship between the Founders' natural rights political philosophy and my construction of the Establishment Clause is a bit more complex. That philosophy directly entails what I have called the "state establishment" prong of the clause's substantive provision. And that prong dovetails with the Free Exercise Clause: Government cannot exercise the functions of a church, because it lacks the authority to do so. Just as individuals do not cede authority over their right to worship according to conscience, they do not grant to government authority to erect or direct the institutions that conduct worship. Therefore, it is not the province of government to regulate religious doctrine, the appointment of ministers, or other matters of internal church governance.

The prohibition against "church establishments" follows from the Founders' natural rights constitutionalism in a different way. Whereas "state establishments" involve government exercising authority not granted to it, "church establishments" involve government giving away authority properly entrusted only to it. The prohibition of "church establishments" follows from the principle of nondelegation, or, to speak more precisely, subdelegation. In the Founders' natural rights social compact theory, the people delegate to the government their lawmaking authority. That delegation is held and exercised by the government in trust and, as such, cannot be subdelegated by the government to a third party. As is helpfully explained by the constitutional scholar Joseph Postell,

> There is only one sovereign power in a free society: the people. When they delegate power to government, they are not creating a sovereign power but merely delegating their sovereignty to be exercised by a trustee. Consequently, in the social compact, the people necessarily designate the government as the endpoint of the flow of power; the government cannot delegate that power on to another body. Only the possessors of power can delegate it....
>
> In short, according to the Framers' political philosophy, the people are the only rightful source of sovereignty, and they cannot relinquish their sovereignty.[71]

The subdelegation of the state's coercive power to churches, or to any other body, subjects the people to rule by agents other than those to whom they have consented.[72] "Church establishments" deprive the people

71. Joseph Postell, "'The People Surrender Nothing': Social Compact Theory, Republicanism, and the Modern Administrative State," *Missouri Law Review* 81 (2016): 1016–17.

72. Philip Hamburger, in *Is Administrative Law Unlawful?* (Chicago: University of Chicago Press, 2014), 380, helpfully explains:

of their natural right of self-government. They undermine the very foundation of a regime based on the principle that all men are created free and equal.

*   *   *

My constructions of the First Amendment's Religion Clauses necessarily have been presented at a fairly abstract level of generality. The next chapter explores how these constructions would adjudicate actual cases. It will also compare my constructions to leading alternatives offered by the Supreme Court. I believe that examining these constructions in a more concrete way will help clarify their meaning and furnish grounds for an evaluation of their strengths and weaknesses.

When a principal delegates power to an agent, the agent ordinarily cannot subdelegate the power to a subagent, as this runs counter to the apparent intent of the principal. In individual circumstances, this is a matter of personal freedom; in politics, it is a foundation of constitutional liberty.

CHAPTER EIGHT

How the Natural Rights Constructions Would Adjudicate Actual Cases

In the previous chapter I offered originalist constructions of the First Amendment's Religion Clauses consonant with the Founders' natural rights political philosophy. This chapter explores how those constructions would adjudicate prominent church-state issues. Addressing actual cases will allow me to clarify the proposed constructions and compare them to various alternatives. We shall see that, taken as a whole, the natural rights approach does not correspond to any existing jurisprudential framework, originalist or otherwise. It consistently produces neither liberal nor conservative results as those classifications are usually understood. Regarding the Free Exercise Clause, it does *not* provide a constitutional right of exemptions for religious believers from generally applicable but burdensome laws. Indeed, the approach permits some laws that single out religion for discriminatory treatment by state actors. Regarding the Establishment Clause, the approach allows forms of state aid to religion that the Supreme Court has prohibited, including financial support of private religious schools, but forbids practices that the Court has allowed, such as legislative chaplains. The natural rights approach is more democratic than leading originalist and nonoriginalist alternatives, while at the same time it imposes a more thorough and categorical form of restriction on state action.

This chapter does not discuss every Supreme Court church-state case or even every church-state issue. It focuses, instead, on how the proposed constructions would resolve a few cases involving some of the most important church-state constitutional issues. Let me acknowledge that the treatment of each case is relatively perfunctory. I attempt only to highlight the essence of the case, narrowly focusing on its central issue. The chapter's purpose is to elaborate the proposed constitutional constructions, not to provide a detailed analysis of their application. Let me also recognize that, even if one accepts the constructions set forth in the previous chapter, one might reach results different from those advanced in this chapter. I offer an application of a framework; for any given case, I may have misapplied the framework, and a more thoughtful application may lead to different results. What follows is a good-faith effort to illustrate in a relatively succinct way the proposed natural rights constructions.

Following the order established in the last chapter, this chapter begins with the Free Exercise Clause and then proceeds to the Establishment Clause. The chapter aims primarily to clarify the proposed constructions in light of actual cases, not to defend their prudence or propriety. How the natural rights constructions would reformulate, modify, or dispense with existing Supreme Court precedent, as well as whether the constructions are choice-worthy, will be addressed in the book's concluding chapter.

How the Natural Rights Construction Would Adjudicate the Free Exercise Clause

In Chapter 7, I constructed the Free Exercise Clause to read as follows:

> Congress and the states shall make no law that exercises jurisdiction over religious exercises as such.

Thus constructed, no government may

- punish religious beliefs or exercise as such.
- prohibit religious beliefs or exercises as such.
- mandate religious beliefs or exercises as such
- regulate religious beliefs or exercises as such.

The construction's jurisdictional character captures the Founders' natural rights political philosophy: the right of worship according to conscience is "unalienable," and so individuals do not grant authority to government over religious worship as such.

TABLE 7. **Adjudication of the Free Exercise Clause**

Free exercise issue Justice	Exemptions *Sherbert, Smith*	Targeting of religious exercises *Lukumi Babalu Aye*	State prayers *Vitale, Weisman, Town of Greece*	Religious exercises on state property *Good News Club*	Non–worship-based exclusion of religion *Locke, Trinity Lutheran*
Natural rights construction	Not required, but allowed	Prohibited	Prohibited	Allowed	Allowed
Scalia	Not required, but allowed	Prohibited CSI/LRM*	Allowed	Allowed	Prohibited
Thomas	Required and allowed	Prohibited CSI/LRM	Allowed	Allowed	Prohibited
Kennedy	Not required, but allowed	Prohibited CSI/LRM	Sometimes allowed, sometimes prohibited	Allowed	Sometimes allowed, sometimes prohibited
O'Connor	Required and allowed	Prohibited CSI/LRM	Prohibited	Allowed	Allowed
Breyer	Required and allowed	Prohibited CSI/LRM	Prohibited	Allowed	Allowed
Ginsburg	Not required	Prohibited CSI/LRM	Prohibited	Prohibited	Allowed and required (EC)
Brennan	Required and allowed	n/a	Prohibited	Prohibited[1]	Allowed and required (EC)[2]

[1]CSI/LRM = subject to "compelling state interest" and "least restricted means" analysis
[2]Position extrapolated from opinions and votes in analogous cases

Table 7 presents the results the natural rights construction would reach in a few key issues and cases. To facilitate comparison, the table also includes an ideological cross-section of recent and current Supreme Court justices.

Does the Free Exercise Clause Require Exemptions?
Reynolds, Sherbert, Yoder, Smith

The leading Free Exercise Clause question remains: Does the First Amendment provide a right of exemptions from generally applicable laws that burden individuals' and institutions' religious beliefs, practices, and commitments? In *Reynolds v. United States* (1879), the Supreme Court answered "no." In *Sherbert v. Verner* (1963), the Court changed course and answered "yes," a position it reaffirmed in *Wisconsin v. Yoder* (1972). The Court then reversed course again and answered no (for the most part) in

Employment Division v. Smith (1990).[1] The *Smith* case and Justice Antonin Scalia's majority opinion provoked Michael McConnell to develop what is considered today the leading originalist case for an exemptionist construction of the Free Exercise Clause, a construction Justice O'Connor adopted in her dissent in *City of Boerne v. Flores* (1997) and Justices Thomas, Alito, and Gorsuch adopted in *Fulton v. City of Philadelphia* (2021).[2]

The natural rights construction would *not* construe the Free Exercise Clause to provide exemptions from generally applicable laws. Exemptions would be constitutionally permissible (say, if provided through legislation), but the First Amendment would not mandate them. As discussed in chapters 2 and 7, the inalienability of the natural right of religious liberty prevents government from exercising jurisdiction over religious worship as such, not from burdening religious believers or institutions through the promulgation of otherwise valid legislation. Thus constructed, the Free Exercise Clause narrowly, but categorically, restricts government action.

The facts of *Reynolds v. United States* (1879), *Sherbert v. Verner* (1963), *Wisconsin v. Yoder* (1972), and *Employment Division v. Smith* (1990) can help illustrate the jurisdictional character of the natural rights approach. In all four cases, religious individuals claimed that a generally applicable statute burdened their religious practices. In *Reynolds*, the federal government prosecuted a member of the Church of Jesus Christ of Latter-Day Saints for violating a federal criminal law against bigamy and polygamy, despite the individual's taking a second wife for religious reasons. In *Sherbert*, the state of South Carolina denied Adell Sherbert's claim for unemployment benefits despite her being fired because she remained faithful to the dictates of her Seventh-Day Adventist religion. In *Wisconsin v. Yoder*, the state of Wisconsin fined parents of Amish children for violating the state's mandatory school attendance laws; the parents had withdrawn their children from formal schooling after their eighth grade, consistent with their community's long-established religious practices. In *Smith*, the state of Oregon denied unemployment benefits to two individuals who had been fired from their jobs for ingesting an illegal drug in a Native American religious ceremony. In none of these cases did the law target

---

1. In this chapter, I omit citations to Supreme Court cases unless needed to refer to a specific passage or issue in the case.

2. Michael W. McConnell, "The Origins and Historical Understanding of Free Exercise of Religion," *Harvard Law Review* 103 (1990): 1409–1517; Michael W. McConnell, "Free Exercise Revisionism and the *Smith* Decision," *University of Chicago Law Review* 57 (1990): 1109–53; *City of Boerne v. Flores*, 521 U.S. 507, 544–65 (1997); *Fulton v. City of Philadelphia*, 593 U.S. ___ (2021) (Alito, J. concurring).

the religious practice it burdened. In every case, the relevant aspect of the challenged law was facially neutral toward religion; but, in its application against religious individuals, each law had the effect of either criminalizing or burdening bona fide religious practices.[3]

Because the natural rights construction only prevents constitutional actors from exercising jurisdiction over religious exercises *as such*, it would sustain each law. In *Reynolds*, the approach would have asked whether the federal law prohibiting plural marriages explicitly targeted religious marriages—say, by prohibiting "Mormon Celestial marriages." Proscribing a specific religious practice or explicitly forbidding practices of a specific religion would violate the Constitution, but assuming the state is acting within its legitimate sphere of jurisdiction—in this case, the regulation of marriage—the fact that a generally applicable law has the incidental effect of burdening or even prohibiting a religious practice or practices has no bearing on its religious-free-exercise constitutional validity. The natural rights approach focuses on whether government possesses legitimate authority to pass a law, not on how the law affects religious believers when implemented. *Reynolds*'s polygamy ban would have been found constitutional, as would have the denials of employment benefits in *Sherbert* and *Smith* and the compulsory school attendance law in *Yoder*.[4] It is within the state's legitimate authority to not extend unemployment benefits to those who do not accept available work, to make drug use illegal, and to require minors to receive an education. Whether these laws are wise or desirable does not inform their constitutionality. What matters is whether the law in question is within the state's competence (in every case it was) and whether it specifically targets religious exercises as such (in every case it did not).

The Prohibition and Prescription of Religious Exercises:
Lukumi Babalu Aye, Vitale, Lee v. Weisman

While in recent years the question of exemptions has dominated scholarly discussion of the Free Exercise Clause, the quintessential free exercise

---

3. A different aspect of the statute challenged in *Sherbert* provided that "no employee shall be required to work on Sunday ... who is conscientiously opposed to Sunday work" if, in times of "national emergency" textile plants were authorized by the state to operate on Sundays. See *Sherbert v. Verner*, 374 U.S. 398, 406 (1963).

4. For an alternative nonexemption construction of the Free Exercise Clause that would reach a different result in *Yoder*, see Matthew J. Franck, "Freedom without Exceptions: A New Jurisprudence of Religious Liberty," in *Diversity, Conformity, and Conscience in Contemporary America*, ed. Bradley C. S. Watson (Lanham, MD: Lexington Books, 2019), 89–118.

case involves state prohibition of religious exercises as such. Such cases are relatively rare, but the Supreme Court decided one in *Church of the Lukumi Babalu Aye, Inc. v. City of Hialeah* (1993).

Lukumi involved a Florida city council's attempt to prohibit Santerían religious exercises. A unanimous Supreme Court found that "the record in this case compels the conclusion that suppression of the central element of the Santería worship service was the object of the ordinances," that the ordinances were drafted in such a way "that almost the only conduct subject to [them] is the religious exercise of Santería church members," and that "the ordinances had as their object the suppression of religion."[5]

The Court struck down the ordinances, but only after evaluating the government's asserted compelling interest and the means used to achieve it. That analysis was required, according to Justice Kennedy's majority opinion, because,

> although a law targeting religious beliefs as such is never permissible, if the object of a law is to infringe upon or restrict practices because of their religious

---

5. *Church of the Lukumi Babalu Aye, Inc. v. City of Hialeah*, 508 U.S. 520, 534, 535, 542 (1993). Santería ("the way of the saints") emerged in the nineteenth century when Yoruba slaves brought to Cuba from Africa infused their traditional religion with elements of Catholicism. It teaches that every individual has a destiny from God that is fulfilled with the aid and energy of spirits called orishas. The basis of the religion is the nurturing of a personal relationship with the orishas, and one of the principal forms of devotion is animal sacrifice. The animals sacrificed—which include chickens, pigeons, doves, ducks, guinea pigs, goats, sheep, and turtles—are killed by the cutting of the carotid arteries in the neck. The sacrificed animal is then cooked and eaten, except after healing and death rituals.

In April 1987, the Church of the Lukumi Babalu Aye announced plans to open a house of worship, school, cultural center, and museum in Hialeah, Florida. The church's president, Ernesto Pichardo, said the church's goal was to bring the practice of the Santería faith, including its ritual of animal sacrifice, into the open. At the time of litigation, the federal district court estimated that there were at least fifty thousand Santería practitioners in South Florida. The prospect of a Santería church in its midst prompted the Hialeah city council to adopt three ordinances that together prohibited animal sacrifice "in a public or private ritual or ceremony not for the primary purpose of food consumption" by any individual or group that "kills, slaughters or sacrifices animals for any type of ritual, regardless of whether or not the flesh or blood of the animal is to be consumed." The ordinances contained an exemption for slaughtering by "licensed establishment[s]" of animals "specifically raised for food purposes." A brief summary of the facts of the case and the ordinances in question can be found in Vincent Phillip Muñoz, *Religious Liberty and the American Supreme Court: The Essential Cases and Documents*, updated edition (Lanham, MD: Rowman & Littlefield, 2015), 404–5. See also David M. O'Brien, *Animal Sacrifice and Religious Freedom:* Church of the Lukumi Babalu Aye v. City of Hialeah (Lawrence: University Press of Kansas, 2004).

motivation, the law is not neutral; and it is invalid unless it is justified by a compelling interest and is narrowly tailored to advance that interest.[6]

Upon finding that the ordinances in question were not neutral, the Court inquired whether the city had a compelling state interest to "restrict practices because of their religious motivation" and, if it did, whether the city employed properly tailored means to do so. The Court determined that the ordinances were both under- and overinclusive in their alleged aim to prevent animal cruelty, which indicated that the city had failed both to identify a compelling interest and to pursue it in a sufficiently narrowly tailored manner.[7]

The natural rights construction also would have struck down the anti-Santería ordinances, but in a more straightforward and decisive manner than did the Court. Assuming the accuracy of the Court's factual findings — that the ordinances in question deliberately targeted and prohibited Santerían religious exercises[8] — the ordinances would amount to an ultra vires action by the Hialeah city council. By prohibiting religious acts as such, the city council exercised an authority not granted to it—in fact, an authority not granted to any political body, according to the Founders' understanding of the inalienable right of worship according to conscience. Under the natural rights construction, the ordinances would be found unconstitutional, and no compelling-state-interest or least-restrictive-means analysis would be undertaken.

In the Framers' natural rights understanding, the rights of religious free exercise cannot legitimately be evaluated in light of or "balanced" against "competing state interests." The state can *never* have a constitutionally compelling interest that allows it to suppress religious exercises as such, because such suppression per se always exceeds the state's jurisdiction. The state's lack of sovereignty over religious exercises means not only that legislators lack authority to directly prohibit religious exercises, but also that judges—who are also agents of the state—lack authority to "balance" elements of the natural right to religious liberty against other state interests, "compelling" or otherwise. The act of balancing itself assumes that the nonalienated rights of religious freedom can be limited by the

6. *Church of the Lukumi Babalu Aye, Inc. v. City of Hialeah*, 508 U.S. 520, 533 (1993).
7. *Church of the Lukumi Babalu Aye, Inc. v. City of Hialeah*, 508 U.S. 520, 542–47 (1993). The Court also determined that the ordinances were not generally applicable.
8. Cf. Lino A. Graglia, "*Church of the Lukumi Babalu Aye*: Of Animal Sacrifice and Religious Persecution," *Georgetown Law Journal* 85 (1996): 31–32, 34–41.

state. The "balancer" places the competing free exercise right and state interests on opposite ends of a scale. Even if the scale is tilted toward religious freedom, as in *Lukumi*, the very act of weighing assumes an authority over religious exercises that the Founders denied. As we have already discussed, this does not mean that all laws incidentally burdening religious interests are unconstitutional, but, rather, that the state may never legitimately exercise direct sovereignty over elements of the natural right to religious liberty. In practice, the natural rights construction would dispense with all compelling-state-interest and least-restrictive-means inquiries. If the Free Exercise Clause is violated, it is violated.

Under the natural rights construction, *Lukumi* is a simple and straightforward case. Once it is determined that the city council's ordinances targeted religious exercises as such, they would be found unconstitutional. Full stop. To repeat, no compelling-state-interest or least-restrictive-means analysis would be undertaken.[9]

Cases such as *Lukumi*, in which the state proscribes religious acts as such, are relatively rare.[10] More commonly, church-state cases have involved state prescription of religious exercises. Such cases have tradition-

---

9. For a construction of the Free Exercise Clause that also rejects as-applied challenges to otherwise valid laws and the compelling-state-interest analysis necessary to implement it, see John Harrison, "The Free Exercise Clause as a Rule about Rules," *Harvard Journal of Law and Public Policy* 15 (1992): 169–79. Harrison writes (p. 173):

> It is easy to make fun of the compelling state-interest test. . . . No one really knows how to distinguish compelling and non-compelling state interests. That is surely a problem—because constitutional rules should be capable of principled, neutral application—but the real problem is that the doctrine, in its old or new form, has no textual hook in the Constitution. It has no place in the Free Exercise Clause.

10. An example of government regulation of religious exercises as such occurred while this chapter was being drafted. In the midst of the 2020 coronavirus pandemic, the governor of the state of Washington issued a memo regulating "drive-in spiritual services." The order, which pertained exclusively to religious services, regulated the manner ("All persons attending the service must drive up in an enclosed vehicle and remain in that same vehicle during the service. Individuals should not get out of their vehicle during the service for any reason"), number of attendees ("No more than 10 people may be in a single vehicle"), and content of religious services ("No food, beverages, or other materials [whether for religious or secular purpose] may be distributed or collected before, after, or as part of the service"). The governor's actions regulated religious exercises as such, and thus violated the proposed construction of the Free Exercise Clause. See "Memo of Governor Jay Inslee regarding Religion and Faith-based Organization Guidelines," May 6, 2020, https://www.governor.wa.gov/sites/default/files/Spiritual%20Drive-in%20Services%20Guidance%20Memo.pdf?utm_medium=email&utm_source=govdelivery (accessed May 12, 2020).

ally been analyzed under the Court's Establishment Clause jurisprudence; and under the proposed Establishment Clause construction they would fall under what I labeled the "state establishment" prong. Under the natural rights construction, they also would raise Free Exercise Clause issues. For the same reason that government cannot prohibit religious exercises, it also cannot prescribe them. Under the natural rights construction, the Free Exercise Clause provides a two-way prohibition: it forbids government both from prohibiting and from prescribing religious exercises as such. The latter prohibits government from directing religious exercises, including in public schools.

Government-organized prayers, such as the one at issue in *Engel v. Vitale* (1962), accordingly present a clear violation of the Free Exercise Clause. The case involved the mandated recitation of the following government-composed prayer at the beginning of the public school day:

> Almighty God, we acknowledge our dependence upon Thee, and we beg Thy blessings upon us, our parents, our teachers and our Country.

Students were not punished for nonparticipation, and they could be excused from the room while the prayer was recited.[11] The Supreme Court struck down the prayer by a 6–1 vote. Justice Black's majority opinion motioned toward "the wall of separation between church and state," and commented on the impropriety of the union of church and state—an alliance, he said, that "tends to destroy government and to degrade religion"[12]— but did not say specifically why the prayer violated the First Amendment.

The natural rights construction would use more precise reasoning to strike down the prayer: the school policy violated the Free Exercise Clause because it exercised jurisdiction over a religious exercise as such. For the same reason, it also would violate the "state establishment" prong of the Establishment Clause. The case would not turn on whether the prayer was coercive. Its constitutionality would not be saved by the facts that students were not required to recite it, or that they could be excused from the room

11. As described in Justice Douglas's concurring opinion, *Engel v. Vitale*, 370 U.S. 421, 438 (1962), along with the prayer, the board of education adopted a regulation that stated, "Neither teachers nor any school authority shall comment on participation or non-participation ... nor suggest or request that any posture or language be used or dress be worn or be not used or not worn." Provision was also made for excusing children, upon written request of a parent or guardian, from the saying of the prayer or from the room in which the prayer was said.

12. *Engel v. Vitale*, 370 U.S. 421, 425, 431 (1962).

in which it was said. The availability of exemptions is inapposite because the state lacked authority to conduct the practice in the first place.

Public school officials also could not instruct a graduation speaker on how to compose a prayer as an official part of a graduation ceremony, as was at issue in *Lee v. Weisman* (1992). The natural rights construction would not ask whether students were psychologically coerced to participate in a prayer, as did Justice Kennedy's majority opinion;[13] rather, it would pose a more clear-cut question: Did the state exercise jurisdiction over religious exercises as such? Given that school officials organized the prayer and then regulated its content (though school officials did not draft the words themselves), the answer in *Lee* would be "yes," and the school district's action would have been held to violate the Free Exercise Clause. Again, whether the prayer was coercive (Justice Scalia contended it was not)[14] is immaterial to the outcome of the case.

For similar reasons, the legislative prayer upheld by the Supreme Court in *Town of Greece v. Galloway* (2014) also would have been found unconstitutional. Lacking jurisdiction over religious exercises, no government body or political subdivision may make prayer an official part of its meetings. In his majority opinion, Justice Kennedy contended that the First Amendment ought to be read in light of historical practices and understandings. "That the First Congress provided for the appointment of chaplains only days after approving language for the First Amendment," he said, "demonstrates that the Framers considered legislative prayer a benign acknowledgment of religion's role in society."[15] Justice Kennedy is correct about how some of the Framers viewed government-sponsored prayer, but as chapter 7 argued, the Free Exercise Clause ought to be constructed in light of the original meaning of the principles that animate it, not in light of select Founding-era practices that may or may not be consistent with those principles.[16]

Just as state officials cannot compose or direct official school prayers, they cannot specifically prohibit religious exercises by private individuals, even on state property. Insofar as students or teachers are acting in

13. *Lee v. Weisman*, 505 U.S. 577, 592–93 (1992).
14. *Lee v. Weisman*, 505 U.S. 577, 637–44 (1992).
15. *Town of Greece v. Galloway*, 572 U.S. 565, 576 (2014).
16. For an approach that emphasizes traditional practices over principles, see Marc O. DeGirolami, "The Traditions of American Constitutional Law," *Notre Dame Law Review* 95 (2020): 1123–81. I further discuss the differences between the natural rights approach and the Supreme Court's use of tradition in the concluding chapter.

their capacity as private individuals, the state cannot forbid them from exercising their religion. High school football coaches, accordingly, cannot be prohibited from saying a prayer after a football game, at least insofar as they do so in their capacity as a private individual. Similarly, when members of the public are allowed to use public school facilities, after-hours-school-use policies cannot forbid religious exercises as such, as did the New York school districts in *Lamb's Chapel v. Center Moriches School District* (1993) and *Good News Club v. Milford Central Schools* (2001). In the latter case, a Christian group was denied access to otherwise available school facilities because a district superintendent determined the proposed use was "the equivalent of religious worship."[17] In both cases, the Supreme Court struck down the exclusionary use policies on free speech grounds. The natural rights construction would have provided grounds independent of free speech analysis to strike down both policies for violating the Free Exercise Clause. The state lacks jurisdiction over religious exercises. It cannot make religious exercises as such the basis of state action. If public school facilities are available for the public's general use, religious exercises as such cannot be prohibited.

State Discrimination in Favor of and against Religious Individuals and Religious Institutions

If religious exercises as such exceed the state's jurisdiction, can the state ever make an individual's or institution's religious affiliation the ground for state action? Can the state exclude religious individuals from civic obligations (e.g., military service, tax obligations), benefits (e.g., state-funded educational scholarships), or even political rights (eligibility for political office) on account of religious status? Madison and Jefferson (at least in their more philosophical writings, though not necessarily in their political practice) thought government ought to be blind to or noncognizant of religion in general, not just religious exercises.[18] Jefferson's 1786 Virginia Statute for Religious Freedom, for example, provides that "no man . . . shall be enforced, restrained, molested or burthened in his body or goods, nor shall

---

17. *Good News Club v. Milford Central Schools,* 503 U.S. 98, 103 (2001).

18. For a discussion of Madison's principle of noncognizance, see Vincent Phillip Muñoz, *God and the Founders: Madison, Washington, and Jefferson* (New York: Cambridge University Press, 2009), 11–48. For discussions of Madison and Jefferson's actions inconsistent with their stated principles, see pp. 37–38, 72–74, 96, 97, 99, 106, 113, 114, 174, and 209 in the same volume.

otherwise suffer, on account of his religious opinions or belief. . . ."[19] The
natural rights construction I have put forth is more limited and does not
fully embrace Jefferson and Madison's "expansive liberalism." The proposed construction prevents the state from exercising jurisdiction over
religious exercises as such, but does not prohibit all legislation that concerns religion or is cognizant of religious status or affiliation. It prohibits
some but not all uses of religion as a classification for state action. The
decisive inquiry is whether a classification exercises jurisdiction over religious exercises as such, not religion in general. The following examples
aim to clarify when and how state actors constitutionally could and could
not employ religion as a criterion for action.

We can start with religious tests for political officeholding, a practice
that clearly violates the Virginia Statute but was commonplace in the
Founding-era states. As discussed in chapter 4, among the original thirteen
states only Virginia did not impose religious restrictions on officeholding.
The Supreme Court has addressed the issue twice, first in *Torcaso v. Watkins* (1961) and then in *McDaniel v. Paty* (1978), striking down the religious tests in both cases. *Torcaso* evaluated Article 37 of Maryland's
Declaration of Rights, which provided, "No religious test ought ever to
be required as a qualification for any office or profit or trust in this State,
other than a declaration of belief in the existence of God." The natural
rights construction would strike down the test for reasons similar to those
offered by the Supreme Court: it required an act of worship, specifically
a profession of belief in God.[20] For the same reasons, state oaths and affirmations of office that include a profession of faith, such as the one prescribed by the 1776 Delaware Constitution, would violate the incorporated
Free Exercise Clause:

I, A B. do profess faith in God the Father, and in Jesus Christ His only Son,
and in the Holy Ghost, one God, blessed for evermore; and I do acknowledge the holy scriptures of the Old and New Testament to be given by divine
inspiration.[21]

19. "A Bill for Establishing Religious Freedom in Virginia," in *Religious Liberty and the
American Supreme Court*, 604–5.
20. *Torcaso v. Watkins*, 367 U.S. 488, 495 (1961).
21. Constitution of Delaware, 1776, Article 22, in *The Federal and State Constitutions, Colonial Charters, and Other Organic Laws of the United States*, 2nd edition, ed. Ben Perley
Poore (Washington: Government Printing Office, 1878), 1:276. See chapter 4 for a discussion
of Founding-era state religious tests for office.

Not every religious test for office, however, involves an actual religious exercise. The challenged provision in *McDaniel v. Paty*, for example, disqualified religious ministers on account of their professional status as ministers. The case involved Reverend Paul McDaniel, an ordained Baptist minister, who was prevented from taking his seat as an elected member to a state constitutional convention on account of a provision of the Tennessee Constitution that provided:

> Whereas Ministers of the Gospel are by their profession, dedicated to God and the care of Souls, and ought not to be diverted from the great duties of their functions; therefore, no Minister of the Gospel, or priest of any denomination whatever, shall be eligible to a seat in either House of the Legislature.[22]

Unlike the religious test at issue in *Torcaso*, Tennessee's minister exclusion rule did not require Reverend McDaniel to make a religious profession. The state's provision avoided exercising jurisdiction over religious exercises as such. Tennessee identified McDaniel as a religious minister and then applied an exclusion based on that status—a status the state could have ascertained in any number of licit ways—for example, from self-reporting or from census or tax data. Because neither the identification of McDaniel's status as a religious minister nor his exclusion from eligibility based on that status required the state to exercise jurisdiction over religious exercises, Tennessee's exclusion would not violate the natural rights construction of the Free Exercise Clause.[23] The same authority that would allow the state to exempt religious ministers from civic obligations such as paying taxes or military service also would allow the state to deny ministers the enjoyment of specific civil privileges.[24] More generally, the use of

---

22. Tenn. Const., Article 8, Section 1 (1796), in *Federal and State Constitutions*, 2:1672. I omit from consideration whether the stated reason for the prohibition passes constitutional muster.

23. For an opinion skeptical of whether constitutionally legitimate distinctions can be based on religious status, see Justice Gorsuch's concurring (in part) opinion in *Trinity Lutheran v. Comer*, 582 U.S. ___ (2017).

24. Though it recognized that Tennessee's exclusion was based on religious status and not religious belief, the Supreme Court still struck down the provision because, in the Court's reasoning, the exclusion erected an unconstitutional condition. According to Justice Burger's majority opinion, McDaniel possessed a free exercise right "to preach, proselyte, and perform other similar religious functions" and a right as a Tennessee citizen "to seek and hold office." "Under the clergy-disqualification provision," Burger concluded, "McDaniel cannot exercise both rights simultaneously because the State has conditioned one on the exercise of another." *McDaniel v. Paty*, 435 U.S. 618, 626 (1978). In this chapter, I mean to suggest only that the

religious status for legal privileges or disabilities is permissible, though not required, under the natural rights construction if the relevant categorization does not lead the state to exercise jurisdiction over religious exercises as such.

Other religion-based classifications can be evaluated similarly. The natural rights Free Exercise Clause construction does not forbid religion-based classifications, but does prohibit classifications that require the state to exercise jurisdiction over religious exercises as such. Tax and other exemptions that use religion as a criterion for qualification are constitutionally permissible as long as the state refrains from classifying religious individuals or institutions on the basis of acts of worship. A municipality might extend a property tax exemption to church buildings because it determines that religion contributes positively to the social fabric of the community, but the municipality could not limit the tax exemption only to church buildings where "acts of sacrifice to God are held." The latter, more focused exemption would require state judgments about religious exercises as such, which the proposed construction forbids.

A few more examples may prove helpful. The conscientious objector legislation upheld in *United States v. Seeger* (1965), which extended draft exemptions to individuals whose opposition to war was based on "religious training or belief," would have been constitutionally valid under the proposed construction. Clearly, raising an army is within Congress's authority. As long as the exempting legislation does not require the government to exercise its own independent judgment about the religious validity of the conscientious objector's perception of his or her religious obligations, the legislation would be constitutionally legitimate. If, for example, an applicant for conscientious objector status claimed that his Catholic faith prevented him from taking up arms, the government's examining board could not determine that the applicant misunderstands the Catholic faith, or that Catholicism, correctly understood, does not prevent him

---

Free Exercise Clause alone would not strike down Tennessee's exclusion. The exclusion might be understood to violate an equal protection provision of Tennessee's laws, the Fourteenth Amendment's Equal Protection Clause, or perhaps the Privileges and Immunities Clause.

On a related matter, the constitutionality of Article 8, Section 2 of the 1796 Tennessee Constitution is doubtful. It provides: "No person who denies the being of God or a future state of rewards and punishments, shall hold any office in the civil department of this state" (*Federal and State Constitutions*, 2:1672). If enacting legislation requires state cognizance of an act of worship, it would fail to pass constitutional scrutiny under the proposed construction of the Free Exercise Clause.

from military service. The examining board could examine the sincerity of the petitioners' beliefs, but not their religious veracity.[25]

For similar reasons, the Religious Freedom Restoration Act (1993) also would be constitutionally valid under the natural rights construction, with an important qualification. RFRA provides for a judicial proceeding to evaluate exemptions claims by individuals and institutions whose religious beliefs or practices are substantially burdened by a neutral and generally applicable law. Presuming that the law itself is within the government's legitimate sphere of action (the Supreme Court case that evaluated RFRA, *City of Boerne v. Flores* [1997], involved a legitimate land-use ordinance), the state can grant exemptions from laws without exercising jurisdiction over religious exercises as such, as long as it refrains from making judgments about the religious validity of the religious practice itself. As drafted, however, RFRA might be interpreted to require such an inquiry insofar as it prohibits the federal government from "*substantially*" burdening a person's exercise of religion. If the law's standard of a "substantial" burden required a state official (including a judge) to make an independent judgment about the degree to which a claimant's religion was burdened—a *substantial* as opposed to an insubstantial amount—then the law likely would require the evaluation of religious exercises as such, and would thus violate the jurisdictional limitations imposed by the proposed construction.[26]

Just as the proposed construction of the Free Exercise Clause would permit religion-based exemptions from generally applicable laws, it also would permit religion-based exclusions—once again assuming state nonjurisdiction over religious exercises as such. In *Locke v. Davey* (2004), the

---

25. The Supreme Court adopted this view in *United States v. Seeger*, 380 U.S. 163, 184 (1965):

> The validity of what he [the conscientious objector applicant] believes cannot be questioned. Some theologians, and indeed some examiners, might be tempted to question the existence of the registrant's "Supreme Being" or the truth of his concepts. But these are inquiries foreclosed to the Government.

26. For discussion of "substantial burdens" in the RFRA context, including a plausible manner to read the provision to be consistent with the Religion Clauses as I have constructed them, see Michael A. Helfand, "Identifying Substantial Burdens," *University of Illinois Law Review* 2016 (2016): 1773–1808. Helfand suggests (p. 1775, emphasis in the original), "that in order to determine whether a burden is substantial, courts must examine the substantiality of *the civil penalties triggered by religious exercise.*" See also Ira C. Lupu, "Where Rights Begin: The Problem of Burdens on the Free Exercise of Religion," *Harvard Law Review* 102 (1989): 933–90.

Court evaluated a Washington state scholarship program that supported low-income, academically promising college students enrolled in public and private postsecondary institutions within the state, including accredited, religiously affiliated colleges and universities. Scholarship recipients were free to pursue any course of study except for a degree in "theology." The Supreme Court (7–2) upheld the exclusion, finding it to fall within the "play in the joints" between the Establishment Clause and Free Exercise Clause.[27] The proposed construction would have reached a similar result. For reasons I will discuss, the Establishment Clause would not have mandated the exclusion of theology students. Nor would the Free Exercise Clause have prohibited it, for Washington could have adopted the exclusion for any number of reasons that do not require jurisdiction over religious exercises as such. State legislators could have decided that it was not in the state's interest to fund residents to acquire more theological knowledge or, as the state contended, that the provision was necessary to comply with the Washington State Constitution.[28]

The examples above reveal that the natural rights construction does not transform the Free Exercise Clause into a religious nondiscrimination provision. In his vigorous *Davey* dissent, Justice Scalia held that at a minimum, the state neutrality demanded by the Free Exercise Clause requires that "a law not discriminate on its face." He continued:

> When the State makes a public benefit generally available, that benefit becomes part of the baseline against which burdens on religion are measured; and when the State withholds that benefit from some individuals solely on the basis of religion, it violates the Free Exercise Clause no less than if it had imposed a special tax.[29]

27. *Locke v. Davey*, 540 U.S. 712, 718–20, 725 (2004).
28. The relevant provisions of the Washington state constitution are:

Article 1, Section 11: "No public money or property shall be appropriated for or applied to any religious worship, exercise or instruction, or the support of any religious establishment."

Article 10, Section 4: "All schools maintained or supported wholly or in part by the public funds shall be forever free from sectarian control or influence."

Constitution of the State of Washington (1889) in *The Federal and State Constitutions, Colonial Charters, and Other Organic Laws of the States, Territories, and Colonies Now or Heretofore Forming the United States of America*, ed. Francis Newton Thorpe (Washington: Government Printing Office, 1909), 7:3974, 3992.

29. *Locke v. Davey*, 540 U.S. 712, 718–20, 726–27 (2004).

Although the Court did not overturn *Davey* in *Espinoza v. Montana* (2020), a five-member majority adopted a version of Justice Scalia's non-discrimination approach in the case. *Espinoza* involved a "school choice" state tuition-assistance and tax credit program that excluded religiously affiliated schools. In his majority opinion, Chief Justice Roberts declared that the "Free Exercise Clause . . . protects religious observers against unequal treatment and against laws that impose special disabilities on the basis of religious status." "Because the Montana Supreme Court applied the no-aid provision to discriminate against schools and parents based on the religious character of the school," the chief justice continued, "the 'strictest scrutiny' is required"—a requirement the state of Montana failed to meet.[30]

The natural rights construction I have offered provides a more focused restriction. Whereas Justice Scalia would construe the Free Exercise Clause to prevent facial discrimination against *religion* and the *Espinoza* majority against religious status, the natural rights construction prevents facial discrimination against *religious exercises as such*. The natural rights construction recognizes that the government lacks jurisdiction only over religious exercises alone, not over religion in general. The natural rights construction, accordingly, is less restrictive than Justice Scalia's nondiscrimination construction. To say the same thing differently, it is more democratic. Under it, majorities may adopt laws that promote religion, exclude religion, or require nondiscrimination on the basis of religion, so long as those laws do not require or prohibit religious acts as such.[31] The natural rights jurisdictional approach, therefore, would concur with Justice Sotomayor's conclusion in *Trinity Lutheran v. Comer* (2017) that the Free Exercise Clause affords "government some room to recognize the unique status of religious entities and to single them out on that basis for exclusion from otherwise generally applicable laws."[32] Just as the state may extend special privileges or exemptions toward religion—as I discuss below, the Establishment Clause would not prohibit such special

---

30. *Espinoza v. Montana*, 591 U.S. ___, slip op. 8, 18 (2020).

31. Cf. Philip B. Kurland, *Religion and the Law: Of Church and State and the Supreme Court* (Chicago: Aldine, 1962), 112, which offers a nondiscrimination construction of the Religion Clauses.

32. *Trinity Lutheran v. Comer*, 582 U.S. ___, slip op. 9 (2017). As I shall discuss below, the proposed construction would clash with Justice Sotomayor's construction of the Establishment Clause in the same case.

consideration—the state may make exclusions on the basis of religion as long as it does not exercise jurisdiction over religious exercises as such. A state, accordingly, could exempt religious individuals and institutions from sexual orientation nondiscrimination laws similar to the one at issue in *Masterpiece Cakeshop v. Colorado Civil Rights Commission* (2018), but the Free Exercise Clause would not *mandate* such an exemption. The Free Exercise Clause protects the inalienable natural right to worship according to conscience; it does not mandate government neutrality or nondiscrimination toward religion in general.[33]

The distinction between religious exercises as such and religion in general may seem artificial or perhaps even arbitrary, but it follows from the very logic of the idea of the inalienability of the right to religious freedom. What is inalienable, precisely speaking, is the individual's sovereignty over his or her worship according to conscience. Authority over worship as such is what cannot be ceded to the state.[34] The state, accordingly, cannot exercise jurisdiction over religious exercises as such. The nonworship elements of religion, however, are not inalienable in the same way. The state, therefore, may exercise jurisdiction over these elements of religion when pursuing otherwise constitutional policies.[35] Abstract as it may seem, the distinction between religious worship and the nonworship elements of religion provides the constitutional logic that explains why government cannot coerce students to pray, but can excuse religious students from school on their respective religious holy days; and why government cannot coerce soldiers to attend religious services, but can exempt religious individuals from the draft. The natural rights construction of the Free Exercise Clause respects the unique status of religious worship and, at the same time, recognizes that some elements of religion are properly subject to governmental authority.

33. For a thoughtful debate on the subject of religious liberty and discrimination among participants who all take a different approach from the one advanced here, see Ryan T. Anderson, John Corvino, and Sherif Girgis, *Debating Religious Liberty and Discrimination* (New York: Oxford University Press, 2017).

34. See chapter 3 for the main philosophical and theological arguments the Founders used to reach this conclusion.

35. The reader might note that the natural rights construction of religious free exercise I have offered differs from Madison's principle of state noncognizance of religion in general. For my reservations about Madison's noncognizance principle, see Muñoz, *God and the Founders*, 220–21.

How the Natural Rights Construction Would
Adjudicate the Establishment Clause

In chapter 7, I labeled the two forms of a constitutionally prohibited establishment of religion as follows:

- "state establishments": government itself exercising the functions of an institutional church, including the regulation of internal church matters such as the content of doctrine and the selection of ministers.
- "church establishments": delegation of government's coercive authority to churches, especially in matters of taxation and financial contribution.

I will refer to these as the "state establishment and "church establishment" prongs of the natural rights construction of the Establishment Clause. As we shall see, these Establishment Clause limitations overlap to a degree with those imposed by the Free Exercise Clause, but they also complement free exercise protections by limiting state action pertaining to churches' institutional integrity. Table 8 presents the results the natural rights construction would reach in some of the cases discussed below. The table also includes an ideological cross-section of recent and current Supreme Court justices.

State Establishments: Governmental Religion

Though the Constitution does not use the phrase, nearly everyone recognizes that the Establishment Clause pertains to the separation of church and state in some vague way.[36] How we ought to conceive of that separation—be it a wall, a line, an intention, a specific effect, a perception, a disposition, a feeling, or a relationship—continues to be much disputed. Nonetheless, virtually everyone agrees that the state cannot act like a church because such authority has not been given by the people to the government.[37] The "state establishment" prong captures this important jurisdictional element of natural rights social compact theory. "State establishments" involve the exercise of religious authority not given to government

36. Cf. Philip Hamburger, "Separation and Interpretation," *Journal of Law and Politics* 18 (2002): 7–64.

37. Virtually everyone, of course, does not mean everyone. See, for example, Adrian Vermeule, "Integration from Within," *American Affairs* 2 (2018): 202–13.

TABLE 8. **Adjudication of the Establishment Clause**

Establishment Clause issue Justice	State chaplains *Marsh*	State aid to religion for civic purposes *Lemon, Zelman*	State-supported religious displays *Allegheny, American Legion*	Regulation of religious ministers *Hosanna Tabor*
Natural rights construction	Prohibited	Allowed	Allowed	Prohibited if direct; allowed if incidental
Scalia	Allowed*	Allowed	Allowed	Prohibited
Thomas	Allowed*	Allowed	Allowed	Prohibited
Kennedy	n/a	Allowed	Allowed	Prohibited
O'Connor	Allowed	Allowed	Sometimes allowed, sometimes prohibited	Prohibited
Breyer	n/a	Sometimes allowed, sometimes prohibited	Sometimes allowed, sometimes prohibited	Prohibited
Ginsburg	Prohibited*	Prohibited	Prohibited	Prohibited
Brennan	Prohibited	Prohibited	Prohibited	n/a

*Position extrapolated from opinions and votes in analogous cases

and the pursuit of religious ends not properly belonging to government, especially vis-à-vis churches in their institutional capacity.

I have already discussed South Carolina's 1778 religious establishment, but we can return to it here to highlight elements of the "state establishment" prong that, as far as I know, have not emerged in a Supreme Court case. Perhaps most obviously, the 1778 South Carolina Constitution violated the proposed construction (again, assuming incorporation) by expressly declaring that "the Christian Protestant religion shall be deemed, and is hereby constituted and declared to be, the established religion of this State," and then by specifying five doctrinal articles of faith to which established religious societies had to agree and subscribe.[38] The declaration

---

38. Constitution of South Carolina, Article 38 (1778), in *Federal and State Constitutions*, 2:1626. The five articles were:

   1st. That there is one eternal God, and a future state of rewards and punishments.
   2d. That God is publicly to be worshipped.
   3d. That the Christian religion is the true religion.
   4th. That the holy scriptures of the Old and New Testaments are of divine inspiration, and are the rule of faith and practice.
   5th. That it is lawful and the duty of every man being thereunto called by those that govern, to bear witness to the truth.

of an establishment and official state-recognized articles of religious faith exceed the state's jurisdiction. Relatedly, South Carolina imposed on churches what today would be recognized as an "unconstitutional condition" by conditioning incorporation on acceptance of the state's official religious tenets. What a state cannot do directly it also cannot do indirectly by withholding an otherwise available benefit.[39]

South Carolina abandoned its official establishment in 1790, and I am aware of no attempt since then by any state to expressly recognize an official church with state-imposed religious tenets. There remain in both the states and the federal government vestiges, however, of establishment practices that would violate the proposed Establishment Clause construction, including the employment of official state ministers. The Nebraska state legislative chaplaincy, which was upheld by the Supreme Court in *Marsh v. Chambers* (1983), offers an example. At the time of litigation, a Presbyterian minister, Robert E. Palmer, had been employed by the state at a salary of $319.75 per month. His duties included beginning each legislative session with a prayer. Insofar as those prayers were an official act of the government, they violated the proposed construction of the Free Exercise Clause. The chaplaincy itself would violate the proposed construction of the Establishment Clause. The natural rights approach holds that government's purposes do not include saving citizens' souls. The state, accordingly, lacks authority to operate its own religious institutions, including the employment of religious ministers to conduct state-run religious exercises. Government-employed military chaplains would also violate the Establishment Clause, at least insofar as the reason for the chaplain's employment is to conduct religious exercises.[40]

Official government chaplains offer a clear example of how the proposed construction reaches different results from interpretive approaches that emphasize tradition and historical practices. Legislative and military chaplains were supported by many if not most of the Founding generation, including several of the drafters of the First Amendment. As commander-in-chief of the Continental Army, George Washington sought not only to

---

39. I overlook here that general incorporation statutes were not yet available at this point in time. For a discussion of the "unconstitutional conditions" doctrine in the context of the Establishment Clause, see Michael W. McConnell, "Unconstitutional Conditions: Unrecognized Implications for the Establishment Clause," *San Diego Law Review* 26 (1989): 255–75.

40. If chaplains were employed for reasons not connected to performance of religious exercises—e.g., as counselors or mental health professionals—they likely would not violate the "state establishment" prong.

procure chaplains for his soldiers but also to ensure that the Continental Congress offered a salary generous enough to "attract men of abilities."[41] The First Congress agreed to the final language of what became the Bill of Rights three days after it authorized the appointment of paid legislative chaplains. According to Chief Justice Burger's majority opinion in *Marsh*, such "historical evidence sheds light not only on what the draftsmen intended the Establishment Clause to mean, but also on how they thought that Clause applied to the practice authorized by the First Congress."[42] Burger correctly captures what we might presume to be the Framers' expected application of the Establishment Clause.[43] Those expectations, however, do not govern the natural rights construction of the text. As I contended in chapter 7, the text's meaning ought to be informed by the underlying original principles that animate the text. Those natural rights philosophical principles do not permit government religious chaplains, even if the Founders themselves legislated such chaplaincies. The Founders' principles are more authoritative than their practices.[44]

The proposed "state establishment" prong also would prohibit the state from levying taxes for the exclusive use of religious institutions in their capacity as religious institutions. Historically, religious taxes often went

41. Muñoz, *God and the Founders*, 51.

42. *Marsh v. Chambers*, 463 U.S. 783, 790 (1983)

43. It should be noted, however, that James Madison, after he left the presidency, called the appointment of taxpayer-funded legislative chaplains by the First Congress a "palpable violation" of constitutional principles. See Elizabeth Fleet, "Madison's 'Detached Memoranda,'" *William and Mary Quarterly*, 3rd Series, no. 3 (1946): 558–62. Madison's "Essay on Monopolies" had been published in *Harper's Magazine* in 1914, but was lost and forgotten until Fleet rediscovered and republished it in 1946 as "Madison's 'Detached Memoranda.'" While its date of composition is unknown, it is thought that Madison drafted it between 1817 and 1832. See also Muñoz, *God and the Founders*, 43–44.

44. In this context I concur with Andrew P. Koppelman in "Phony Originalism and the Establishment Clause," *Northwestern University Law Review* 103 (2009): 738, who writes:

> The fact that someone in the Founding generation did something does not prove that it was constitutionally permissible even then. You have to say what the clause means before you can tell whether it has been violated.

Regarding the problems of interpreting the original meaning of a constitutional provision on the basis of a law passed after its adoption, see Ellis M. West, *The Free Exercise of Religion in America: Its Original Constitutional Meaning* (Cham, Switzerland: Palgrave Macmillan, 2019), 25–29.

The inclusion of religious professions as part of state oaths of office is a second widespread Founding-era practice that does not comport with the Founders' own natural rights principles of religious liberty.

hand in hand with state appointment of religious ministers—religious taxes funding state-appointed ministers.

An episode from early American history provides an example of the type of governmental financial support of religion that the natural rights construction of the Establishment Clause would prohibit. In 1784, Patrick Henry proposed for the state of Virginia "A Bill Establishing a Provision for Teachers of the Christian Religion." As I describe in *God and the Founders*, Henry's bill constituted a property tax the exclusive purpose of which was to fund religious ministers.[45] Under its provisions, each property owner was to specify the Christian denomination toward which he wished his tax directed. The sheriffs of the several counties would then distribute the taxes accordingly, minus five percent for administration. If a taxpayer failed or refused to specify a Christian society, the tax would go to the public treasury "to be disposed of under the direction of the General Assembly, for the encouragement of seminaries of learning . . . and to no other use or purpose whatsoever." Similarly, taxes received by the various denominations were to be "appropriated to a provision for a Minister or Teacher of the Gospel, or the providing of places of divine worship, and to none other use whatsoever." An exception to this rule was made for Quakers and Mennonites, who were allowed to place their distribution in their general funds because they lacked the requisite clergy. The restrictions on how funds were to be distributed, with the noted exceptions, derived from the bill's stated educational purpose. The bill began,

> WHEREAS the general diffusion of Christian knowledge hath a tendency to correct the morals of men, restrain their vices, and preserve the peace of society, which cannot be effected without a competent provision for learned teachers. . . .

While Henry's bill might seem like a clear Establishment Clause violation—and it certainly would be under any number of the "tests" devised by the modern Supreme Court—it is a close call under the proposed construction. What I have called the "state establishment" prong prohibits the government from exercising church functions; taxation for the sole purpose of funding ministers' salaries would seem to fall within that prohibited category. Yet Henry's bill also claimed to advance a legitimate civic end—"to

45. The following summary of Henry's bill is taken from Muñoz, *God and the Founders*, 21–22. Henry's bill can be found in the same volume on pp. 229–30.

correct the morals of men, restrain their vices, and preserve the peace of society." If the end be legitimate, are not all means rationally related to that end constitutional?[46] And is it not plausible that funding Christian ministers is a reasonable means by which to foster moral education, especially before the advent of public education?

As discussed in chapter 4, what I labeled the "narrow republican" understanding held tax support of religion, including the funding of religious ministers, to be compatible with due respect for religious freedom. Nonetheless, the proposed construction would strike down Henry's bill, at least if something similar were proposed today and we assume incorporation. The constitutional infirmity lies in the lack of a nexus between the asserted end—moral education—and the adopted means—a tax subsidy for religious ministers. The bill's educational rationale was not present in the bill's original version, which was designed to support Christian ministers, churches, and worship. A drafting committee added it, probably to increase the bill's appeal.[47] While that modification makes the constitutional question more difficult, it does not seem to be enough to save the bill. Even with the educational preamble, ministers who received appropriations were not required to use them for educational purposes. In practice, the bill granted a direct subsidy to Christian clergymen reminiscent of the religious establishment that existed prior to the Revolutionary War.[48] While the bill may have posited a legitimate end, the means employed did not necessarily or sufficiently advance the end. Indeed, it appears that the end itself was asserted as a pretext to justify the means.

The natural rights construction would allow the state to fund religion as a means to foster legitimate state ends, but the state cannot manufacture ends to legitimize funding religion. Such pretextual analysis is neces-

---

46. Recall Chief Justice John Marshall's statement in *McCulloch v. Maryland*, 17 U.S. (4 Wheat) 316, 421 (1819):

> Let the end be legitimate, let it be within the scope of the constitution, and all means which are appropriate, which are plainly adopted to that tend, which are not prohibited, but consist with the letter and spirit of the constitution, are constitutional.

47. Thomas E. Buckley, S.J., *Church and State in Revolutionary Virginia* (Charlottesville: University Press of Virginia, 1977), 105. Cf. Eva Brann, "Madison's 'Memorial and Remonstrance,'" in *The Past-Present: Selected Writings of Eva Brann,* ed. Pamela Kraus (Annapolis, MD: St. John's College Press, 1997), 210.

48. It should be noted that Henry's legislation was more ecumenical than the establishment of Anglicanism in colonial Virginia. For a description of the latter, see Buckley, *Church and State in Revolutionary Virginia,* 8–16.

sarily contextual and heavily dependent on the facts of a given case, but it provides one way to identify unconstitutional forms of governmental financial support of religion.

While the natural rights construction would prohibit state chaplaincies, it would permit many forms of government support of religious institutions that the Court has found suspect. Take *Everson v. Board of Education* (1947), the Supreme Court's first modern Establishment Clause case. The case involved state-funded reimbursements to parents who paid their children's transportation costs to and from public or Catholic schools. The Court narrowly upheld the program, 5–4, but all nine justices agreed with Justice Black's construction that the Establishment Clause erects a "wall of separation" between church and state and, therefore, that "no tax in any amount, large or small, can be levied to support any religious activities or institutions, whatever they may be called, or whatever form they may adopt to teach or practice religion."[49] To the four dissenters, "no tax" meant no tax; they concluded that the Establishment Clause "forbids any appropriation, large or small, from public funds to aid or support any and all religious exercises."[50]

"No aid to religion" has become a dominant aspect of "strict separationist" jurisprudence, an approach championed in recent times by Justices Ginsburg and Sotomayor. The proposed construction is more limited. It would allow government to fund religious individuals and institutions as an instrumental means to further otherwise legitimate civic interests, provided that a nexus exists between ends and means and that state actions do not establish jurisdiction over religious exercises as such. Under the proposed construction, *Everson* would be a straightforward case. The state clearly has an interest in facilitating the safe transportation of children to and from school, no matter the school's religious affiliation. Reimbursing parents for city bus fares is a reasonable way to further that interest. No relationship of privilege and control is established between church and state. The *Everson* funding scheme, accordingly, would not violate the natural rights Establishment Clause.

Other government aid to religious individuals and institutions would be addressed in the same manner. In *Lemon v. Kurtzman* (1971), perhaps the Court's most famous no-aid-to-religious-schools decision, the Court struck down Rhode Island and Pennsylvania policies that funded, among

49. *Everson v. Board of Education*, 330 U.S. 1, 16 (1947).
50. *Everson v. Board of Education*, 330 U.S. 1, 41 (1947) (Rutledge, J., dissenting).

other things, salary supplements to teachers of nonreligious subjects in Catholic schools. The Court found that the administrative requirements necessarily caused a constitutionally impermissible "excessive entanglement" between church and state even though the programs might have had a legitimate secular purpose.[51] The proposed construction would reject the Court's demand in *Lemon* that "the State must be certain, given the Religion Clauses, that subsidized teachers do not inculcate religion." All that would be required, again, is that the state advance a legitimate civic end (in this case, instruction in nonreligious subjects such as mathematics) and adopt means reasonably related to those ends (salary supplements for math teachers). Those requirements clearly would have been met in *Lemon*.[52]

The proposed construction also would not categorically forbid religious individuals and religious groups from participating in state funding programs. Special needs students could receive state-funded sign language assistance, even in religious schools (*Zobrest v. Catalina Foothills School District* [1993]). Religiously oriented college newspapers could receive state university student activity funds, even if those newspapers included essays proselytizing the student body (*Rosenberger v. University of Virginia* [1995]). Religious schools could participate in government-funded school voucher programs (*Zelman v. Simmons-Harris* [2002]). Churches could receive state funds for safety improvements for their playgrounds, even if religious instruction or religious play were facilitated thereby (*Trinity Lutheran v. Comer* [2017]).[53] In all such cases, the proposed construction would *not* require the justices to inquire whether the funding in question had the effect of aiding or endorsing religion. The "state establishment prong" only forbids the state from functioning like a church

---

51. *Lemon v. Kurtzman*, 403 U.S. 602, 616–24 (1971).

52. Dropping the Court-constructed "non-advancement" of religion requirement would likely evaporate the "excessive entanglement" aspect of the case. To the extent that regulations accompanying tax dollars persisted, those regulations themselves would be subject to scrutiny. If they established an improper relationship of state control of religious institutions, a constitutional remedy would be to grant state funds without the regulations. I omit analysis of the specific regulations imposed in the case, in part because they were promulgated in response to judicial reasoning in earlier separationist Establishment Clause cases (e.g., *Everson, Schempp*) that would not be supported by the advanced constructions.

53. As noted above in my discussion of the natural rights Free Exercise Clause construction, religious institutions in some cases could also be excluded from generally available programs. My discussion in this context pertains only to whether the receipt of government funds by religious organizations in cases such as *Rosenberger* and *Trinity Lutheran* violates the Establishment Clause as constructed.

and pursuing spiritual as opposed to civic ends, a standard that is met by demonstrating the existence of a legitimate state interest pursued using reasonable and related means.

Another instance of a "state establishment" arises when the state itself prescribes or prohibits religious exercises as such. Here the Establishment Clause's prohibitions overlap with those of the Free Exercise Clause. On the proposed construction of the Free Exercise Clause, official state religious exercises—such as legislative prayers or state-directed prayers in public schools—would be unconstitutional. For the same reasons, so would decrees by family courts mandating or prohibiting religious worship.[54] Those decrees also would violate the natural rights Establishment Clause for the simple and straightforward reason that, in making them, the state assumes the functions of a church by directing religious exercises.

A related type of prohibited "state establishments," which might not quite amount to religious exercises as such, occurs when the state uses its resources to proselytize or preach the truth about religion for religious reasons. Here again, the line between an unconstitutional "state establishment" and the constitutional advancement of morality is fuzzy. It lies beyond the state's jurisdiction to preach religious doctrines for religious reasons; it is permissible, however, for the state to recognize the religious identities of citizens, and even to nurture and advance the religious character of the people for the purpose of inculcating the moral character that sustains a constitutional republic. In actual cases, context would matter. It would be unconstitutional, for example, to post the Ten Commandments in grade school classrooms for the purpose of inculcating observance of Exodus's teaching that "You shall have no other gods before me. You shall not make for yourself a graven image, or any likeness of anything that is in heaven above." Posting religious material as a means to foster moral behavior in general, however, would be permissible. The proposed construction, accordingly, would adjudicate cases such as *Stone v. Graham* (1980), which struck down a Kentucky law that required the Ten Commandments to be posted in each public elementary school, by examining the purpose of the legislation. As was true of my analysis of Patrick Henry's proposed tax-funding of clergymen, the law would be unconstitutional if its purpose were to foster religious observance for religious reasons; but it would be

54. See, e.g., the Washington State Supreme Court case *Muñoz v. Muñoz*, 79 Wn. 2nd 810 (1971), in which a divorce court prohibited Mr. Muñoz from bringing his children to Catholic religious services as part of a child-custody settlement. The provision was overturned by the Washington Supreme Court and, as far as I know, was not obeyed while it was in effect.

constitutionally permissible if its purpose were to foster the moral character requisite for democratic citizenship.

Government-sponsored religious displays would be addressed in a similar manner. Government may not sponsor religious exercises or attempt to inculcate religious truths for spiritual reasons, but the proposed constructions would not prohibit religious displays that are part of governmental programs to recognize the identity of the people or what is dear to them, to acknowledge aspects of the nation's history, or to advance otherwise legitimate state interests. The natural rights Establishment Clause would recognize that state acknowledgment of the religious character(s) of the people does not violate the Establishment Clause any more than the recognition and celebration of ethnic or racial heritages violates the Equal Protection Clause. A state-sponsored creche during the Christmas season or a menorah during the time of Chanukah, to reference the displays at issue in *County of Allegheny v. ACLU* (1989), would not violate the proposed Establishment Clause construction. The Bladensburg World War I "Peace Cross" Memorial sustained in *American Legion v. American Humanist Association* (2019), similarly, would be found constitutional. In religious display cases, *why* the state acts when it aims to advance religion is crucially important. The state may employ religious imagery or symbols to foster otherwise legitimate civic ends, so long as the means used are rationally related to the ends pursued. What would violate the Constitution is state promotion of religion for religious purposes, including the inculcation of religious dogmas, in respect of which the state is jurisdictionally incompetent to legislate.

Church Establishments: Delegation of State Authority to Churches

The proper separation of church and state requires not only that the state not act like a church, but also that the state not delegate its authority to a church. The "church establishment" prong prohibits such delegations.

Perhaps the clearest example of a "church establishment" is the delegation of taxing authority to churches, though I know of no Supreme Court case that has addressed the issue. Just as the state cannot impose religious taxes akin to those in Patrick Henry's proposed bill, the state cannot grant churches authority to impose tithing rates that are then legally enforceable on the church's membership. This is not to say that churches are forbidden from entering into or enforcing contracts otherwise legally made; under the proposed construction, churches could be incorporated and enjoy the same rights and privileges as other similarly situated corporate bodies. The "church establishment" prong ensures that churches, so far as civil law is concerned, remain voluntary associations and that, in particular, financial contributions to churches are given voluntarily, not imposed by the church and then legally enforced by the state.

Other forms of improper delegation can arise in domains where the state exercises its authority, including licensing and public education. In *Larkin v. Grendel's Den* (1982), the Court struck down, 8–1, a delegation to churches of the state's alcohol licensing authority. Massachusetts state law provided that "premises . . . located within a radius of five hundred feet of a church or a school shall not be licensed for the sale of alcoholic beverages if the governing body of such church or school files written objection thereto."[55] Grendel's Den's liquor license application was denied for the sole reason that Holy Cross Church, which was located just ten feet away from the bar, objected. The proposed construction would have struck down the ordinance for the simple fact that it subdelegated the state's legal authority to churches. By statute and in practice, the ordinance vested in the governing bodies of churches and schools the power to veto the approval of liquor license applications from establishments within a five-hundred-foot radius of their premises.

A second example of an unconstitutional "church establishment" can be found in one of the Court's early Establishment Clause cases, *McCollum v. Board of Education* (1948).[56] Illinois public schools, like many public schools at the time, operated a "released time" program for religious education. During the official school day, members of the Jewish, Protestant, and Catholic traditions taught their respective faiths to students who enrolled in the classes via parental consent. Students who did not take a religion class were expected to remain in school while the once-a-week, forty-five-minute classes were in session. At the time, Illinois enforced a compulsory school attendance law, punishable by fines, which with certain exceptions required parents to send their children to tax-supported public schools or private or parochial schools that met state educational

55. The relevant text of the Massachusetts law can be found in *Larkin v. Grendel's Den*, 459 U.S. 116, 117 (1982). As reported in the Court's opinion (p. 117–18n1), the law defined "church" as "a church or synagogue building dedicated to divine worship and in regular use for that purpose, but not a chapel occupying a minor portion of a building primarily devoted to other uses."

56. *Illinois ex rel. McCollum v. Board of Education*, 333 U.S. 203 (1948).

standards. By law, pupils were to remain in attendance during regular school hours.

Given the state's mandatory school attendance laws, the state effectively delegated its coercive authority to religious authorities. The constitutional violation lies not in the fact that the state promoted or endorsed religious instruction, but that the instruction took place during the official school day when students were required by law to remain in the building. Even though attendance of religious education classes was not mandatory, school attendance was. Religious authorities thereby effectively possessed the state's power to compel attendance for the portion of the school day during which religious classes were held. For the same reason, the New York "released time" program, which was upheld 6–3 by the Court in *Zorach v. Clauson* (1952), also is an unconstitutional "church establishment" under the proposed construction. The New York program took place off public school property but during the regular school day. School officials took part in administering the program by releasing students upon parental request to attend religious instruction classes. Only those students who attended religion classes were permitted to leave school grounds, and participating religious groups were required to report to the public schools the names of children who failed to attend their assigned religious classes, presumably so that the schools could enforce mandatory attendance policies. The constitutional violation, again, lies not in governmental promotion or endorsement of religious education, but in the delegation of its coercive authority to church authorities. The New York program, like the Illinois program, ultimately rested on the government's authority to compel students to attend school. The "church establishment" program prohibits delegation of that authority to church groups, even if participation in the program is via parental consent.

Alternative programs in which public schools facilitated religious instruction in ways *not* dependent on mandatory school attendance laws would not violate the "church establishment" prong of the natural rights construction. A program of religious instruction that took place after the official end of the school day but in public school classrooms would be permissible if the state did not require students to be present at school during the time of instruction. Because it would be after the official school day, no delegation of state authority would take place. Similarly, the proposed construction would permit public schools to end the school day an hour early for all students on a given day of the week, thus facilitating a program of religious instruction (on or off public school grounds).

The "church establishment" prong does not mandate state neutrality toward religion or prohibit governmental advancement or endorsement of religion; it only prohibits the delegation of state authority to religious authorities.

Religion in the Public Square, Church Autonomy,
and Government Entanglement with Religion

Since *Lemon v. Kurtzman* (1971), a prohibition against "excessive entanglement" by the state with the church has been a part of the Supreme Court's Establishment Clause doctrines.[57] The judicial remedy for an entanglement violation has been to disassociate the state from the church, which typically has meant preventing religious organizations from receiving state funds, as was mandated in *Lemon*. A different type of entanglement has been prohibited by the "church autonomy" doctrine.[58] Under it, matters of internal church governance, including the selection of ministers, are shielded from the state's legal reach. The doctrine was recognized by a unanimous Supreme Court in *Hosanna-Tabor Evangelical Lutheran Church and School v. EEOC* (2012) and further developed in *Our Lady of Guadalupe School v. Morrissey-Berru* (2020). In the former case, Hosanna-Tabor Evangelical Lutheran Church and School had fired a "called" schoolteacher with the formal title "minister of religion, commissioned," an action that an EEOC investigation found to have likely violated the Americans with Disabilities Act. The Court preempted EEOC litigation, finding that "both Religion Clauses bar the government from interfering with the decision of a religious group to fire one of its ministers." A "ministerial exception," the Court declared, "precludes application of such [employment nondiscrimination] legislation to claims concerning the employment relationship between a religious institution and its ministers." One can certainly appreciate the Burger Court's desire to prevent "excessive entanglement" of church and state, and the Roberts Court's

57. Although, like the *Lemon* test as a whole, it has been frequently ignored. For a discussion of *Lemon*'s longevity and irrelevance, see Justice Alito's opinion in *American Legion v. American Humanist Association*, 588 U.S. ___ (2019).

58. For a particularly thoughtful account of the "church autonomy" doctrine, see the scholarship of Richard W. Garnett, including "The Freedom of the Church," *Journal of Catholic Social Thought* 4 (2007): 59–86; "Religious Freedom, Church Autonomy, and Constitutionalism," *Drake Law Review* 57 (2009): 901–7; "'The Freedom of the Church': (Towards) an Exposition, Translation, and Defense," *Journal of Contemporary Legal Issues* 21 (2013): 33–57.

recognition that "requiring a church to accept or retain an unwanted minister, or punishing a church for failing to do so . . . interferes with the internal governance of the church, depriving the church of control over the selection of those who will personify its beliefs."[59] Nonetheless, the natural rights Establishment Clause would not support the entanglement and church autonomy doctrines as constructed by both Courts.

The natural rights construction establishes what Matthew Adler has termed "rights against rules," not shields from specific types of treatments.[60] The rules the proposed construction prohibits are those in which the state exercises spiritual dominion over its subjects. The proposed construction enforces the jurisdictional boundaries by policing the reasons or ends of state action. It prohibits the state from exercising the functions of the church, but it does not prohibit it from regulating church functions when it adopts otherwise constitutional legislation. When the state acts within its legitimate sphere and pursues legitimate civic ends, its actions can apply to churches. Though the state cannot pass laws that specifically regulate how religious ministers are to be selected (as was done in Founding-era states such as South Carolina, Massachusetts, and New Hampshire), it can apply generally applicable employment regulations to church employment contracts. The scope of the natural rights Establishment Clause construction thus mirrors that of the Free Exercise Clause. Just as the Free Exercise Clause prohibits state actions that directly regulate religious exercise but does not shield religious individuals from otherwise valid but burdensome legislation, the Establishment Clause prohibits direct state regulation of how ministers are selected but does not shield religious believers from generally applicable non-discrimination legislation that (from the church's perspective) might be quite burdensome and disruptive.

The same logic means that religious institutions and individuals can receive state benefits and participate in state-funded programs if they otherwise qualify to do so. Private religious schools, as I have noted, could receive state funds to supplement mathematics instruction (to use one of the programs struck down in *Lemon*). Religious ministers could even be funded by the state under certain circumstances. I write this as the world is

---

59. *Hosanna-Tabor Evangelical Lutheran Church and School v. Equal Employment Opportunity Commission*, 565 U.S. 171, 181, 188 (2012).

60. Matthew D. Adler, "Rights against Rules: The Moral Structure of American Constitutional Law," *Michigan Law Review* 97 (1998): 1–173. See also Harrison, "The Free Exercise Clause as a Rule about Rules."

engulfed in the 2020 coronavirus pandemic. As part of its economic recovery program, the US Congress has drafted a "paycheck protection" program that would extend forgivable governmental loans to employers for the purpose of keeping employees on their payrolls. Under the proposed construction, and assuming that they otherwise qualify, churches would be eligible to participate in such a program and receive funds to pay their employees, including their ministers.[61] Just as churches can be subject to generally applicable governmental regulations, they can participate in and receive generally available governmental benefits.

*   *   *

The natural rights constructions of the First Amendment's Religion Clauses developed in chapter 7 and applied in this chapter do not correspond to any existing jurisprudential approach. Their distinctiveness is illuminated by comparing how they would adjudicate leading Religion Clause cases to the outcomes reached by Justices Scalia and Ginsburg— justices considered to be at different ends of the judicial-ideological spectrum, especially on church-state matters. The natural rights approach would agree with both justices that the Free Exercise Clause does not provide a constitutional right to religious exemptions from neutral but burdensome laws (*Smith*). It would disagree with both justices, however, regarding the "ministerial exception" they voted to construct in *Hosanna-Tabor*. It would agree with Justice Scalia and disagree with Justice Ginsburg that religious exercises can be hosted on state grounds (*Good News Club*), but disagree with Scalia and agree with Ginsburg that the state may exclude religious individuals from state funded-programs (*Locke v. Davey*). It would disagree with Justice Scalia and agree with Justice Ginsburg that a city council meeting cannot begin with an official prayer, but agree with what we would presume to be Scalia's position and disagree

---

61. Details of the 2020 "Paycheck Protection" legislation were not readily available at the time of this writing. An early document published by the United States Small Business Association immediately after the legislation was passed stated:

> Faith-based organizations are eligible to receive SBA loans regardless of whether they provide secular social services. That is, no otherwise eligible organization will be disqualified from receiving a loan because of the religious nature, religious identity, or religious speech of the organization.

https://www.sba.gov/sites/default/files/2020–04/SBA%20Faith-Based%20FAQ%20Final.pdf (accessed on April 17, 2020).

with Ginsburg that that same city council could fund religious displays (*American Legion*) and even, in some cases, religious schools (*Trinity Lutheran*). If we add additional judges to the comparison, we get a similar pattern of some agreement and some disagreement. For example, the natural rights approach would disagree with Justices O'Connor and Breyer on exemptions, but agree with their conclusions concerning the impermissibility of state prayers and the permissibility of religious exercises on state property.

What these comparisons do not reveal is *why* the natural rights approach produces such distinctive results. As I will discuss in the concluding chapter, the approach demands a sort of judicial inquiry that is different from any existing approach. It produces neither liberal nor conservative results in the contemporary political sense, because it does not focus on mandating a particular relationship between church and state (such as "neutrality") or producing particular outcomes (such as "separation," "accommodation," nonentanglement, or noninterference). Rather, the approach focuses on the jurisdictional limits of state power—a consideration that is all but ignored by existing approaches to church-state jurisprudence, but central to the Founders' understanding of religious liberty.

Should We Adopt the Natural Rights Constructions?

In the past few years, the US Supreme Court and America as a whole have divided over whether prayers can be said at city council meetings, whether a Christian baker must design a wedding cake for a same-sex couple, and whether it is proper for the government to maintain on state property a war memorial featuring a forty-foot Cross.[1] Such disputes and the disagreements underlying them are nothing new. Before the most recent clashes, Americans fought over whether "under God" could be included in public-school recitations of the Pledge of Allegiance, whether Ten Commandments displays could be placed on public property, and whether religious individuals and institutions have a right to exemptions from religiously burdensome laws.[2] Before that, it was prayer in public school and religious participation in state-funded programs.[3] Since the Supreme Court declared in the 1940s that the First Amendment erects a "wall of separation between church and state," we have been debating the proper height

---

1. *Town of Greece v. Galloway*, 572 U.S. 565 (2014); *Masterpiece Cakeshop v. Colorado Civil Rights Commission*, 585 U.S. __ (2018); *American Legion v. American Humanist Association*, 588 U.S. __ (2019).

2. *Elk Grove School District v. Newdow*, 542 U.S. 1 (2004); *Van Orden v. Perry*, 545 U.S. 677 (2005); *McCreary County v. American Civil Liberties Union of Kentucky*, 545 U.S. 844 (2005); *City of Boerne v. Flores*, 521 U.S. 507 (1997); *Employment Division, Department of Human Resources of Oregon v. Smith*, 494 U.S. 872 (1990).

3. See, e.g., *Engel v. Vitale*, 370 U.S. 421 (1962); *Lemon v. Kurtzman*, 403 U.S. 602 (1971); *Wallace v. Jaffree*, 472 U.S. 38 (1985); *Rosenberger v. Rector and Visitors of the University of Virginia*, 515 U.S. 819 (1995); *Locke v. Davey*, 540 U.S. 712 (2004).

and width of that wall and even whether it should be torn down.[4] Justices across the ideological spectrum have agreed that the Founding Fathers' thought ought to guide our construction of the Constitution's religious freedom protections. That shared commitment to our Founding history has not, however, generated agreement about the Constitution's meaning, nor a consistent, coherent, and compelling jurisprudence of the First Amendment's Religion Clauses.

This Book's Argument in Summary

Our church-state constitutional confusion results, in part, from the Court's failures to understand how the Founders agreed about religious liberty but disagreed about the separation of church and state. This book attempts to provide that understanding and construct the First Amendment's Religion Clauses on the basis of the Founders' shared political philosophy of religious freedom, while remaining cognizant of and open to their (and our) disagreements about the separation of church and state.

Part 1 set forth the Founders' natural rights political philosophy of religious freedom. I attempted to show that

- the Founders held the right to worship according to conscience to be a natural right possessed by all individuals.
- the Founders understood this right to be inalienable, meaning that authority over religious worship was not granted, and could not be granted, to governing authorities.
- the Founders reached an "overlapping consensus" about the inalienable character of the right to religious worship through Enlightenment philosophy (e.g., Jefferson), natural theology (e.g., Madison), and Protestant theology (e.g., Isaac Backus).
- the Founders' agreement on the inalienable character of the right to worship did not preclude disagreement on how far natural rights protections extended. "Narrow republicans" (George Washington, Patrick Henry) understood the scope of the right to be more limited, and therefore took a more republican disposition to church-state public policies such as state funding of religion. "Expansive liberals" (James Madison, Thomas Jefferson) held a more expansive view of the

4. *Everson v. Board of Education*, 330 U.S. 1, 16 (1947).

right of religious liberty, and thus a more robust view of how it limited government action.[5]

Part 2 explained how the Founders' agreements and disagreements help elucidate the original meanings of the First Amendment's Religion Clauses. I found that

- the Framers designed the Establishment Clause to enforce two rules:
  - Congress shall make no law erecting a religious establishment.
  - Congress shall make no law concerning state-level religious establishments.
- the Framers designed the Free Exercise Clause to recognize and protect the principle of religious liberty.

Part 2 concluded that, although we can know something about the text's original design, there is no clear, unambiguous, original public meaning of what constitutes an "establishment" of religion or the "free exercise" thereof. For reasons that have to do with the politics surrounding the adoption of the Bill of Rights, the Founders didn't need to be precise when they drafted the Religion Clauses. They could agree to draft text that prohibited the national government from violating an unspecified right to the free exercise of religion (whatever that might be), from making a religious establishment (whatever that might be), and that did not interfere with existing state-level church-state practices (thus agreeing to disagree about the proper separation of church and state). The underdetermined nature of the First Amendment's church-state provisions requires that both the Establishment Clause and Free Exercise Clause be "constructed," to use the nomenclature of contemporary constitutional theory.

In part 3, using a method I call "design originalism," I constructed the Religion Clauses in a manner that coheres with the First Amendment's text, is consistent with what we can discern about the text's original meaning, and is grounded in the Founders' natural rights political philosophy. I constructed the Free Exercise Clause to prohibit laws that exercise jurisdiction over religious exercises as such. I constructed the Establishment Clause to forbid legislation creating relationships of privilege and control between government and institutional churches. I accepted the incorporation of the First Amendment against the states, which for the Establishment Clause

5. In this context I use "liberal" in the sense of classical liberalism, not modern progressivism.

necessitated dropping the Framers' original concern with federalism. Thus constructed:

- The Free Exercise Clause prohibits the government from punishing, prohibiting, mandating, or regulating religious beliefs or exercises as such.
- The Establishment Clause prohibits
  - "state establishments": government itself exercising the functions of an institutional church, including the regulation of internal church matters, such as the content of doctrine and the selection of ministers.
  - "church establishments": delegation of governmental coercive authority to churches, especially in matters of taxation and financial contribution.

In chapter 8, I explained how the natural rights approach would adjudicate some of the most notable church-state cases that have reached the Supreme Court. The approach would not provide a presumptive right to exemptions from laws that burden but do not exercise jurisdiction over religious exercises as such. It would allow forms of state aid to religion (such as state aid to religious elementary schools) that the Supreme Court has prohibited, and would forbid practices (such as legislative chaplains) that the Court has allowed.

The Distinctiveness of the Natural Rights Constructions

Before discussing some of the ways the natural rights constructions may be attractive or unattractive, let me highlight three ways the approach is distinctive from most alternative Religion Clause constructions.

Protecting the Right of Religious Liberty through Jurisdictional Limits on State Power

The construction's most distinctive element is its implementation of the Founders' philosophy of inalienable natural rights through jurisdictional limits on state action. A comparison of how the natural rights Free Exercise construction and current US Supreme Court jurisprudence address laws that directly target religious worship manifests this distinctiveness.

The Supreme Court currently adjudicates such cases within the framework of "strict scrutiny." The definitive precedential passage is found in Justice Anthony Kennedy's unanimous opinion in *Church of the Lukumi Babalu Aye* (1993):

Although a law targeting religious beliefs as such is never permissible, if the object of a law is to infringe upon or restrict practices because of their religious motivation, the law is not neutral; and it is invalid unless it is justified by a compelling interest and is narrowly tailored to advance that interest.[6]

The natural rights construction, by contrast, would simply strike down all laws that directly target religious worship. Because government lacks jurisdiction over religious worship, it cannot directly legislate on it as such. Unlike the Court in *Lukumi Babalu Aye*, the natural rights approach would not employ compelling-state-interest and least-restrictive-means analysis.

While the two approaches reach the same outcome in *Lukumi Babalu Aye*, they do so via fundamentally different reasoning. The Court's strict-scrutiny approach allows the state to target religious practices on account of their religious character if it has a really good reason to do so (a "compelling state interest") and does so in the right manner ("least restrictive means"). The mechanism of strict scrutiny brings religious exercises as such into the state's jurisdiction, quietly erasing the limit imposed by the inalienable natural rights understanding.[7] In principle, the Court's current approach imposes no categorical limit on what the state can do vis-à-vis religious exercises. The natural rights construction, by contrast, imposes a categorical subject-matter restriction on state action vis-à-vis religious beliefs *and* religious worship as such.[8] It starts from the idea that individuals retain sovereignty over their religious exercises when they enter the social compact.

---

6. *Church of the Lukumi Babalu Aye, Inc. v. City of Hialeah*, 508 U.S. 520, 533 (1993).

7. While it lies beyond the scope of this study, in future work I hope to explain how "strict scrutiny" analysis itself is a product of an approach to constitutionalism that rejects natural rights. For a thoughtful recent account of strict-scrutiny analysis, including a discussion of its relatively recent adoption by the judiciary, see Richard H. Fallon Jr., *The Nature of Constitutional Rights: The Invention and Logic of Strict Judicial Scrutiny* (New York: Cambridge University Press, 2019).

8. To my knowledge, the Court has never addressed a case involving a law that explicitly targeted religious belief as such. If it did, I suspect it would deploy strict scrutiny analysis. See, e.g., Justice Sotomayor's call for heightened scrutiny review in *Trump v. Hawaii*, 585 U.S. ___, slip op. p. 15–16 (2018). Justice Sotomayor viewed the case as an instance of governmental targeting of religious beliefs.

The Supreme Court's distinction between religious beliefs and religious actions dates to *Cantwell v. Connecticut*, 310 U.S. 296, 303–4 (1940) and, ultimately, to the Court's reliance on Thomas Jefferson in *Reynolds v. United States*, 98 U.S. 145, 164 (1879). The distinction has no basis in the Constitution's text or in the Founders' natural rights political philosophy as set forth in chapters 1 and 2. Whether the distinction itself withstands rigorous scrutiny even in Jefferson's own thought is also questionable. See Vincent Phillip Muñoz, *God and the Founders: Madison, Washington, and Jefferson* (New York: Cambridge University Press, 2009), 96.

The government therefore has no authority "to infringe upon or restrict practices because of their religious motivation."

The Prohibitive and Democratic Character of the Natural Rights Constructions

While the jurisdictional character of the natural rights constructions imposes a thorough separation between religious worship and state action, it paradoxically also facilitates a democratic disposition toward governmental action concerning religion. When the natural rights constructions prohibit state action, the prohibitions are total; when they allow state action, they allow democratic majorities to adopt the church-state policies they favor. The constructions adopt the Founders' principled limitations on government authority, but they adopt only *those* limitations. By doing so, they leave considerable room for democratic deliberation on how best to separate church from state.

The limited scope of the natural rights approach can be seen clearly with regard to the Free Exercise Clause. By focusing on jurisdiction, the approach looks only to the subject matter, not the effects, of legislation.[9] It prohibits the state from legislating on matters of religious exercise as such; it is silent when the state legislates on matters within its jurisdiction, even if that legislation turns out to be particularly burdensome to religious individuals and institutions. If the state acts within its legitimate jurisdiction, the natural rights Free Exercise Clause is not in play. It allows, but does not constitutionally *require*, the political branches to grant exemptions to religious individuals and institutions. In the case of the military draft, for example, it would allow the legislature to exempt Quakers and other religious and nonreligious pacifists, but it would not *mandate* such exemptions.

In other church-state matters, the natural rights constructions also respect democratic self-government. The constructions do not demand inclusion or exclusion of religion from generally applicable governmental programs. A state-funded tuition scholarship program for college students could exclude students majoring in theology (*Locke v. Davey* [2004]), and state-funded educational vouchers could be used at private religious schools (*Zelman v. Simmons-Harris* [2002]). Conversely, theology college students

---

9. Cf. the approach taken by Justices Thomas, Alito, and Gorsuch in *Fulton v. City of Phila-delphia*, 593 U.S. ___ (2021) (Alito, J., concurring), which necessarily examines the effects or impact of legislation on those who are religious.

could be included and the private religious schools excluded. The natural rights construction requires only that the grounds for inclusion and exclusion not be based on religious exercises as such. Many issues concerning religion in the public square, including state funds flowing to religious organizations and religious displays on state property, would remain within the majoritarian political process.

Limited Judicial Role

Correspondingly, the jurisdictional character of the natural rights constructions fosters a relatively limited role for the judiciary. Rather than managing or supervising church-state relations, judges would enforce jurisdictional boundaries. Regarding the Free Exercise Clause, judges would ask whether a given state action exercised jurisdiction over religious worship as such; if it did not, the action would pass free exercise scrutiny. Similarly, to enforce the "state" and "church" prongs of the Establishment Clauses, judges would inquire whether the state acted like a church (e.g., by prescribing religious doctrines, hiring religious ministers, or collecting church tithes) or delegated its coercive authority to a church, thus improperly empowering a church to act like the state. The approach does not require judges to investigate how otherwise legitimate public policies affect religious individuals "as applied." The constructions provide protections against *types* of governmental policies; they do not provide shields from the particular outcomes of otherwise constitutional policies.

The natural rights constructions thus eschew the managerial role for the judiciary that alternative approaches permit or require. To take a leading example, Chief Justice Burger viewed an underlying purpose of the Court's enforcement of the First Amendment to be the prevention of political divisions along religious lines. In *Lemon v. Kurtzman* (1971), he wrote:

> Ordinarily political debate and division, however vigorous or even partisan, are normal and healthy manifestations of our democratic system of government, but political division along religious lines was one of the principal evils against which the First Amendment was intended to protect. The potential divisiveness of such conflict is a threat to the normal political process. To have States or communities divide on the issues presented by state aid to parochial schools would tend to confuse and obscure other issues of great urgency. We have an expanding array of vexing issues, local and national, domestic and international, to debate and divide on. It conflicts with our whole history and tradition to permit

CONCLUSION

questions of the Religion Clauses to assume such importance in our legislatures and in our elections that they could divert attention from the myriad issues and problems that confront every level of government.[10]

Whatever may be the dangers attendant upon the formation of political divisions along religious fault lines, the natural rights constructions do not grant to the judiciary authority to manage democratic disagreement.[11] They do not ask judges to decide whether the people can safely align politically along religious lines, or to decide for the people which "vexing" political issues they should prioritize. The approach places squarely out of bounds specific subjects of legislation (religious worship, religious doctrines, manner of selecting church leadership) and types of governmental arrangements (collecting taxes specifically for churches, delegating coercive power to churches), and it does so by recognizing categorical limits on governmental power. In those domains in which the government can properly exercise authority, the natural rights constructions let the people govern themselves, even if they do so differently in New York than in Idaho.

For similar reasons, the natural rights constructions do not authorize the judiciary to scrutinize state action for the perceptions it produces or the attitudes it reflects. The approach does not require subjective analyses as to whether a reasonable observer would perceive state action to "endorse" religion or "psychologically coerce" someone to participate in a religious exercise.[12] It does not attempt to evaluate whether government officials and their legislation are properly "neutral" toward religion.[13] Such approaches implicitly understand religious freedom primarily to consist in a type of acceptance, recognition, or nondisparagement (to put it in negative terms) by government. They elevate attitudes and "inclusiveness," to use a currently fashionable term. The natural rights approach, by contrast, directs the jurisprudential inquiry toward the topic of government's jurisdiction, not the

10. *Lemon v. Kurtzman*, 403 U.S. 602, 622–23 (1971). For a thorough critique of the divisiveness construction of the Establishment Clause, see Richard W. Garnett, "Religion, Division, and the First Amendment," *Georgetown Law Journal* 94 (2006): 1667–1724.

11. I note in passing that Burger's jurisprudence arguably inflamed political division along religious lines.

12. Cf. Justice O'Connor's endorsement test for the Establishment Clause in, e.g., *Lynch v. Donnelly*, 465 U.S. 668, 687–94 (1984), and Justice Kennedy's psychological coercion analysis in *Lee v. Weisman*, 505 U.S. 577, 592–97.

13. For recent church-state appeals to "neutrality," see *Trump v. Hawaii*, 585 U.S. ___, slip op. at 1 (2018) (Sotomayor, J., dissenting); *Masterpiece Cakeshop v. Colorado Civil Rights Commission*, 584 U.S. ___, slip op. at 2–3 (2018).

attitudes or feelings of state actors or the individuals affected. The focus on jurisdiction therefore limits the role of the judiciary relative to other church-state approaches.

Are the Natural Rights Constructions Good Constructions?

Should the Supreme Court and other constitutional officers adopt the natural rights constructions? For the originalist—at least the originalist who accepts the legitimacy of judicial constitutional constructions—the answer principally turns on the accuracy of the historical account set forth in part 1 and part 2 and the soundness of that history's deployment via the constructions offered in part 3. But what about for the "faint-hearted" originalist or the nonoriginalist?

Like most constitutional questions, the answer depends on what one considers to be good constitutional law and which aspects of constitutionalism one prioritizes. Below I offer concluding thoughts about the merits of the natural rights constructions on the basis of seven considerations I believe may be of interest to originalists and nonoriginalists alike. First, the natural rights constructions cohere well with the First Amendment's text (especially when compared to alternative constructions); but, second, they cohere less well with the reasoning the Court has used in some of its leading precedents. Third, while incorporation of the Establishment Clause is not fully faithful to the text's original design and necessarily nationalizes "the separation of church from state," incorporating the proposed Establishment Clause construction would enhance protections for the natural right of religious liberty. Fourth, as is true of all constructions, a natural rights approach is subject to manipulation and thus to the substitution of judicial will for judgment, but perhaps no more so (and arguably less so) than the alternatives. Fifth, some will find the approach anemic, which it admittedly is, but it is also more democratic and more categorical than might be appreciated. Sixth, a potentially significant drawback of the approach lies in the possible incoherence of adopting natural rights constructions for the Religion Clauses without a broader commitment to natural rights constitutionalism. Finally, the natural rights approach is teleological in that it is premised upon a reasoned judgment affirming a moral order that we discover, not create—an order in which we have obligations to our Creator. It thus parts ways with conceptions of religious freedom or liberty of conscience that are grounded primarily in human autonomy and willfulness.

Coherence with the First Amendment's Text

One of the stronger arguments in favor of the natural rights constructions is their coherence with the First Amendment's text. First, the text is categorical. "Congress *shall make no law*" commands that, whatever "respecting an establishment religion" and "prohibiting the free exercise thereof" mean, Congress cannot make *any* law that does those things. From a textual perspective, it makes no sense to talk about limiting, abridging, burdening, or balancing First Amendment freedoms, even if this has been the Court's usual manner of thinking. Take as just one example Justice Kennedy's language in the recent Free Exercise case *Masterpiece Cakeshop*, which involved the enforcement of a nondiscrimination ordinance against a Christian cakemaker who declined to design a wedding cake for a same-sex couple. Kennedy writes,

> The Court's precedents make clear that the baker, in his capacity as the owner of a business serving the public, might have his right to the free exercise of religion limited by generally applicable laws.[14]

Kennedy's summation of the Court's precedents is accurate; they do make clear that an individual's "right to the free exercise of religion [might be] limited." But compare that to the plain meaning of the First Amendment's text, which declares that "Congress *shall make no law* ... prohibiting the free exercise" of religion. As I noted in chapter 7, the scope of the First Amendment's church-state provisions is different from the Fourth Amendment's protection against "unreasonable" searches and seizures or the Fifth Amendment's protections against deprivations of life, liberty, and property "without due process of law." The First Amendment affords no constitutional space for "reasonable" prohibitions of religious free exercise if "due process" is afforded or if, to use modern terminology, "compelling state interests" are pursued in appropriately tailored ways. The text of the First Amendment does not support precedents holding that an individual's "right to the free exercise of religion [might be] limited." Its categorical character comports with a jurisdictional construction that either simply prohibits or allows categories of state action.[15] Given its categorical character, it also

14. *Masterpiece Cakeshop v. Colorado Civil Rights Commission*, 584 U.S. ___, slip op. at 2–3 (2018).
15. For a similar analysis of the text, see Philip Hamburger, "Separation and Interpretation," *Journal of Law and Politics* 18 (2002): 53–56. Justice Alito's textual analysis of the Free

stands to reason that the First Amendment's protections must be relatively narrow in scope.

The natural rights construction also gives effect to the words "respecting an" in a manner that is consistent with the evidence available from the drafting record. Many constructions of the Establishment Clause either ignore the words and read the text as if it stated that "Congress (and the states through incorporation) shall not establish a religion," or offer an implausibly loose construction of "respecting an." Justice Wiley Rutledge took the latter route in an especially influential way when, in *Everson v. Board of Education* (1947), he constructed "respecting an" to mean something like "anything tending toward an establishment." "Not simply an established church," Rutledge asserted, "but any law respecting an establishment of religion is forbidden." He continued:

> The Amendment's purpose was not to strike merely at the official establishment of a single sect, creed or religion, outlawing only a formal relation such as had prevailed in England and some of the colonies. Necessarily it was to uproot all such relationships. But the object was broader than separating church and state in this narrow sense. It was to create a complete and permanent separation of the spheres of religious activity and civil authority by comprehensively forbidding every form of public aid or support for religion.[16]

It is difficult to know why precisely the First Congress adopted the words "respecting an." Rutledge might have been correct that the words were designed to broaden the prohibition beyond prohibiting only a formal relation such as had prevailed in England. As chapter 5 documented, the House and Senate had adopted different language in their final versions — a "law establishing Religion" (the House) and a "law establishing articles of faith or a mode of worship" (the Senate). Accordingly, I constructed "respecting an" to encompass both types of establishments — what I labeled "church" and "state" establishments. But there is no evidence from the drafting record to support Rutledge's reading that "respecting an" was intended to communicate the prohibition of "every form of public aid or support for religion." Such a broad construction goes far beyond the evidence available from the drafting record.[17]

Exercise Clause in *Fulton v. City of Philadelphia*, 593 U.S. ___, (2021) (Alito, J., concurring), fails to confront this point.

16. *Everson v. Board of Education*, 330 U.S. 1, 31–32 (1947) (Rutledge, J., dissenting).

17. Cf. Ellis M. West, *The Religion Clauses of the First Amendment: Guarantees of States Rights?* (Lanham, MD: Lexington Books, 2011), 104–9; Ellis M. West, *The Free Exercise of*

The available evidence does support reading "respecting an" to communicate a jurisdictional purpose—that Congress shall make no law on the subject of religious establishments. As we noted in chapter 5, this reading comports with the Constitution's other use of the term "respecting"—"The Congress shall have power to dispose of and make all needful rules and regulations respecting the territory or other property belonging to the United States" (Article 4, Section 3). It comports also with the concerns of some members of the First Congress that the text not be misinterpreted and applied against the states.

A textual critic of the natural rights approach might focus on how it constructs the Free Exercise Clause as a two-way provision, forbidding any governmental action that directly prohibits *or* directly promotes religious exercises. "Congress shall make no law . . . *prohibiting* the free exercise" of religion would seem to permit the state to make laws that *promote* religious exercise. Does the text not support a one-way restriction—the state cannot prohibit, but it can promote? Such a construction is not an implausible reading of the text alone; however, it fails to appreciate the most basic reason why the state cannot directly prohibit religious exercises. The government is forbidden from making laws that prohibit the free exercise of religion because it lacks jurisdiction over religious exercises as such. The government therefore also lacks the authority to promote religious exercises as such. The inalienable character of the right to worship imposes a jurisdictional restriction on state action that is necessarily a two-way prohibition.

To construe "prohibit" to mean "may promote," moreover, is exactly the type of reading the Ninth Amendment was designed to foreclose. Recall *Federalist* 84. Publius warns that a bill of rights "would contain various exceptions to powers not granted; and, on this very account, would afford a colorable pretext to claim more than were granted." He continues:

> Why, for instance, should it be said that the liberty of the press shall not be restrained, when no power is given by which restrictions may be imposed? I will not contend that such a provision would confer a regulating power; but it is evident that it would furnish, to men disposed to usurp, a plausible pretense for claiming that power. They might urge with a semblance of reason, that the Con-

---

Religion in America: Its Original Constitutional Meaning (Cham, Switzerland: Palgrave Macmillan, 2019), 265–76.

stitution ought not to be charged with the absurdity of providing against the abuse of an authority which was not given, and that the provision against restraining the liberty of the press afforded a clear implication, that a power to prescribe proper regulations concerning it was intended to be vested in the national government.[18]

Publius feared that if the Constitution stated that the government could not restrain the freedom of the press (or prohibit the free exercise of religion), some would construe that prohibition to mean that the government could regulate the press in a nonrestraining manner (or promote religious exercises in a nonprohibitory manner). Such a construction, Publius makes clear, would be a misconstruction and would improperly augment governmental power. To the extent that Congress has power to accommodate religion, it is not given by the First Amendment, but rather resides elsewhere. Congress's power to grant exemptions from the draft, for example, lies within its Article 1, Section 8 power "to raise and support armies."

Disjointed Relationship with Precedent

One of the stronger arguments against the practicability of the natural rights constructions is that they do not easily cohere with many leading Supreme Court precedents. The Court constructed its Establishment and Free Exercise Clause jurisprudence—both in majority opinions and leading dissents—without concern for the jurisprudential aspects of natural rights constitutionalism. Even when the natural rights constructions would not produce different outcomes, they would often reach those outcomes for different reasons. To implement the natural rights constructions, accordingly, the Supreme Court would have to revisit and be willing to reconceptualize why the First Amendment prohibits Congress and the states (assuming incorporation) from making an establishment or prohibiting the free exercise of religion. To give a sense of how the Religion Clauses would have to be reconceptualized, let me highlight a few of the ways the natural rights approach would reformulate, modify, or dispense with the alternative approaches to the Religion Clauses, in particular those that have guided significant church-state precedents.

18. Alexander Hamilton, James Madison, John Jay, *The Federalist Papers*, ed. Clinton Rossiter, introduction by Charles R. Kesler (New York: Signet Classics, 2003), 513.

THE NATURAL RIGHTS CONSTRUCTIONS AND "STRICT-SEPARATIONISM."   In
Everson v. Board of Education (1947), the Supreme Court constructed the
Establishment Clause to mean "at least" the following:

> Neither a state nor the Federal Government can set up a church. Neither can
> pass laws which aid one religion, aid all religions, or prefer one religion over an-
> other. Neither can force nor influence a person to go to or to remain away from
> church against his will or force him to profess a belief or disbelief in any reli-
> gion. No person can be punished for entertaining or professing religious beliefs
> or disbeliefs, for church attendance or non-attendance. No tax in any amount,
> large or small, can be levied to support any religious activities or institutions,
> whatever they may be called, or whatever form they may adopt to teach or
> practice religion. Neither a state nor the Federal Government can, openly or se-
> cretly, participate in the affairs of any religious organizations or groups and vice
> versa. In the words of Jefferson, the clause against establishment of religion by
> law was intended to erect "a wall of separation between Church and State."[19]

The adoption of the natural rights construction of the Establishment Clause
would not require overturning *Everson*'s result, which allowed state funding for the transportation of school children to Catholic schools, but it would
significantly narrow or reject elements of *Everson*'s reasoning. Specifically,
the natural rights construction (assuming its incorporation to apply against
the states) would agree and disagree with *Everson*'s construction as follows:

- *"Neither a state nor the Federal Government can set up a church."* Agree. Such
  action would constitute a "church establishment."
- *"Neither can pass laws which aid one religion, aid all religions, or prefer one religion over another."* Disagree. What is constitutionally relevant in the natural rights
  construction is not whether legislation aids, hinders, or prefers some or all religions, but whether the state erects a "church" or "state" establishment. Under
  the natural rights construction, the state can pass legislation that has the effect
  of helping some religions (e.g., salary supplements for math teachers in private
  schools, which might disproportionately aid Catholic schools) or hindering others (e.g., mandatory military service, which disproportionately hinders Quakers and other religious pacifists). The law's effects are not the grounds of its
  constitutionality.
- *"Neither can force nor influence a person to go to or to remain away from church
  against his will or force him to profess a belief or disbelief in any religion."* Mostly

19. *Everson v. Board of Education*, 330 U.S. 1, 15–16 (1947).

agree. Legislation that exercises jurisdiction over religious exercises or beliefs as such, including legislation that coerces individuals to exercise religion against their will, would violate the Free Exercise Clause. Whether otherwise constitutional legislation "influences a person to go to or remain away from church" is not constitutionally significant.

- *"No person can be punished for entertaining or professing religious beliefs or disbeliefs, for church attendance or non-attendance."* Agree.

- *"No tax in any amount, large or small, can be levied to support any religious activities or institutions, whatever they may be called, or whatever form they may adopt to teach or practice religion."* Disagree. To repeat, what is constitutionally relevant is not whether legislation aids, hinders, or prefers some or all religions, but whether the state erects one of the specified relationships of privilege and control between church and state.

- *"Neither a state nor the Federal Government can, openly or secretly, participate in the affairs of any religious organizations or groups and vice versa."* Mostly agree, but it depends how "participate" is construed. The Court's dictum here is vague, but direct state regulation of matters of internal church governance and state delegation of its taxing authority to churches would violate the Establishment Clause.

The natural rights construction would transform *Everson*'s vague standard of a "wall of separation" into rules prohibiting specific relationships of privilege and control between church and state. Correspondingly, the natural rights construction would partially support but mostly reject how the Supreme Court itself later transformed *Everson* into more focused standards.

In *Lemon v. Kurtzman* (1971), the Court specified that *Everson* and its progeny set forth a three-pronged test for adjudicating a law's constitutionality: state action must have a "secular legislative purpose," "its principal or primary effect must be one that neither advances nor inhibits religion," and it "must not foster an excessive entanglement with religion."[20] The natural rights construction would cohere with and diverge from the *Lemon* test as follows:

- *"Secular legislative purpose"*: Agree with modification. The dichotomy between "secular" and "religious" is not one the Founders used, and it does not cleanly map on to the categories the Founders did use.[21] The Founders excluded from the

---

20. *Lemon v. Kurtzman*, 403 U.S. 602, 612–13 (1971).

21. Take, for example, the Declaration of Independence. If the purpose of the Declaration is to communicate the American people's political independence according to "the Laws of Nature and Nature's God," and thereby to better secure the unalienable rights "endowed by their Creator"—and if in doing so, the American people appeal "to the Supreme Judge of the

state's authority jurisdiction over religious exercises as such. The natural rights construction, accordingly, would ask not whether legislation has a "secular" or "religious" purpose, but rather whether it lies within the state's legitimate civic jurisdiction—or, alternatively, improperly exercises jurisdiction over religious exercises or establishes a prohibited relationship of privilege and control between church and state. The natural rights construction has the flexibility to "smoke out" pretextual purposes that smuggle otherwise unconstitutional legislation under the guise of a legitimate civic purpose. As discussed in chapter 7, Patrick Henry's proposed Virginia bill that effectively funded religious clergy under the pretext of fostering education would be such an example. Such analysis would function much like the *Lemon* test's "secular purpose" rule, with the noted modifications.

- "*Principal or primary effect must be one that neither advances nor inhibits religion*": Disagree, for the reasons stated above. The natural rights construction does not monitor the effects of legislation.
- "*Excessive entanglement*": Might agree, provided significant specification, including the omission of "excessive." The natural rights construction prohibits only specific forms of state entanglement with churches. Most relevant to *Lemon*'s analysis, the state cannot directly regulate the internal religious affairs of churches, for example, by passing legislation that specifically regulates how ministers are elected. The natural rights construction would only prohibit the type of entanglements that result from what we have called "state establishments" and "church establishments." They do not require judicial monitoring of legislation to ensure that it neither advances nor inhibits religion, which is what led to the constitutional violation in *Lemon*.

The adoption of the natural rights construction would require dispensing with Justice Sandra Day O'Connor's "endorsement" test, the doctrine she constructed to modify the *Lemon* test.[22] For reasons already discussed, the natural rights construction of the Establishment Clause does not scrutinize state action for the perceptions it produces. Whether the state seeks or appears to "endorse" religion is immaterial. But not every decision reached under the endorsement test would need to be overturned. As discussed in chapter 8, religious displays that are part of governmental programs to recognize the identity of the people or what is dear to them, to acknowledge aspects of the nation's history, or to advance otherwise legitimate state

---

world for the rectitude" of their intentions, and explicitly rely "on the protection of Divine providence"—have they acted with a "secular" or "religious" purpose?

22. *Lynch v. Donnelly*, 465 U.S. 668, 687–89 (1984) (O'Connor, J., concurring).

interests would be constitutional. The Christmas display (which included a creche) that the Court narrowly upheld using the endorsement test in *Lynch v. Donnelly* (1984), for example, would be upheld under the natural rights constructions. Unlike the endorsement test, moreover, the natural rights approach would not need to fabricate a "ceremonial deism" exception to uphold the constitutionality of acts like public school recitations of the Pledge of Allegiance.[23]

The natural rights constructions would reach the same results as most strict-separationist decisions on prayer in public schools, but would reach them via a different course of reasoning. The government-composed prayer recited at the beginning of the public school day in *Engel v. Vitale* (1962), and the government-directed prayer at a public school graduation in *Lee v. Weisman* (1992), would violate both the "state establishment" prong of the natural rights Establishment Clause and the jurisdictional limits imposed by the Free Exercise Clause.

THE NATURAL RIGHTS CONSTRUCTIONS AND "ACCOMMODATIONISM." In contrast to "separationism," "accommodationism" holds that the Constitution does not require the strict exclusion of religion from the public square and, therefore, that government can accommodate religion in a variety of ways. Like separationism, however, no version of accommodationism exactly parallels the natural rights constructions. The natural rights and accommodationist approaches would sometimes reach the same results in a given case, but in no case would they employ the same analysis.

Justice William Rehnquist offered "non-preferentialism" as one of the early accommodationist alternatives to "separationism." In a scathing dissent in *Wallace v. Jaffree* (1985), in which a public school's practice of a moment of silence for prayer or voluntary meditation was found unconstitutional, Rehnquist held that the Establishment Clause "had acquired a well-accepted meaning" based on the Founders' design and early interpretations:

> It forbade establishment of a national religion, and forbade preference among religious sects or denominations. . . . [It] did not require government neutrality between religion and irreligion nor did it prohibit the Federal Government from providing nondiscriminatory aid to religion.[24]

---

23. *Elk Grove School District v. Newdow*, 542 U.S. 1, 37 (2004) (O'Connor, J., concurring).

24. *Wallace v. Jaffree*, 472 U.S. 38, 106 (1985). Rehnquist cited nineteenth-century dictionaries to support his finding that an establishment was defined as "the act of establishing, founding, ratifying or ordaining," such as the "episcopal form of religion, so called, in England."

"Non-preferentialism" never commanded a Supreme Court majority, but Justice Clarence Thomas adopted a modified version of it in his opinion for the Court in the government aid to religious schools case *Mitchell v. Helms* (2000), and Rehnquist adopted a modified version of it himself in his majority opinion in the school choice case *Zelman v. Simmons-Harris* (2002). Both Thomas in *Mitchell* and Rehnquist in *Zelman* conducted their analysis within *Lemon*'s broader framework, evaluating whether government aid to religious schools had the unconstitutional purpose or effect of advancing religion by measuring whether such aid is "neutral" toward religion.[25] In both cases, the Court found the challenged aid to be constitutional: 6–3 in *Mitchell* and 5–4 in *Zelman*.

As I discussed in the context of explaining how the natural rights approach differs from *Lemon*, the natural rights construction of the Establishment Clause does not ask whether legislation is "neutral" toward religion.[26] In cases that involve government aid flowing to religious organizations, the natural rights approach demands only that the government act to foster ends within its legitimate jurisdiction, and that a reasonable nexus exist between those civic ends and the means used to pursue them. The natural rights construction would uphold the results reached by the Court in *Mitchell* and *Zelman* because in each case the state employed means (funding schools) reasonably related to a legitimate civic end (education). The approach would prohibit some forms of legislation that are not neutral toward religion (for example, the delegation of taxing authority), but "neutrality" itself would not be the criterion by which legislation is judged.

THE NATURAL RIGHTS CONSTRUCTIONS AND "TRADITION."   One example of "accommodationist" legislation that the natural rights construction would strike down is the state chaplaincy at issue in *Marsh v. Chambers* (1983). In *Marsh*, the Court ignored *Lemon* and other precedents to uphold Nebraska's practice of opening each legislative day with a prayer led by a chaplain paid by the state. The Court found that the "unique history" of the First Congress itself—which authorized legislative chaplains for each chamber—justified the practice.[27] More recently, the Court invoked tradition

    25. *Mitchell v. Helms*, 530 U.S. 793, 809–15, 829–30 (2000); *Zelman v. Simmons-Harris*, 536 U.S. 639, 649, 652, 662 (2002).
    26. Cf. West, *Free Exercise of Religion in America*, 296, which suggests that a jurisdictional approach to the Religion Clauses would support the Supreme Court's "neutrality" jurisprudence.
    27. According to Justice William Brennan's dissent in *Marsh v. Chambers*, 463 U.S. 783, 796 (1983):

to uphold the practice of beginning a monthly town board meeting with a prayer. Writing for the Court, Justice Kennedy clarified that *Marsh* teaches "that the Establishment Clause must be interpreted 'by reference to historical practices and understandings.'"[28] Kennedy continued:

> *Marsh* stands for the proposition that it is not necessary to define the precise boundary of the Establishment Clause where history shows that the specific practice is permitted. Any test the Court adopts must acknowledge a practice that was accepted by the Framers and has withstood the critical scrutiny of time and political change.

Inquiring "whether the prayer practice in the town of Greece fits within the tradition long followed in Congress and the state legislatures,"[29] he led a five-member majority to find the town's prayer practice constitutional.

A difficulty with Justice Kennedy's reasoning is that it provides no basis for a "critical scrutiny" that would identify those practices accepted by the Framers but which "time and political change" have demonstrated to be unconstitutional. Once one admits that some Founding-era practices might be unconstitutional, tradition alone cannot be the decisive standard; some criterion must exist for distinguishing constitutional from unconstitutional traditions. Functionally, Justice Kennedy's tradition standard upholds those practices that have been upheld in the past, but continues to find unconstitutional those practices that have been previously struck down. This simply begs the question of what standard justified the Court's earlier decisions. Legislative chaplains (upheld by the Court in 1983 in *Marsh v. Chambers*) and minister exclusions from political office (struck down by the Court in 1978 in *McDaniel v. Paty*) are both traditions inaugurated by the Founders. Why is the former constitutional and the latter unconstitutional? Kennedy's appeal to tradition cannot provide an answer, because it fails to articulate clear rules by which the Court can "define the precise boundar[ies]" of the Religion Clauses.

This Court makes no pretense of subjecting Nebraska's practice of legislative prayer to any of the formal "tests" that have traditionally structured our inquiry under the Establishment Clause. That it fails to do so is, in a sense, a good thing, for it simply confirms that the Court is carving out an exception to the Establishment Clause rather than reshaping Establishment Clause doctrine to accommodate legislative prayer.

28. *Town of Greece v. Galloway*, 572 U.S. 565, 576 (2014), quoting *County of Allegheny v. American Civil Liberties Union Greater Pittsburgh*, 492 U.S. 573, 670 (1989) (Kennedy, J., concurring in judgment in part and dissenting in part).

29. *Town of Greece v. Galloway*, 572 U.S. 565, 577 (2014).

The most fundamental tradition of American constitutionalism, more-over, is not reliance on tradition. The Founders themselves were not tradi-tionalists, especially in church-state matters. As I showed in chapters 1 and 2, they established the American constitutional tradition of religious lib-erty not by invoking tradition, but by adopting natural rights social compact political philosophy. To follow the Founders requires that we follow their philosophical thinking. America's most authoritative and most distinctive church-state tradition, in fact, is the political philosophy of natural rights, not the specific political practices that existed at the time of the Founding. Accordingly, I have concluded that it is *not* decisive that some members of the First Congress expected legislative chaplains to be consistent with the Establishment Clause. The Founders' expectations do not determine the natural rights constructions; natural rights philosophical thinking does. For reasons I have already discussed, state chaplaincies and official prayers said or orchestrated by state officials assume jurisdiction over religious worship as such, and therefore violate the natural rights constructions of both the Free Exercise Clause and the Establishment Clause.

THE NATURAL RIGHTS CONSTRUCTIONS AND FREE EXERCISE CLAUSE PRECE-DENTS.   Having already addressed the subject earlier in this chapter when discussing the approach's distinctiveness, I will only briefly explain here how the natural rights construction relates to leading Free Exercise Clause precedents. It would confirm the outcomes in *Employment Division v. Smith* (1990) and *Lukumi Babalu Aye* (1993), though it would not employ the same reasoning the majority did in these cases. Regarding *Smith*, it would offer the reasons for the Court's nonexemptionist result that Justice Scalia's majority opinion failed to provide. The natural rights construction would also reach the same result as the Court in *Locke v. Davey* (2004), but would reject much of Chief Justice Rehnquist's faulty historical reasoning. Rehn-quist contended that Founding-era states "that sought to avoid an establish-ment of religion ... placed in their constitutions formal prohibitions against using tax funds to support ministry." Citing as one example Georgia's 1789 Constitutional provision, "All persons shall have the free exercise of reli-gion, without being obliged to contribute to the support of any religious profession but their own," he averred that "the plain text of these constitu-tional provisions prohibited any tax dollars from supporting the clergy."[30]

30. *Locke v. Davey*, 540 U.S. 712, 721, 723 (2004). Chief Justice Rehnquist also cited Arti-cle 2 of the 1776 Pennsylvania Constitution.

Such texts, however, did not actually prohibit "any tax dollar from supporting the clergy." As we discussed in chapter 4, seven states at the time of the
Founding (New Jersey, Delaware, Pennsylvania, North Carolina, Georgia,
South Carolina, Vermont) prohibited compelled financial support without
consent or contrary to conscience. Of these states, some legislated religious
taxes; others did not. Georgia's 1777 Constitution included language that
was virtually the same as that which would appear in its 1789 Constitution:
all persons "shall not, unless by consent, support any teacher or teachers
except those of their own profession."[31] In 1785, the Georgia legislature
adopted a property tax "for the regular establishment and support of the
public duties of religion."[32]

None of this history would have been necessary for the natural rights
constructions to affirm *Locke*'s conclusion that the exclusion of theology
majors from a state-funded scholarship program is permitted by the Free
Exercise Clause and not required by the Establishment Clause. As I noted
in chapters 7 and 8, the natural rights constructions do not demand that
religious and nonreligious interests be treated equally. The constructions
would allow states to include or exclude religious individuals as long as the
criterion for participation is not based on religious exercises as such. The
approach would not agree, accordingly, with Justices Scalia and Thomas's
nondiscrimination construction of the Free Exercise Clause.[33]

Because the natural rights construction does not require neutrality toward religion, it also would not sustain the outcome or support the reasoning employed by Justice Kennedy in his majority opinion in *Masterpiece
Cakeshop v. Colorado Civil Rights Commission* (2018). Kennedy found

31. Constitution of Georgia, 1777, Article 56, in *The Federal and State Constitutions, Colonial Charters, and Other Organic Laws of the United States*, 2nd edition, ed. Benjamin Perley
Poore (Washington: Government Printing Office, 1878), 1:383. The 1789 Georgia Constitution
more clearly stated that "all persons shall have the free exercise of religion, without being
obliged to contribute to the support of any religious profession but their own" (Article 4, Section 5 in *Federal and State Constitutions*, 1:386).

32. *The Colonial Records of the State of Georgia*, ed. Allen D. Candler (Atlanta: Chas P.
Byrd, 1911): 19(2): 395–98. Cf. West, *Free Exercise of Religion in America*, 202–3. The existence
of Georgia's 1785 church tax, Vermont's 1783 church tax, and efforts to legislate a similar tax
in Delaware in 1786 refute West's contention that "there is no external evidence to support"
the interpretation that constitutional language such as Georgia's was understood to be compatible with some forms of religious taxation.

33. *Locke v. Davey*, 540 U.S. 712, 726–27 (2004). For defenses of a nondiscrimination construction of the Religion Clauses, see Philip B. Kurland, *Religion and the Law: Of Church and
State and the Supreme Court* (Chicago: Aldine, 1962); Vincent Phillip Muñoz, "Establishing
Free Exercise," *First Things* 138 (2003): 14–20. Cf. West, *Free Exercise of Religion in America*,
296–97.

that Colorado state officials acted with "clear and impermissible hostility toward the sincere religious beliefs" of the cakeshop owner in the case.[34] While Kennedy's appraisal of the state's attitudes might have been correct, such attitudes alone would not constitute a Free Exercise Clause violation. The natural rights approach would instead leave to the democratic political process both the existence of nondiscrimination laws and the degree to which religiously motivated beliefs and actions are exempt from their reach. The natural rights approach allows the state to include or exclude religion from participation in public programs, and to subject or exempt religion from governmental regulations in order to facilitate the political common good.

Incorporation of the Establishment Clause
and the Nationalization of Church-State Separation

In chapter 4, I argued that Founding-era state declarations of rights demonstrate that the Founders agreed that the right to worship according to conscience is an inalienable natural right. This conception is the core of the Founders' principle of religious liberty and, as such, I used it to construct the First Amendment's Free Exercise Clause. I also argued that Founding-era state declarations of rights and constitutions reveal that the Founders disagreed about the proper separation of church and state. I mapped that disagreement by categorizing the Founders as "narrow republicans" and "expansive liberals." "Narrow republicans," such as George Washington and Patrick Henry, held a narrower view of the scope of the natural right of religious liberty, and thus a less stringent view of the constitutional limitations it imposed. "Expansive liberals"—"liberal" here referring to classical liberalism, not modern progressivism—held a more expansive view of the scope of the natural right of religious liberty, and thus a more stringent view of its constitutional limitations.

The Founders themselves dealt with their disagreement primarily through federalism; they agreed to disagree. Virginia adopted the "expansive liberal" understanding by adopting Jefferson's 1786 Virginia Statute for Religious Freedom. Massachusetts and New Hampshire were governed by their respective "narrow republican" constitutions. Other states adopted middling positions. One of the original purposes of the Establishment Clause was to enshrine this agreement to disagree. As I documented in chapter 5,

---

34. *Masterpiece Cakeshop v. Colorado Civil Rights Commission*, 584 U.S. ___, slip op. at 12 (2018).

the Establishment Clause was originally designed (1) to recognize that the national legislature could not establish a religion and (2) to keep most church-state affairs at the state level. By keeping most church-state questions at the state level, the Founders did not need to resolve their differences regarding the proper separation of church and state.

Incorporating the Establishment Clause to restrict state government practices necessarily clashes with the Establishment Clause's original design. It transforms text that was designed to recognize the states' authority into a restriction on the states' authority. As I discussed in the previous chapter, the path most consistent with the Establishment Clause's original design would be to apply its limitations only against the national government; the Free Exercise Clause alone would be incorporated to restrict state governments.[35] The availability of that path depends on the meaning of the Fourteenth Amendment and its relationship to the Establishment Clause, a topic that exceeds the scope of this study.[36] If we accept the Establishment Clause's incorporation—either because it is mandated by the Fourteenth Amendment or because it is an accomplished fact—the Founders' path of federalism is foreclosed to us. Incorporation nationalizes constitutional questions pertaining to what I have colloquially called "the separation of church from state."[37]

35. While the Free Exercise Clause also originally applied only against the national government, no similar tension exists in applying it against the states. Incorporation of the Free Exercise Clause extends the provision's original purposes to apply against the states. Incorporation of the Establishment Clause *undermines* one of the text's original purposes.

36. It is possible that those who adopted the Fourteenth Amendment intended to apply a nonestablishment prohibition against the states. If so, they either did not understand the text's original federalism purpose, or sought to revoke that purpose. I take no position on the actual original meaning of the Fourteenth Amendment vis-à-vis the Establishment Clause, though my review of the scant available evidence leads me to concur with Carl H. Esbeck in "The Uses and Abuses of Textualism and Originalism in Establishment Clause Interpretation," *Utah Law Review* 2011 (2011), 597n452, that there "is paltry evidence that the Thirty-Ninth Congress gave thought to the meaning of the Establishment Clause when the Fourteenth Amendment was debated in 1866–1867." See also Kent Greenawalt, *Religion and the Constitution: Establishment and Fairness* (Princeton, NJ: Princeton University Press, 2008), 2:33–39.

Perhaps the most thoughtful attempt to harmonize an originalist account of the Establishment Clause with the Fourteenth Amendment's original meaning has been offered by Kurt T. Lash, "The Second Adoption of the Establishment Clause: The Rise of the Non-Establishment Principle," *Arizona State Law Journal* 27 (1995): 1085–1154. For a thoughtful approach to the Establishment Clause's incorporation from a different point of view, see Frederick Mark Gedicks, "Incorporation of the Establishment Clause against the States: A Logical, Textual, and Historical Account," *Indiana Law Journal* 88 (2013): 669–722.

37. Note that federalism is not exhaustive of the Establishment Clause. As I discussed in chapter 5, the Establishment Clause imposed a substantive restriction on Congress. With the adoption of the First Amendment, Congress could no longer establish a religion in the federal

The natural rights argument for applying the constructed Establishment Clause's prohibitions against the states is that it would ensure, beyond the Free Exercise Clause's prohibitions, that state governments respect the jurisdictional limitations correlating to the individual's nonalienated right to worship according to conscience. The "state establishment" prong prohibits state actors from exercising religious authority. The "church establishment" prong prohibits state actors from delegating its coercive authority to churches, a delegation that leads to religious authority being enforced by law. Preventing "state" and "church" establishment facilitates protection of the natural right of religious liberty by keeping governmental power in its proper sphere. While the authors of the First Amendment did not design the Establishment Clause to impose these restrictions against the states, the natural rights constructions offer an approach to the Establishment Clause's incorporation consistent with the deepest currents of the Founders' political philosophy of religious freedom.

The reader may have noticed that the Establishment Clause construction I have presented does not precisely correspond to either "narrow republicanism" or "expansive liberalism," but borrows elements from both. Like "narrow republicanism," the construction allows religion-based classifications, such as exemptions for religious conscientious objectors from military service, that an "expansive liberal" approach would prohibit. Take Jefferson's Virginia Statute, which provided that an individual's religious opinions or beliefs "shall in no wise diminish, enlarge, or affect their civil capacities."[38] A strict application of "expansive liberalism's" principle would prohibit religion-based exemptions that "enlarge" "civil capacities" on the basis of religious beliefs or opinions; it would require complete blindness or state noncognizance toward religion. The natural rights approach is not as restrictive.[39] At the same time, the natural rights construction imposes stricter limits than "narrow republicanism" on certain forms of government involvement with religion. Like "expansive liberalism," it would prohibit the state from employing religious chaplains to conduct religious services,

territories where it otherwise would have had the constitutional power to do so. The Establishment Clause, accordingly, would still require construction even if it were not incorporated, though absent incorporation the stakes would be considerably lower.

38. "A Bill for Establishing Religious Freedom in Virginia," in *Religious Liberty and the American Supreme Court: The Essential Cases and Documents*, updated edition, ed. Vincent Phillip Muñoz (Lanham, MD: Rowman & Littlefield, 2015), 605.

39. For a brief consideration of how Madisonian "expansive liberalism" overreaches and exceeds the requirements of protection of the inalienable natural right to worship according to conscience, see Muñoz, *God and the Founders*, 220–21.

and would prohibit official state prayers. The approach acknowledges that the state may be cognizant of religion and may even support religion as a means to accomplish otherwise legitimate civic ends; but also that the state lacks authority over religious exercises as such, and thus can neither function as a church nor delegate its authority to religious authorities. This natural rights construction attempts to be faithful to the Founders' philosophy of natural rights, cohere with the First Amendment's text, and also recognize the historical development of the doctrine of incorporation.

Are the Natural Right Constructions Too Elastic or Too Susceptible to Judicial Willfulness?

Some originalists, especially those whose originalism is motivated by the desire to restrain the judiciary, balk at the idea of invoking natural rights or natural law. They fear that this would allow judges to roam wildly and impose their own view of natural justice on the Constitution's text.[40] I have attempted to construct relatively specific rules to cabin the natural rights constructions, though it must be recognized that any jurisprudential rule can be manipulated in such a way as to provide the interpreter with wide discretion. Doctrinal rules alone can't guarantee their good-faith application. For conservatives who prioritize judicial restraint, the proposed constructions will likely be viewed as a mixed bag. The constructions' jurisdictional and democratic character calls for a relatively limited judicial role, which the proponents of judicial restraint should appreciate; at the same time, the approach sanctions judicial constitutional constructions, which some "restraintists" hold to be illegitimate. Michael Stokes Paulsen, for example, contends that the judiciary should not enforce underdetermined text and that, when faced with underdetermined text such as the Religion Clauses, judges should defer to constructions made by the political branches.[41] I justify judicial constitutional constructions by the same reasons that would justify constructions by the more democratic branches: the Constitution is supposed to govern. If the Constitution's provisions are not given meaning

40. See, e.g., Robert H. Bork, "Natural Law and the Constitution," *First Things* 21 (1992): 16–20; Antonin Scalia, "Natural Law," in *Scalia Speaks: Reflections on Law, Faith, and Life Well Lived*, ed. Christopher J. Scalia and Edward Whelan (New York: Crown Forum, 2017): 243–49. Cf. Diarmuid F. O'Scannlain, "The Natural Law in the American Tradition," *Fordham Law Review* 79 (2011): 1513–28.

41. Michael Stokes Paulsen, "How to Interpret the Constitution (and How Not To)," *Yale Law Journal* 115 (2006): 2057.

and enforced by the officers of government, including the courts, they do not govern.

Those who oppose judicial constructions must admit that some branch of government must construct underdetermined constitutional provisions if those provisions are to govern us. Even if judges don't construct the Religion Clauses, other state actors must develop some operative understanding of their meaning if they are to be governed by the First Amendment's restrictions. So even if one holds that the judiciary should not be the first branch to construct underdetermined text, and instead should defer to constructions first made by the political branches, legislators and executive branch officials will still need to construct the Religion Clauses. The reality of underdetermined text and the logic of constitutionalism *require* constructions. The preference for constructions by the political branches reflects a preference for majoritarian democracy and a distrust of the judiciary. These may be defensible preferences, but they are not required by a commitment to constitutionalism. Indeed, the "restraintist" position strays from the Founders' political philosophy insofar as the Founders conceived America to be a constitutional republic devoted to the protection of natural rights, not simply a constitutional democracy.

One can recognize the legitimacy of constitutional constructions, including those performed by the judiciary, and also appreciate the concern that judges may make bad constructions or even abuse their power. Once one admits that judges must go beyond the text, there is no telling where they might go, even if they are supposedly identifying and applying the original meaning of the Constitution. Church-state jurisprudence is a case in point. Anyone who cares to look can see that originalism as practiced has not effectively constrained judicial willfulness. Historical examples and references have been used with impunity to support constructions that have no foundation in the Founders' political or constitutional thought. The jurisprudential record is now sufficiently complicated and convoluted, moreover, that a nod to supposedly originalist precedents can produce almost any result a judge wants. Philosophical history, like any method, can be abused. "Design originalism" is no different.

Are the Natural Rights Constructions Too Anemic?

I suspect a likely criticism of the natural rights constructions is that they are too anemic. Many, especially those on the left, are committed to *Everson*'s construction of the Establishment Clause as gospel truth—that the separation of church and state means that government cannot support religion in any way, shape, or form. Religious individuals and institutions, in this view, must be treated differently from other similarly situated individuals and institutions, because the combination of state and church power is uniquely dangerous to democracy. Even if government promotes other forms of racial, ethnic, and cultural identity and practice, it cannot promote religious identification or belief. The natural rights construction rejects much of separationism's dictate that religion be excluded from the public square. Others, especially contemporary social conservatives, will view the natural rights Free Exercise Clause as too feeble. Given the growth of the modern regulatory state over the last hundred years and, more recently, the legal enshrining of the norms of the sexual revolution, many social and religious conservatives hold that the protection of religious liberty demands religious exemptions from generally applicable laws. Separationists construct the Establishment Clause to exclude religion from the ever-expanding sphere in which government operates; exemptionists seek to construct the Free Exercise Clause to insulate religiously inspired beliefs and practices from the effects of the modern regulatory state.[42]

Both sides eschew republican self-government in matters of church and state. From their own perspectives, it may be strategically sensible to do so. Allowing a creche to be displayed in the public square or tax dollars to fund religious schools may lead Americans to embrace more traditionally religious moral views and thus to reject the further advancement of LGBT rights or expansive abortion laws. Alternatively, not providing a constitutional right to exemptions may subject some (especially more traditional) religious believers to nondiscrimination laws that make it effectively impossible for them to participate in governmental programs, certain licensed professions, certain types of voluntary associations, or the marketplace without contradicting their religious beliefs. If applied to the employment contracts of Catholic priests, gender nondiscrimination laws would make the all-male Catholic priesthood illegal. Compared to these combative alternatives, the natural rights approach allows government to both benefit and restrain religion. It leaves to the people the authority over

42. It should be noted that exemptionism is also defended by a number of prominent left-leaning jurists, notably Douglas Laycock and Andy Koppelman. See, e.g., Douglas Laycock, "Liberty and Justice for All," in *Religious Freedom, LGBT Rights, and the Prospects for Common Ground*, ed. William N. Eskridge Jr. and Robin Fretwell Wilson (New York: Cambridge University Press, 2018), 24–37; Andrew Koppelman, *Defending American Religious Neutrality* (Cambridge, MA: Harvard University Press, 2013).

church-state matters that many on the left and the right would rather the people, operating through majoritarian political institutions, *not* possess.

Democratic republicanism in church-state matters might be insufficiently protective of liberty for reasons those on both the left and the right fear. It ought to be recognized, however, that these fears reflect a distrust of republican self-government and the American people themselves, or at least of those who govern as the representatives of the American people. It also should be recognized that these criticisms, from both Establishment Clause separationists and Free Exercise exemptionists, implicitly place enormous trust and authority in the legal professional class that exercises disproportionate influence through judicial power. Both sides — for different reasons — prefer church-state matters to be governed through the judiciary rather than through majoritarian politics.

Leaving aside for the moment the principle of protection for the core inalienable natural right of religious liberty, the case for (and against) the natural rights constructions rests in no small part on their democratic character. In many areas of church-state legislation, the constructions themselves do not produce any particular result; they respect the authority of the people to decide for themselves the proper role of religion in the public square. Exemptions from generally applicable laws, state funding for religious schools, religious displays on governmental property, the inclusion or exclusion of religious organizations from governmental programs: these issues, for the most part, would be addressed through the democratic political process. Religious pacifists could be exempted from military service, but they need not be. Religious employers could be subject to nondiscrimination laws or exempted from them. Private religious schools could receive supplemental funds to improve mathematical education, or they could be excluded. Cities could host religious displays during the holiday season, or they could exclude them. The examples are numerous. One's judgment of the prudence and wisdom of the natural rights approach will depend largely on which institutions of government one wants to exercise decision-making power, one's evaluation of the character and fairness of the American people, and, relatedly, one's estimation of the virtues and vices of representative democracy as applied to matters of religion and politics.

The natural rights approach vests authority to make many (though not all) church-state decisions in the people. The approach sets hard constitutional boundaries on what the people can do through their representative institutions (e.g., no coercion of worship, no delegation of taxing authority to churches), but as long as those institutions operate within their legitimate jurisdiction, the people can increase protections for religious liberty or erect more extensive barriers separating church from state. To emphasize the former point: that the natural rights constructions do not provide a constitutional right to exemptions from otherwise legitimate but religiously burdensome laws *does not mean* that exemptions cannot be legislated. The First Amendment's protections can be augmented through ordinary legislation and executive action. First Amendment limitations are just one way — and certainly not the only way — that the Constitution was designed to protect religious liberty.

We might observe this last point in a different manner. Those who find the natural rights constructions anemic are likely to do so because they conceive the First Amendment to address a different and more robust mischief than that posited by the approach I have presented. Take the Free Exercise Clause. The natural rights construction conceives the Free Exercise Clause to address a specific mischief: state action that exercises jurisdiction over religious exercise as such, thus violating individuals' inalienable natural right to worship according to conscience. It does not hold that the Free Exercise Clause was designed to protect religious individuals and institutions from every law that might burden religious interests. Its limited scope corresponds to the limited albeit fundamentally important mischief it was designed to remedy.[43]

Alternative constructions hold the Free Exercise Clause to address a different mischief. Douglas Laycock, a leading proponent both of Free Exercise exemptionism and Establishment Clause separationism, defends a "substantive neutrality" approach because he holds that the underlying purpose of the Religion Clauses is "to minimize the extent to which it [government] either encourages or discourages religious belief or disbelief, practice or nonpractice, observance or nonobservance."[44] Jocelyn Maclure and Charles Taylor advance an exemptionist construction of the Free Exercise Clause in order to allow every individual "to choose and realize his or her own conception of what a successful life is."[45] Bill Galston, similarly, argues that an exemptionist approach to free exercise is needed to prevent the mischief of government encroachment on what he calls "expressive

43. For an extraordinarily helpful account of the "mischief rule," see Samuel L. Bray, "The Mischief Rule," *Georgetown Law Journal* 109 (2021): 967–1013.

44. Douglas Laycock, "Formal, Substantive, and Disaggregated Neutrality toward Religion," *DePaul Law Review* 39 (1990): 101.

45. Jocelyn Maclure and Charles Taylor, *Secularism and Freedom of Conscience* (Cambridge, MA: Harvard University Press, 2011), 71.

liberty," which he defines as the freedom of individuals to live their lives in ways that express their deepest beliefs about what gives meaning or value to life.[46] While less grand and philosophical, Justices Alito, Thomas, and Gorsuch reach a similar doctrinal rule through textual analysis that finds "the ordinary meaning of 'prohibiting the free exercise of religion' was (and still is) forbidding or hindering unrestrained religious practices or worship."[47] These approaches offer a stouter conception of the Free Exercise Clause because they construct it to remedy a more unbounded mischief.

The natural rights approach does not necessarily deny the concerns articulated by scholars such as Laycock, Maclure, Taylor, and Galston or Justices Alito, Thomas, and Gorsuch, but it denies that the Free Exercise Clause is the proper vehicle through which to address all of them. As I have already suggested, it would direct most of these concerns to the ordinary political process, relying on the various structural mechanisms established by the Constitution to preserve liberty, including representation, separation of powers, and federalism. The natural rights construction gives the Free Exercise Clause a fundamentally important but relatively limited role in America's constitutional system of government, policing the jurisdictional boundaries of government that correspond to the inalienable character of the right to worship.

The natural rights constructions also recognize that, at least in practice, expanding the scope of constitutional protections has made them more porous. It is typically thought that constructing the Free Exercise Clause to include exemptions simply expands the provision by offering religious individuals and institutions some protections from otherwise valid but burdensome legislation. Exemptions, however, come with a jurisdictional price. Constructing the Free Exercise Clause to include protection for religious believers from generally applicable but particularly burdensome laws requires state actors to "balance" or otherwise limit such protection. Almost any law or regulation can impose burdens on the religious beliefs of some individual, which means that every law is potentially subject to a Free Exercise challenge. Since it is impractical to relieve every burden or accommodate every litigant, the availability of religious exemptions must be joined with an exemption-denial mechanism. As implemented by the Supreme Court, infringements of the free exercise of religion can be justified

---

46. William A. Galston, *Liberal Pluralism: The Implications of Value Pluralism for Political Theory and Practice* (New York: Cambridge University Press, 2002), 28.

47. *Fulton v. City of Philadelphia*, 593 U.S. ___, slip op. at 25 (2021) (Alito, J., concurring).

by "compelling state interests" pursued via properly tailored means. Once again, in the words of Justice Kennedy, writing for a unanimous Supreme Court:

> If the object of a law is to infringe upon or restrict practices because of their religious motivation, the law is not neutral; and it is invalid unless it is justified by a compelling interest and is narrowly tailored to advance that interest.[48]

Exemptions thus do not only expand the breadth of the Free Exercise Clause's protection. They also reduce its depth by allowing laws "to restrict practices because of their religious motivation" as long as the state does so for "compelling" reasons pursued in the right manner. While the natural rights construction of the Free Exercise Clause is more limited than the exemptionist approach in one sense, it is more robust and complete in another. It *never* allows the state to target religious exercises because of their religious motivation. In affirming this categorical barrier on all state action, it establishes the primary jurisdictional restriction necessary for the maintenance of limited government.[49]

Is It Coherent to Adopt Natural Rights Constructions Only for the Religion Clauses?

Religious liberty is not the only categorical barrier the First Amendment imposes. Congress (and the states, assuming incorporation) also shall make no laws "abridging the freedom of speech, or of the press, or the right of the people peaceably to assemble, and to petition the government for a redress of grievances."[50] The First Amendment makes clear that the Constitution's protection of religious freedom is part of a larger whole. Whether it makes sense to adopt natural rights constructions for the Religion Clauses alone, absent a larger commitment to construing the Constitution in a natural rights framework, is not a simple question to answer.

---

48. *Church of the Lukumi Babalu Aye, Inc. v. City of Hialeah*, 508 U.S. 520, 533 (1993).

49. See also Vincent Phillip Muñoz, "Two Concepts of Religious Liberty: The Natural Rights and Autonomy Approaches to the Free Exercise of Religion," *American Political Science Review* 110 (2016): 378–80.

50. For an excellent presentation of a natural rights understanding of freedom of speech, see Jud Campbell, "Natural Rights and the First Amendment," *Yale Law Journal* 127 (2017): 246–321.

The complexities of the issue can be illustrated by considering a number of different cases, but let me use *Masterpiece Cakeshop* as an example. The case involved a Colorado cakeshop owner who refused to design a wedding cake for a same-sex couple. As I noted in chapter 8, the natural rights Free Exercise Clause would not shield the cakemaker from the state's nondiscrimination ordinances. It is conceivable, however, that a natural rights construction of other constitutional provisions might have protected the cakemaker—say, perhaps, the Free Speech Clause or the First Amendment's protection of freedom of assembly, or even the Fifth Amendment's protection of property rights. Let us say, for the sake of argument, we have good reason to conclude that the First Amendment was originally designed to protect the natural right of free speech and that, so constructed, the Free Speech Clause would have protected the baker. Let us also stipulate that settled precedents foreclose that result and the adoption of a natural rights construction of the Free Speech Clause. Should a champion of natural rights adopt the natural rights Free Exercise Clause, and thus *fail* to reach the result that the natural rights Free Speech Clause should have achieved? Or should that champion *distort* the Free Exercise Clause in order to restore, in some sense, the protection that should have been provided by the natural rights Free Speech Clause?

I have argued that the Free Exercise Clause was designed to protect only a narrow slice of our natural liberty. Other constitutional provisions were designed to work in tandem with the Free Exercise Clause. I have not discussed those other provisions; I have presented only natural rights constructions for part of one amendment. Whether it is coherent to adopt these constructions in the absence of a more general acceptance of the natural rights approach to other constitutional provisions (or, indeed, the entire Constitution) would require a more comprehensive analysis than I have attempted. For a champion of natural rights, it would require comprehension of how the various provisions of the Constitution relate to one another, and the degree to which those provisions are currently construed (or likely to be construed) toward the common end of the protection of natural rights.

The Natural Rights Constructions and the Worship of God

Insofar as the natural rights constructions limit Free Exercise Clause protections to traditional conceptions of religious belief and practice, they might be considered narrow in another way as well. While some contend that liberal constitutionalism requires special restrictions on religion in the public square, others, such as Micah Schwartzman, argue that "religion cannot be distinguished from many other beliefs and practices as warranting special constitutional treatment."[51] Jocelyn Maclure and Charles Taylor espouse what is probably the prevailing position among contemporary political and legal theorists:

> Within the context of contemporary societies marked by moral and religious diversity, it is not religious convictions in themselves that must enjoy a special status but, rather, all core beliefs that allow individuals to structure their moral identity.[52]

As I have already discussed, most advocates of this view envision the Free Exercise Clause to mandate a robust scheme of exemptions for religiously and nonreligiously inspired conscientious beliefs and practices.[53]

In chapters 7 and 8, I did not directly define "religion" or identify precisely what beliefs ought to be considered "religious" for the purposes of First Amendment protections.[54] The most philosophically persuasive argument that justifies the inalienable character of the right to religious liberty would require "religion" to be defined narrowly and to not include beliefs and practices divorced from the conception of a Creator God. To see this, we need to revisit Jefferson and Madison's natural rights philosophical arguments.

As I discussed in chapter 3, Jefferson and Madison state that religious exercises are to be directed only by "reason and conviction." They derive that conclusion from the freedom of the human mind—from our capacities for reason and free choice. Their argument holds that human beings' capacities for reason and freedom allow us to be self-directed moral agents,

---

51. Micah Schwartzman, "What if Religion Is Not Special?" *University of Chicago Law Review* 79 (2012): 1353.

52. Maclure and Taylor, *Secularism and Freedom of Conscience*, 89. See also Christopher Eisgruber and Lawrence Sager's conception of "equal liberty," which similarly "denies that religion is . . . a category of human experience that demands special benefits and/or necessitates special restrictions." Christopher Eisgruber and Lawrence Sager, *Religious Freedom and the Constitution* (Cambridge, MA: Harvard University Press, 2007), 6.

53. See, e.g., Galston, *Liberal Pluralism*, 28; Martha Nussbaum, *Liberty of Conscience: In Defense of America's Tradition of Religious Equality* (New York: Basic Books, 2008), 168–70.

54. For a list of citations to how the Supreme Court and various scholars have defined "religion" in the context of church-state jurisprudence, see West, *Free Exercise of Religion in America*, 9n22–25.

not simply unreflective slaves of our instincts or passions. As Jefferson says in his Virginia Statute, even God, "lord both of body and mind," chose not to coerce man, but rather to teach him by and through reason.[55] Our ability to apprehend moral principles and norms (including those that are divinely revealed), and our freedom to choose to follow them, make possible a distinctly human manner of worship. Man can worship God freely according to his conviction and conscience. This capacity to worship freely — which, of course, includes the capacity to choose not to worship — suggests that, if men do have the duty to worship God, that duty can only be discharged through worship animated by conscientious conviction. The only worship fittingly expressed toward a God that created us and authored our nature is a movement of mind and heart that is freely chosen and pursued. This natural theology is implicit in Madison's understanding, and is reflected in his 1813 presidential proclamation calling for a day of "public humiliation and prayer":

> If the public homage of a people can ever be worthy [of] the favorable regard of the Holy and Omniscient Being to whom it is addressed, it must be that, in which those who join in it are guided only by their free choice, by the impulse of their hearts and the dictates of their consciences; ...

A reasonable inference from our capacities of reason and freedom is that our creator would settle for nothing less than freely given worship that reflects conscientious convictions. Only worship "freed from all coercive edicts" and "free-will offerings of humble supplication, thanksgiving and praise," Madison continues in his proclamation, "can be acceptable to Him whom no hypocrisy can deceive, and no forced sacrifices propitiate."[56]

As I discussed in chapter 3, that religious duties can only be fulfilled according to conviction and conscience leads Madison to conclude that freedom of worship is an inalienable right. His argument for the inalienable character of the freedom to worship is premised upon the possibility and knowability of a creator god, as well as the normative status of nature. From these premises — that God authored nature (including human nature), and that this nature establishes moral guidelines for human behavior — Madison reasons that religious duties can only be fulfilled ac-

---

55. "A Bill for Establishing Religious Freedom in Virginia," in Muñoz, *Religious Liberty and the American Supreme Court*, 604.

56. Presidential proclamation, July 23, 1813, in *Papers of James Madison: Presidential Series*, ed. J. C. A. Stagg et al. (Charlottesville: University of Virginia Press, 1984), 6:458–59.

cording to conviction and conscience. Thus conceived, religious freedom is oriented toward the divine. Its purpose is to secure for individuals the freedom to fulfill their obligations to their Creator. The natural rights understanding does not and cannot exhaustively determine the content of those obligations or specify how they are to be discharged, other than in freedom and according to conscience. It is grounded, however, in a moral reality that accepts reason's ability to discern an objective moral order. It therefore understands the natural moral law to establish the boundaries of the legitimate use of freedom: as discussed in chapter 2, in the Founders' understanding, natural rights have natural limits. It also defines what types of beliefs and practices are protected by the right of religious freedom: those that are directed toward the discharge of duties toward the Creator. Thus understood, the original meanings of the Religion Clauses do not pertain to "all core beliefs that allow individuals to structure their moral identity," to use Maclure and Taylor's phrase—at least not if that moral identity is separated from a concept of the divine or necessitates actions opposed to the natural moral law.

The Founders grounded the natural right to religious liberty in duties to God and the moral fabric of the human nature, of which they understood God to be the author. Their conception of religious freedom is oriented toward the divine; individuals require freedom so they can worship according to conscience. This does not imply that the Founders thought political authorities could legitimately suppress religious freedom if individuals blasphemed or committed idolatry. It also does not exclude nonbelievers and atheists from the Religion Clauses' protections; the liberty to worship freely also includes the freedom not to worship. But the Founders understood religious freedom to be an endowment from the Creator. While establishing religious liberty is a great political accomplishment, it is not the final end or even an end in and of itself. The purpose or telos of protecting religious freedom is to make possible the worship of God according to conviction and conscience. Our rights are oriented toward the fulfillment of our duties.

This book has attempted to show how the First Amendment's Religion Clauses might be constructed to facilitate that end. The best justifications for these constructions are the philosophical arguments for the existence of the inalienable right to worship according to conscience.[57] If those

57. Michael Uhlmann, one of the most perceptive originalist critics of academic originalism, stated the matter better than I can:

arguments are sound, then developing constitutional law to recognize and respect that right advances the cause of justice, which one hopes is the final cause of any method of constitutional interpretation.

I set forth the Founders' philosophical and theological arguments for the natural right of religious liberty in chapter 3. Those arguments are likely to seem foreign to us, in part because we have grown accustomed to the social fact of pluralism and are committed to the belief that "reasonable disagreement" cannot be overcome by reasoned arguments.[58] These intellectual commitments—held as if they were articles of faith—lead some to believe that only state neutrality toward religion can secure a peaceful society. The Founders disagreed. They held a contrary and more optimistic view about the power and authority of reason, and they designed the Constitution accordingly.

This book is an attempt to recover the Founders' reasoning and thereby, in the spirit of Publius, to make the Founders' constitutional principles and design once again the object of our reflection and choice.

At the end of the day, words in a legal text, without more, cannot carry the philosophical weight that originalists place upon them. It is one thing to point out, as originalists do most effectively, that such-and-such a phrase had, and was meant to have, a particular, relatively fixed meaning at the time of its adoption. Persuading others that the identified meaning has, or should have, binding effect in our own day is another argument altogether. Ultimately, that argument must rest on the reaffirmation of the enduring, self-evident truths that must undergird the case for limited government, that is, on premises that are not explicitly identified in the constitutional text itself. A true originalism, in short, must look beyond the Constitution to justify the ground of its intellectual authority.

Michael Uhlmann, "The Supreme Court v. the Constitution of the United States of America," *Claremont Review of Books* 6 (2006): 37. If the Founders' inalienable natural rights principle of religious liberty is true, moreover, then the "dead hand fallacy" is answered. As explained by Christopher L. Eisgruber, "The Living Hand of the Past: History and Constitutional Justice," *Fordham Law Review* 65 (1997): 1613:

I believe . . . the central and most damaging fallacy of modern constitutional theory [is] the "Dead Hand Fallacy." The Dead Hand Fallacy holds that the purpose of the Constitution is to subordinate present-day politics to the will of past supermajorities. . . . This result is sometimes justified by reference to ideas about popular sovereignty, which I find exceedingly odd, since the whole people who made the Constitution's most important provisions are all dead.

If respect for and protection of the natural right of religious liberty is a matter of justice, Eisgruber's criticism of misapplied popular sovereignty is rendered irrelevant.

58. John Rawls, of course, is the academic philosopher most associated with this position.

Acknowledgments

I initially presented this book's argument over the course of several days at Princeton University as the 2020 Charles E. Test, M.D. '37 Lectures. Providentially, my lectures were scheduled the week before the world shut down on account of the COVID-19 pandemic. I am grateful to Robby George, Brad Wilson, Matt Franck, and Princeton's James Madison Program in American Ideals and Institutions for the invitation to deliver the Test Lectures, and to Michael Moreland for commenting on them.

Don Drakeman also commented on my Princeton Test Lectures and repeatedly provided feedback to me as I developed my arguments. His always gentle but painfully incisive criticisms have made my work better. His friendship is a great blessing to me.

Time to think through and write this book was provided through a fellowship from the National Endowment for the Humanities. I am deeply grateful for the NEH's support, and to the American taxpayers who provided the funds. I am also grateful to Notre Dame's de Nicola Center for Ethics and Culture and its intrepid leader, Carter Snead, for a grant that supported the completion of this book. Notre Dame's Institute for Scholarship in the Liberal Arts graciously provided funds to create the index.

I have been fortunate to receive feedback from scholars at a number of academic workshops. For these opportunities I would like to thank Paul Carrese, Carol McNamara, Adam Seagrave, and Arizona State University's School of Civic and Economic Thought and Leadership; Rich Avramenko and the Center for the Study of Liberal Democracy at the University of Wisconsin; George Thomas and Claremont McKenna College's Henry Salvatori Center for the Study of Freedom in the Modern World; and Mike Andrews and the Jack Miller Center. I also received helpful comments and criticisms on a draft of the entire manuscript at a workshop sponsored by the Institute for Humane Studies and the Law and Liberty Center at George Mason University's Antonin Scalia Law School. Thank you to Helen Alvare, JoAnn Koob, John Snider, Betty Gallagher, Maria Rogacheva, and the scholars who participated in the workshop.

Beyond the professional lectures and workshops, I have been blessed by many friends and colleagues who generously have given their time, support, and advice to help me think more deeply and present my ideas more clearly. Some commented on parts of the manuscript, others patiently listened to and challenged my arguments or provided other forms of advice and support. I am particularly thankful to Hadley Arkes, Jeremy Bailey, Mark Blitz, Sonu Bedi, Eric Claeys, Marc DeGirolami, Colin Devine, Justin Dyer, Carl Esbeck, Rick Garnett, Fred Gedicks, Tom Hardiman, Charles Kesler, Andy Koppelman, Kurt Lash, Sai Prakash, Ralph Rossum, Rodgers Smith, Jim Stoner, John Witte, Stephen Wrinn, and Michael Zuckert.

Chuck Myers, Sara Doskow, and Holly Smith of the University of Chicago Press were a pleasure to work with. Chuck secured three extraordinarily thorough and thoughtful reviews. I wish to thank him and the reviewers, who remain unknown to me.

Former and current Notre Dame students initially helped me edit the manuscript. Rebecca Devine is a superb editor; I recommend her enthusiastically (writewithrebecca.squarespace.com). Michael Bradley, an ND law student, has a first-rate legal and philosophical mind, not to mention a sharp eye for unnecessary words. Becca, Michael, and John Petrakis, an outstanding ND PhD student, provided valuable suggestions, corrections, and criticisms.

At Notre Dame I serve as the director of the Center for Citizenship and Constitutional Government. I work with a terrific staff whose professional excellence allowed me to concentrate on this book. Thank you especially to Jen Smith. This book has greatly benefited from the hours of conversation I've had with my associate director, Soren Grefenstette, an impeccable young intellectual whose thoughtful criticisms I deeply appreciate.

I lost a dear friend and mentor before I completed this project. Michael Uhlmann was an enthusiastic supporter and a continual source of encouragement. I regret not being able to share the finished manuscript with him. I think he would have liked it; I know it would have been better had he commented on it. I also lost my mother a few weeks before I submitted the final manuscript, and my father while the book was in production. I remember Michael and my parents with a heavy heart. They all would have wanted me to dedicate the book to my wife, Jennifer. This book is as much hers as it is mine. I would not have been able to finish it without her love, support, and devotion, for which I am profoundly thankful.

*   *   *

In writing this book, I have borrowed from my previously published scholarship, though the attentive reader might notice that I have modified and refined some of my positions. I have cited my publications when appropriate. I wish to acknowledge and thank the journals and collections for the use of material that originally appeared in their pages under the following titles: "The Original Meaning of the Establishment Clause and the Impossibility of Its Incorporation," *University of Pennsylvania Journal of Constitutional Law* 8 (2006): 585–639; "The Original Meaning of the Free Exercise Clause: The Evidence from the First Congress," *Harvard Journal of Law and Public Policy* 31 (2008): 1083–1120; "Church and State in the Founding-Era State Constitutions," *American Political Thought* 4 (2015): 1–38; "If Religious Liberty Does Not Mean Exemptions, What Might It Mean? The Founders' Constitutionalism of the Inalienable Rights of Religious Liberty," *Notre Dame Law Review* 91 (2016): 1387–1418; "Two Concepts of Religious Liberty: The Natural Rights and Moral Autonomy Approaches to the Free Exercise of Religion," *American Political Science Review* 110 (2016): 369–81; Vincent Phillip Muñoz and Kevin Vance, "How the Founders Agreed about Religious Freedom but Disagreed about the Separation of Church and State," ed. Barbara A. McGraw, in *The Wiley Blackwell Companion to Religion and Politics in the U.S.* (West Sussex, UK: John Wiley and Sons, 2016), 85–97.

Vincent Phillip Muñoz
November 14, 2021

Index